HOW TO DO COMPARATIVE THEOLOGY

Comparative Theology / *Thinking Across Traditions*

SERIES EDITORS

Loye Ashton and John Thatamanil

This series invites books that engage in constructive comparative theological reflection that draws from the resources of more than one religious tradition. It offers a venue for constructive thinkers, from a variety of religious traditions (or thinkers belonging to more than one), who seek to advance theology understood as "deep learning" across religious traditions.

HOW TO DO COMPARATIVE THEOLOGY

FRANCIS X. CLOONEY, S.J.,
AND KLAUS VON STOSCH, EDITORS

Fordham University Press NEW YORK 2018

Visit us online at www.fordhampress.com.

Library of Congress Cataloging-in-Publication
Data available online at https://catalog.loc.gov.

Printed in the United States of America
20 19 18 5 4 3 2 1

First edition

CONTENTS

III Recognizing Comparative Theology by Its Fruits

HOW TO DO COMPARATIVE THEOLOGY

Introduction

Francis X. Clooney, S.J., and Klaus von Stosch

The fifteen essays collected in *How to Do Comparative Theology* are the fruits of an August 2014 conference in Paderborn, Germany, which itself was part of a larger conversation involving senior and junior scholars in the field over the five years before that. The conference brought together scholars in the field of comparative theology in the United States and Europe to share their work in this emerging field, and to reflect together on the nature and best methods current today by listening to how each of us actually does it.

Comparative theology is, after all, a challenging endeavor: From the perspective of the authors of this volume, it is *theology*, which may be briefly described as faith seeking understanding, grounded in community, cognizant of claims regarding truth, and open to the implications of study for spiritual advancement and practice; and it is *comparative*, familiar with and respectful of the best work in comparative studies of religion today, yet also committed to learning from both outside and within one's own community in a way that remains theologically sensitive and conducive to mutual transformation in study. Regardless of how this balance is achieved, however, in convening the Paderborn conference we also realized that the question of "Why?" implicit in the "How?" remains a pressing one. Accordingly, it is important to profile more clearly the intellectual and practical benefits of the field for individuals, for the academy, and for religious communities themselves. Methods, purposes, and results are intertwined.

The 2014 conference was motivated also by our recognition that while exciting comparative theological work is being done in both North America and Europe, there have been only a few links connecting these groups of scholars. This gap is remedied, in part, by our current work together, culminating thus far in *How We Do Comparative Theology*. The conference was distinctive also in offering younger scholars from both continents—those with completed doctoral degrees and those still in studies—the opportunity to share their work, take an active role in interrogating the field as it stands today, and help shape its future.

In the aftermath of the conference, excited by the conversations we had, and yet also alert to the challenges that became all the more apparent in Paderborn, we decided it would be useful—for ourselves and potential readers—to gather in a single volume the key presentations from the conference so as to record and highlight the issues before the field today. Hence this volume, which we are delighted to have appear in Fordham University Press's *Comparative Theology: Thinking Across Traditions* series. Given the diversity in the field and in our conference—a part of which is manifest in these essays—early on we decided to focus on method, how we—this group of interested theologians, so diverse among ourselves—each has decided to do comparative work, with which priorities and ends in mind. By advancing the project of developing common criteria in comparative theology in light of our various approaches, we thereby hope to further refine its character as an academic discipline.

The common criteria recurring across these essays—including faith- and tradition-groundedness, responsibility with respect to doctrinal implications, epistemic humility in one's encounter with the other, patience with and respect for the particulars, attentiveness to experiential and practical outcomes—should not be understood as an exclusive or easily coded set which we all share entirely and which might be easily implemented by readers. These criteria stand rather as a group of family resemblances—such as Ludwig Wittgenstein so famously described—which bring together our different approaches to comparative theology. Some of these resemblances have to do with our shared ways of relating the theologies of different traditions and with our concern to attend to the praxis of religious believers, including how they do (or might) respond to our modes of study. Other resemblances resonate include our common concern to take experience seriously, foster pastoral relevance, and keep up with the religious and spiritual sentiments of younger generations, even among our contributors, and with emerging trends in the understanding and practice of religion. Many, if not all, of our contributors are confident that even in pursuing very particular case studies, the expected results still shed light on larger issues of wider interest. And so on.

All our authors share a commitment to comparative work, and all are concerned that our work remain clearly and solidly theological. Yet we differ among ourselves in how we go about this. We also differ among ourselves in other ways: gender (seven women, eight men), age (a span of more than forty years from the oldest to the youngest), religious background and commitment (Jewish and Christian of various denominations), Muslim, and some with strong Buddhist and Hindu affinities), place of residence and academic work (continental Europe, the United Kingdom, the United States), and expertise in varying traditions (Judaism, Christianity, Islam, Hinduism, Buddhism). While we can certainly imagine greater diversity (involving, for instance, East Asian cultures and religions and African cultures and religions), we are content that this set of fifteen authors provides a rich panorama for how comparative theology can be thought about and practiced today.

It will be evident to the reader, then, that differences in approach and explanation remain, even if all the essays are the fruits of an increasingly shared conversation. It would have been very difficult to compose a finalized list of attributes necessary to comparative theology. In the end, however, our tentativeness is not a weakness but a rather sensible vote of confidence in the field, as vital and growing even or especially in areas lacking specificity. If we interpret "comparative theology" in accord with Wittgenstein's concept of family resemblances, we can see that it is neither necessary nor possible to consolidate a single and final list of components essential to comparative theological method.

The volume thus fills a niche in a growing field that in recent years has seen a number of collections of essays that describe and exemplify the field: *The New Comparative Theology: Interreligious Insights from the Next Generation*, edited by Francis X. Clooney, S.J. (Continuum Publishing, 2010); *Comparative Theology in Europe*, edited by John H. Berthrong and Francis X. Clooney (MDPI Publishing, 2014); *Teaching Comparative Theology in the Millennial Classroom: Hybrid Identities, Negotiated Boundaries*, edited by Mara Brecht and Reid Locklin (Routledge Research in Religion and Education, 2015); *Comparative Theology: Insights for Systematic Theological Reflection*, edited by Michelle Voss Roberts (Fordham University Press, 2016); and many of the essays in the *Beiträge zur Komparativen Theologie* series edited by Klaus von Stosch (Ferdinand Schöningh, 2011–16). *How We Do Comparative Theology* aptly complements those volumes, while remaining distinctive in highlighting issues of method in comparative work.

The volume divided naturally into three parts that aid us in thinking about each essay in proximity to those it more closely resembles: "Doing Comparative Theology—As Theology," "Comparative Theology Is What Comparative Theology Does," and "Recognizing Comparative Theology by Its Fruits." The three parts of the volume mark three moments, even graded steps, in the project of unfolding the significance of this field.

Doing Comparative Theology—as Theology

The essays in Part I are concerned particularly with the relationship between the work of comparative theology and doctrinal theology. The goal here is to be honest about the implications of seeing comparative theology as theology, to further the conversation about interfaith learning as relevant and responsible to doctrinal theology, and thereby also to ensure that comparative theology is taken seriously by mainstream, non-comparative theologians.

In Chapter 1, "The Problem of Choice in Comparative Theology," Catherine Cornille lays out the challenges inherent in developing a unified focus and method for comparative theology. While the possibilities for comparison between religions are almost unlimited, the approaches to the discipline range along a continuum from explicitly confessional to what she calls meta-confessional. In this open situation, some moderate constraints are of great value. Focusing primarily on the confessional grounding of the discipline, Cornille develops a typology of the different ways in which the exercise of comparative theology may lead to new theological insight and growth. She proposes addressing the problem of choice and fragmentation in the field by focusing on certain pressing theological questions or problems within one's religion and exploring how another religion might shed light on those problems. She points also to the continued importance of the theology of religions as integral to comparative theology.

In Chapter 2, "Reflecting on Approaches to Jesus in the Qur'ān from the Perspective of Comparative Theology," Klaus von Stosch illustrates very concretely what Cornille is suggesting. He urges us to do comparative theology in a way that is oriented to problems, rather than proceeding just by case studies. The extended example he introduces, though interesting as exemplifying a certain kind of comparative work, is primarily aimed at making a constructive contribution to Christian Christology with the help of the Qur'ān, by working through one of the fundamental problems in Muslim-Christian understanding: the meaning of Christ. von Stosch aims to take the Islamic appreciation of Jesus of Nazareth as seriously as possible, to face the problems arising as directly as possible, and, in the end, to ask whether or not that Islamic appreciation can be integrated into Christian theology without abandoning Christian claims of truth. For this purpose, von Stosch seeks to clear the historical ground so as to better understand influences and differences pertinent to Islam in its earliest eras, and then to do theology constructively with the specific of the original and contemporary situations in mind. It is this constructive work that he sees as the final purpose of comparative theology. This Christian comparative theology, at its best, seeks to develop its insights in a dialogical and fruitful way, as the Christian author seeks to involve Muslim colleagues in every step of his reflections. Yet too, a third party situated outside the dialogue—in this case, the Middle Eastern Studies scholar Angelika Neuwirth—is drawn into the conversation in order to interrogate further the tentative results of the dialogue. Thus, von Stosch invites us to see how comparative theology is to be done when it seeks to develop a theological position through dialogue with theologians from other religions.

In Chapter 3, "The Moment of Truth: Comparative and Dogmatic Theology," Aaron Langenfeld further generalizes the point made by Cornille and von Stosch. He reflects on how the discipline of comparative theology should be related to the normative grounds for religious truth claims to which theology as a whole is committed. Confirming a fundamental characteristic of comparative theology, he proposes that this challenge cannot be met if the question of truth is neglected; rather, it must be preserved as the central focus in concrete comparative work. To justify this proposition, in his Christian-Muslim work on salvation Langenfeld elaborates a fundamental insight regarding the Muslim critique of Christian anthropology, particularly regarding the concept of original sin, which is presumed in the Christian understanding of salvation and redemption. The evident differences are then elaborated in four phases common to comparative theological reflection and dogmatic theological reflection: the development of an original theological concept, an internal irritant or external provocation urging us to deconstruct the presumed concept, a grappling with the irritant or provocation, and a reconstruction of the original concept, considering the newly gained insights. Understood in this way, Langenfeld suggests, we can see more easily how comparative theology really does proceed like other substantive forms of theology, and thus is fairly measured by familiar theological standards, even if breaking new ground interreligiously.

The next three essays in Part I problematize in different ways the turn to doctrine, although these authors do not dispute in principle the doctrinal significance and responsibility of comparative theology. In Chapter 4, "Rhetorics of Theological One-Upsmanship in Christianity and Buddhism: Athanasius's Polemic Against the Arians and Vasubandhu's Refutation of Pudgalavāda Buddhism," Hugh Nicholson explores some perhaps unexpected parallels in the work of doctrine-making in two texts representative of the early Christian Arian controversy and of the Buddhist Personalist controversy. He elucidates common underlying motivational and rhetorical structures of two materially dissimilar religious concepts, namely, the Christian doctrine of the Son's consubstantiality with the Father, and the Buddhist doctrine of no-self. In doing so, he foregrounds what might be called the "objective," as opposed to the confessional, dimension of comparative theology. He argues that Athanasius and Vasubandhu shared similar motivations, despite the obvious dissimilarity of the doctrines of consubstantiality and no-self. In doing so, he dispels the notion that comparative work must be arbitrary—a vexing impression that has contributed to its marginalization in both Christian theology and the study of religion writ large. Comparative theology evades the charge of arbitrariness, argues Nicholson, by avoiding two pitfalls of the "old" comparativism: minimalizing religious differences and failing to attend to concrete religious expressions.

In Chapter 5, "'An Interpreter and Not a Judge': Insights into a Christian-Islamic Comparative Theology," Axel Marc Oaks Takács takes a different tack, asking why theological comparisons with the Buddhist or Hindu religious traditions seem to be far more fruitful, productive, constructive, and imaginative than comparisons engaging the Islamic religious tradition. He steps away from the ordinary subject matter and methods of Muslim-Christian relations as these have been manifested throughout history, and argues that modern Christian comparative theology engaging the Islamic religious tradition has more often than not been overly constrained by the historically received interactions between the traditions and, as a result, too narrowly confined to the creedal concerns of orthodoxy: for example, a triune as opposed to a non-triune God, or "Jesus the Son of God" as opposed to "Jesus the prophet," and so on. Christian theologians who are heirs to Orientalism have tended to focus on *'ilm al-kalām*—which has been translated as "dialectical theology"—to the exclusion of other Islamic discursive traditions, such as the philosophical Sufism, which more closely approximates concerns at home in Christian theology. Consequently, Takács seeks to challenge and unsettle both standard Islamic-Christian interreligious scholarship and the concept of "method" as it relates to the practice of theology, comparative or otherwise. In the words of Hans Urs von Balthasar, objective teaching (part of a uniform *theologia spiritualis*) must "be realized in practice, in the life of faith, hope and charity." Ultimately, comparative theology will be judged by its fruits. Attentive to the relative strengths and weaknesses of a doctrinal focus, Takács seeks to clear a more direct path to fruitful practice by redirecting the energies of the Christian-Muslim exchange into a different range of topics. He exemplifies this fresh approach by the close reading of a text by the thirteenth-century mystic-philosopher, Muḥyiddin ibn al-ʿArabī.

In Chapter 6, "On Some Suspicions Regarding Comparative Theology," Glenn Willis also reflects on comparative theology and its claims from a different angle. He suggests that comparative theologians, in order to be theologians at the service of communities wider than the small circle of comparative theology itself, need to consider two points insufficiently discussed in comparative theological conversations thus far. First, theological obligations notwithstanding, we need also to take seriously the robust and ongoing questioning of comparative work in general, articulated in recent years by scholars such as George Lindbeck and Jonathan Z. Smith. According to Willis, comparative theologians must show that comparative work does more than favor similarities, lest the discipline be linked too closely with the hopeful but too often naïve search for an underlying common ground. Comparativists need to keep making the more sophisticated case for their discipline in the wider realm of scholarship on religion, and to do this, they must take more seriously the problem of difference. They must also acknowledge the danger that comparison, eager in its selectivity, risks neglecting or dishonoring the integrity of the other. Second, Willis adds, systematic clarity will not be the sole sufficient way to sustain a vital comparative theology. Shortfalls in theological clarity and system may turn out also to be excellent teaching tools. Indeed, comparativists who honestly face a problem, imperfection, or confusion within their own tradition may travel to the other tradition with a sense of acute vulnerability born from need rather than overflowing confidence. Comparison in theology—risk-taking, border-crossing—then offers itself as a distinctive and vital way of engaging passionately the problems and desires of imperfect human lives and communities. Although there is the risk of denigrating the home tradition at the moment of appreciating the other, these chastened seekers are actually better positioned to speak convincingly back to their own tradition in a relevant way. This is overall prudent advice too: while the quest for scientific clarity and evident expertise may keep the scholar of theology institutionally safe for a time, the university hardly seems likely to honor that compact for much longer; some risk and some vulnerability are essential, if comparative theology, and even theology itself, are to remain relevant among academic scholars as well as believers.

Comparative Theology Is What Comparative Theology Does

The essays in Part II highlight specific instances of comparative theology: Catch comparative theology in the act, so to speak; understand the discipline by working through specific cases. These keep the actual work of comparative theology in front of us; they show us the distinctiveness of this field and its theological contribution, whether or not doctrinal clarifications come swiftly to the fore. The contributors to this section share the conviction that unless we are engaged in the actual doing of comparative theology and reflection on it, our discussion of it will slip away into generalities applicable to theology in general, to theology of religions and interreligious dialogue, or back into a use of comparative study simply for the sake of clarifying one tradition's doctrines.

In Chapter 7, "Embodiment, Anthropology, and Comparison: Thinking-Feeling with Non-Dual Saivism," Michelle Voss Roberts takes to heart the simple insight that theologians are, in fact, always drawing on various ways of knowing; comparative theology is no exception, and its multifaceted epistemology expects corresponding complexities in theological anthropology. Accordingly, she devotes the core of her essay to the constructive development of such an anthropology with respect to the human faculties by Thomas Aquinas and the Kashmir Saiva theologian, Abhinavagupta. His system resonates with Aquinas's anthropology, generating resonances that are enhanced by their epistemologies' nuanced and flexible epistemological contribution to theologies of the body, the senses, and other faculties. In this light, constructive comparative theology can be seen as a practice of thinking-feeling with the categories and questions of another tradition. At the conclusion of her essay, Voss Roberts highlights the value of attending to various embodied faculties, including reason itself, awareness of the elements, the physical senses, the emotions, and even limit cases such as apophatic unknowing.

In Chapter 8, "Comparative Theology After the Shoah: Risks, Pivots, and Opportunities of Comparing Traditions," Marianne Moyaert begins by noting that relatively few comparative theologians engage Judaism and that few consciously post-Holocaust theologians do comparative theology. There is work to be done here because comparative theology and post-Shoah theology, though usually intertwined with Christian-Jewish dialogue, have not yet joined forces in an effort to overcome supersessionist theologies. In fact, this is not entirely surprising because post-Shoah theologians are quite conscious of the violent potential of comparative readings and may for that reason refrain from doing theology comparatively in order to avoid the violence of odious comparisons. Moyaert shows the potentially violent nature of comparisons between Jewish and Christian scriptures by recollecting the story of the sibling rivalry between Jacob and Esau and exploring how it has been interpreted. She notes some classical Christian (and anti-Jewish) readings of this story, which to her mind are exemplary of what Hugh Nicholson has termed the "old comparative theology." Consequently, she formulates some ground rules for comparative theology after the Shoah, such as may help minimize the problem of violence in the comparative use of another's tradition. In the last section of her chapter, she makes the proposed ground rules come alive by returning to the Jacob and Esau saga. A careful study of this story together with rabbinic interpretations—including contemporary readings such as that of Rabbi Jonathan Sacks—not only interrupts thought patterns of replacement and substitution but also initiates constructive theological reflections about the relation between Esau and Jacob, Church and Synagogue, and Christians and Jews.

In Chapter 9, "Using Comparative Insights in Developing Kalām: A Personal Reflection on Being Trained in Comparative Theology," Muna Tatari presents her personal and autobiographical encounter with comparative theology and how it influenced the writing of her Ph.D. dissertation. We learn that at the beginning of her work in comparative theology, she came to realize that not only did she need to learn much about Christian theology, its doctrines and methods, but that she also had a quantitative and a qualitative lack of knowledge of her own Muslim religious tradition. In regard to current philosophical discourses and theories of cognition, Tatari felt herself inadequately equipped with the requisite knowledge, thus facing the challenge of playing catch-up with those academic discourses, which are crucial to theology, particularly in Germany, if theology is to play a part in academic and public discourse and not be marginalized as a special but largely irrelevant science. Tatari elaborates two theological categories, justice and mercy, in order to demonstrate how comparative insights are fruitful in developing kalām as the way of study and reflection that illuminates these categories. To elucidate her method, Tatari discusses five major insights arising in her dissertation that were inspired by comparative theology; she shows how she used tools and insights from Christian theology and late-modern philosophy to reconstruct Islamic thought on a specific topic.

In Chapter 10, "Difficult Remainders: Seeking Comparative Theology's Really Difficult Other," Francis Clooney aims to break new ground in his ongoing series of instances of a Christian comparative theology that engages Hinduism. In doing so, he illustrates how comparative theology, done in the particular and by cases rather than by a turn to large doctrinal matters, can be fruitful even when difference trumps similarity and a common ground is hard to find. To accentuate valuable difficulties, he engages the highly rational and highly exacting thinking of Hinduism's Mīmāṃsā, a distinctive mode of Hindu ritual analysis that is clear and rational, exact and conclusive, and in a way that resists any easy borrowing by Christian comparativists. In taking up a set of twenty Mīmāṃsā cases devoted to the seemingly abstruse matter of ritual remainders (consecrated leftovers that need to be disposed of after a ritual is finished), he illustrates the possibilities and problems arising when we engage a religious other that is clear and logical, but at every step unfamiliar, its tenets articulated by a vocabulary prepared to resist relocation to a terrain more familiar to Christian theologians. Concerns for revelation and obligation, the coherence of faith and reason, and the subtleties of right performance are all operative in the Mīmāṃsā. Yet such matters are articulated and debated in thick ritually attuned debates at times nearly impenetrable by the novice learner. Following a method he has used elsewhere, Clooney puts his reader to work, providing in his essay a translated primary text of the twenty cases on what to do with ritual remainders. Clooney is asking us to read, to learn slowly how ritual remainders are to be recognized and handled, if we wish then to think through a mode of revelation inscribed in and dependent upon particulars. This kind of good but very difficult comparison can, in fact, fail. But even when the comparative project, grounded in reading rather than concern for doctrines, reaches its limits and remains incomplete, thwarted, on edge, we are still doing our theology well and constructively.

In Chapter 11, "*Sagi Nahor*—Enough Light: Dialectic Tension Between Luminescent Resonance and Blind Assumption in Comparative Theology," Shoshana Razel Gordon-Guedalia, who has studied with Clooney, furthers and deepens the turn in comparative theology to liturgy and ritual reasoning by drawing the same Mīmāṃsā reasoning into relation with Rabbinic reasoning. Her juxtaposed reading of cases in Mīmāṃsā and Rabbinic legal reasoning validates a sense of similarity in ritual-legal hermeneutics, and also illumines the systemic understanding of each by discovering new categorical possibilities forged when the details of one system-specific case are applied to those of another. Gordon Guedalia compares cases enunciated in verses of the fourteenth-century *Garland of Jaimini's Reasons* with sixth-century Talmudic and twelfth-century Maimonidean cases pertaining to the competing oughts of ritual agency and efficacy, and in doing so rethinks as complimentary several concepts formerly thought to have been singular to one or the other of these traditions. The deeper riches of these instances of legal reasoning become visible, although neither tradition is confined by inappropriate labels or antithetical categories. Such reading promises further opportunities for mutual text examination through fresh generative lenses. As a scholar with a passion for comparative ritual hermeneutical reasoning and as a woman of faith seeking understanding, Gordon Guedalia seeks to show us how this quest for a deeper grasp of ritual and legal particulars, rather than doctrines, is a manner of doing comparative theology of potentially great significance.

Recognizing Comparative Theology by Its Fruits

The essays in Part III are most concerned with the fruits of comparative theology. They assess the field and our pursuit of it by the measure of what it achieves, and for whom. While these authors share basic sensitivities with the authors in the preceding two sections about the doctrinal groundedness of comparative theology on the one hand, and on the other, the need actually to do comparative theology in the particular, these authors pick up on another widely recognized dynamic in contemporary theology: the turn to experience, individual and social. They call to our attention the importance of putting to the fore pastoral criteria for theology in general and comparative theology in particular.

In Chapter 12, "Methodological Considerations on the Role of Experience in Comparative Theology," Emma O'Donnell explores the implications of the fact that comparative theology primarily based in textual studies has to date been the norm in comparative theology. While textual study tends to be central to most theological work and has provided strong foundations for comparative theology, too, the operative intellectual virtues—close attention to detail, reflective and patient learning, openness to change—can also be taken outside the text, so to speak, in order to pave the way for a new methodology attuned to the richer and living contexts in which texts are composed, read, and lived. Accordingly, O'Donnell explores the possibility of comparative theological work grounded in the experiential elements of faith. A comparative study of religious experience, for instance, has the capacity to bring to light specific aspects of interreligious relationships such as will not be evident simply through textual study. The turn to reflectively considered experience also helps keep comparative theology in alignment with the general tendency of theology today toward the experiential aspects of religion and its performative and material aspects as well.

In Chapter 13, "Incarnational Speech: Comparative Theology as Learning to Hear and Preach," Brad Bannon argues that comparative theology both challenges and enables us to think differently about *how* scriptural revelation takes place. He begins by considering how to reformulate Christian theological questions through comparative theology. A half-century ago, Lutheran theologian Rudolf Bultmann provocatively answered "no" to a question he posed: Can the *written* words of John's Gospel reveal the Word-become-*flesh*? Through an engagement with classical Vedānta texts, Bannon encourages us to reformulate Bultmann's question: How might scriptural revelation occur as an event in the community's midst, aside from—or subsequent to—the (necessary) activity of reading? While Bultmann rightly presents a Johannine paradox of Word-become-flesh-become-text, after and in light of Vedānta's embodied pedagogy, Bannon encourages us to rethink Christian homiletics as sensual, revelatory, and incarnational speech that inspires a congregation's thirst for social justice. Bannon then explores the question and possible answers in two primary and very influential instances of Hindu and Christian theological works: Śaṇkara's commentarial Vedānta and a sermon by Nicholas of Cusa. By (re)incarnating the Word (whether Johannine or Vedic), the preacher and guru envision revelation as taking place beyond and subsequent to the activity of reading, in the lived and practiced word. In this way Bannon reflects on his own practice. To do comparative theology effectively one should be in academic dialogue with theologians from one's own tradition (in his case, the United Church of Christ, Congregationalist), attentive to the novel implications of theologies proposed in another tradition, and ready to address issues (such as social justice and interreligious understanding) that are timely and pertinent in today's world.

In Chapter 14, "Living Interreligiously: On the 'Pastoral Style' of Comparative Theology," Michael Barnes, S.J., proposes fruitful parallels between comparative theology and pastoral theology. Both can provide reflection on the inner or contemplative dialogue provoked by the myriad relationships that make up the Church's "outer life"—relationships with the poor, the marginalized, the disadvantaged, the unbeliever—and that remain essential even alongside efforts to build relationships with those who profess different religious faiths. As Barnes sees it, contextual pastoral responsibility and interfaith engagement are practices of faith characteristic of a Church called to engage in serious witness to and learning from the people among whom we actually dwell. This vital contextualization broadens the context for the work of "reading" in comparative theology: In today's pluralist world, "living interreligiously" demands attention not just to the traces of divine wisdom revealed in ancient texts, but also to places and monuments, ancient artifacts and contemporary cultural icons that shape and deepen faith within a community, while also instigating conversation and debate beyond familiar boundaries.

Finally, in Chapter 15, "Theologizing for the Yoga Community? Commitment and Hybridity in Comparative Theology," Stephanie Corigliano addresses the issues of religious belonging and commitment by comparing and contrasting "rooted" and "aerial" modes of comparative theology. Corigliano first examines the "rooted" comparative theological methods of four founding scholar-practitioners: James Fredericks, Paul Knitter, Catherine Cornille, and Francis Clooney, and then attends to the differently configured experiences and theological potentials of a younger generation that is "aerial," more agile and fluid in its instincts. Even if initially religious commitment or "rootedness" sensibly formed a natural criterion for comparative theology, nevertheless, as the scope of the field expands, this criterion must cede some space to the fact of less rooted, more fluid realities in one's own community and life, and in those of our religious others. Testing comparative theology in the classroom and using it as a tool for examining new religious and spiritual movements suggests that it can no longer be limited to exchanges between persons from established religious traditions. If the goal of comparative theology is to discover new ways of thinking about one's own tradition/practice and to foster creative and compassionate means for living with diversity, then the field must more successfully represent that diversity. By way of example, she examines her own research on yoga as abiding in a middle space because she participates in a necessary and ongoing Christian theological conversation, and yet, too, in the lively conversation occurring in the wider yoga community.

How to Do Comparative Theology: Let the Reader Choose

The rich array of topics arising in the fifteen chapters of *How to Do Comparative Theology* makes it clear that none of these essays, nor the set of them, offers a definitive recipe for the best way to do comparative theology. They examine methodology in detail, but still only in light of a wider range of issues pertaining also to content and intention. The essays in Part I do not really dwell in purely doctrinal spaces; the essays in Part II still face the difficulties inherent in finding just the right balance between the theological grounding that might be expected of all scholars and the work of doing something new, which requires fresh expertise, experimental thinking, and a good bit of professional and personal daring. The essays in Part III end up assessing theological fruitfulness in terms of how comparative theology works in detail, and what it is for. All the essays, even when striving for solid competence in related sub-disciplinary matters, agree that the history of religions and general field of the study of religion cannot provide all of what we need and want as comparative theologians committed to theological and not area studies discourses. And those disciplines are indispensable, and so we abide in-between the challenges posed by academics on the one side and those posed by faith communities on the other. All of these merit serious attention if the discipline is to thrive.

It will also be clear that the essays do not all agree with one another, even if the volume has arisen from our shared conversation. The essays in Part I, for instance, urge direct connection to doctrinal discourse (even if Nicholson, Takács, and Willis interrogate and rethink that connection from fresh angles). As such, they stand in contrast to the essays in Part II that deliberately *do not* travel a direct path back to doctrine—perhaps because of a concern that if this (re)turn is taken too directly and too quickly it will slip back into the already-established categories of (Christian) doctrine, preemptively diminishing the power of the new learning arising from experiments that do not fit previous theological models. The authors writing in Part III may be read as keeping a distance from both the doctrine-centeredness of Part I and the elite practice of Part II, instead allying themselves with our contemporary cultural and theological preference for experience and for practical and pastoral applications. Comparative theologians all struggle with the same issues of doctrinal grounding, enactment in good practice, and real-world relevance that challenge any serious theology today, and there is no reason to expect an easier or quicker consensus, even on method, than is achieved by other theologians in other fields. *How We Do Comparative Theology* thus honestly assesses the field as it is today, its continuities and differences rendered evident.

We are also aware of the fact that not all theologians who are doing comparative work are represented in this volume. There are other styles and methods than those proposed here, holding other attitudes toward faith and community, for instance, and different measures of rapprochement to the comparative study of religion and other pertinent disciplines. Other traditions of Christian theology will generate other modes of comparative theology—and we have hardly touched at all upon the myriad starting points in other traditions where religious intellectuals do theology differently (if they do it at all). We happily concede that there are other voices, requiring other volumes; yet we do not believe that there can be an unlimited set of possibilities, if the discipline is to remain both comparative and theological in some meaningful sense.

By the work of these essays, we are hoping to share with our readers something of the intensity, challenge, and deep pleasure of our learning at Paderborn, thereby inviting readers to take up the same comparative theological work, balancing the interreligious and the theological in their own way. The very idea of sharing in a common project of comparative theological work remains only partially realized; needed are further clarifications of the criteria that have allowed this work to be a partially realized common enterprise. We can only hope that our different and mutually illuminative case studies will show the way forward for a new generation of comparative theologians, arriving from many different religious traditions and parts of the world, and eager to get on with the work of learning interreligiously, for the sake of a still deeper comprehension of the truths of our own traditions, and a common good that will benefit us all.

PART I

Doing Comparative Theology—as Theology

1 The Problem of Choice in Comparative Theology

Catherine Cornille

The discipline of comparative theology is steadily growing and diversifying. While it is often seen as originating within Christian, and predominantly Roman Catholic, theological circles, it is increasingly practiced by Christians of other denominations and by other religious traditions. And comparative theologians of any one tradition are presented with a seemingly endless possibility of choice in terms of which tradition, which text, or which aspect of that tradition to engage in comparative work. Once other religions are recognized as possible resources for constructive religious reflection and insight, there is no limit to where such truth or insight might manifest itself—in old or new religions, large or small ones, scriptural or non-scriptural. Moreover, the other religion need not even be regarded as a source of truth for comparative theological effort to yield interesting conclusions. Even more exclusivist theologians such as Karl Barth have been used in comparative theological work for fruitful comparative theological work.[1] In addition to the diversity of choice among different traditions and different aspects of other traditions, the discipline of comparative theology has also developed a diversity of approaches, from confessional to meta-confessional approaches, or from tradition-specific to more philosophical approaches.

This diversity of approaches to comparative theology may be regarded as an asset and as a necessary or logical component of the discipline. Not only does it facilitate engagement with any aspect of other religions, but it also allows for the possibility of enriching any of the traditional fields of theology: ethics, systematics, pastoral theology, historical theology, biblical studies, and so on.[2] It also allows for the various approaches to comparative theology to enrich one another and for the discipline as a whole to remain conscious of its particular methodology.

However, the diversity within comparative theology may also lead to fragmentation and to trivialization. As scholars of comparative theology are becoming experts in ever more diverse traditions, it becomes more difficult for them to speak to one another and to their respective traditions. Christian comparative theologians engaging Buddhism may have little to say to Christian comparative theologians engaging Islam, just as Hindu comparative theologians engaging Christianity may have little to say to Hindu comparative theologians engaging Buddhism. Even among comparative theologians engaging the same tradition, there may be little overlap or food for conversation if they are focused on different schools of thought or different aspects of the other tradition. And in all of this, traditional theologians and believers may have little or no involvement in the discussions happening among specialized comparative theologians. For those not immediately involved in comparative theology, the choice of particular religious traditions, topics and insights might appear arbitrary or random and thus only of marginal interest. One of the main challenges for comparative theology is thus that of maintaining or establishing its broader theological relevance.

In this article, I will focus mainly on the challenge or problem as it presents itself for Christian theology, fully conscious that comparative theology presents different challenges for different religious traditions.

Diversity of Approaches

Most comparative theologians are on the same page in terms of the difference between comparative theology and comparative religion. While the latter focuses on understanding and/or explaining a particular religious phenomenon, the former seeks to grasp or advance the Truth. While comparative religion is based on historical methods and maintains the ideal of religious neutrality, comparative theology is a normative discipline that reflects not only on the meaning but also on the truth of particular beliefs and practices. The difference between comparative theology and comparative religion in this regard has been questioned by Hugh Nicholson when he states that "as scholars of religion begin to recognize that the nontheological study of religion is grounded in a set of normative commitments, commitments, moreover that are not inherently inimical to those of theology, the disciplinary boundary between religious studies and theology becomes considerably less clear-cut, and indeed more arbitrary, than previously presumed."[3] While this is undoubtedly the case, there remains a fundamental difference between the two disciplines in that comparative theology fully embraces its religious presuppositions whereas comparative religion still seeks to minimalize their impact.

If we presume the normative nature of comparative theology, the varying approaches to the discipline are based largely on different conceptions of religious truth. Some view comparative theology as a means to gaining a more universal understanding of truth, while others regard it as a way to deepen or enrich the truth as revealed within a particular tradition. The former may be referred to as a "meta-confessional" and the latter as a "confessional" approach to comparative theology.[4] Meta-confessional comparative theologians tend to distinguish their approach from that of classical theology. As Keith Ward puts it, comparative theology is to be understood "not as a form of apologetics for a particular faith but as an intellectual discipline which inquires into ideas of the ultimate value and goal of human life, as they have been perceived and expressed in a variety of religious traditions."[5] In his definition of comparative theology, John Thatamanil states that the goal is "not only to understand better these traditions but also *to determine* the truth of theological matters through conversation and collaboration" (my italics).[6] Here, the aim is thus not only to shed new light on the truth of a particular religion, but to actually discover or decide the truth through dialogue.

The meta-confessional approach to comparative theology seeks to attain to a deeper truth behind the various religious expressions. This approach is exemplified in the volumes of the Comparative Religious Ideas Project, where Robert Neville and Wesley Wildman use the data presented by scholars from different religions to develop broader philosophical and theological theories which attempt to capture the core of a particular religious phenomenon. Here, "comparison is used to develop, probate and improve appropriately vague terminology, most of which is inherited from past discussions, and then systematically tweaked."[7] From developing "vague categories," this approach then proceeds to propose theological or philosophical theories that attempt to capture the core of a particular religious phenomenon. The purpose of this type of comparative theology is not merely speculative but also spiritual and moral, understood in terms of bringing about "cultural and personal change through mutual understanding."[8]

In abandoning a confessional stance while still pursuing questions of truth, this approach to comparative theology is akin to comparative philosophy or philosophy of religion in general. Raimon Panikkar also speaks of his own work as "imparative philosophy" involving an "open philosophical attitude ready to learn from whatever philosophical corner of the world, but without claiming to compare philosophies from an objective, neutral and transcendent vantage point."[9] While he does not claim a neutral perspective, neither is it solely grounded in his original Christian tradition. His theology consists of a highly original synthesis of elements drawn mainly from the Hindu, Christian, and Buddhist traditions. In that regard, his work can also be classified as an example of meta-confessional comparative theology.

The confessional approach, on the other hand, starts from the truth of a particular revelation, which it seeks to elucidate through dialogue with another religion. This approach is reflected in the work of Francis Clooney, who defines comparative theology as

> acts of faith seeking understanding which are rooted in a particular faith tradition but which, from that foundation, venture into learning from one or more other faith traditions. This learning is sought for the sake of fresh theological insights that are indebted to the newly encountered tradition/s as well as the home tradition.[10]

The confessional nature of comparative theology here manifests itself in different ways. It is first of all expressed in a sense of accountability toward a particular faith tradition. As Clooney also puts it, the community to which the theologian belongs

> should be able to see in the work of the comparative theologian a concern for the truth that is known and revered within the theologian's faith tradition. Her work must in some meaningful way contribute to a receptive community's effort to understand more deeply the truths of its faith.[11]

But this confessional character of comparative theology also appears in the choice of topics and the point of departure for comparison. Clooney indeed starts the work of comparative theology from distinctly Christian texts and topics. In *Hindu God, Christian God*, he affirms the Christian nature of the book as follows: "Not only have I begun my chapters with Christian theologians, but I frame the questions and discover answers that fit nicely into the categories and expectations of the Christian theological tradition."[12] The confessional approach to comparative theology starts from a particular theological question, problem, or text within one tradition, which it seeks to elucidate and deepen through exploring the resources and insights of other religions. It requires in-depth knowledge of another religion, but that knowledge is ultimately used to gain a deeper understanding of one's own tradition.

The difference between meta-confessional and confessional approaches is at times subtle because meta-confessional approaches are often still based on clear religious presuppositions, and because confessional approaches do not always carry out the normative implications of their approach. Clooney, for example, at times moves away from a strictly confessional understanding of comparative theology. In *Beyond Compare*, he states that a consequence of reading texts from different traditions side by side is that the "reader becomes distant from the totalizing power of both texts, precisely because she or he knows both, cannot dismiss either, and does not submit entirely to either."[13] Comparative theology is practiced in a vulnerable place between religious traditions where

> we acquire a surfeit of scriptures, yet have no Scripture; multiple languages and words and images, yet no tested, effective manner of speaking; a wealth of theological insights, yet no sure doctrine; not one but two rich religious traditions from which to benefit, and yet—because we know too much—no single normative tradition that commands our attention.[14]

This thus suggests a departure from or at least an ambivalence toward the idea of a clearly confessional starting point and goal for comparative theology. In *Seeing Through Texts*, he suggests that it may not be the time to make final theological judgments on the truth of particular texts and traditions. Rather, he proposes that "one may also consider whether it would be a good idea to entertain a new, larger narrative which encompasses both traditions without (intentionally) privileging either one of them. Though early on this too may be an explanatory venture which aids future scholarly work, at a root level it may also be a step toward the composition of the new canon, the telling of a larger story—for, and in the formation of, a new community beyond both traditions."[15] The idea of forming a new community also reappears in more recent works where he states that comparative theology "may create a liminal religious community that seeks to understand faith that is complexified by comparative learning. This new community will have roots in multiple communities, even if it usually remains its participants' second community. As the number of persons living this complicated intellectual and spiritual life grows larger, the fixed boundaries separating religions become all the less plausible, not due simply to demographics or social change, but now also because the theological insights arising in comparative study will push the boundaries."[16]

Clooney seems to suggest that comparative theology naturally leads away from an explicitly confessional position when he states that "Even if a comparative theologian is determined to adhere faithfully to the tradition into which she has been born and to the academic community in which she is employed, simple loyalties become more difficult after we have actually engaged in the very learning across religious borders that rootedness in a tradition has made possible."[17] Rather than clearly belonging to a particular tradition, he speaks of comparative theology as leading to a "cultivated hybridity"[18] in which "deference to two traditions means that she in a way belongs to both, without belonging fully to either."[19] This approach seems to move in the direction of Tinu Ruparell's notion of interstitial theology, which he defines as "a mode or methodology for the comparative philosophy of religion which exploits the structure of metaphor and aims at the construction of liminal, hybrid perspectives or standpoints for continuing the conversation of religions in a creative and open-ended way."[20] Ruparell sees this form of comparative theology or comparative philosophy of religion as evolving into the formation of new, "recombinant" religious traditions, based on the hybrid religious beliefs and practices of its adherent. This hybrid approach to comparative theology thus moves away from an explicitly confessional to an inter-confessional approach which focuses on the common ground between two traditions, or else oscillates between the normativity of one and the other tradition.

It is not surprising that the discipline of comparative theology has come to develop various goals and approaches, and that the theoretical views of the discipline at times diverge somewhat from the practical applications. The practice of comparative theology requires a variety of skills and methods (linguistic, historical, philosophical, and theological) that all pull the scholar in different directions. Though the practice of comparative theology may generate some methodological fluidity, the basic difference between the goals of confessional and meta-confessional comparative theology remains clear. Whereas confessional comparative theologians attempt to remain within the boundaries of orthodoxy of their own traditions, meta-confessional theologians feel less restrained by such theological strictures. This is why the dialogue between these two approaches may at times be difficult, but also fruitful.

Diversity of Traditions and Topics

As data regarding different religious traditions has become readily available, the choice of tradition and topic for the comparative theological enterprise has become dazzling. The world of religious diversity indeed includes thousands of religions, old and new, scriptural and oral, large and small, local and transnational. Many religions contain multiple subtraditions and schools, that at times have themselves spawned breakaway religions. The general recognition of goodness and truth in other religions (as, for example, in the document *Nostra Aetate*) opens the door to engaging a vast plethora of religious teachings and practices. Serious engagement with another religion of course requires study of its language, history, and traditions, which tends to limit the work of the comparative theologians to his or her particular competency. To date, the religions that have received the lion's share of comparative theological interest are Hinduism and Buddhism.[21] In *The New Comparative Theology*, Daniel Joslyn-Semiatkoski laments the fact that Judaism has received comparatively little comparative theological interest.[22] He ascribes this to a latent supersessionism. However, it may also simply be due to the newness of the field and to a sense of prudence in not wanting to appear as (again) using Jewish texts for Christian theological purposes.[23] The study of Islam and Confucianism is also becoming an integral part of Christian comparative theology. However, this still leaves open an immense world of possibility that is difficult to manage or control.

In practice, the choice of a tradition is generally based on one's personal interest, and/or on the vicissitudes and requirements of academic training (which traditions happen to be taught at particular institutions). This appeal of a certain religion may already suggest a certain resonance or promise and potential for constructive engagement. But the actual focus then on a particular aspect of the tradition, on a certain text, teaching, or practice seems to occur fairly haphazardly. To be sure, the comparative theologian will present compelling reasons why he or she has chosen particular texts or teachings for comparative theological reflection. But this still leaves open an infinite array of other possibilities, both within and beyond a particular religion. Comparative theology is indeed subject to some of the same methodological difficulties and challenges as Jonathan Z. Smith outlined in his famous article "In Comparison a Magic Dwells."[24] As in comparative religion, the choice of topic in comparative theology is often governed by what Smith calls a quasi magical "recollection of similarity":

> often, at some point along the way, as if unbidden, as a sort of déjà vu, the scholar remembers that he has seen "it" or "something like it" before; he experiences what Coleridge described in an early essay in *The Friend* as the result of "the hooks-and-eyes of the memory." This experience, this unintended consequence of research, must then be accorded significance and provided with an explanation.[25]

In discussing the method of comparative theology, Clooney states that the process "ordinarily starts with the intuition of an intriguing resemblance that prompts us to place two realities—texts, images, practices, doctrines, persons—near one another, so that they may be seen over and again, side by side."[26] The occasion for learning remains a virtually chance occurrence in which what one encounters in the other religion strikes a chord of resonance with what one happens to know within one's own tradition. Clooney also admits that this is a "necessarily arbitrary and intuitive practice." Whereas the historian of religion may proceed from similarity to contiguity, and the comparativist to more general theories on the nature of the particular phenomenon or belief, the comparative theologian explores similarities and differences that may shed new light on one's own tradition or that may generate new insight. Still, it would be difficult to establish a natural or necessary connection between the texts or topics guiding comparative theological work. Because comparative theology may involve both a process of learning from and theological critique of the other, just about any aspect of any religion may lend itself to comparative theological reflection.

A review of the list of topics that have been the object of comparative theological exercise reveals that there is indeed little or no continuity or coherence. Some works compare the central objects of devotion in different religions (Amida and Christ; Baby Krishna, Infant Christ, and so on) while others compare texts touching on similar subjects; some compare theological ideas or concepts (reincarnation and Christian eschatology, God and emptiness) while others compare significant figures (Mechtild and Lalleshvari; Ramanuja and Schleiermacher; Eckhart and Shankara).[27]

This seemingly infinite diversity of choice raises the question of the relevance or impact of this approach to comparative theology. As the discipline is becoming more and more diversified, with scholars working in different traditions and on different topics, there is increasingly less occasion for comparative theologians with different expertise (even in one other religion) to speak to one another, let alone to the mainstream theologians within their tradition. The requirements of specialization moreover work against the possibility for dialogue and correction within the tradition, and the theological conclusions drawn often remain marginal to the theological discussions taking place within a tradition. This should be a topic of concern for confessional comparative theology, which seeks to advance the theological project of a particular tradition.

In order to address this challenge, I have elsewhere suggested that comparative theologians might focus on topics that are of central concern to mainstream theologians in a particular tradition at a particular time. Comparative theologians may then bring the insights from other religions to bear on that particular topic, thereby demonstrating the relevance of the field for broader theological reflection.[28]

Diversity of Method and Purpose

The method of comparative theology has been carved out and established largely in opposition to or contrast with other disciplines focused on the reality of religious diversity. It distinguishes itself from the secular and historical approaches to the study of religion by its normative focus on questions of truth, which it shares with other theological disciplines. And it distinguishes itself from Theology of Religions by its focus on actual comparisons between religious texts, teachings, or rituals, and from earlier, nineteenth-century approaches to comparative theology by its greater mutuality, its receptivity to the presence of truth in other religions, and openness to the possibility of learning from them. At times, the new comparative theology is also placed in opposition to traditional religious apologetics, which establishes the truth of one's own tradition over against the falsehood or incoherence of the other. Though this is certainly not the main goal or method of comparative theology, the pursuit of truth probably cannot advance without some degree of apologetics.

Beyond these general and contrastive outlines, there has been little by way of a common method in the practice of comparative theology. There is general agreement that it involves in-depth study of another religion, which includes linguistic and historical competencies. But how that understanding of the other religion is then related to and brought to bear on one's own tradition differs significantly from one comparative theologian to the next. Some focus on close textual comparisons, while others compare particular concepts, ideas, or practices across traditions; some focus on close historical and contextual comparisons, while others engage in a wholesale reinterpretation of one tradition in light of the worldview and philosophical categories of another. Though the term "comparative theology" as understood in the preceding text has only become current since about the last decade of the twentieth century, it has been practiced before (as well as since) by scholars who do not use that designation for their own work. Focusing only on the engagement of Christianity with Hinduism, theologians such as Upadhyaya, Johanns, Le Saux, Griffiths, Klostermaier, Chenchiah, Chakkarai, Thomas, De Smet, Grant, Panikkar,[29] and so on were deeply involved in comparative theology without using the disciplinary category. It is thus important that these pioneers of the discipline are not forgotten and that their methods are also taken into consideration. In attempting to develop a distinctive method, some European scholars moreover prefer the term "interreligious theology" to "comparative theology." All of this adds to the methodological complexity of comparative theology.

Comparative theology has tended to focus on texts, whether canonical texts or philosophical or spiritual treatises. While this textual focus has been attributed to a typically Christian (and Protestant) privileging of scriptural revelation,[30] there are also more generic reasons to turn to texts. For one, they represent the most stable data of any religion. While ritual forms and material artifacts change through time, texts offer a continuous basis for reflection. To be sure, the interpretation of sacred texts changes and differs, but at least they offer a basis from which to study those differences and consider their significance for one's own comparative theological reflection. This, of course, does not mean that oral or non-scriptural traditions are less relevant for comparative theology, or that rituals might not be rich food for comparative work. But it is only to point out that the focus on texts is not purely arbitrary or unjustifiable. However, besides texts, comparative theology may also focus on ritual forms, on material culture, institutional and social structures, and on general philosophical principles and systems (usually also elaborated in texts).

If the ultimate purpose or goal of comparative theology is to advance in one's religious self-understanding through learning from other religious traditions, then one may distinguish four different types of learning, which are also exemplified in the work of particular comparative theologians.

A first form of learning involves a process of *intensification* through the bringing together of texts, teachings, or practices of different traditions. It is exemplified in the work of Francis Clooney, who foregrounds this approach to comparative theology in all of his works. In *The Way, the Truth and the Life*, for example, Clooney states that "Proximity enhances intensity, and with intensification, all their meanings become sharper and clearer, even as the possibilities of a single meaning and single conclusion seem all the more unlikely because now we see clearly what is involved."[31] Similarly, in *Beyond Compare, St. Francis de Sales and Sri Vedanta Desika on Loving Surrender to God*, Clooney suggests that "although these two reading experiences do not require each other, once both are read in proximity this doubled intensity deeply affects the reader twice over, such that each text intensifies and magnifies the other rather than diluting its impact."[32] And in the conclusion of his latest book, *His Hiding Place is Darkness*, in recapturing the intense experiences of love in separation expressed in both the *Song of Songs* and in the *Tiruvaymoli*, Clooney argues that "This doubling of memories intensifies rather than relativizes the deep yet fragile commitments of our singular, first love."[33] Here, the reading of texts from different traditions side by side amplifies the meaning of each. This may take the form of reinforcing the religious meaning and truth of a particular experience or text through its recurrence in other traditions, or through its very specificity. Or it may take the form of highlighting the specificity of the symbols and ideas advanced in one's own religious texts. It thus points to the religious or spiritual implications and consequences of the comparative study of religions, without, however, proposing any shifts or changes in the meaning of religious texts or teachings.

A second type of learning involves a process of *recovery* or *rediscovery* of elements embedded in one's own tradition. The engagement with other religions indeed often refers one back to figures or practices or beliefs that for various reasons had been forgotten, neglected, or marginalized in the course of history. The resurgence of interest in figures such as Meister Eckhart or Marguerite Porete, for example, has much to do with an interest in unitive mystical experiences, ignited by a fascination for non-dual strands of Hinduism or Buddhism. And the appeal of practices of yoga and meditation has similarly reawakened interest in the Hesychast tradition and in the Jesus prayer. This often leads to a critical re-evaluation of the causes or reasons for their neglect and to their revaluation in the tradition. It allows individuals who were being drawn into another tradition to find new sources of inspiration and spiritual nourishment in their own tradition. As such, comparative theology may bring the unsuspected richness of the tradition to the fore. In recovering elements of one's own tradition through the eyes of the other, it may also bring with it new levels of understanding of traditional texts, teachings, or practices. It may thus also offer a new lens through which the rest of the tradition is understood and interpreted. But as such, it merely shines light on particular aspects of the tradition, without changing them.[34]

A third approach to comparative theology involves the actual *reinterpretation* of one tradition in light of another. Here, the philosophical categories of one tradition are used to interpret another. To be sure, in the course of history, religions have habitually borrowed philosophical categories from one another and adjusted them to make sense of their own beliefs and practices. In the context of comparative theology, this may be done more self-consciously and on a broader scale. As such, some Christian theologians have used the philosophical systems of Hindu Advaita Vedanta or Buddhist Madhyamika in order to reinterpret all of Christian thought and practice. This tends to be justified by pointing to the accidental process by which Christianity was originally interpreted in Hellenistic terms and by the importance of establishing the true universality of Christianity by expressing it in different philosophical terms.[35] Such process of reinterpretation opens new avenues of understanding and experience, while also raising challenges and questions with regard to certain fundamental Christian teachings. Short of a wholesale interpretation of one tradition in light of the philosophical categories of another, comparative theology may also involve a more limited use of particular concepts of another tradition, which may shed fresh light on one's own teachings and practices. This process has been operative wherever categories from another religion are used to translate one's own tradition in a different culture. In the current attempts at inculturation, categories borrowed from another tradition are not merely emptied of their original meaning, but allowed to enrich Christian self-understanding. This thus requires comparative theological engagement, and a process of negotiation between original and Christian interpretations. Reinterpretation thus points to a genuine potential for change and growth of the tradition through comparative theology. It plays a role in every type of comparative theology because by putting texts side by side, or by seeing one tradition through the eyes of another, new meanings are naturally accrued.[36]

A final form of learning through comparative theology may consist of the actual *appropriation of new insights,* experiences, and practices derived from engagement with another religion. This may present a particular challenge to religions, as it might be thought to suggest some degree of insufficiency or lack, which clashes with religious claims to doctrinal certainty and ritual efficacy. The incorporation of elements from another religion is thus generally understood as a further elaboration of established teachings or practices, or as a development of elements that were already in essence present in the tradition. Thus, when drawing from Buddhist teachings and practices of wisdom and mindfulness, Aloysius Pieris draws from Thomas Aquinas in emphasizing the necessary balance between love and wisdom.[37] And John Keenan grounds the possibility of interpreting Christian faith through Mahayana categories in the mystical theologies of Gregory of Nyssa and Pseudo-Dionysius.[38] For Catholic comparative theologians, the permission to learn something new from other religions may be found in the Vatican II document *Nostra Aetate,* which recognizes "rays of that truth which enlightens all men" in precepts and doctrines "differing in many ways from her own teaching" (2).[39] To be sure, these practices and teachings cannot contradict Christian faith, and at times may have to be reinterpreted to fit within a Christian religious framework. But comparative theology may lead to the appropriation of insights and experiences that had previously not been developed or cultivated in the tradition. This tends to occur mainly within the areas of spirituality and ethics.

All of these forms of learning in comparative theology are of course not mutually exclusive. Reading texts side by side may lead not only to intensification but also at times to reinterpretation of one text in light of the other. And the rediscovery of neglected or forgotten traditions may also involve certain subtle shifts of interpretation leading to the incorporation of genuinely new meaning. The difference between appropriation, reinterpretation, and rediscovery may also at times be blurred as texts and teachings are at times used for the single purpose of advancing new theological ideas which may be only partly explicit in the text.[40] Regardless of the method employed, comparative theology is to contribute to and be an expression of systematic theological reflection which seeks to advance the self-understanding of the tradition.

Traditional Theology and Comparative Theology

One of the important challenges for comparative theology lies in establishing its place and function in relation to traditional theology. This challenge does not necessarily apply to the meta-confessional approach to theology. Such "theology without walls" or "global" or "conviviencia" theology by definition views itself as beyond the traditional understanding of theology as based on a particular revelation or set of foundational religious principles. It views traditional theology at best as a set of ideas or practices from which to borrow in the process of developing a higher synthetic system.

However, in so far as the confessional approach to comparative theology is focused on enhancing theological reflection within a particular religious tradition, its constructive relationship to traditional theology is of vital importance to its self-understanding. Several challenges present themselves in this pursuit. First, the fragmentation within the field of comparative theology makes it difficult for classical theologians to know how or where to connect with the work of comparative theologians. Second, classical theologians may not know how to judge the importance and validity of particular comparative theological works because they are not themselves experts in the other traditions. Third, comparative theology may not be perceived as intrinsic to Christian theological reflection. It may still be regarded as a threat, or at best as a luxury that is not essentially relevant for Christian theological reflection. Comparative theologians themselves of course bear some responsibility for addressing each of these challenges. An additional or related challenge for comparative theology is that, unlike feminist or liberation theology, it does not have a clear and unifying material object, as my discussion of the problem of choice has made clear. While its focus is on theological enrichment through dialogue with other religions, it does not have a specific religion, problem, or question to consider. This may render the discipline somewhat ethereal or unmanageable for traditional theologians.

This is where the discipline of theology of religions plays an essential role. It establishes the theological foundation for engaging with other religions and for the possibility of learning from them. If indeed God's spirit and grace are at work in other religions, then it would be necessary for Christian theologians to engage in theological dialogue with other religions in order to discern the presence of truth in them. In both critically reflecting on the traditional Christian attitudes toward other religions and providing a theological foundation for engaging them in a constructive manner, theology of religions will thus continue to represent an important bridge between traditional and comparative theology.

There are also ways in which comparative theologians may themselves work to illustrate the importance of comparative theology for traditional constructive theology. Rather than pursue any possible avenue of choice in terms of topic and tradition, comparative theology may become more attentive to the particular questions and topics which occupy the broader theological community. Because the possibilities for comparative theology are indeed vast, one way of contributing to the broader theological discussion is to focus on particular burning issues and demonstrate how engagement with perspectives from other religions may indeed enhance and enrich the discussion. This may also enhance the communication between comparative theologians specialized in different traditions, who may then bring various religious insights into a theological discussion, and thus form communities of theological research.

A second avenue for greater dialogue with traditional theologians is through continued engagement and pursuit of theological feedback. It is through submitting the fruits of their comparative theological efforts to the tradition at large that comparative theologians may remain part of critical theological discussions and may indeed hope to have an impact on the broader theological tradition.

Conclusion: Choice of the Problem in Comparative Theology

Comparative theology by its very nature tends toward internal diversity and fragmentation. The term may cover different approaches: historical, theological, or philosophical. The number of traditions and topics to be explored is almost limitless. And the mode and outcome of the comparative theological exercise are equally varied. I have identified four general goals or effects of comparative theology (intensification, recovery, reinterpretation, and appropriation), each of which will, however, yield different results depending on the topic and on the traditions involved.

This diversity and unpredictability of the field may be regarded as a source of richness. Each new comparison, however pursued, adds new insight to the tradition and enhances the discipline itself. However, this radical diversity in methods and contents also presents significant challenges. First, it makes it difficult for the discipline to establish itself among other theological disciplines. There is among theologians still some confusion about the nature and goals of comparative theology, and some suspicion about its genuine theological orientation. As such, a greater clarity about the discipline and its various approaches, and maybe also a different nomenclature for confessional and meta-confessional or inter-confessional approaches may be in order. Because the term "comparative theology" has generally come to be defined as a confessional discipline, non-confessional approaches might, for example, be called "interreligious theology."

Second, growing specialization and diversification inhibits dialogue and exchange among the scholars involved in the field. If every scholar pursues his or her own individual topic of choice in his or her own way, there is little opportunity for mutual correction and collaboration. One way to address this is through greater collaboration around particular theological questions or problems, which are ideally also alive in and pertinent to the broader theological community. This would thus generate various circles of dialogue, with scholars from another religion, with comparative theologians of one's own tradition, and with traditional theologians from one's own tradition. Not only will this demonstrate the immediate relevance of comparative theology, but it will also provide more opportunity for critical feedback and reflection on one's comparative theological insights.

While comparative theology may yield rich and challenging new insights, it takes time for a tradition to absorb those insights and findings. The problem is thus how to control or contain the infinite possibility of choice in comparative theology so as to allow for traditions to keep pace with the discipline, and to allow the discipline itself to develop in a methodologically coherent manner.

I have suggested that the problem of choice in comparative theology may thus be abated by a proper choice of a problem for comparative theological inquiry. This may be difficult to achieve because the interest in comparative theology often evolves from a personal fascination with a particular text, teaching, or practice, and because the expertise required to engage two traditions in depth does not tend to generate a critical mass of scholars interested in the same topics. Moreover, one may argue that the fruits of comparative theological labor may only manifest themselves in the long run. However, like every area of theology, comparative theology would itself also benefit from critical feedback and response from the broader theological community. Not only would this aid in the process of discernment, which is a critical part of comparative theology, but it would also enhance the impact of comparative theology and ensure its integral role within the broader theological reflection.

Notes

1. See Ensminger, *Karl Barth's Theology as a Resource for a Christian Theology of Religions* and Clooney, *Hindu God, Christian God*, 129–62.
2. The work of many Biblical scholars who attempt to understand the Hebrew Bible in the contexts of broader Near Eastern religions may, in fact, be regarded as a form of comparative theology.
3. In Nicholson, "The Reunification of Theology and Comparison in the New Comparative Theology," 635.
4. In his 1987 entry to the *Encyclopedia of Religion*, David Tracy distinguishes two different approaches to comparative theology, one involving a comparison of theological concepts and systems and the other a more strictly theological and confessional enterprise in which one religion is critically correlated with another. While the comparison of theological systems is still an important part of comparative theology, it is generally viewed as a prelude to or an expression of a particular theological question. The comparison of theological systems and beliefs as such would be classified as comparative religion.
5. Ward, *Religion and Revelation*, 40.
6. Thatamanil, *The Immanent Divine*, 3.
7. Neville and Wildman, "On Comparing Religious Ideas," 10.
8. Wildman and Neville, "Our Approach to Comparison," 214.
9. "What Is Comparative Philosophy Comparing?" 127.
10. Clooney, *Comparative Theology*, 10.
11. Ibid., 157
12. Clooney, *Hindu God, Christian God*, 181
13. Clooney, *Beyond Compare*, 209.
14. Ibid.
15. Clooney, *Seeing Through Texts*, 302.
16. Clooney, *Comparative Theology*, 161–62.
17. Ibid., 161.
18. Ibid., 160.
19. Ibid., 156.
20. Ruparell, "Inter-Religious Dialogue and Interstitial Theology," 121.
21. The volumes in the series of Christian Commentaries on non-Christian sacred texts have also so far focused exclusively on Hindu and Buddhist texts, which can only be partly explained by the multiplicity of texts in these traditions.
22. Josely-Semiatkoski, "Comparative Theology and the Status of Judaism: Hegemony and Reversals," 89.
23. This was at least the response I received from the Christian Scholars Group, which is deeply engaged in the dialogue with Judaism and post-Holocaust theology. When presenting my series of Christian Commentaries on non-Christian Sacred Texts, they

commented that this would not (yet) be possible with Rabbinic texts for fear of giving the impression of supersessionism and hegemony.

24. The article was originally published in 1982 in Smith's book *Imagining Religion: From Babylon to Jonestown* (19–35) and later republished with responses in *A Magic Still Dwells*, 23–44.
25. Smith, "Prologue: In Comparison a Magic Dwells," 25–26.
26. Clooney, *Comparative Theology*, 11.
27. See Largen, *Baby Krishna, Infant Christ*, Voss Roberts, *Dualities: A Theology of Difference*, Sydnor, *Ramanuja and Schleiermacher*, Henri De Lubac, *Amida*, Otto, *Mysticism East and West*.
28. Cornille, "The Confessional Nature of Comparative Theology."
29. Upadhyaya, *The Writings of Brahmabandhab Upadhyaya*; Johanns, *To Christ through the Vedanta*; Le Saux, *Saccidananda: A Christian Approach to the Advaitic Experience*, Griffiths, *Marriage of East and West*; Klostermaier, *Hindu and Christian in Vrindaban*; Chenchiah, *Ashrams Past and Present*; Thomas, *The Acknowledged Christ of the Hindu Renaissance*; De Smet, *La Quête de l'Éternel, Approches Chrétiens de l'Hinduisme*; Sara Grant, *Toward an Alternative Theology: Confessions of a non-Dualist Christian*; Panikkar, *The Rhythm of Being*.
30. Holdrege, "What's Beyond the Post? Comparative Analysis as Critical Method," 84–86.
31. Clooney, *The Truth, the Way, the Life*, 182.
32. Clooney, *Beyond Compare*, 183
33. Clooney, *His Hiding Place is Darkness*, 126.
34. An example of this may be found in John Main's Christian Meditation Movement, which, through encounter with Buddhist and Hindu forms of meditation led to a recovery of Christian Hesychast forms of meditation.
35. Keenan, "The Promise and Peril of Interfaith Hermeneutics."
36. An example of this is Keenan's *The Meaning of Christ: A Mahayana Theology*.
37. Pieris, *Love Meets Wisdom*.
38. Keenan, *The Meaning of Christ*.
39. *Vatican Council II*, ed. A. Flannery (New York: Costello Publishing Co, 1975), 739.
40. See, for example, Voss Roberts's book *Dualities: A Theology of Difference*, in which through a comparative theological engagement with Lallesvari and Mechthild of Magdeburg, she advances feminist theological insights regarding divine fluidity, which neither woman themselves explicitly develops.

2 Reflecting on Approaches to Jesus in the Qur'ān from the Perspective of Comparative Theology

Klaus von Stosch

Choosing the Topic and Way of Proceeding

The first issue to which comparative theology must respond when its methodology is questioned is choosing a topic for discussion. As religions offer such great variety of starting points for discussion, these points should not be chosen only according to the preference of the researcher or institution, if comparative theology wants to show its relevance to the Church and society. In my opinion, theology, like any other science, should try to solve problems and to respond to contemporary issues. Therefore, I see three legitimate starting points for comparative theology: problems of society, problems of theology, and problems that arise out of the interaction of people with different religious backgrounds.

Dealing with topics important to society provides the possibility for comparative theology to show its specific knowledge of religious traditions and to point out different religions' ideas on how to respond to these problems. To do this, comparative theology relies on its knowledge of different religious traditions. Challenges in the economic sector or the environmental sector can therefore be better accepted with the help of comparative theology's guidance—especially if different religions argue for the same response to a common problem, but by drawing on their respective traditions. However, if the participants do not learn from the other religions anything that enhances concepts in their own religions, such an approach should not be called comparative theology. I think that the term "comparative theology" should be restricted to theological contributions that are shaped and enriched by comparison. Thus, topics such as those mentioned previously can become comparative theology if specific resources of the other religion are taken into account to correct or expand one's own response to a problem.[1]

A second legitimate reason to practice comparative theology is the desire for reflection on a problem in one's own religious tradition. This chapter therefore deals with a discourse within Christianity that has become problematic for many contemporary Christians: Christology. Many contemporary Christians find it difficult to understand Jesus as truly human and at the same time truly divine. For them, the question of a consistent theory of the hypostatic union, which always has been a problem dogmatically, arises on an existential level. Taking the Qur'ān into account in order to respond to this issue shows great potential because the Qur'ān also points out and criticizes notions that challenge Christian dogmatics.[2] However, this essay does not focus on further developing Christology; I focus my discussion on a different issue that is very much in line with a last possibility of comparative theology.

This third possibility of practicing comparative theology refers to problems arising out of the interaction among people with different religious backgrounds. In Islamic-Christian relations, Christology is generally considered the decisive point of difference between both religions. For Christians, it is essential to believe that Jesus Christ is the Son of God; the rejection of this confession seems to be a constituent part of Muslim identity. This is why the discussion about Jesus seems to lead necessarily to points of controversy central to Islamic-Christian dialogue.

Engaging in a dialogue about Jesus with Islamic theology should not, of course, aim to change other people's views to fit one's own. Neither can the dialogue negate the differences between the religions. Nonetheless, I hope to show that Christians can learn a lot through a deeper look at the perception of Jesus in the Qur'ān. That the Qur'ān can indeed contribute to a better understanding of Jesus of Nazareth is exactly what different Muslim scholars—for example Mahmoud Ayoub, the American pioneer in Islamic research regarding Jesus of Nazareth—claim when speaking of a legitimate Christology on the basis of the Qur'ān.[3] So, too, the Qom-based Shiite theologian Muhammad Legenhausen, arguing that the time has come for Muslims to engage in discourse about Christology,[4] contributes to this engagement. Legenhausen is of the opinion that through such engagement, the similarities and differences of Islam and Christianity can be looked at in a different light. Moreover, he asserts that Muslims may be able to help Christians to better recognize Jesus as healer and savior.[5]

Therefore the question arises whether something can be learned from the Qur'ānic understanding of Jesus of Nazareth, or whether, at this point, the difference is so essential to the formation of a religious identity that the depreciation of the other's belief is indispensable. This chapter intends a first attempt to respond to these questions from the perspective of comparative theology. Contributing to a Christian comparative theology, this chapter aims to take the Islamic appreciation of Jesus of Nazareth as seriously as possible in order to ask whether this appreciation can be integrated into Christian theology without abandoning one's own claims on truth. In other words, what is important is whether the Qur'ānic approach to Jesus of Nazareth can be accepted and whether it can be granted a place in reflection on Christian belief. Moreover, this chapter wants to ask whether this unfamiliar approach might enrich one's own identity.[6]

At this point, the danger of expropriating the other and making the other's religion a means to an end also has to be taken into account. Therefore, I suggest using comparative theology as a methodological tool for the review of one's own work, and also for finding a way to include the arguments of theologians of other religions in this project. According to my own definition of comparative theology, it is important that comparative theology not happen through solitary research—even if extensive knowledge of the other religion is already present—but by developing a theological position through dialogue with theologians from other religions. It is clear that the ideas of these theologians can also be accessed through reading their books or commentaries, but I think that more cooperative work between theologians of different religions should be done. Scholars can evaluate each other's work and help to improve it. I have applied these suggestions by writing this chapter in dialogue with Islamic theologians.[7]

How do we have to do comparative theology? I am suggesting that we work in a way that is oriented toward problems and toward dialogue, as well as working micrologically, i.e., by turning to case studies. Participants in a comparative theological conversation have to be willing to engage the others' traditions and to debate one another. Moreover, a third party situated outside the dialogue needs to be involved in the process in order to challenge the dialogue's results and to question the temporary results of the dialogue. The Middle Eastern Studies scholar Angelika Neuwirth is the third party involved in this chapter, as I deal with Jesus in the Qur'ān. She encouraged us to work more diachronically in our study of the Qur'ān and to examine individual verses in the context of the respective surah.[8] A diachronic reading means a reading that follows the chronological order of the emergence of the verses in the Qur'ān. This requires much historical work, which I cannot do in this first approach to the verses. Although the first results of this study have already been published, until now I had not taken into account all the implications of this new methodological approach.[9] Thus, I see that what is particularly desirable—but what this paper cannot yet carry out satisfactorily—is a diachronic investigation of the Qur'ānic references to Jesus of Nazareth and their location in the context of each surah. But for the time being, I consider the option for a synchronic interpretation of the Qur'ān to be legitimate for the purposes of a first orientation—i.e., I will look at all the relevant verses of the Qur'ān at the same time. Therefore I will go into diachronic aspects of exegesis only at particularly salient passages.

This chapter is structured in the following way: First, I acknowledge the Qur'ānic appreciation of the person of Jesus of Nazareth by looking at the Qur'ānic attributions as "Prophet," "Servant of God," "Messiah," "Healer," "Word," and "Spirit from God". Second, I look more deeply into the Qur'ānic rejection of Jesus as Son of God, and into other seemingly anti-Christian interpretations of Jesus of Nazareth, in order to locate these in their original historical context. Third, a short conclusion offers first results regarding the prospects and limits of a Qur'ānic Christology.[10]

Acknowledging the Qur'ānic Appreciation of Jesus of Nazareth

Jesus of Nazareth is one of the prophets most frequently mentioned in the Qur'ān. Martin Bauschke notes 15 surahs, 6 Meccan and 9 Medinan, and 108 verses in total, which speak of Jesus directly or refer to him.[11] In this chapter, I cannot, of course, discuss all these verses in detail. Therefore, I confine myself to those central to the evaluation of Qur'ānic Christology. In this section, I will concentrate on the most important titles, attributes, and names given to Jesus of Nazareth in the Qur'ān.

JESUS AS PROPHET AND SERVANT OF GOD

What may be the most famous characterization of Jesus and what is stressed time and again in the Qur'ān is his identification as prophet

(19:30; 33:7).[12] Only from the Medinan period onward is Jesus also recognized as having been sent by God (*rasûl*) (3:48f.; 4:171; 5:75.111; 57:27; 61:6). Being named prophet is already one of the highest honors given by the Qur'ān; when this is combined with other titles, it becomes even more obvious that in the Qur'ān Jesus holds the highest honor possible for a human being.[13]

From a Christian point of view, the title "prophet" lies at the heart of the New Testament.[14] Still, the Qur'ānic characterizations of Jesus as prophet or as *rasûl* find only little enthusiasm with Christians. This can be explained by the fact that the Qur'ān acknowledges Jesus only as one among other prophets. It repeatedly declares programmatically: "We make no distinction among any of them" (2:136 and 3:84). Although this declaration is relativized elsewhere and the importance of Jesus is stressed,[15] the fact that he, like all others, "was but an apostle" (5:75) cannot be ignored. Therefore, the title does not seem adequate for appreciating the uniqueness of Jesus, but it can be helpful in reminding Christians of an important aspect of the mission of Christ.

Another title repeatedly applied to Jesus of Nazareth in the Qur'ān is "servant of God." As early as in the cradle, Jesus declares himself to be servant of God (19:30). At this point he also emphasizes that he, as servant of God, will always be blessed by God, wherever he goes (19:31). It is especially striking that Jesus is a role model for Israel; he is the one who can save it from its contentiousness (43:58f) due to his position as servant. He is the servant radiating peace and renouncing violence (19:32f). Using titles[16] and concepts that identify him as servant of God, therefore, brings him closer to the servant of God we know from Isaiah, presumably also very important to the historical Jesus and his self-understanding.

The self-predication of Jesus as servant of God is also a correction of exaggerated claims put into Jesus's mouth in the apocryphal infancy gospels. Here, just as in many other passages of the Qur'ān, every exaggeration in the adoration of Jesus is rejected. At the same time, the identification of Jesus as servant of God does not indicate a depreciation of his person but is rather like the first, early Christian formula of confession which did not say, "Jesus is the Kyrios," but "Jesus is the Servant of God."[17] As a matter of fact, at this point, the similarity to statements of Paul is striking.[18] Even if there are no specific allusions to Paul in the Qur'ān,[19] specifically Pauline notions, such as the connection between Jesus's being servant and being lord and having authority, can also be found in the Qur'ān. Jesus is not only depicted as servant but also as someone to be heeded (by the Jews): "Remain, then, conscious of God, and pay heed unto me" (3:50; 43:63). The Qur'ān repeatedly emphasizes this.

Certainly, by these same claims, the Qur'ānic talk of Jesus is always strictly theocentric. Jesus, precisely in being servant, radically points away from himself and toward God; in being obedient to Him, Jesus is always engaged in the service of God (cf. 3:51). In this respect, Jesus is a role model for the essence of Islam because of his total devotion to God.[20] Similarly, Mahmoud Ayoub defines Jesus as a model of fulfilled humanity;[21] in him, the destiny of humankind and the model of humankind's relationship to God are mirrored[22] :"The human spirit in all its richness, its faith and hope, its love and creativity, is mirrored and indeed celebrated in the life of Jesus."[23] This forms, according to Ayoub, the exceptional nature of Jesus. By this interpretation, Jesus "is much more than a mere human being, or even simply the messenger of a Book."[24] In the Islamic tradition, his exceptional nature lies precisely in his radical humanity, such as is expressed through attributes such as "love" and "meekness."[25]

Regarding newer approaches to Christology by theologians such as Wolfhart Pannenberg or Karl Rahner (in his "searching Christology"): What becomes clear is the fact that the focus on Jesus's humanity can indeed be in tune with a modern Christology. It is well known that Karl Rahner emphasized Jesus's particular nature as a human being as the starting point of Christology. Modern Christian approaches to Christology do not link the divinity of Jesus to any supernatural or superhuman properties, but precisely to his human nature. The Qur'ānic emphasis of Jesus as servant of God, therefore, should not be prematurely rejected. This opens much space for a new encounter between Muslims and Christians.

JESUS AS MESSIAH AND HEALER

What seems to be even more compatible with Christology, in addition to the titles "prophet" and "servant of God," is the fact that the Qur'ān repeatedly describes Jesus as Messiah. The description of Jesus as Messiah can be found in the Qur'ān eleven times, primarily in the Medinan suras.[26] Islamic Studies now take for granted that this title originated in Jewish Christianity[27] and that it is a literal translation of the title of Christ,[28] but it is assumed that "messiah" here has no conceptual meaning, but is only a proper name.[29] However, during the formation of the Qur'ān, it was not unknown that the "Messiah" title could evoke a number of Christological connotations. Indeed, the traditional commentators on the Qur'ān are also aware of the fact that the "Messiah" title indicates a theological appreciation of Jesus. What is normally understood by this appreciation is that Jesus is the one blessed by God and the one without sin.[30] Admittedly, from a traditional Muslim's point of view, being without sin is not only assigned to Jesus; this is, in fact, an indispensable feature of all prophets and imams in Shiite Islam. Still, it is noticeable how the central singularity of Jesus in Christian belief, his being without sin, is taken up. A crucial point of reference for an Islamic appreciation of the exceptional nature of Jesus of Nazareth is thus put in place, compatible with modern concepts of Christology.

However, in the Qur'ān, Jesus is not only described as Messiah but also appreciated through the use of another characteristic, which is central to the Christian understanding of the Messiah: He is experienced as healer and savior. The Qur'ān reveals that Jesus heals blind people and lepers and brings the dead back to life.[31] Since the Qur'ān does not link the name and honorary title of Jesus to the apocalyptic exegetical tradition pertaining to the Messiah, the title is being placed in a new context. In this way, the Qur'ān alludes to some crucial characteristics of Jesus as a charismatic faith healer; it also adopts the biblical way of understanding the miracles as symbols. In light of this, Mahmoud Ayoub notes that all miracles of Jesus are targeted to a specific purpose and always have a symbolic function.[32] Mehdi Bazargan points to the fact that in this way the Qur'ān grants an exceptional position to Jesus, one "that it does not grant any other prophet."[33] Therefore, Jesus seems not to be one prophet among many, but receives a unique position through his healing and saving. In this context, Mahmoud Ayoub understands the actions of saving and redeeming as emanating from healing, and thus takes up the Christian idea of the Messiah: "He is the savior of us all, for what is salvation but healing?"[34] Of course, some Christians will say that "saving" is more and even different from "healing," but the idea is not entirely foreign to Christian theology. It is interesting for example that in African Christology today the notion of healing is a key to the idea of salvation.[35] Perhaps we have to learn this lesson in the West again and be more aware of salvation as something that has to do with our daily lives and our bodies. Moreover, Muslim theologians are also aware of the spiritual dimension of the idea of salvation. For example, Muhammad Legenhausen goes so far as to describe Jesus as savior from sins, although he does not ascribe to Jesus the ability to forgive sins that one expects in the Christian perspective.[36] All in all, the Qur'ānic depiction of Jesus as Messiah cannot be dismissed as lacking theological import. On the contrary, we can learn a lot from the Qur'ānic point of view. We can rediscover Jesus as savior through healing, we can rediscover his divinity in his servanthood, and we can appreciate anew the importance of being a messenger from God, the importance of being the person who is coming from God and pointing to him. For a Christian, however, the most exciting characterization of Jesus in the Qur'ān is probably his appreciation as the "Word from God."

JESUS AS WORD, SPIRIT, AND SYMBOL FROM GOD

In the last section, I pointed to the fact that the Qur'ān, in accordance with the biblical understanding, maintains the symbolic function of Jesus's miracles. From a Christian point of view, however, Jesus not only delivers divine symbols, but is the symbol. Jesus does not only speak the Word of God, but is the Word. In this, he is the incarnate divine word of promise to the world. Is there also any evidence for this perspective in the Qur'ān?

To discover this evidence, many strands of reasoning in the Qur'ān need to be considered. First, it is indeed the case that Jesus—in one of the earliest suras from the Medinan period (3:45)—is described as a word from (or of) God. Only a little later, he is even called "His Word" because he apparently has been this word from God since shortly after his birth.[37] Early commentators in particular have seen this depiction of Jesus as a hint of the exceptional nature of Jesus's creation, thereby distinguishing him from all other human beings.[38] Some scholars even claim that this title is intended to reveal Jesus as the "embodiment of the good news of God's mercy"—a claim very close to the core of the Christian interpretation.[39] "Râzî . . . [for instance] understands Jesus as Word and Spirit in the sense that he as a person would embody the good news of God's mercy."[40] This interpretation has, since then, been only rarely brought forward in the course of Islamic history of theology, and not only for apologetic reasons, but also because some verses in the Qur'ān seem to show that its prophetology always thinks of messengers as persons who get a message. Thus, it is quite unusual for a prophet to be a message.

The aforementioned fact makes it even more interesting that interpretations of this kind are again winning ground in contemporary Iranian theology. Muhammad Legenhausen, for instance, critically engages with the positions of the extremely influential modern theologian Tabataba'i. In Legenhausen's further development of Tabataba'i's arguments, all of which Legenhausen considers to be equally legitimate, he distinguishes three different manners in which Jesus could be interpreted as the Word from God. First, he refers to an interpretation that describes Jesus as the Word from God because he is seen as the fulfillment of God's promise to the prophets of the Old Testament.[41] And, in fact, some passages of the Qur'ān can be found to suggest that Jesus is the fulfillment of the Torah. For instance, the Qur'ānic Jesus declares: "And [I have come] to confirm the truth of whatever there still remains of the Torah, and to make lawful unto you some of the things which [aforetime] were forbidden to you" (3:50). Another passage about Jesus reads: "And we have vouchsafed onto him the Gospel, wherein there was guidance and light, confirming the truth of whatever there still remained of the Torah; and as a guidance and admonition unto the God-conscious. Let, then, the followers of the Gospel judge in accordance with what God has revealed therein" (5:45f.). Thus, the authority of Jesus for those living according to the Gospel is explicitly affirmed, and Jesus appears to be the affirmation and fulfillment of the Torah. In this way, Jesus has the same function for Christians that the Torah has for the Jews. This definition of the Jewish-Christian relationship has plenty to offer from the perspective of modern Christian hermeneutics, especially for the dialogue with Jews.[42]

Another interpretation of the description of Jesus as Word from God supported by Legenhausen is that Jesus is described as Word from God due to his receiving the divine revelation. And finally, he presents the possibility that Jesus is described as Word from God due to his virgin birth—a reading that is also favored by Tabataba'i. In this reading, the virginal conception suggests his birth to be directly from God and, in fact, to be a direct expression of divine power. Through the virginal conception, Jesus obtains an exceptional honor.[43] Moreover, the creation of Jesus is quite noticeably paralleled with the creation of mankind. In both cases God says: *Kun fa yakūn* ("'Be'—and he is.").[44]

From the Qur'ānic perspective, the title "God's Word" can therefore be understood as in contrast to the Christian confession of Jesus as the Son of God. But this contrast is not intended as open opposition, but rather intends to focus on another aspect that the Qur'ān apparently considers more important and deems less ambiguous.

Indeed, in accordance with Muhammad Legenhausen, one can maybe even speak of a similar meaning in the Biblical and Qur'ānic speeches, if we leave aside for the moment the Qur'ānic denial of Jesus's sonship, which I will consider shortly.[45] Moreover, it is interesting that the Qur'ān confesses Jesus not only as "God's Word," but also as His spirit, therefore combining and mixing distinctions made in Christian Trinitarianism. According to the Qur'ān, Jesus is a spirit from God (4:171). Therefore, not only the Qur'ān's identification of Jesus as the Word from God, but also his identification as spirit, distinguishes Jesus from all other human beings.[46] Aside from these direct identifications of "word" and "spirit," which are obviously directed against exaggerated Trinitarian speculations, God's spirit in the Qur'ān is described as having a very similar relation to Jesus of Nazareth as the relationship between the Spirit and Jesus depicted in the Bible. The confession that Jesus is conceived from the Holy Spirit is very similar to that made in the Gospel of Luke. This is especially noticeable (21:91), even as the parallel with Adam is relativized (15:29). Moreover, the Qur'ān considers Jesus as being strengthened by "the spirit of holiness" (2:87; 2:253; 5:110). He is strengthened through this spirit in order to proclaim God's message throughout his life—"in thy cradle, and as a grown man" (5:110). It is the spirit of God that strengthens the one sent by God and announces the conception of Jesus. Traditionally, this spirit is identified as Gabriel, but this identification is never explicitly confirmed by the Qur'ān itself (26:192f; 58:22; 70:4; 78:38; 97:4).

Beside these interesting remarks about the spirit of God, what is even more important for the understanding of the Qur'ānic speech about Jesus as Word from God is, I suggest, the Qur'ānic theology of symbols. According to this theology, the whole world is full of "symbols" (*âyât*) pointing to God's benevolence and almightiness. Jesus is given a special standing because he is described as symbol of God not just once but three times in the Qur'ān. First, the Qur'ān emphasizes that God makes Jesus a symbol for mankind to express the divine mercy; indeed, he is a symbol virtually embodying it (19:21). As "symbol [of Our grace] unto all people" (21:91; Cf. 23:50), Jesus not only seems to be important to Israel or Christianity, but also to bear universal significance. Jesus, therefore, is a divine symbol for the world, not merely a miracle.[47] Moreover, this not only applies to his birth but also to his whole life.[48] As Martin Bauschke puts it: "Jesus is entirely God's human being and as such a 'symbol' of God in his being, conduct, and speech."[49] "Jesus, even already before his birth, is a symbol pointing to God's almightiness,"[50] similar to Adam and the whole creation which is also a sign of the very same almightiness because it is done out of nothing. As in the Pauline tradition, where Jesus is a symbol and image of God (cf. Col.1.15), the Qur'ān emphasizes that Jesus is a symbol for humanity.[51] Here, the Qur'ān evidently sees a peculiarity in Jesus, setting him apart from the other prophets. This presents another argument regarding why Jesus alone is described as the Word from God. Maybe the Qur'ān could be interpreted in a way that sees Jesus as the personified communication of God for humankind, through whom humankind can symbolically (in the sense of Karl Rahner) experience His merciful closeness. Thus, reading the Qur'ān from a Christian perspective can contribute to some fresh insights in our perception of Jesus. It can help us to rethink some of our basic concepts and to search for a deeper meaning. Thus, it seems that agreeing with some of the Qur'ānic interpretations of the person of Jesus would be possible, if it were not for other passages arguing against a pro-Christian interpretation, for it seems that another series of Qur'ānic passages repeatedly and explicitly rejects those specifically Christian conceptions. The following section therefore discusses some of these anti-Christian demarcations. Only if those anti-Christian demarcations can be understood constructively, from a Christian point of view, will it make sense to appreciate the Qur'ān as possibly being the word of God also for Christians.

REJECTION OF JESUS AS SON OF GOD AS AN ANTI-CHRISTIAN DEMARCATION?

The Qur'ān repeatedly rejects the identification of God with Christ: "Indeed, the truth deny they who say, 'Behold, God is the Christ, son of Mary'" (5:17 and 5:72; similarly 19:35). However, in Catholic orthodoxy too, Jesus is not seen as identical with God. By a Christian understanding, Jesus is indeed not the triune God, but only the incarnation of the divine Logos, the divine Word of promise to humankind. He is in a sense God's "body language," but it does not make sense to identify him with the Trinity. In this context, Christian speech can therefore tie in with the Qur'ānic understanding of Jesus as Word of God, and make clear that Jesus is precisely this word from God in human form. As a matter of fact, there is not a single biblical passage directly identifying God with Christ.[52]

?

But the Qur'ān not only opposes the identification of God with Christ but also the belief that Jesus is the Son of God. It declares: "God is but One God; utterly remote is He, in His glory, from having a son" (4:171). For God does not need an intermediary (10:68; 2:116f.). Therefore, the Qur'ān repeatedly emphasizes that Jesus of Nazareth is a normal human being, "but an apostle" (5:75) and thus consequently describes him as "son of Mary" (2:87, among other passages).[53]

However, the context of these demarcations in the given passages needs to be considered. Upon reflection, it becomes doubtful whether the Qur'ān really opposes a properly understood Christianity or really criticizes orthodox Christology in the sense of Catholic belief, for example. When the Qur'ān, for instance, emphasizes the human nature of Jesus in 5:75, it argues for it by pointing to the fact that Jesus, just as his mother, had a totally normal diet. What seems to be important to the Qur'ān, therefore, is that Jesus and Mary are real human beings with real human needs. This, however, is not contested by Christianity—neither for Mary nor for Jesus. Moreover, the Qur'ān opposes the view, also not claimed from a Christian side, that God would need a son to turn toward humankind (10:68). Later, the Qur'ān warns against the substitution of human beings for God.[54] What becomes clear in the context of this warning, however, is that it is first concerned with the deification of scribes and priests. The scene appears to be somewhat surreal because the Jews are accused of worshiping Ezra as Son of God (9:30). This, however, does not apply to any Jews in history or any Jews known to me in the present day. Here, the Qur'ān obviously has very specific groups of Jews and Christians in mind and makes clear to them that they must not substitute anything for God. One may question, though, whether Qur'ānic criticism on Jesus's sonship really addresses an understanding of this sonship as understood by orthodox Christianity.

According to Kenneth Cragg "the logic by which, for the Qur'ān, Jesus can never be 'Son' to God, is precisely the logic by which, for Paul and the New Testament, he is."[55] One difference between Christians and Muslims, of course, is the fact that Muslims find the divine in Jesus without deifying him.[56] What seems open to question, however, is whether one therefore needs to go so far as to deny entirely the exceptional nature and uniqueness in Jesus.[57] And it is not his deification but the exceptional nature of his humanity, which in modern theology is the most important path to his divinity, as I explained previously. Thus, Christians should be ready to learn from the Qur'ān. We can also ask: To whom is the Qur'ānic criticism of aberrations in Christology and the doctrine of the Trinity addressed? At this point, it seems to be helpful to me to cast a glance at the historical situation of the seventh century on the Arabian Peninsula. Even if it is assumed that the Qur'ān is the ultimate Word of God, one needs to understand to whom it is actually addressed and to which specific situations its message refers.[58]

SEVENTH-CENTURY CHRISTOLOGY ON THE ARABIAN PENINSULA

In the seventh century, the majority of Christians on the Arabian Peninsula were the so-called Jacobites. They opposed the Council of Chalcedon and are therefore also referred to as anti-Chalcedonians. However, after "pacification" by the Persians in 570, Nestorian influence was present mainly in the capital city San'a and was therefore only a marginal phenomenon on the Arabian Peninsula as a whole.[59]

The anti-Chalcedonians' (i.e., Jacobites') presence on the Arabian Peninsula was characterized by weak hierarchies in their churches and also by their popularity with believers, especially those within the Ghassanids-Residences.[60] The Ghassanids of North-West Arabia also appear to have been Anti-Chalcedonians.[61] Christians in South Arabia likewise seem to have been dominated by anti-Chalcedonian notions; this group includes Christians settled in Nağran in mid–fifth century.[62] Scholars assume that there were anti-Chalcedonian clergy in Nağran, whereas there were no Chalcedonian clergy on the Arabian Peninsula.[63] Ethiopia, which converted to Christianity in mid–fourth century,[64] acted as a protecting power for south Arabian Christians.[65] It is reasonable to assume that Christians in the southern region of Arabia, integrated into the Anti-Chalcedonian movement during the second wave of mission,[66] were predominately Anti-Chalcedonian.

Christianity in Ethiopia also seems to have been influenced significantly by Jewish-Christianity.[67] Abyssinian theologians seem to have cultivated the notion that the "chosen people" status of Israel had been transferred, such that Abyssinian Christians were God's chosen people.[68] They especially emphasized Jesus's dignity as the messiah, such that the title "messiah" in Abyssinia conveyed a meaning similar to the meaning conveyed by the title "Logos" in the Byzantine Empire.[69] Their theology and piety were oriented in such a way that "in some cases Mariology is overemphasized to the extent that even a Eucharistic anaphora is stylized marianically."[70] Oriental Studies therefore regards the Abyssinian church as a church wherein "Mary—as the successor of Isis—is venerated in a manner that differs from any other branch of Christianity."[71]

The anti-Chalcedonians under Syrian influence belonged to the west Syrian Orthodox Church of Antioch. Their Christology asserts Christ to be "an incarnated nature (or Hypostasis) of the God-Logos . . . Polemicists accused them of mixing and called them Monophysites and Eutychianists."[72] However, it seems more appropriate to call them "Miaphysites" or "anti-Chalcedonians"[73] because they did not follow Eutychianism's heretic teachings, but Cyril of Alexandria's Christology.[74] By the second half of the sixth century, anti-Chalcedonians had been separated into groups condemning each other.[75] Everything points toward this situation having become worse in the seventh century. How widespread the Miaphysite approach was in the Syrian Church becomes apparent in the disputation of Antioch (596), which asserted that Jesus's human nature was pre-existent.[76] In the predominant contemporary Christology, this notion is absolutely unacceptable. Anti-Chalcedonianism suffered the secession of so-called tritheism in the middle of the sixth century. These tritheistic views were shaped by John Philoponus's philosophical notions.[77] During the formation of the Qur'ān, tritheism seems to have been especially common among the anti-Chalcedonians in Syria. In contrast to contemporary teachings of the Church, tritheism claims that the persons of the Trinity are three inner-triune hypostases, each with its own *ousia*, *physis*, and divinity. Alois Grillmeier states that "another monk named Polycarp spread this 'Polytheism' in parts of Asia and Caria. Even the emperor's family was prone to these speculations, as John [Philoponus] found an enthusiastic follower in Athanasius, the grandson of empress Theodora."[78] We can therefore assume that tritheism from Syria influenced Christology on the Arabian Peninsula. Therefore, it is reasonable to conclude that Qur'ānic references allude to this particular understanding of Christology rather than Chalcedonian formulations.

Moreover, closely related to the aforementioned idea is the divine reverence shown to Mary in Miaphysitism since the times of Cyril of Alexandria. For example, according to Martin Bauschke:

> [Epiphanus of Salamis mentions] a group of Thracian women emigrating to Arabia and showing divine reverence to the Mother of God . . . Analogous to the ritual eating of the body of Jesus they offered (bread)/

> cake . . . to Mary. According to Theodor Klauser it is "as good as certain that the forming of this sect based on the assumption that Mary's, at that time popular, title as Theotokos was meant to express her divinity."[79]

There are also similar tendencies in Jewish-Christian, Coptic, and Syrian theology, to identify the Holy Spirit with Mary, thus resulting in a triadic conception of God as Father (God)—Mother (Spirit)—Son (Jesus).

The Christology of West-Syria emphasizes Jesus Christ's divine nature while marginalizing his human nature—probably as a polemic self-differentiation from the allegedly Nestorian theology of East-Syria: "In fear of Nestorianism, Jacob [of Sarug, one of the best-known West Syrian theologians—KvS] describes Christ's human characteristics very cautiously—perhaps even obscures them."[80]

Sources other than the Qur'ān offer only a few insights into how Christianity spread in Mecca and Medina. It can be assumed that Mecca, as the center of trade, was in contact with Syria, and at least two caravans per annum travelled between Mecca and Syria.[81] Christianity appears to have had only little influence in Mecca and there is no proof that Christian churches existed at that time in Mecca. According to Theresia Hainthaler, "[t]he Christians we know about were a number of slaves, adventurers, merchants and wine-sellers,"[82] but according to Henri Lammens, there were also doctors, surgeons, and dentists.[83] It is certain that Christian merchants had business in Mecca, at least for a time.[84] According to Lammens, Mecca was at times occupied by Christian Abyssinians before the Hijra. Moreover, Mecca was strongly connected to Nağran and other Christian centers of Jemen. This becomes apparent in the meaning of the Nağranites in the early reports on the life of Muhammad and early exegesis of the Qur'ān.[85] Amongst the Quraysh Shia tribes, the Banu Asad clan, in particular, seems to have sympathized with Christianity,[86] provided that some of them also were affiliated with the Ghassanids.[87] Despite all this, Christianity seemed to have had little presence in Mecca before the Hijra. Therefore, Muhammad knew about its existence, but could not or did not want to make a theological distinction.[88] This changed only in Medina, especially due to the presence of Judaism.[89] Until now, accounts of the history of Christianity conclude that Christianity had only little presence in Medina. Theresia Hainthaler argues: "There have only been a few Christians in Medina whose names are barely known, and surely there was no structured Christianity."[90]

Since the Arabic tribes and the Chalcedonian bishops became known through a strong anti-Chalcedonian tendency,[91] it can be assumed that Muhammad probably came into contact with miaphysite Christianity in Medina. Moreover, as Arabia had been a melting pot for Christian heresy since the fifth century,[92] it can be assumed that other heterodox notions of Christianity also played a role in influencing Muhammad's perception of Christianity. Therefore, a careful analysis of the qur'anic text is required to clarify the situation. But also in Arabia itself, there was opposition to Miaphysitism—not so much through the orthodoxy but considerably more through the Nestorians, who were opponents of the Miaphysites at the council of Ephesus. In 484 at the synod of Beth Lapat, the Nestorian-oriented church in eastern Syria, for instance, officially revoked the Council of Ephesus and identified Mary's title, "Theotokos," as the root of all evil. This Nestorian Christianity spread from Southern Arabia after its conquest by the Persians in 597, and thus had a substantial influence in Arabia at the time of Muhammad.[93]

In light of these historical disputes, it therefore becomes clear that the statements of the Qur'ān are directed against Monophysitism and its tritheistic tendencies. Therefore, Monophysitic Christians, who naturally invoked Christ with phrases such as "our God" or even "almighty God," will have been the addressees of the accusation of disbelief in sura 5:17 and 5:72.[94] It is therefore uncertain whether the Qur'ān only rejects the triadic-tritheistic conceptions of God of Oriental Christian piety or if it indeed opposes orthodox Trinitarian theology as well.[95] Regarding the historical context, what does become clear is that the Qur'ānic judgments concerning Christology cannot be unequivocally classified as anti-Christian, even though they may appear anti-Christian at first sight.

Prospects

In this first reflection on Qur'ānic statements about Jesus of Nazareth, by comparative theology I have tried to establish that these statements are, in many cases, in greater correspondence with modern Christian theology than scholars have thus far assumed. Therefore, it can be asked whether rejecting the Christian confession of Jesus as Christ must be a constituent part of Muslim identity. On the contrary, Islamic appreciations of Jesus offer ample possibilities that can be integrated into an orthodox Christology.

Since those Islamic appreciations also offer Christians important insights into the characteristics of Jesus, I do not want to say that the Qur'ān is not addressing orthodox Christianity at all. The Qur'ān is inviting Christians to a revision of their ideas and concepts without being in complete contradiction to them. For instance, a greater appreciation of Jesus's role as prophet and servant of God is such an invitation and this seems—from my point of view—to be very rewarding for Christology. In this context, developments during the last decades have shown the importance of Jesus's humanity as a starting point for a convincing Christology. Both the Muslim interpretation of Jesus as the embodiment of God's mercifulness and the emphasis on his peacemaking power are notions that offer great insight, as does understanding salvation as healing and saving. But now the danger of devaluing Christian soteriology needs attention. The development of indigenous Christologies in Africa and Latin America indicates the fruitfulness of rediscovering Jesus as a healer. Finally, speaking about Jesus as a word and sign from God could be an addition to the traditional view of Jesus as son, and thus could open up interesting possibilities if received into a modern Christology.

As a whole, Qur'ānic Christology challenges the Christian approach to Jesus of Nazareth, as it tends to bring him in line with God's messengers and, in this way risks the loss of his exceptional nature. Even if a Christian point of view detects certain dangers in this approach, it could nevertheless be a valuable starting point for making Jesus of Nazareth more accessible in the wider biblical tradition and to the wider human family. By appreciating him as a child of Israel, it could further people's understanding of him. After all, by its dogmatic formulas, traditional Christian speech about Jesus is always in danger of removing Jesus so far from the individual human being and his own religion that his healing and saving power can no longer be experienced.

An interesting question for Islamic theology in this context is whether it is also willing to give serious consideration to the Christian understanding of Jesus of Nazareth, and how then Muslims might redefine their relationship to the biblical tradition. Would Muslims be willing to take the biblical religions into account and thus acknowledge Jews and Christians as their older brothers and sisters who also believe in the one God, just as Christians have acknowledged Jews? Would Islamic theology be willing to acknowledge the intrinsic power of the Bible, and, for instance, seek to make the Gospels hermeneutically productive for a

Muslim understanding of Jesus? If such willingness exists, it would become possible for Muslims to appreciate Jesus of Nazareth's exceptional nature and acknowledge his unique role.[96] This is the case even if the Christian approach to Jesus may always remain offensive and seem exaggerated to Muslims. Even so, after comparative theological reflection, it will no longer seem necessary to distance Islam so sharply from Christianity. Based on the Qur'ān, degrading this other religion does not seem necessary. On the contrary, the Qur'ān offers possibilities for appreciating Jesus's exceptional nature. This appreciation has the potential to promote discussion about Jesus as the Christ.

Notes

1. For additional information about this in the context of ethics and economy, see Stosch, *Wirtschaftsethik interreligiös*. For additional information about the theology of liberation in this context, see Stosch and Tatari, *Gott und Befreiung*.
2. In this essay, I discuss a problem rooted in Christian dogmatics. However, other theological disciplines can also be starting points for issues of comparative theology.
3. See Ayoub, *A Muslim View of Christianity*, 156: "there is an authentic Islamic understanding of Christ that deserves careful consideration as a legitimate christology."
4. See Legenhausen, *Preface*, 27f: "[T]he time has come for Muslims to begin work in this area, as well. Through the development of an Islamic Christology we can come to a better understanding of Islam as contrasted with Christianity, and Islam in consonance with Christianity, too."
5. See ibid., 30: "The Muslim always seems to appear as a stranger to the Christian, but perhaps it is from the stranger that the Christian can best come to know his saviour."
6. For the methodology of comparative theology, see Stosch, *Komparative Theologie als Wegweiser*, 203–8.
7. The basis for a first draft of this essay was the seminar for Muslim and Christian students at the University of Paderborn, which I conducted with Mahmoud Ayoub in the summer of 2011. I am very grateful to my colleague Ayoub for the inspiring dialogues that occurred during that seminar. Later, I further developed my thoughts through dialogue with some of my Islamic colleagues in Germany, and presented the paper at several universities in Iran. At the moment, my Islamic colleagues and I are preparing our ideas for publication by appreciating him as a child of Israel in several co-authored books. This essay is therefore still a "work-in-progress," which I present, even while exploring it further with respect to its methodological background.
8. For research on a diachronic reading of the Qur'ān and which includes context of its origin in late antiquity, see the extremely helpful analyses of Neuwirth, *Der Koran als Text der Spätantike*.
9. See my earlier publication, which tries to consider these diachronic notions, Stosch, "Versuch einer ersten diachronen Lektüre der Jesusverse des Qur'ān."
10. Most of the following passages are a translation from my own text "Jesus im Qur'ān. Ansatzpunkte und Stolpersteine einer qur'ānischen Christologie," 109–33.

11. Bauschke, *Jesus—Stein des Anstoßes*, 22. Also, if we consider indirect references, 15 additional verses can be added, making it 18 surahs and 123 verses.
12. Surah and Verse numbers of the Qur'ān appear within parentheses throughout the text. All numbers refer to the translation by Muhammad Asad.
13. See Antepli, "Muslim Mary and Jesus," 301.
14. See Pöhlmann, "Jesus im Islam und Christentum," 499.
15. See 2:253: "Some of these apostles have We endowed more highly than others . . . and some he has raised yet higher. And we vouchsafed unto Jesus, the son of Mary, all evidence of the truth."
16. The Hebrew title for servant "Ebed" corresponds to Arabic "Abd".
17. See Schedl, *Muhammad und Jesus*, 565 [my translation].
18. See Pöhlmann, "Jesus im Islam und Christentum," 499.
19. See Gnilka, *Die Nazarener und der Koran*, 91; Bauschke, *Jesus—Stein des Anstoßes*, 162, fn. 170.
20. See Ayoub, *A Muslim view of Christianity*, 117: "Jesus is a model of true Islam, or total submission to God."
21. Therefore, in Islamic tradition, Jesus is not only regarded as "the example of piety, love, and asceticism . . . , but also the Christ who exemplifies fulfilled humanity" (ibid., 152). "The humanity of Jesus is evident in the narrations of the Shi'ah, but it is a humanity transformed, a perfected humanity, and as such there is no denying its supernatural dimension" (Legenhausen, *Preface*, 30).
22. See Ayoub, *A Muslim view of Christianity*, 115.
23. See ibid., 111
24. See ibid., 152.
25. Triebel, "Das koranische Evangelium," 276.
26. See Bauschke, *Jesus—Stein des Anstoßes*, 107, for instance in 3:45.
27. Additional information on the meaning of Jewish Christians for the Qur'ān, see Gnilka, *Die Nazarener und der Koran*, 111f.
28. See Bauschke, *Jesus—Stein des Anstoßes*, 108.
29. See Gnilka, *Die Nazarener und der Koran*, 117; Triebel, *Das koranische Evangelium*, 277.
30. See Khoury, *Jesus Christus im Koran*, 467; Ayoub, *A Muslim View of Christianity*, 117.
31. 3:49; 5:110. See Antepli, *Muslim Mary and Jesus*, 308; Triebel, "Das koranische Evangelium," 274. The Qur'ān emphasizes that Jesus can only do those miracles with God's permission. From a Christian point of view, this could be understood as criticism of Jesus's particular claim to authority. However, the Qur'ānic emphasis can be accepted as natural to a Christian because the biblical Jesus also understands himself fully from God and toward Him and receives his authority only from Him.
32. See Ayoub, *A Muslim view of Christianity*, 112.
33. Bazargan, *Und Jesus ist sein Prophet*, 26.
34. Ayoub, *A Muslim view of Christianity*, 115.
35. Aklé et al., *Der Schwarze Christus. Wege afrikanischer Christologie*, 73–137.
36. See Legenhausen, *Preface*, 28: "Muslims accept Jesus as savior, along with all the other prophets, for the prophetic function is to save humanity from the scourge of sin . . . Islam denies that salvation is through redemption resulting from the crucifixion."

37. See Bürkle, "Jesus und Maria im Koran," 579, referring to 4:171: He is "his promise which he had conveyed unto Mary." Jesus talking to his mother shortly after his birth seems the most probable interpretation (see Bauschke, *Jesus—Stein des Anstoßes*, 118).
38. See Ayoub, *A Muslim View of Christianity*, 129: "While earlier commentators saw a special creation in Jesus as 'the Word of God', more recent ones have consistently attempted to play down any distinction between Jesus and the rest of humankind."
39. Eißler, "Jesus und Maria im Islam," 177; see Imbach, *Wem gehört Jesus?*, 93.
40. See Bauschke, *Jesus—Stein des Anstoßes*, 115 [my translation].
41. See Legenhausen, *Preface*, 14: "According to the promissory interpretation, Jesus is called the Word of God because he was the fulfillment of God's promise to the Hebrew prophets that he would send a Messiah. According to the revelatory interpretation, Jesus is the Word of God because he was the recipient of divine revelation. According to the creative interpretation, Jesus is the Word of God because God created Jesus without a father. 'Allamah argues in favor of the creative interpretation and rejects the others. To the contrary, I would suggest that all three are consistent."
42. See Stosch, "Philosophisch verantwortete Christologie als Komplizin des Antijudaismus?" 370–86.
43. See Cragg, *Jesus and the Muslim*, 32.
44. See ibid., referring to 3:59; Eißler, "Jesus und Maria im Islam," 177. What is interesting in this context is that this verse also chronologically seems to be the first one revealed that makes reference to Jesus of Nazareth.
45. See Legenhausen, *Preface*, 15: "So, since the Qur'ān uses the expression 'Word of God' where the Bible uses 'Son of God' and the Biblical term is used to explain the virgin birth, we could consider the phrase of the Qur'ān as having a similar significance minus the idea of divine fathering to which the Qur'ān objects."
46. See Flannery, "Christ in Islam," 34: "for the Qur'an no other being is said to be Kalima of God, ruh of God."
47. See Legenhausen, *Preface*, 17.
48. See Shomali, "Mary, Jesus and Christianity," 73.
49. Bauschke, *Jesus—Stein des Anstoßes*, 192 [my translation].
50. Ibid., 114 [my translation]. Sayyid Qutb also confirms the exceptional nature of Jesus as being a symbol of God (see ibid., 193).
51. See Brinkmann, "Christian-Muslim dialogue," 108.
52. Imprecise translations of John 1.1 could create the impression that, in this passage, the "Logos" is identified with God. But in fact, the passage only confesses the word as being with God (HO THEOS). Moreover, it is only identified with THEOS—without a definite article—so that this passage should better be translated in the way that the word is divine, but not that it is God. So, too, when Thomas says in John 20.28, "My Lord and my God," he is not addressing Jesus because the Greek is not using the vocative, but the nominative. Thus, even in the Gospel of John there is no verse claiming that Jesus is God.
53. In the context of the Qur'ānic definition of Jesus as being "son of Mary," Martin Bauschke describes the Jesus of the Qur'ān as the fatherless one *per se*, without divine or worldly father (see Bauschke, *Jesus—Stein des Anstoßes*, 124). Like many other interpreters, he explains that the speech about Jesus, as being son of Mary, has the pur-

pose to form an opposition to the speech of him being son of God (Triebel, "Das koranische Evangelium," 278). However, "Son of Mary" could also be a link to a particular veneration of Mary, and influenced by Ethiopian Christians (see Bürkle, "Jesus und Maria im Koran," 578).

54. "Such are the sayings which they utter with their mouths, following in spirit assertions made in earlier times by people who denied the truth! 'May God destroy them!' [. . .] They have taken their rabbis and their monks—as well as the Christ, son of Mary—for their lords beside God, although they had been bidden to worship none but the One God [. . .]" (9:30f.).
55. Cragg, *Jesus and the Muslim*, 30; for a corroborative view, see Flannery, "Christ in Islam," 31.
56. See Legenhausen, *Preface*, 27.
57. Against Shomali, "Mary, Jesus and Christianity," 81: Shomali disapproves of singling Jesus out. He argues that this would oppose the Muslim view of all prophets having the same message and function. In the aforementioned arguments, I have argued why in this context Q 2:253 can be put forward against Shomali's disapproval.
58. See Rahman, *Islam and modernity*, 6.
59. Tardy, *Najrân*, 165f. Tardy assumes that this kind of Monophysism was influenced by Julianism (ibid., 172). Julianism—named after its founder Juliana's—taught the immortality of Jesus's body. This position will again be discussed in light of Q 5:75. Theresia Hainthaler also confirms that Nestorianism after 570 was "found in the cities and especially in the harbors of Jemen; but there is no proof that it had spread to the countryside," [my translation]. (Hainthaler, *Christliche Araber vor dem Islam*, 134).
60. Hainthaler, *Christliche Araber vor dem Islam*, 57.
61. See ibid., 79.
62. See Grillmeier, *Jesus der Christus im Glauben der Kirche. Bd. 2/4*, 312. See also Schmucker, *Die christliche Minderheit von Nāğran und die Problematik ihrer Beziehungen zum frühen Islam*; Schedl, *Muhammad und Jesus*, 374–97. In the Islamic tradition, *Nāğran*'s Christians are considered as the reason for the revelation in Q 3:61–62.
63. Hainthaler, *Christliche Araber vor dem Islam*, 129.
64. See Grillmeier, *Jesus der Christus im Glauben der Kirche. Bd. 2/4*, 306.
65. See ibid., 309.
66. See ibid., 308.
67. See Hainthaler, *Christliche Araber vor dem Islam*, 139. For information on Jewish-Christian influences on Islam, see Neuwirth, "Imagining Mary," 412. Neuwirth, in contrast to François de Blois, for example, does not believe that Jewish-Christians had a great influence on the Qur'ān.
68. See Grillmeier, *Jesus der Christus im Glauben der Kirche. Bd. 2/4*, 345.
69. See ibid., 344.
70. See ibid., 402 [my translation].
71. Andrae, *Der Ursprung des Islam und das Christentum*, 205 [my translation].
72. Hainthaler, *Christliche Araber vor dem Islam*, 31.
73. See ibid., 33.
74. See Oeldemann, *Die Kirchen des christlichen Ostens*, 23.
75. Grillmeier, *Jesus der Christus im Glauben der Kirche. Bd. 2/3*, 403.

76. See ibid., 436.
77. Hainthaler, *Christliche Araber vor dem Islam*, 32.
78. Grillmeier, *Jesus der Christus im Glauben der Kirche. Bd. 2/3*, 280f. [my translation]. Philoponus also claims that the "Father, Son and Spirit [are] three hypostases in the shape of individual natures" (ibid., 290).
79. Bauschke, *Jesus—Stein des Anstoßes*, 154f.
80. Ibid., 655.
81. See Hainthaler, *Christliche Araber vor dem Islam*, 137n2.
82. Ibid., 138 [my translation].
83. See ibid., 140, referring to Lammens, "Les chrétiens à la Mecque à la veille de l'hégire," 29, which she believes to be the best and most extensive source about Christianity in Mecca up to the present day.
84. See Trimingham, *Christianity Among the Arabs in Pre-Islamic Times*, 260. Because Mecca was the center of slave trading, the existence of Christian slaves is likely (see Lammens, "Les chrétiens à la Mecque à la veille de l'hégire," 12).
85. See Lammens, "Les chrétiens à la Mecque à la veille de l'hégire," 16.
86. See ibid., 37.
87. See ibid., 38.
88. There could be strategic reasons for not making precise theological statements in the revelation's early stage because these would be likely to open a debate.
89. See Lammens, "Les chrétiens à la Mecque à la veille de l'hégire," 48.
90. Hainthaler, *Christliche Araber vor dem Islam*, 140 [my translation].
91. "Their main representatives were Peter the Iberian, his biographer, John Rufus, who later became bishop of Maiuma, Romanus, and Gerontius." (Grillmeier, *Jesus der Christus im Glauben der Kirche. Bd. 2/3*, 160).
92. See Hainthaler, *Christliche Araber vor dem Islam*, 56.
93. See ibid., 156, referring to Andrae, *Der Ursprung des Islam und das Christentum*, 7ff., 201ff., and Brock, "The Christology of the Church of the East in the Synods of the fifth to early seventh centuries," 125–42.
94. See Bauschke, *Jesus—Stein des Anstoßes*, 151. Ṭabarî also reads this passage as opposing Monophysite Jacobites (see ibid., 152).
95. With regard to this interesting question, see Tatari and Stosch, *Trinität—Anstoß für das muslimisch-christliche Gespräch*.
96. In Paderborn, we are working in a research group of Muslim and Christian scholars to give a response to this challenge. The Muslim members of the group—Zishan Ghaffar, Mouhanad Khorchide, Hamideh Mohagheghi and Muna Tatari—are all committed to comparative theology and try to use this approach to reshape their perspective on Jesus.

3 The Moment of Truth

COMPARATIVE AND DOGMATIC THEOLOGY

Aaron Langenfeld

In European theological discourse, the various projects of comparative theology often are confronted with two reproaches: first, that they are not distinguishable from a pluralistic theology of religions,[1] and second, that they are not distinguishable from some types of religious studies.[2] The interesting point is that both assertions are traceable to the same fundamental critique, even if they obviously diverge in its specific interpretation. This criticism addresses the apparent relativization of Christology as the dogmatic normative core of all Christian theology. Confronting this objection against the comparative projects, in the first part of the paper I will address comparative and dogmatic theology as intertwined aspects of the very same theological project of *fides quaerens intellectum*.[3] I will argue that comparative theology must always have a dogmatic impact and, reciprocally, that dogmatic theology necessarily has to argue in a comparative way. If this holds true, both aforementioned reproaches will fail because comparative theology will neither be suspected of an *a priori* pluralism, nor lose its normative claims. The second part of the paper will elaborate on the consequences of this proposition by reflecting upon some methodological aspects of comparative and dogmatic work. To provide a better understanding of the abstract methodological reflections, I will outline my thoughts with reference to a specific example of my comparative work, the problem of salvation in Christian-Muslim dialogue.

The Normativity of Comparative Theology: Criteriological Presumptions

First of all, it seems useful to clarify what is understood by the Anselmian term of *fides quaerens intellectum*. In my viewpoint, the specific task of theology is the reflection on and analysis of the rationality of a certain religious faith. Thus, theology *as a whole* is challenged to seek the rationality of faith. Consequently, any study of religious belief that is not involved in this specific attempt may not be called theology. Theology can be understood as a systematic elaboration of the contents of a certain religious belief, which by definition concerns all parts and disciplines of theological work. In this perspective, Christian theology as a whole has to face the task of justifying the rationality of the fundamental Christian belief that God has revealed Himself in the person of Christ Jesus, a belief dogmatically elaborated in the commitments of Nicaea and Chalcedon and their theological interpretations.[4] Thus, all parts of Christian theology refer to dogmatic theology as the inner core of justifying Christian faith. Therefore, I argue, the same holds true for comparative theology, which has to be involved in the effort of establishing reason for the rationality of faith if it is truly to be called theology.[5]

But even as dogmatic theology determines the foundations for all theology, the explanations of its insights are bound to certain language games within specific historical and cultural contexts which respectively change the mode of systematic reflection, even if not the content that is reflected on. In other words, the justification of the rationality of faith is only possible in the given words of our time, and in our social and cultural contexts.[6] If this applies, then dogmatic theology, and theology as a whole, have changed completely since the Enlightenment and its critique of metaphysics. Insofar as the critique, especially the one of Immanuel Kant, included the demonstration of the impossibility of all proofs of the existence of God,[7] the rationality of faith had to transform itself to keep working on the theological task. The only alternative would have been to ignore the landmark philosophical insights and thus refuse dialogue, which would actually signify a refusal to partake in the language games of modernity. This refusal would have been nothing other than an evasion; theology thereafter would be fideistic—and thus seemingly in contradiction with the aforementioned basic concern of theology. Theology, as a result, had to learn to work with atheist and agnostic philosophical concepts to preserve an understanding of its own truth claims, which were no longer self-evident.[8] For European theology, the philosophical tradition of transcendental criticism[9] became an especially important interlocutor, as different and even contradictory truth claims were addressed over and over again until sufficient answers were found—until, that is to say, differences were adequately understood and unexpected opportunities for mutual understanding had been discovered. The questioning of religious truth by philosophy thus became a source for the development of a theology able to ground the consistency of faith in an adequate language.[10]

The important insight for comparative work, then, is that the questioning of truth and the emphasis on different possible concepts of truth seem to be necessary for a development of one's own perspective on and understanding of dogmatically asserted truth. Similarly, the focus on truth is very important for a deeper and honest understanding of the other because I am only able to know and to appreciate the other if the two of us also talk about the differences in our worldviews. If this holds true, theology has to be both dogmatic and comparative: *dogmatic for the sake of the rationality of faith, comparative for the sake of questioning one's own and the truth of the other's faith*. Thus, a comparative theology that is conceived as dogmatic theology cannot lose the dogmatic normativity necessary for any theological project (i.e., the reasoning of a certain system of religious convictions). Accordingly, the aforementioned accusation regarding comparative theology's identification with pluralistic positions or with religious studies fails. Of course, this reflection is still formal and abstract, and a demonstration must follow. If it is true that Christian comparative theology has to deal with the fundamental dogmatic claims of Christian theology, the most important parts of comparative work seem to be those in which the *seemingly* most problematic interreligious differences are analyzed.[11] From a Christian point of view, this might be the negation of the Christian concept of salvation and redemption by Judaism and Islam. Whenever the Christian concept of salvation is questioned, Christian theology as a whole is challenged because the *theologumenon* of salvation—which is fundamentally linked to a concept of redemption—expresses the relevance of the action of God in his self-revelation for humanity.

Because the understanding of salvation as a problematic in Christian-Muslim dialogue has not yet been elaborated sufficiently, I will now focus on this particular dialogical constellation, with the purpose of finding a deeper understanding of comparative theology as dogmatic theology.

Comparative Theology's Dogmatic Orientation: Four Formal-Methodological Phases of Reflection

In the light of the aforesaid, I argue that comparative theological work includes the posing of a *provocation*[12] *to the respective other, so that that other gives reasons for his or her specific understanding of truth.* For our subject, the Muslim critique of the Christian use of the term "salvation" is a fundamental provocation. Conversely, the Christian explanation of soteriology can itself be understood as a fundamental provocation posed to Islamic theology. As we will see, this (mutual) provocation is the beginning and the end of the four comparative phases, which I will now introduce very briefly. They are, of course, only inductive examples for the purpose of my research, but perhaps they will be helpful for the shaping of a theology that claims to be dogmatic and comparative. Likewise, the model of four phases is shaped by a certain, presumed understanding of comparative and dogmatic theology. If dogmatic theology can be described as the inner justification of a system of religious convictions, its genuine work can be categorized in four specific phases: 1) the development of an original theological concept, 2) an internal irritation or external provocation which urges a de-construction of that concept, 3) engagement with the irritation or provocation, and 4) a re-construction of the original concept, after consideration of the newly gained insights. My understanding of comparison as normative, dogmatic theology, is that it includes the very same periods of 1) elaboration, 2) opening, 3) discourse, and 4) reconstruction as the reaction to an external (interreligious) provocation. Confrontation with other truth claims and questions posed to one's own theological concepts compel a rethinking of these concepts.

For the outline of the different phases, one preliminary note is necessary: The phases are epistemologically distinct and only hypothetically follow each other. In practice, they may occur at the very same time or in a different order. Thus, the following description does not claim to reflect a defined procedure but rather aspects constitutive to a theological comparison.

ELABORATIVE PHASE

In this phase, the dogmatic concept of a certain theological topic must be developed. Thus, it is at the same time a descriptive and a normative phase: descriptive in the sense of giving an exposition of one's own understanding of a certain religious conviction for the dialogical purpose, normative in the sense of grounding reasonably the pertinent (dogmatic) truth claim. Obviously, this phase may follow from a preceding one of questioning, which in turn makes necessary a new understanding of the specific content. Because the theologian in this first phase is already trying to answer a prior question, it becomes clear that these two comparative phases are intertwined and refer to each other. Consequently, the "elaborative phase" may stand at both the beginning and end of the comparative work.

In our example, the original provocation would be the Muslim critique of Christian anthropology, particularly the concept of original sin, which is presumed in the Christian understanding of salvation and redemption.[13] A fundamental interpretation of the human as corrupted by sin from the day of his birth, thereby making him in need of a special redemptive act by God, seemingly does not match the Muslim concept of *fitra*, the natural human orientation to God.[14] The objection against the classical (Augustinian) anthropology raises questions that are intriguingly similar to the critique of original sin during the period of the Enlightenment:[15] If the presupposition of sin is free will, then only the person himself can commit sin; the idea of a transferred sin is self-contradictory.

Such questions urge us to reframe Christian anthropology and original sin in regard to a theory of human free will. This is accomplished in the work of Thomas Pröpper, who argues that the human need for salvation is not determined by original sin, but by the unfulfillable human reaching out for unconditional meaning.[16] According to this concept, salvation does not, first of all, mean redemption from sin; rather, in a more existential philosophical way, it means the gift of meaning for a potentially absurd human existence. Pröpper points out that humankind would also be in need of God's saving word to the world, even if there were no sin causing depravity in history because the mere existence of the human is a question for meaning that cannot be answered by the human himself, but only by the unconditional being itself.[17] Consequently, the act of redemption is completely identified with the meaning-giving act of God's self-revelation in which God gives His unconditional affirmative word to human existence. The human need for salvation is not grounded in one's sinful depravity but in the *conditio humana* itself, which entails also the inseparable opportunity of sin. From this point of view, the communicative, affirmative life praxis of Jesus and his death and resurrection may be understood as God's own unconditional, meaningful dedication to humankind. This act of self-revelation is the act of salvation, and vice versa.

As this example demonstrates, the development of a dogmatic position, which was initially evoked by an Islamic critic, leads from the comparative theological act of interreligious provocation to a new conception of a truth in one's own tradition. Consequently, the "elaborative phase" is actually, from the start, a dogmatic theological reflection.

THE QUESTIONING PHASE

By elaborating a certain dogmatic subject, the language game of *being questioned and giving reason* is opened up. In the second period, the "questioning phase," the results of the preceding analysis are presented to the dialogue partner, raising questions that are gathered from the elaboration for the concrete discourse. In our example, one could focus on the consequences of the Christian-anthropological shift: If the concept of God's self-revelation is so important for a Christian understanding of salvation, how might Muslims integrate this concept? If it is a philosophically consistent thought that the human, and of course not only a Christian but every human, is in need of God's affirmative and meaning-giving self-revelation—which is pointed out as the act of salvation itself—and if this act is identified in Christian theology with the life, death, and resurrection of Jesus Christ, how might Muslims address this assertion, insofar they do not understand Jesus as the self-revelation of God? Is there a possibility of accepting the fundamental need for salvation, understood as a need for God that can only be fulfilled by his revelation? Is there a way of considering divine self-revelation in Islamic terms? If yes, how might such a theology of the Qur'ān be formulated compared to the Christian concepts developed in dogmatic Christology? If not, then how might Muslims understand salvation? Is not every concept of salvation that does not posit divine self-revelation as its fundamental category deficient?

It is obvious that this stage is still connected with the "elaborative phase" and not separable from it. It is included in the heuristic attempt to understand one's own dogmatic system of beliefs by asking how other systems of theological reflection resolve similar problems, or by asking if the problems are even realized as such in these frameworks. Of course, the questions raised may already anticipate possible answers within the original hermeneutical horizon which elucidates the interweaving of the different stages, even as we acknowledge the subjective shape of all perception. In this regard, especially in the "questioning phase," a real willingness of the theologian not to be limited by his or her hermeneutical presuppositions is required. Even if he or she will never be able to completely leave that epistemological framework (what could be called a hermeneutic inclusivism), a real openness for the (possibly irritating) truth of the other must be taken as a given.[18]

THE DISCOURSE PHASE

The "discourse phase" is the stage of genuine comparative theological work. The dogmatic-hermeneutical background, the problems arising in the "questioning phase" included, is now confronted with concrete theological reflections arising in the other tradition, in answer to the questions raised.[19]

If the idea of self-revelation, the meaning-giving redemptive devotion of God to the world, can be determined to be the central Christian concept required for an understanding of salvation through alterations in anthropological presuppositions, then the questions to Islamic theology mainly concern the Muslim concept of revelation and the anthropological preconditions for an adequate comprehension of divine action in the world. Because the Christian perspective on salvation is shaped by contemporary theology and philosophy, it seems appropriate also to examine contemporary Muslim concepts of revelation.

One interesting discourse partner could be the Afghan-German Islamic philosopher Milad Karimi,[20] whose revelation-theology distinctly depends on Navid Kermani's aesthetic understanding of the Qur'ān.[21] For Karimi, the Qur'ān reveals the beauty of God and, by this, the beauty and the goodness of creation at the same time. In the act of Qur'ānic recitation the beauty of God becomes palpable right now in the middle of a seemingly absurd existence.[22] The verses of the Qur'ān are not self-explanatory but must be interpreted in accord with this original aesthetical experience of beauty.[23] Karimi compares this act of revelation with a love letter from God to humankind in which the creator Himself becomes present.

On the one hand, we can notice a close resemblance to the Christian understanding of revelation as salvation: By revealing God's presence in human history, God breaks the "reasonless silence" (Albert Camus) of a potentially absurd world by revealing Himself as unconditional affirmation of human existence in the person of Jesus Christ *and* by revealing Himself as the unconditional beauty of all existence. On the other hand, Karimi denies an Islamic equivalent to the idea of a "need of salvation"—be it articulated in the theological system of original sin or even in the existential philosophical sense of reaching out for meaning. In Islam, the aforementioned concept of *fitra* means the primordial gift of salvation for humans. Accordingly, humankind does not need any form of redemption other than remembrance of having already been saved by God. Christian anthropology, Karimi accordingly continues, knows a determination of the human based on neediness and sin, while Islamic anthropology just knows a determination by grace that has already happened. The Christian needs grace to act well, whereas the Muslim just needs to act well because he or she already has the grace of God.[24]

Christian theologians, of course, will raise objections to this interpretation, but they would also agree on some aspects of Karimi's diagnosis of Christian soteriology (probably regarding the essential axiom of human neediness) and defend them against his downplaying of the sinfulness of the human condition. This leads us to the last stage, but first, let me summarize where we are.

This third phase of a dogmatic and comparative-theological project includes the most challenging part for theologians because it is the stage in which the religious other may be discovered as a source for a new understanding of one's own theological concept. This is so, even if the process of interreligious learning has already begun in the prior stages. It requires an intensive examination of sources and an openness to changing fundamental convictions within one's worldview and thus, too, in one's presumptions about the other's truth claims. Changes as such may only occur if one is really able to understand the basic rules of the other's language games, and this requires knowledge and expertise regarding language, culture, philosophy, and so forth. The most important consequence is this: If it is true that dogmatic and comparative theology are aspects of the same theological project of faith seeking understanding, then seeking a deeper understanding of one's own dogmatic truth claims in practice excludes any avoidance of engaging another tradition (philosophy, culture, and so on) and all the implications that follow from such avoidance. Consequently, interreligious comparison is a constitutive method of dogmatic reflection and a necessary part of theological education.

THE RETURNING PHASE

The final methodological phase is the "returning phase," in which the insights of the "discourse phase" are brought back to the original dogmatic reflection. Standard reflections at this stage will be something like these: Where did new provocations arise? Can the understanding of my own theological concept be improved or deepened? Are there points that have been overlooked? Obviously, the "returning phase" overlaps with the "elaborating phase." This circumstance illustrates that the comparative project is not fully defined, and thus, too, that the dogmatic theology is not fully defined.

As I mentioned before, new provocations for a Christian theology could be a reproach to a negative Christian anthropology. Christian theologians will have to explain that the original *conditio humana*, too, can be seen as determined by the grace of God. In addition, they will have to state that human nature is nevertheless still also influenced by sin. Explanatory concepts useful here could be Karl Rahner's idea of supernatural existential and his idea of structural sin.[25] In this process of reflection, another dogmatic elaboration begins. At the same time, questions arise for Muslim anthropology: Why does God reveal His presence in human history if it is useless for a humankind that is already saved from the beginning? How can it be explained that God reveals His presence in the recitation of the Qur'ān, when the experience of unconditional beauty can easily be explained in accord with a naturalist worldview?[26] The game of raising and answering questions becomes a permanent process of understanding and (re-)constructing systems of religious identification. Of course, there is more to be said, and the interweaving of all four methodological steps might be further elucidated at this point.

Conclusions

This essay has reflected on two key aspects of comparative theological work, one of which is criteriological and the other methodological. Both were addressed in a very formal and abstract way. Conversely, the categories to which I have referred are the fruit, gained inductively, from my comparative work on Christian-Muslim dialogue on salvation. Some short points will reflect the results:

(a) The first criteriological insight has been the immediate connection of dogmatic and comparative theology as aspects of the same theological project, understood as the reflection and analysis of the rationality of a certain religious faith. Consequently, comparative theology includes normative dogmatic purposes which indicate possible research areas for comparative work, if it is still to be understood as theology.

(b) The second result, regarding criteria, is the understanding of comparative theology as a constitutive part of dogmatic reflection. A theology that does not examine other possible religious truth claims must be recognized as evasive. Not only for the sake of understanding one's own tradition in a deeper way but also with respect to scientific standards, theology is obliged to show skill in dealing with different interpretations of reality and a plurality of worldviews.

(c) The methodological insights follow from this second point, in order to describe the formal methodology of a dogmatic and comparative theology. Together, the four phases will help to structure the process of comparison. Even if the stages are actually heuristic, they seem to correlate with the experience of successful theological discourses and fruitful dialogue processes.

(d) The methodological suggestion is adequate for an understanding of comparative theology as dogmatic and vice versa. There is no need for an a priori assumption of interreligious commonalities, nor can the exclusion of their appearance in the process of comparison be taken for granted. The method demands a real openness to similarities and differences among religions, with respect to specific theological systems and reflections. But the inquiring character of comparison acknowledges the preliminary nature of such perceptions, and so they may be permanently revisable. This marks the normative core of the presented method: The continuing questioning of truth claims is an effort to get a better understanding of truth itself.

Notes

1. Because it is a goal of this book to connect American and European perspectives, I will mainly refer to contributions to the European discourse. Cf. to the critique of comparative theology as pluralism—for example Menke, *Das unterscheidend Christliche*, 108–13. Even some comparative theologians would agree on the identification of comparative theology and a pluralistic option within the field of theology of religions. Cf., for example, Winkler, *Projekt*, 159.
2. This possible distinction addresses, for example, von Stosch, *Komparative Theologie*, 230–38.
3. This argument, of course, is not really original. It is, for example, also presumed in the works of Francis X. Clooney, S.J. Cf., for example, Clooney, *Comparative Theology*. But in my perspective, the strong focus of comparative theology as dogmatic theology is

not that present in these works. It seems, for instance, to be more attended in the research of Catherine Cornille even though I disagree with her on the necessary connection of a dogmatic commitment to one tradition with an inclusivist position. Cf. Cornille, *The Im-possibility*, 84.

4. Of course, one could widen the list of councils and dogmatic determinations. However, Nicaea and Chalcedon seem to have already fixed the normative core of Christian faith that God revealed Himself in the person of Jesus.
5. This, of course, does not mean, that the other theological disciplines would have to adapt a dogmatic methodology. Exegesis, for example, needs to reflect the biblical texts philologically and historically. But as a theological discipline, at some point exegetical work must also be related to dogmatic theology to connect the philological analysis with the Christian understanding of Gods revelation in history, which is made explicit in the systematic perspective of dogmatic theology and which on the other hand is permanently directed to exegesis as the foundation of its reflection. Consequently, the relation between dogmatic theology and the other theological disciplines, comparative theology included, can be described as a constitutively dialectical one. For a detailed reasoning for this position, cf. Rahner, *Exegese und Dogmatik*.
6. Currently, this seems to be common hermeneutical ground. For the justification of this argument, refer to Wittgenstein, *Philosophische Untersuchungen*, even though he would have avoided expressing this observation of the status of human language games as a universal epistemological claim. For a theological adaption of Wittgenstein's philosophy, see von Stosch, *Glaubensverantwortung*.
7. Cf. Kant, *Kritik*.
8. Especially the challenges of Friedrich Nietzsche and Albert Camus became important for the evolution of theology. Cf., for example, Werbick, *Gebetsglaube*.
9. For the understanding of contemporary theological concepts in Germany and Europe, the transcendental philosophical tradition necessarily has to be considered and its influence even for the current discourses needs to be emphasized. This seems to make for a significant difference to the American theological context, which is seemingly more dependent on pre- or post-critical metaphysics and which, consequently, does not really deal with the critique of transcendental philosophy.
10. This does not, of course, mean that all questions already are discovered and answered. But the continuing discourse with contemporary philosophy opens opportunities for systematic reflection of current theological problems.
11. However, this already implies that there are dogmatically non-problematic areas of interreligious dialogue and similarities between the religions and denominations that somehow are a precondition for a fruitful discourse because only similarities enable interlocutors to share a common language game. Consequently, these parts of original and mutual understanding are not excluded from the theological work, but an enrichment of the whole project of *fides quaerens intellectum*. But because theology deals with questions of truth, it needs to focus on different concepts of truth claims to avoid a pretended dialogical harmony. Thus, the comparative work needs to include dogmatic theological questions.
12. I use the term "provocation" in the positive sense of summoning the other to engagement in a common discourse about specific problems. By this understanding, "provocation" is

not confined to the dialogue of two religions because the two religions may be provoked to a certain reaction by a third instance. Finally, "provocation" also implies the heuristic intention of enabling the other to become sensitized to obscurities in his explanation of specific (religious) convictions. Thus "provocation" in the context of comparative theology basically means the opening of a discourse that is concerned with at least seemingly different truth claims.

13. Cf. the critique of Karimi, *Zur Frage der Erlösung*, 31–33.
14. It is clear that many different subjects in Christian-Muslim dialogue that are concerned with the question of salvation could be discussed here. The focus on anthropology and original sin just demonstrates the change of perspectives during the comparative work. A Christian soteriology that is developed in discourse with Islamic theology needs, for instance, to refer to the meaning of crucifixion and to a concept of sacrifice because both are constitutive parts of a Christian theory of salvation. Cf. to the whole project of a Christian soteriology in discourse with Islam Langenfeld, *Das Schweigen brechen*.
15. Cf. Kant, *Die Religion*.
16. Cf. Pröpper, *Erlösungsglaube*; Thomas Pröpper, *Theologische Anthropologie*.
17. Pröpper does not try to give proof for the existence of God. He just shows how the human needs God—whether he exists or not.
18. This principle of epistemological openness matches with the virtues of interreligious dialogue that are elaborated by Cornille, *The Im-possibility*. Cf. for a summary von Stosch, *Komparative Theologie*, 155–68. Cornille and von Stosch name: Doctrinal and epistemological humility, confessional affinity with the own tradition, assumption of commensurability and perception of differences, emphatic and caring attention, and hospitality for the potential truth of the other.
19. At this point, a fundamental ongoing discussion between comparative theologians takes place. The question is, if the work with *texts* from the other tradition should be preferred to find deeper insight in the tradition or if a normative confrontation of theological systems, represented by certain *persons*, is more fruitful for the theological discourse. Both perspectives may claim prominent representatives. Clooney, *His Hiding Place* could be an example for the first approach, Fredericks, *Buddhist and Christians* for the second. I would argue that the focus on the intertwined aspects of dogmatic and comparative theology urges to emphasize the confrontation of theological reflections from a religious insiders' perspective. The immediate examination of the basic texts of another tradition seemingly also opens an immediate understanding in the system of convictions of the other but, in fact, it is just opened to one's own hermeneutical approach. Consequently, the comparative theologian is in need of a (theological) "native speaker" of the certain religious language game to collate his interpretation of the text of another tradition with an insider's perspective on the texts. Comparison, however, in this context does not mean simply a descriptive outline of another truth claim but also a normative analysis of the other's explanation of his understanding of truth.
20. Regarding the subsequent part: Karimi, *Hingabe*; Karimi, *Die Beziehung von Mensch und Gott*; Karimi, *Versuch einer ästhetischen Hermeneutik*.
21. Cf. Kermani, *Gott ist schön*.

22. It is notable that Karimi is equally influenced by classical and modern Islamic philosophy and theology but also by German philosophy, in particular Hegel and Heidegger. His understanding of Islamic philosophy and theology is very much shaped by these philosophical approaches and—vice versa—his Islamic references shape his interpretation of Hegel and Heidegger in a remarkable way. The mutual influence of Islamic and German philosophical sources could be called an elliptic framework in which both foci are constitutive parts of understanding the whole theological system. Cf. Karimi, *Identität.*
23. For a better understanding of this hermeneutical principle, a short example might be helpful: The early Meccan Sura 82 is an apocalyptic vision about the day of judgment and its outcome: "The pure of heart will be in bliss / The hard of heart will be in blazing fire / the day of reckoning, burning there—they will not evade that day," (Sura 82,15). (Quoted by Sells, *Approaching the Qur'ān*, 52.) Karimi would argue that the announcement of the eschatological punishment has to be understood in the context of the prior idea of God's revelation of His beauty and thus, the criterion for a theological understanding of God's justice is His loving devotion to the world. Consequently, the text cannot mean a real physical punishment in the hereafter, but it seems to be a description of the sinner's experience of encountering the love of God in the revelation of His beauty. This specific interpretation is much influenced by Karimi's colleague Mouhanad Khorchide. Cf. Khorchide, *Das Jenseits.*
24. Cf. Karimi, *Zur Frage der Erlösung*, 31.
25. Cf. Rahner, *Grundkurs des Glaubens.*
26. This critique, of course, challenges every aesthetical theology, thus, also sacramental theology. It becomes very clear that interreligious provocations may lead to common problems, which may be solved in common theological projects. It becomes also clear that the naturalist philosophical critique can be understood as a provocation to comparative work, which is why comparative theology already includes dialogue with philosophy. This example also shows that a third discourse partner often can identify problems that would have been ignored by just two parties. Cf. to the "instance of the third," especially von Stosch, *Komparative Theologie*, 208–11.

4 Rhetorics of Theological One-Upsmanship in Christianity and Buddhism

ATHANASIUS'S POLEMIC AGAINST THE ARIANS AND VASUBANDHU'S REFUTATION OF PUDGALAVĀDA BUDDHISM

Hugh Nicholson

I

The name of our discipline contains a methodologically significant ambiguity. As David Tracy remarked a number of years ago in his encyclopedia article on "Comparative Theology," "theology" in this designation can refer either to the object or the subject of the activity of comparison.[1] To the extent that theology forms the *object of comparison*, Comparative Theology represents a subfield or a specific focus within Comparative Religion or the History of Religions (for my present purposes, I consider these two designations to be roughly equivalent). That is, Comparative Theology in this sense denotes the study of the intellectual or doctrinal dimension of the larger phenomenon of religion.[2] Conversely, to the extent that theology forms the *subject* of comparison, data from more than one theological tradition are compared on theological grounds and incorporated into a constructive theological vision.

def. of comp theo

Comparative Theology contains both of these dimensions. Even an avowedly confessional Comparative Theology incorporates a historical or contextual study of theological data. Conversely, inasmuch as there is no truly disinterested comparison, the theological interests and concerns of the comparative theologian will be operative even in the objective or contextualist phase of the comparative theological project, if only in the selection of theological examples to compare. Because it contains both theological-religious and contextual-historical dimensions, Comparative Theology must negotiate a tension between the two. Nowhere is this tension between the religious and the historical more starkly expressed than in the historian of religions Bruce Lincoln's well-known "Theses on Method":

> Religion, I submit, is that discourse whose defining characteristic is its desire to speak of things eternal and transcendent with an authority equally transcendent and eternal. History, in the sharpest possible contrast, is that discourse which speaks of things temporal and terrestrial in a human and fallible voice while staking its claim to authority on rigorous critical practice.[3]

From such a historicist perspective that regards religious institutions, discourses, and practices as human products conditioned by human interests, religious claims to transcendent, more-than-human status are ipso facto ideological. The History of Religions thus becomes a species of critical inquiry.[4] Or, as Lincoln himself puts it, "to practice history of religions [. . .] is to insist on discussing the temporal, contextual, situated, interested, human, and material dimensions of those discourses, practices, communities, and institutions that characteristically represent themselves as eternal, transcendental, spiritual, and divine."[5] We can infer that for Lincoln, theology is a particular form of religious discourse that claims transcendent authority.[6] Theology epitomizes ideology.

However, as Tyler Roberts argues, this understanding of theology as a religious discourse that disavows its human, conditioned, and interested character is a caricature.[7] An interest in shoring up a sharp disciplinary boundary between theology and the academic study of religion discourages an acknowledgment of the great variety of contemporary theologies, only a few of which conform to such an implicit "ideological" conception of theology. Roberts cites Kathryn Tanner, Rowan Williams, and Francis Fiorenza as three examples of "relatively mainstream Christian theologians who in one way or another explicitly acknowledge the immanent, historical, and therefore fallible character of religious discourse in general and of theology in particular."[8] Internal ideology critique, in particular, forms an integral component of liberation and political theologies. It also forms an integral component of Comparative Theology, particularly as our discipline must confront issues like the hegemonic nature of the representations of traditions (inasmuch as conventional representations of a tradition invariably privilege the self-representation of the dominant factions within that tradition at the expense of others) and the asymmetrical nature of inter-religious relations in today's neo-colonial global context.[9] Thus, the tension between the historical and the theological components of the comparative theological project is not quite as sharp as some polemical conceptions of the academic study of religion—those that define the discipline over against a theological-religious "other"—might suggest.

My current research project is guided by the proposition that a full and unflinching acknowledgment of what might be called the ideological dimension of theological discourses—that theological doctrines, whatever else they might do, function to mobilize social identity—need not interfere with an appreciation of their capacity, when integrated into suitable regimens of practice, to redescribe human experience in potentially liberating ways. I shall argue, in fact, that an acknowledgment of the role of social identity processes in doctrinal development sheds light on the process by which a tradition's best minds are often able to develop theological insights beyond what earlier generations could have anticipated.

II

My comparative example concerns two doctrines that are about as different substantively as two doctrines can be. The first of these is the Christian doctrine of the consubstantiality of the Son with the Father, a doctrine that forms the basis of the orthodox doctrine of the Trinity. The second is the Buddhist doctrine of No-self (Skt. *anātman*, Pali *anattā*), which claims that the personality is reducible to its impersonal physical and psychological constituents.

While these two doctrines differ radically on a substantive or material level, the discursive strategies used to establish and defend them are remarkably similar. Both doctrines were the products of hegemonic struggles within their respective traditions. Both doctrines, moreover, give expression to successful attempts on the part of their proponents to maximize, in an effort to gain the upper hand over their in-group rivals, the contrast with the "other" of their respective traditions, namely: Judaism (invidiously defined by its rejection of Christian messianic claims) for the one, and Brahmanical Hinduism (with its doctrine of the deathless self or *ātman*) for the other. I shall examine two texts that exemplify these discursive processes. The first is Athanasius of Alexandria's first two *Orations Against the Arians*, one of the classic texts of the so-called Arian Controversy of the fourth century. The second is Vasubandhu's "Treatise on the Negation of the Person" (*Pudgala-pratiṣedha-prakaraṇa*), a classic statement of the No-self doctrine that comprises the ninth and final chapter of his paradigmatic text of Abhidharma Buddhism, the *Abhidharmakośabhāṣ ya*.

III

The first two *Orations*—the third was a slightly later work[10] and the fourth was not written by Athanasius—constitute one of the most extensive and powerful refutations of the subordinationist current of fourth century theology to which Athanasius attaches the tendentious label of "Arian" after the Alexandrian priest condemned at the Council of Nicaea in 325. Admittedly, the extent of Athanasius's influence on later Trinitarian theology is considerably less clear than is typically assumed.[11] Nevertheless, Athanasius's insistence in this text, against his "Arian" adversaries, that the Son "proper to the substance of the Father" (ἴδιος τῆς τοῦ Πατρὸς οὐσίας) forms one of the underlying presuppositions of the orthodox doctrine of the Trinity. The latter is enshrined in the so-called Nicene-Constantinopolitan Creed, which is traditionally associated with the Council of Constantinople in 381.[12]

The first two *Orations* were probably written around 340–41, shortly after Athanasius arrived in Rome during the second of his five exiles.[13] He had been condemned and deposed from his Alexandrian see a little over a year before, in 338–39, by a council of bishops with the emperor Constantius present.[14] The reasons for Athanasius's exile had to do with the bishop's abuse of authority—perhaps the most serious of the improprieties cited was that he had ordered the desecration of the altar of a rival's church—and the vicissitudes of ecclesial-imperial relations, rather than with theological differences.[15] Timothy Barnes suggests that one of Athanasius's motivations for writing the *Orations* was to transpose his personal political struggles onto the theological plane.[16] The text presents its author, not as an embattled prelate seeking to mobilize support among the bishops of Asia Minor for his restitution, but rather as a champion of orthodoxy against an implacable heretical movement intent on destroying the Church.[17]

Accordingly, Athanasius begins the *Orations* by placing his own struggle in the larger narrative of the Church's fight against heresy:

> Although we all are Christians, and are so called, Marcion, an inventor of heresy, was long ago expelled. Those who stood fast with the expellers of Marcion remained Christians. But the followers of Marcion were no longer Christians. Thereafter they were called Marcionites. Thus Valentinus, Basilides, Manes, and Simon Magus have given their name to their followers. [. . .] Thus Meletius, expelled by Peter the bishop and martyr, no longer called his followers Christians but Meletians. So after blessed Alexander had cast out Arius, those who stayed with Alexander remained Christians. Those who united with Arius bequeathed the name of the Savior to us who were with Alexander. Thereafter they are called Arians. See, then, after Alexander's death, those who are in fellowship with Athanasius, who succeeded Alexander, and those with whom Athanasius is in fellowship—all have the same standard. They do not have the name of Athanasius. [. . .] For though we would have a succession of teachers, and become their disciples, being taught by them the things of Christ, we are nothing less than Christians and so called. But the followers of heretics, though they would have countless successors, nevertheless bear the name of the inventor of the heresy. Although Arius has died and many of his own have succeeded him, still they who think the same as Arius, acknowledged from Arius, are called Arians.[18]

This passage evinces a hegemonic struggle for the Christian name. None of Athanasius's contemporary readers would be prepared to recognize any of the second- and third-century figures he mentions—Marcion, Valentinus, Mani, et al.—as Christians, despite the self-understanding of each of these figures as such. Nor, Athanasius contends, should they extend the same honor to Athanasius's enemies, a group that includes, on the one hand, the Melitians, a schismatic sect in Egypt that had refused to recognize the legitimacy of Athanasius's bishopric, and, on the other, the target of the present treatise, the loose alliance of theologians that he calls Arians. The label is highly misleading. None of Athanasius's current theological adversaries—in particular, the bishop Eusebius of Nicomedia and the theologian Asterius—nor any other post-Nicaea theologian for that matter, identified with the disgraced figure of Arius, who ceases to be relevant after his condemnation in 325.[19] Arianism, as scholars have come to realize, was largely the invention of Athanasius and, at least initially, his one-time associate, Marcellus of Ancyra.[20]

Athanasius presents Arianism as what Rowan Williams calls the archetypical heresy.[21] In what has to rank among the most audacious misrepresentations in the history of religious polemic, Athanasius attributes what would have been, at least before the fourth century, an unremarkable feature of his rivals' theology, namely, their subordination of the Son to the Father, to a demonically inspired animus against the Savior. As the theological expression of a will to denigrate Christ, Arian subordinationism epitomizes heresy in general. This characterization of Arian subordinationism, moreover, allows Athanasius to link his rivals to Christianity's quintessential "other," Judaism. Athanasius homologizes the "Arian" subordination of the Son to the Jewish rejection of Jesus's messianic status.[22] In a tour de force of polemical rhetoric, Athanasius thus constructs a double genealogy for his mid-fourth century opponents: to the condemned heretic Arius, on the one hand, and to the New Testament Jews who allegedly had Jesus crucified, on the other.[23] Needless to say, once the Arians are characterized as "enemies of Christ" (χριστομάχοι)[24] there is no question of calling them "Christians."

Athanasius's arguments exploit what I would call, borrowing a phrase from George Lindbeck, a rhetoric of Christological maximalism against his adversaries. One could say that the fundamental theological achievement of Athanasius, and of "pro-Nicene" theology more generally, is problematizing a feature of virtually all pre-Nicene theology, namely, the subordination of the Son to the Father.[25] It is important to recognize that, while virtually all non-Gnostic Christian theology before the mid-fourth century would be subordinationist from the perspective of Nicene orthodoxy, most exalted the Son as much as possible within whatever pre-Nicene theological paradigm they were working with.[26] When seen in its original context, the force of Origen's doctrine of eternal generation, for example, was not to subordinate the Son to the Father but rather to push in precisely the opposite direction, "to make the Son intrinsic to the being of God."[27] From the perspective of later orthodoxy, however, Origen's hierarchical, Neo-Platonic conception of the Son and Spirit as successive and ontologically distinct emanations of the Father would become unacceptably subordinationist. Eusebius of Nicomedia, Eusebius of Caesarea, Asterius, and, as far as we can tell, even Arius himself represented an established Christian theological trajectory.[28] Like most early fourth-century theology, in fact, this "Eusebian" trajectory presupposed the Origenist hierarchical model of the relation between the Father and Son. Within this hierarchical paradigm, the notion of Christ or the

Word as the "first-born of creation," a conception supported by the plain sense of biblical texts like Colossians 1:17, Romans 8.29, and, above all, Proverbs 8:22 ("The Lord created me at the beginning of his work, the first of his acts of old") gave expression to Christ's uniqueness.[29] Such a conception exalted Christ high above the other works of God's creation. Arius expressed this idea in a formula that Athanasius cites: "He is a creature, but not as one of the creatures; a work, but not as one of the works; an offspring, but not as one of the offsprings."[30] In the paradigm change initiated by Alexander and Athanasius, however, this notion of Christ as the first-born of creation will take on an entirely different aspect. By classifying Christ as a creature, albeit the most exalted thereof, this notion was tantamount to a denial of Christ's divinity.[31] Accordingly, Athanasius dismisses Arius's caveat ("a creature, but not as one of the creatures") as a sophism.[32] Athanasius is obliged to reinterpret passages such as Proverbs 8:22 away from their plain sense.[33] That Athanasius feels the need to devote the better part of the second *Oration* (pars. 18–82) to the (re)interpretation of Proverbs 8:22 testifies to the extent to which the plain sense of this text supports the Arian position.

In the original Arian controversy, Alexander and, following him, Athanasius, did not begin with a new theological paradigm in mind. Alexander and Athanasius, no less than Arius and the two Eusebioi, were also working within a broadly Origenist paradigm, although they chose to emphasize different aspects of that legacy than their rivals.[34] Alexander and Athanasius simply recognized a weakness of Arius's theology that they exploited in their effort to assert episcopal authority in the new context of an imperial Church, a context in which orthodoxy—right belief—had become, after Constantine's conversion, a matter of political import.[35] Their critique of the "Arian" subordination of the Son to the Father would have something of a cascade effect on the rest of Christian theology, eventually necessitating a rethinking of every major theological issue, from the principles of biblical exegesis to the nature of God, from the ontological status of the Spirit to the nature of Christ.

The weakness that Alexander and Athanasius exploited was an inference from the concept of divine Sonship that Arius must have regarded as thoroughly unproblematic, indeed banal: namely, that the Father, precisely as Father, had logical priority over the Son. To assert, as one of Alexander's slogans had it, that "always God, always Son" (ἀεὶ θεὸς ἀεὶ υἱός),[36] Arius argues, is to admit two unbegotten, divine principles, an unacceptable breach of the monotheistic principle.[37] Arius reconciles the priority of the Father with the preexistence of Christ by making a distinction between what we might call logical priority and temporal priority. That is, the Son's generation takes place in an atemporal dimension, "before times and ages."[38] "The Son was begotten timelessly before everything (ἀλλ᾽ ἀχρόνως πρὸ πάντων γεννηθείς)."[39] Intent on shoehorning Arian Christology into an invidious dichotomy between the view of Christ as "one of the originated or as united with the Father" (τῶν γενητῶν ἕνα λέγειν αὐτὸν, ἢ τῷ Πατρὶ συνάπτειν αὔτον),[40] Athanasius dismisses the Arian distinction between temporal and atemporal priority as specious. "Why," he taunts his adversaries, "intimating time, do you not say clearly, 'There was a time when the Word was not?' You omit the term 'time' to deceive the guileless, but you do not hide your own thought. [. . .] You intimate time when you say, 'There was once when he was not' and 'He was not before he was begotten.'"[41]

Nowhere is Athanasius's mastery of the rhetoric of Christological maximalism more apparent than in his argument against his adversaries' characterization of God as "unoriginate."[42] He contrasts the characterization of God as unoriginate with the characterization of God as Father. The former term defines God with reference to his works, the latter with reference to the Son who reveals him.[43] His adversaries' preference for the unscriptural term "unoriginated" as the primary title for God betrays an ignorance of the Son[44]; like the Greeks, the Arians' knowledge of God is based only on his works.[45] Construing their preference for "unoriginated" as a willful rejection of Father-Son language, Athanasius imputes to his adversaries an intention to dishonor the Son.[46] The concept of "unoriginate," after all, marks a distinction between God and all originated beings, a group that includes the Son as well as creatures. Thus, this concept implicitly classifies the Son with created works.[47]

For Athanasius, nothing less is at stake in this dispute with the "Arians" than salvation itself. Contrasting his incarnational or descent Christology with the adoptionist Christology that he imputes, probably inaccurately, to his opponents,[48] Athanasius declares, in a celebrated formulation, that it was not that Christ was man and later became God, but rather, "being God, he later became man, that instead he might glorify us."[49] Were one to concede the Arian adoptionist understanding of Christ, "we would not, having been redeemed from sins, rise from the dead, but we would remain dead beneath the earth."[50]

Much of Athanasius's argumentation in the first two *Orations*, particularly the second, is exegetical in nature. It is not possible to examine these exegetical arguments in detail here. Let me simply mention the hermeneutical strategy that Athanasius uses to reconcile texts like Proverbs 8:22 that would seem to favor an Arian interpretation with his contention that the Son is intrinsic to the Father's being. Athanasius distinguishes between passages that speak of Christ with reference to his divinity and those that speak of Christ with reference to his humanity.[51] This principle of New Testament exegesis[52] clashed with the non-Nicenes' assumption that Christ spoke with one voice.[53] Ironically, by raising the Son's divinity to the level of the Father, the doctrine of consubstantiality effectively relegated a good number of Jesus's statements to the category of the merely human.[54]

IV

As the title of this chapter of the *Abhidharmakośabhāṣya* (*AKBh.*) indicates, the primary target of Vasubandhu's "Treatise on the Negation of the Person" (*Pudgala-pratiṣedha-prakaraṇa*)[55] is the doctrine of the person (*pudgalavāda*) espoused by the Vātsiputrīya and Saṃmitīya monastic orders. To appreciate what is at stake in Vasubandhu's refutation, it is important to dispel the common misconception that Pudgalavāda Buddhism was a renegade fringe movement whose doctrine of the person deviated, thanks either to an inability to accept one of the Buddha's most demanding teachings or a pragmatic desire to assimilate to their Hindu surroundings, from the Buddha's putatively original teaching of selflessness. Far from being a fringe movement, Pudgalavāda Buddhism appears to have been well-established in India between the third century BCE and the eleventh CE.[56] According to the seventh-century Chinese pilgrim Hsüan-tsang, a quarter of the monks in India belonged to the Pudgalavāda Sāṃmatīya school, making it the largest non-Mahāyāna school there at the time.[57] Nor should it be assumed that Pudgalavādins deviated from the Buddha's original teaching. This representation of the Pudgalavādins as "philosophical renegades"[58] rests on the assumption that the *anātman* doctrine belongs to the earliest period of Buddhism, long a topic of vigorous debate in Buddhist studies. Because a discussion of this thorny debate lies outside the scope of the present essay, let me just state what I think is the most reasonable hypothesis on the issue.

doctrine der. out of social context.

While some of the earliest Buddhist discourses do indeed call into question the notion of an enduring self at the core of the personality,[59] the "orthodox" *anātman* doctrine most likely developed dialectically in the context of a series of hegemonic struggles within Buddhism. The *anātman* doctrine, like its Christian counterparts, was probably the product of a developmental process. Only such a developmental hypothesis can account for the rather obvious fact that the Pudgalavāda schools were able to interpret the word of the Buddha (*buddhavacana*), to their satisfaction at least, without the "orthodox" *anātman* doctrine. To imagine otherwise would be to effectively concede the polemical view that the Pudgalavādins were too confused, their commitment to authentic Buddhism too compromised, for them to grasp the Buddha's authentic teaching.

Vasubandhu's text locates the refutation of Pudgalavāda in the larger context of a repudiation of Brahmanical arguments in favor of the doctrine of the self or *ātman*. Given the conventional wisdom that Buddhist thought, and the *anātman* doctrine in particular, developed in reaction to Brahmanism,[60] it is surprising that Vasubandhu's fourth-century (CE!) treatise appears to be one of the first extant Buddhist texts to engage explicitly with the non-Buddhist *ātmavāda*.[61] Vasubandhu's engagement with the doctrine of the self anticipates a larger shift in Buddhist intellectual history in which prominent Buddhist intellectuals "suddenly start addressing non-Buddhist philosophies and religious doctrines in a systematic way."[62] Vincent Eltschinger suggests that this "heresiological turn" was a response to a growing Brahmanical hostility toward Buddhism and other non-Brahmanical movements during the declining years of the Gupta Dynasty in the fifth and early sixth centuries.[63] This shift to an extra-sectarian polemical focus is mirrored in contemporary Brahmanical thought, particularly in the early Nyāya school.[64] Inasmuch as it integrated the science of the self (*ātmavidyā*) with the method of reasoning and argumentation,[65] early Nyāya, together with the allied Vaiśeṣika system, was the Brahmanical school ideally suited to—if not expressly designed for—the task of defending Brahmanical thought, symbolized by its doctrine of the *ātman*, against the Buddhist challenge. Vasubandhu's refutation of *ātmavāda* here in the *Abhidharmakoṣa* thus represents a significant moment in a transgenerational dialectic between Buddhists and Nyāyakas on the question of the self.[66]

In the programmatic opening paragraph, Vasubandhu, much like Athanasius, tells us that nothing less than liberation is at stake in the ensuing debate on the question of the self:

> Now, then, is there no liberation [from the round of *saṃsāra*] to be found outside this [teaching of the Buddha]? No, it is not. Why so? Owing to a preoccupation with false views of self. For [our opponents] have not determined that the conceptual construction "self" refers to the bundle continuum (*skandha-santāna*) alone. What then? They imagine that the self is a discrete substance (*dravyāntaram evātmānaṃ parikalpayanti*). Moreover, the negative afflictions are born from grasping-as-self.[67]

The afflictions (*kleśa*) that prevent the occurrence of liberation have their origin in the belief in self. We could say that *ātmavāda*, like "Arianism," is for Buddhists the "archetypical heresy" in the sense that it is the fundamental presupposition of all the misguided views (*dṛṣṭi*) that preclude liberation.

Vasubandhu frames his refutation of Pudgalavāda in terms of a stark contrast between, as the concluding verses put it, "the wise who heed the doctrine of the Buddhas" and "the blind Tīrthikas who act in accordance with various false views."[68] The doctrine in question, of course, is that of selflessness (*nirātmatā*), the only doctrine that "abides in the city of nirvāṇa."[69] Vasubandhu's basic argumentative strategy against the Pudgalavādins will be to reject as vain and specious their effort to differentiate their doctrine of the person from the Brahmanical doctrine of the substantial self. Pudgalavāda is reducible to *ātmavāda* and the Pudgalavādins, accordingly, are far from salvation.[70]

The leading question with which he confronts his Vātsīputrīya Pudgalavādin opponent establishes this dichotomy between self and no-self right from the outset. Does the person exist as a substance (*dravyataḥ*) like physical form and other existents (*dharma*)? Or does it exist conceptually (*prajñaptitaḥ*) like milk and other aggregative entities (*samudāya*)? If the former, then the view of the Tīrthikas—*ātmavāda*—follows as the inevitable consequence. If, on the other hand, his opponent, desirous of remaining within the Buddhist fold, opts for the latter alternative, then he will find himself unwittingly affirming Vasubandhu's own position. Here, we have a beautiful example of a discourse intended to secure in-group hegemony. If one takes an authentic Buddhist position, it will coincide with Vasubandhu's. If, on the other hand, one takes issue with Vasubandhu's position, then one finds oneself, willy nilly, outside the pale. Like Athanasius's Arian opponents, the Pudgalavādins are depicted as outsiders within. Later on, in a clever word-play on their sectarian designation, Vātsīputrīya ("sons of Vātsīputra"), Vasubandhu declares that his opponents are not sons of the Buddha (*śākya-putrīyā*).[71] The implicit contrast here between the followers of Vātsīputra and those of Śākyamuni recalls Athanasius's invidious decision to designate rival, "heretical" expressions of Christianity by the name of their founders rather than that of Christ.

Vasubandhu's Pudgalavādin opponent rejects the choice between substantial and conceptual existence as a false dichotomy; the person, he says, exists as neither.[72] Rather, the person is conceived in reliance upon (*upādāya*) the present constituents that are personally acquired.[73] The key phrase in this statement is "in reliance upon," which, as James Duerlinger explains, marks the crucial distinction between the Pudgalavādins' position, on the one hand, and Vasubandhu's contention that the person is the same in existence as the constituents, on the other.[74] In the lengthy exchange that follows, Vasubandhu attempts to show that the distinction marked by the Pudgalavādin's understanding of *upādāya* is specious or, as Vasubandhu himself puts it, "ignorant talk with obscure meaning" (*andha-vacanam unmīlita-arthaṃ*). However this notion of reliance is understood, the conception of the person refers only to the aggregates, just as the conception of milk refers only to the various constituents of milk.[75] Here I cannot go into the specific arguments that Vasubandhu marshals against his opponent, which are involved, often obscure, and sometimes specious. Let me simply highlight the overall aim of Vasubandhu's argumentation. His aim is to show that the Pudgalavādin's effort to chart a middle course between the *ātmavāda* of the Tīrthikas and the *anātmavāda* (in the sense of *skandhamātravāda*) of Vasubandhu is in vain. Perhaps implicitly responding to the Pudgalavāda objection that the latter constitutes the heretical view of annihilationism, Vasubandhu concludes his refutation of *pudgalavāda* by presenting his doctrine of the person as "the same in existence as the constituents" as the middle way between two extreme views that have arisen in the Buddha's dispensation.[76] Pudgalavāda ("grasping the person"—*pudgala-grāha*) represents the eternalist extreme, the doctrine of the non-existence of everything (*sarva-nāstitā-grāha*), possibly a tantalizingly unelaborated (and caricatured) allusion to the teaching of Nāgārjuna's Madhyamaka school, the annihilationist.[77]

Pace Vasubandhu, the Pudgalavādins' conception of the middle path between the extremes of eternalism and annihilationism might very well have conformed more closely to the spirit of the ancient Buddhist sūtras (as preserved in the extant Pali Suttapiṭaka) than Vasubandhu's. Their doctrine of the person as undetermined (*avyākṛta*) or inexpressible (*avācya*; *avaktavya*) with respect to the constituents[78] appears to have been based on the so-called undetermined or unanswered (*avyākṛta*; Pali *avyākata*) questions of the Buddha.[79] In numerous sūtras the Buddha is depicted as refusing to commit to a series of ten questions, the most consequential of which are two questions concerning the relation between the soul and body (Pali *jīva* and *sārīra*, respectively): Are the soul and body one and the same (*taṃ jīvaṃ taṃ sarīram*) or is the soul one thing and the body another (*aññaṃ jīvam aññaṃ sarīram*)? The tradition has associated the first of these propositions with the "heresy" of annihilationism, that is, the proposition that there is nothing that survives the body, thus rendering meaningless the notions of rebirth and karmic retribution. The latter corresponds to the heresy of eternalism, the belief in an eternal principle that does not participate in karmic processes. The Buddha's refusal to commit to either of these positions, accordingly, gives expression to the doctrine of the Middle Way.[80] The Pudgalavāda doctrine of the inexpressibility of the person as neither the same as nor other than the constituents, again, would seem to be based directly on this tradition.

Vasubandhu's Pudgalavādin opponent, in fact, appeals to the Unanswered Questions in order to call the *anātman* doctrine into question. "If the person is nothing more than the constituents," he asks, "then why did the Blessed One not answer the question about whether the soul was the same or different from the body?"[81] For the Pudgalavādin, Vasubandhu's *anātmavāda* (=*skandhamātravāda*) clearly implies an affirmative response to the first of these questions the Buddha refused to answer, namely, whether the soul is the same as the body. Vasubandhu meets this objection with an explanation that has become so commonplace in the secondary literature that its innovative character is easy to miss. Citing a tradition that goes back at least as far as the *Milindapañha* (1st century?),[82] Vasubandhu argues that the Buddha rejected the questions because they each presuppose the existence of the self which the tradition rejects.[83] To ask whether the soul is the same as the body is akin to asking whether a tortoise's hair is hard or soft[84] or whether the son of a barren woman is dark or fair.[85] The difference in the interpretation of the Unanswered

Questions here corresponds to a distinction in the understanding of "views" (Skt. *Dṛṣṭi;* Pali *diṭṭhi*). The original sense of the Unanswered Questions—to which, as I have suggested, the Pudgalavāda refusal to specify the person as either the same as or different from the aggregates closely conforms—corresponds to what appears to have been an ancient tradition that rejected all views, without exception, as karmically conditioned.[86] Vasubandhu's interpretation of the Unanswered Questions, by contrast, corresponds to a distinction between right view and wrong view (Pali *sammā-diṭṭhi* and *micchā-diṭṭhi*, respectively), the latter category presupposing the false belief in the self as the cognitive expression of attachment. And here we return to the theme announced at the beginning of Vasubandhu's refutation, namely, that the false view of self (*vitathā-ātma-dṛṣṭi*), as the root cause of the afflictive obstructions (*kleśa*) to liberation, represents the archetypical "view" or heresy.

V

Let me draw from the foregoing analysis a few comparative observations.

1. Both texts give expression to hegemonic struggles within their respective traditions. Vasubandhu's "Treatise on the Negation of the Person" reflects a struggle between the VaibhåΣika tradition and the Vātsiputrīya, presumably the most influential Pudgalavāda school in the area where Vasubandhu was active. Athanasius's *Orations* reflects a struggle for influence in an imperial Church in the process of formation. The two parties are, on the one hand, Athanasius and his allies (in particular, Marcellus, destined to be written out of the history of the Church as an embarrassment to "pro-Nicene" theology, and Athanasius's supporter, Julius, bishop of Rome) and, on the other, a loose alliance of ecclesiastics and theologians who opposed Athanasius for theological, ethical, and political reasons (notably, the two Eusebioi and Asterius).

2. The doctrine at the center of each debate is considered a sine qua non for the highest religious goal in their respective traditions. For Athanasius, Christ's coeternality with the Father represents the condition for the possibility of salvation. For Vasubandhu, the afflictions that obstruct the attainment of liberation have the belief in self (*ātmadṛṣṭi*) as their basis. Both authors present the positions of their adversaries—the Arians' alleged refusal to recognize Christ's divinity for the one, the Pudgalavādins' effective adherence to a theory of a self for the other—as the most fundamental or archetypical heresy in their respective traditions.

*In group gets
that rew[...]
to out.*

3. In both cases, the proximate in-group rival is rhetorically assimilated to the out-group "other." In other words, both authors depict their rivals as "outsiders-within." Homologizing the "Arians'" alleged denigration of Christ to the Jewish rejection of Jesus's messianic status, Athanasius calls the former the "new Jews." Similarly, Vasubandhu presents his Vātsiputrīya Pudgalavādin rivals as effectively teaching the *ātmavāda* of the Tīrthikas (outsiders, "heretics") under another name.

4. Accordingly, the general argumentative aim of both polemics is to undermine as specious the distinctions by which their rivals sought to distinguish themselves from their respective out-groups. As we have seen, Athanasius rejects Arius's qualification of Christ's creaturely status—namely, that "He is a creature, but not as one of the creatures"—as a vain and hypocritical attempt to exalt Christ within an anti-Christian paradigm. Likewise, he rejects the distinction between logical priority and temporal priority with which Arius attempted to preserve the preexistence, and thereby the divinity, of Christ. Vasubandhu, for his part, takes great pains to undermine the Pudgalavādins' claim that the person relies on the constituents (thereby distinguishing it from the autonomous *ātman* of the Tīrthikas) and yet is not reducible to them, as Vasubandhu insists. Both distinctions are presented as vain and specious attempts to have it both ways.

5. In both polemics, the argumentation is driven by a rhetoric of one-upmanship. Athanasius's depiction of his Eusebian rivals' hierarchical understanding of the relation between Father and Son as denigrating Christ exploits what I have called a rhetoric of Christological maximalism. All things being equal, when given a choice between two conceptions of Christ, Christians will invariably opt for the one that exalts Christ more. The genius of Athanasius was his ability to imagine, in an effort to gain a rhetorical upper hand over his Eusebian rivals, a Christologically more maximal conception of Christ than that allowed in the prevailing hierarchical Origenist paradigm. A similar rhetoric is at work in Buddhist works such as Vasubandhu's, although this rhetoric is harder to detect in the restrained, scholastic style of the Sanskrit śāstric genre. Vasubandhu's characterization of Pudgalavāda Buddhism as equivalent to non-Buddhist *ātmavāda* embodies a rhetoric of maximizing selflessness, if I can put it like this. Put crudely, Pudgalavāda Buddhism was not "selfless" enough. Ironically, Vasubandhu's style of Abhidharma Buddhism was itself invidiously subjected to this rhetoric of maximal selflessness in Mahāyāna polemic. Whereas the former recognizes the absence of

an enduring self in persons (*pudgala-nairātmya*), the Mahāyāna carries the concept of selflessness to its logical conclusion in its recognition of the absence of self in (all) things as well (*dharma-nairātmya*). In Mahāyāna understanding, the latter becomes a sine qua non for liberation: it is impossible to abandon the obstructive afflictions (*kleśāvaraṇa*) without realizing the selflessness—or emptiness—of things.[87]

6. The claims of traditionalist historiography notwithstanding, both "Arian" Christianity and Pudgalavāda Buddhism represent more traditional expressions of Christianity and Buddhism, respectively, than the "orthodox" forms that came, whether by their greater intrinsic appeal or simply by historical accident, to supplant them. As Rowan Williams concedes, there is a sense in which Arius could be regarded as a theological conservative[88] and Athanasius, conversely, could be regarded, at least by his rivals, as something of an extremist.[89] On the Buddhist side, there are features of an admittedly hypothetical pre-canonical stratum of Buddhist thought, such as a cosmological duality between a temporal and impermanent sphere of form (*rūpa*) and a placeless and unchanging realm of truth (*dharma*), that cohere better with a Pudgalavāda or, more accurately, a proto-Pudgalavāda perspective than with an orthodox *anātmavāda* one.[90] Both examples exemplify the thesis articulated by Walter Bauer in his classic study, *Orthodoxy and Heresy in Earliest Christianity*, namely, that expressions of a religion that will come to be labeled as heretical in many instances pre-date their orthodox counterparts.[91] Or, put differently, what was mainstream and taken to be orthodox for one generation could become heterodox for a later one.[92] There are, of course, many causes at work behind the ascendency of one theological (or Buddhological) paradigm over another. Whatever effect the rhetorics of one-upsmanship might have on shaping religious attitudes and mobilizing support for one theological trajectory over another, these effects do not eclipse the impact of non-discursive factors like the ascendency of a particular emperor or changes in economic conditions that favor one particular religious community over another.[93] Apart from the purely contingent factors at work, however, both Arian Christianity and Pudgalavāda Buddhism can be regarded, at least on the level of discourse, as casualties of the ratcheting effect of the aforementioned rhetorics.

7. The ratcheting effect of the rhetoric of one-upsmanship exacerbates existing tensions within a system of belief and in some cases introduces new ones. As I remarked previously, Alexander and Athanasius's rhetoric

of Christological one-upsmanship over Arius and his allies in the original Arian controversy had a focused and "occasional" character. They sought to gain the upper hand over their adversaries at any cost, postponing a consideration of the systematic implications of certain key anti-Arian statements until Arius's threat to episcopal authority had been neutralized. In particular, the doctrine of the consubstantiality of Father and Son exacerbated the tension between the humanity and divinity of Christ. The Christological controversies of the fifth century were the dubious legacy of the Trinitarian controversies of the fourth. On the Buddhist side, the *anātman* doctrine stands in considerable tension with the core Buddhist doctrines of karmic retribution and rebirth. In this regard, we must judge Pudgalavāda, like pre-Nicene Christology, to be more intuitive than its orthodox counterpart. The counter-intuitive character of doctrines like Nicene consubstantiality and *anātmavāda* can be explained, at least in part, as a consequence of these dynamics of polemical struggle.

8. Such tensions become particularly manifest in the area of scriptural exegesis. As a tradition's doctrines develop in accordance with social identity processes, they can find themselves at odds with some of the foundational teachings enshrined in that tradition's scriptures. I mentioned previously how Athanasius had his work cut out for him arguing against this more obvious Arian interpretation of such texts like Proverbs 8:22 and Colossians 1:17 that speak of Christ as the first-born of creation. More generally, Athanasius reconciles texts that imply or presuppose the temporality of Christ by distinguishing between the things Jesus said and did by virtue of his divine nature and those he said by virtue of his divine nature as God's preexistent Word. On the Buddhist side, there are texts, like the famous "Burden Sutta,"[94] which allegorizes the bearer of burden to be set down to the person (*puggala*), that seem to cohere better with the doctrine of the person than with that of No-self. The Buddhist solution to the problem of reconciling the *anātman* doctrine with those texts in which the Buddha speaks of persons being reborn or, alternatively, attaining release was a metalinguistic distinction that itself became a central Buddhist doctrine, namely, the distinction between conventional and ultimate truth (Skt. *Saṃvṛti*[95]- and *paramārthika-satya*, respectively).

9. Religious traditions devote a great deal of intellectual energy and creativity to reconciling such tensions. Much of this activity can appear to unsympathetic observers as attempts to square the circle with ad hoc

distinctions. And yet, politically generated theological problematics can occasion, like the spandrels of evolutionary theory, genuine insights destined to ground a distinctive way of experiencing and understanding the world. An example would be the Christian trinitarian conception of God, according to which God's self-manifestation (represented by the Person of the Son) belongs to God's very essence and whose relational trinitarian structure, moreover, serves as a paradigm for all reality.[96] To the extent that the application of the principle of conditionality to the problematic of rebirth-without-self transformed the former into a comprehensive cosmological principle,[97] the doctrine of Dependent Origination (Skt. *Pratītya-samutpāda*) would also exemplify this phenomenon.

The value of the foregoing comparative generalizations consists in their ability to sharpen our perception of each of the phenomena being compared. Throughout the comparative process, our interest remains focused on the compared traditions; these are not set aside, like scaffolding, once they have yielded a theory. Looking at the No-self doctrine in light of the Christian doctrinal disputes of the fourth century allows us to formulate a hypothesis about doctrinal development that in turn allows us to move beyond the increasingly unproductive debate in Buddhist studies over whether ancient Buddhism did or did not deny a self. Conversely, looking at a text like Athanasius's *Orations* in light of Vasubandhu's "Negation" has the effect of foregrounding certain aspects of the former's argumentation that might otherwise escape notice. In particular, looking at Athanasius's polemic in light of the structure of Vasubandhu's treatise, in which the refutation of Pudgalavāda Buddhism is placed in the larger context of a refutation of non-Buddhist *ātmavāda*, allows us to see that Athanasius's characterization of the Arian Christ as a mere creature carries an implicit reference to the non-Christian—in particular the Jewish—refusal to recognize Christ's divinity. The foregoing comparison suggests that Athanasius' invidious comparisons between the "Arians" and the Jews do not simply embellish his argumentation, but rather manifest its underlying structure.

VI

I have suggested that No-self and the consubstantiality of the Son with the Father were each the products of hegemonic struggles within their respective traditions, and that each of these doctrines, moreover, represented successful attempts to maximize, in an effort to gain the upper hand over their rivals, the contrast with the respective "others" of each tradition. I anticipate the objection that this thesis, at least as formulated, is theologically unpalatable. These doctrines, it might be argued, express a truth above and beyond their social function; indeed, even if one is willing to acknowledge the social identity processes behind their development, such an analysis misses the point. One might even argue that constructive theological reflection requires that one bracket such causal analyses.

Such a proposal presupposes something analogous to the distinction between the context of discovery and the context of justification in the philosophy of science. That is, the process by which scientific truths are discovered may be undisciplined and "irrational," but the truth of those claims need not be vitiated by the disorderly path that led to their discovery so long as those truths can subsequently be tested in accordance with rational procedures. This distinction between the contexts of discovery and justification corresponds to Imre Lakatos's historiographical distinction between the internal and external histories of science. Lakatos argues that one can rationally reconstruct the history of science in accordance with a particular normative philosophy or methodology of science[98]—this is its internal history. Whatever elements cannot be understood or justified according to that philosophy will be relegated to its external, social history. Applying this model to the study of religious doctrine, one might argue that the social identity process I have highlighted in the foregoing analysis could be safely relegated to the external history of doctrine.[99]

Internal histories of doctrine need not be "Whiggish" narratives that suppress the contingencies of history in an effort to present the past as an inexorable march to the present. A rational reconstruction of doctrine that nevertheless acknowledges the extra-theological factors influencing doctrinal development is continuous with the venerable theological project of arguing for the "fittingness" of the contingent facts of the biblical narrative. Nevertheless, I contend that an understanding of identity-sustaining doctrines like No-self and consubstantiality should be permeable to externalist, sociological analyses like the foregoing.[100] For only by forthrightly acknowledging the role of social identity processes in doctrinal development can one appreciate the mechanism of theological creativity alluded to in the ninth point in the preceding section. There I suggested that consubstantiality and No-self exemplify the way in which doctrines that develop in accordance with social identity processes can find themselves standing in considerable tension with other teachings of a tradition. Such doctrines therefore challenge a tradition to look for creative solutions to the problematics they create. Just as the juxtaposition of the two categorically dissimilar terms in metaphor encourages an imaginative break from an ordinary vision of reality that perceives no kinship between the two terms,[101] or the way that the resistance of a recalcitrant medium summons forth and reveals the creative powers of the artist, so too can a politically generated problematic—how to reconcile Christ's full divinity with monotheism, or how to imagine rebirth without a vehicle of transmigration—challenge the best minds of a tradition to glimpse a perspective in which the seemingly contradictory claims make sense.

Abbreviations

AKBh.	*Abhidharmakośabhāṣya* of Vasubandhu. Śāstri, Swāmī Dwārikādās, ed. *Abhidharmakośa and Bhāṣya of Ācārya Vasubandhu with the Sphuṭārthā Commentary of Ācārya Yaśomitra.* Varanasi: Bauddha Bharati, 1973. References to the *AKBh.* include the page and line numbers in Śāstri's edition—for example, *AKBh.* 1189.1–3 is page 1189 of Śāstri's edition, lines 1–3. Translation of the ninth and final chapter, the *Pudgala-pratiṣedha-prakaraṇa*, is given in Duerlinger, *Indian Buddhist Theories of Persons: Vasubandhu's "Refutation of the Theory of a Self."*
C. Ar.	*Orations Against the Arians,* of Athanasius of Alexandria. *S. P. N. Athanasaii: Opera Omnia Quae Exstant.* J. P. Migne, ed. Paris, 1887. Translation: NPNF, vol. 4.
D.	*Dīgha Nikāya.* References are to the volume and page numbers in the Pali Text Society (PTS) edition.
M.	*Majjhima Nikāya* (PTS).
NBh.	*Nyāya-Bhāṣya* of Vātsyāyana. *Gautamīyanyāyadarśana with Bhāṣya of Vātsyāyana.* Anantalal Thakur, ed. New Delhi: Indian Council of Philosophical Research, 1997.
NPNF.4	*Nicene and Post-Nicene Fathers of the Christian Church: Volume IV: St. Athanasius: Select Works and Letters.* Philip Schaff and Henry Wace, eds. New York: The Christian Literature Company, 1892.

NS.	Nyāya Sūtra. *Gautamīyanyāyadarśana with Bhāṣya of Vātsyāyana*. Anantalal Thakur, ed. New Delhi: Indian Council of Philosophical Research, 1997.
S.	*Saṃyutta Nikāya* (PTS).
Sn.	*Sutta Nipāta* (PTS).
U.	Hans-Georg Opitz, ed, *Urkunden zur Geschichte des arianischen Streites*. Vol. 3/1 of *Athanasius Werke*. Berlin and Leipzig, 1934–35. References are given as "Opitz, U," followed by document, page, and line numbers—for example, Opitz, U.6, 13.10–12 refers to the sixth document (Arius's Letter to Alexander of Alexandria), page 13, lines 10–12. Translations of most of these documents are found in Rusch, *Trinitarian Controversy*.

Notes

1. Tracy, "Comparative Theology," 446.
2. For example, Jordan, *Comparative Religion*, 27; Tiele, "On the Study of Comparative Theology," 76.
3. Lincoln, *Gods and Demons*, 1.
4. Griffiths, "On the Future of the Study of Religion," 73.
5. Lincoln, *Gods and Demons*, 1.
6. Roberts, "Exposure and Explanation," 148.
7. Roberts, "Exposure and Explanation," 147–51.
8. Roberts, "Exposure and Explanation," 150–51. To say nothing of theologians like Gordan Kaufman and Sheila Greeve Davaney, who each foreground historicism as a central presupposition of Christian theological reflection.
9. At the same time that an engagement with religious others heightens the demand for an awareness of the extent to which religious discourses, including that of comparative theology itself, function ideologically to conceal the interests of their proponents, comparison provides a particularly effective tool for its detection. Given that one mark of the effectiveness of ideology is its ability to render itself invisible to those subject to it, it is generally easier to recognize the ideological products of other cultures. An exposure to these can help one discern in the home tradition similar ideological patterns and tendencies that might otherwise escape notice (Lincoln, *Gods and Demons*, 2).
10. Ayres, *Nicaea*, 110.
11. M. R. Barnes, "Fourth Century," 53–54; Ayres, *Nicaea*, 117.
12. We lack any direct evidence that the creed was actually composed and ratified at the council of Constantinople in 381. This lack of evidence has led some scholars, most notably F. J. A. Hort and A. Harnack, to question the traditional association between the creed and the council. Against these scholars, Kelly (*Early Christian Creeds*, 313–31) argues for the traditional association of the creed with the council.

13. Lienhardt, "Did Athanasius Reject Marcellus?," 70.
14. T. Barnes, *Athanasius*, 45.
15. Hanson, *Search*, 258, 261; Wiles, *Archetypal Heresy*, 6.
16. T. Barnes, *Athanasius*, 53.
17. T. Barnes, *Athanasius*, 54–55.
18. *C. Ar.* I.3; trans. Rusch, *Trinitarian Controversy*, 65.
19. Williams, *Arius*, 82; Ayres, *Nicaea*, 56; Wiles, *Archetypal Heresy*, 5–6; Hanson, *Search*, xvii.
20. M. R. Barnes, "Fourth Century," 53.
21. Williams, *Arius*, 1–2; see, for example, *C. Ar.* I.7.
22. For example, *C. Ar.* I.38.
23. *C. Ar.* 1:8.
24. *C. Ar.* I.55; cf. I.7.
25. This is not to say, of course, that pre-Nicene theologies did not recognize the divinity of Christ. There is evidence, in fact, that early Christians worshipped Jesus from very early on in the movement. Larry W. Hurtado, for example, argues that "the resurrected Jesus is treated as divine for all practical purposes from the first decades of the Christian movement" ("Christ Devotion," 28 and passim; see also Hengel, *The Cross of the Son of God*, 2 and passim). Nevertheless, Hurtado concedes that even the exalted Christological statements found in a late-first-century text like the Gospel of John presuppose the subordination of Jesus to God the Father (*Lord Jesus Christ*, 52). The difficulty contemporary Christians have in recognizing a subordinationist theology that nevertheless affirms Christ's divine status testifies to the influence of Athanasius's rhetoric and, more broadly, to the power of Nicene orthodoxy in fostering an "all or nothing" concept of divinity.
26. Both J. N. D. Kelly and Lewis Ayres make the point that to accuse pre-Nicene theologians of subordinationism is inappropriate if the charge implies an *intent* to subordinate the Son to the Father (Kelly, *Early Christian Doctrines*, 100–1 [concerning the second century Apologists]; Ayres, *Nicaea*, 21–23, 27–28 [concerning Origen]).
27. Ayres, *Nicaea*, 23.
28. See Ayres, *Nicaea*, 52–61.
29. Williams, *Arius*, 20.
30. *C. Ar.* II.19; NPNF.4, 358.
31. Here there was a subtle narrowing of the concept of creation. As Wiles (*Archetypal Heresy*, 13) perceptively remarks, the spirit of the "Arian" reading of such texts was that creation was "the appropriate generic term, with begetting as a way of indicating the unique and intimate nature of this primary act of divine creation—the bringing into being of a distinct divine Word or Wisdom or Son."
32. *C. Ar.* II.19–20.
33. *C. Ar.* II.62–65. For example, *C. Ar.* II.44: "Therefore it is necessary to unfold the sense of what is said, and to seek it as something hidden, and not nakedly to expound as if the meaning were spoken 'plainly,' lest by a false interpretation we wander from the truth" (trans. NPNF.4, 372; cf. also *C. Ar.* II.77).
34. Williams, *Arius*, 154–57; Ayres, *Nicaea*, 20–30.
35. Williams, *Arius*, 82–91.

36. Opitz, U.1, 2.1; trans. Rusch, *Trinitarian Controversy*, 29.
37. Opitz, U.6, 13.12; trans. Rusch, *Trinitarian Controversy*, 32.
38. Opitz, U.6, 13.4; trans. Rusch, *Trinitarian Controversy*, 31.
39. Opitz, U.6, 13.10; trans. Rusch, *Trinitarian Controversy*, 32.
40. *C. Ar.* I.9; trans. Rusch, *Trinitarian Controversy*, 71.
41. *C. Ar.* I.13, trans. Rusch, *Trinitarian Controversy*, 76.
42. Athanasius treats the two Greek terms ἀγέννητος and ἀγένητος as synonyms. Later theologians will use these two terms to mark a distinction between generation and creation: Only the Father is ἀγέννητος (ungenerated), but all three divine Persons are ἀγένητος (uncreated). See Ayres, *Nicaea*, 113, no. 23.
43. *C. Ar.* I.33.
44. *C. Ar.* I.33.
45. *C. Ar.* I.34.
46. *C. Ar.* I. 33; cf. I.30, I.18.
47. *C. Ar.* I.30.
48. There is little evidence for an adoptionist Christology apart from Athanasius's description (Ayres, *Nicaea*, 56; Williams, *Arius*, 113).
49. *C. Ar.* I.39, trans. Rusch, *Trinitarian Controversy*, 102; cf. *C. Ar.* I.41, I.43.
50. *C. Ar.* I.43, trans. Rusch, *Trinitarian Controversy*, 107; cf. *C. Ar.* II.43.
51. For example, *C. Ar.* I.50, 60, 62, 64; II.1, 7, 11, 46, 47, 52, 62, 66, 75. Cf. Ayres, *Nicaea*, 113–14; Vaggione, *Eunomius*, 109–10.
52. See Hanson, *Search*, 26; see also Simonetti, *La Crisi Ariana*, 478–79.
53. Vaggione, *Eunomius*, 110–13; see also 120. According to Arius, "[Christ's] divinity was reduced enough to be able to encounter suffering without ceasing to be divine." (Hanson, *Search*, 25; see also 26, 32.)
54. Vaggione, *Eunomius*, 110–11.
55. Kapstein, *Reason's Traces*, 347.
56. Priestley, *Pudgalavāda Buddhism*, 1.
57. Priestley, *Pudgalavāda Buddhism*, 2, 31; Maclean, *Religion and Society in Arab Sind*, 7–10; Eltschinger and Ratié, *Self, No-Self, and Salvation*, 37–39. There is also suggestive but admittedly inconclusive evidence that other schools may originally have held Pudgalavāda views (Priestley, *Pudgalavāda Buddhism*, 37–39; cf. Bareau, *Les Sectes Bouddhiques*, 156). Vasumitra (second century) in his *Samayabhedoparacana-cakra* attributes a belief in the existence of an ultimately real person (*paramārtha-pudgala*) to the Sautrāntikas (Walleser, *Die Sekten*, 48; Priestley, *Pudgalavāda Buddhism*, 37). Bhāvaviveka (sixth) attributes a personalist doctrine to the "original Sthaviras" (*pūrvasthaviras*) and to the Haimavatas (Walleser, *Die Sekten*, 84; Priestley, *Pudgalavāda Buddhism*, 37–38).
58. Kapstein, *Reason's Traces*, 81.
59. Kapstein, "Śāntarakṣita's Tattvasaṃgraha," 320.
60. The most articulate advocate of this view is Richard Gombrich; see, for example, his *How Buddhism Began*. See also Collins, *Selfless Persons*, 29–33, 39–40, 80–84, and passim. A compelling challenge to this assumption is found in two important studies of Johannes Bronkhorst, *Greater Magadha* and *Buddhism in the Shadow of Brahmanism*.
61. Eltschinger and Ratié, *Self, No-Self, and Salvation*, 86.

62. Eltschinger, "Dharmakīrti," 432–33.
63. Eltschinger, "Dharmakīrti," 398–99, 433.
64. Eltschinger, "Dharmakīrti," 432. Vātsyāyana/Pakṣilasvāmin's *Nyāya-Bhāṣya* (late fourth century), the formative text of early Nyāya, integrated an ancient tradition of disputation (*vāda*) with the doctrine of the *ātman* as the most consequential object (*prameya*) of salvific knowledge (Oberhammer, "Pakṣilasvāmin's Introduction," 310; Ruben, "Zur Frühgeschichte," 352; Slage, "Niśreyesam im alten Nyāya," 170–71). In his effort to give shape to the nascent discipline of Nyāya, Vātsyāyana retrieves the earlier concept of *ānvīkṣiki*, described by Kauṭilya in the *Arthaśāstra* as an investigative method of reasoning (see Hacker, "Ānvīkṣikī," 55; cf. *NBh.* 3:12–13). Vātsyāyana reinforces and disambiguates earlier associations of *ānvīkṣikī* with the Vedic-Upaniṣadic science of the self (*ātmavidyā*) (Oberhammer, "Der frühe Nyāya," 340–43; Wilhelm Halbfass, *India and Europe*, 274–79; Hacker, "Ānvīkṣikī," esp. 73–74; cf. *NBh.* 2:20–3:1).
65. Ruben, "Zur Frühgeschichte," 354; Oberhammer, "Pakṣilasvāmin's Introduction," 302–3; 316–17; 321–22; Oberhammer, "Der frühe Nyāya: 345.
66. Vātsyāyana argues for the existence of the self against an unnamed Buddhist opponent in his comment on *NS.* I.1.10 (Kapstein, *Reason's Traces*, 376, 378–79; *NBh.* 26:16–20). Vasubandhu answers this challenge in this section of the *Abhidharmakośa*, in turn inviting a counter-response from the fifth-century Nyāya philosopher Uddyotakara in the latter's subcommentary on the *Nyāya Sūtra*, the *Nyāyavārttika*.
67. Trans. Kapstein, *Reason's Traces*, 350; *AKBh.* 1189:2–5.
68. *AKBh.* 1232:4–6; cf. 1189:2–3.
69. *AKBh.* 1233:1–2.
70. *AKBh.* 1215:3–4.
71. *AKBh.* 1203:14.
72. *AKBh.* 1192:7: *naiva hi dravyato 'sti, nāpi prajñaptitaḥ.*
73. *AKBh.* 1192:7–8.
74. Duerlinger, *Indian Buddhist Theories of Persons*, 133.
75. *AKBh.* 1193:1–2.
76. Duerlinger, *Indian Buddhist Theories of Persons*, 126.
77. *AKBh.* 1215:6–8.
78. Priestley, Pudgalavāda Buddhism, 6; Châu, "Les Réponses des Pudgalavādin," 40–42.
79. Cf. Eltschinger and Ratié, *Self, No-Self, and Salvation*, 67.
80. See, for example, S.ii.60–62.
81. *AKBh.* 1209:6–7.
82. Curiously enough, the fragment Vasubandhu cites is not found in the extant Pali text of the *Milindapañha*. See Skilling, "A Note on King Milinda," 95–96.
83. Collins, *Selfless Persons*, 132–33; cf. Schayer, *Ausgewählte Kapitel*, xxvi–xxvii.
84. *AKBh.* 1209:9.
85. *AKBh.* 798:1–2.
86. This "apophatic" rejection of views can be found in two of the oldest texts of the Pali Canon, the Pārāyana- and the Aṭṭhaka-vaggas of the *Sutta-Nipāta* (see Gómez, "Proto-Mādhyamaka," 140–41, 153 and passim; Collins, *Selfless Persons*, 129). Another important text for this understanding of views as karmically conditioned is the Brahmajala Sutta of the *Dīgha Nikāya*. See Collins, *Selfless Persons*, 128.

87. See Lopez, "Do Śrāvakas Understand Emptiness?," 65–105; P. Williams, *Mahāyāna Buddhism*, 52–55. This view was not universal, however. For example, Bhāvaviveka, the sixth-century Svātantrika Mādhyamika, conceded that a realization of the selflessness of persons was sufficient for liberation, a view that was premised on the claim that the doctrine of emptiness was unknown to the Hīnayāna canon. A realization of the selflessness of phenomena was required to attain Buddhahood. See Lopez, "Do Śrāvakas Understand Emptiness?," 68–69 and passim.
88. Williams, *Arius*, 232.
89. Williams, *Arius*, 82. Williams (*Arius*, 232 and passim) qualifies this assessment of Arius as a conservative, however.
90. Schayer, "Precanonical Buddhism," 476–77, 508, 511; Keith, "Pre-Canonical Buddhism," 4; Regamey, "Le problème du bouddhisme primitif," 53; Christian Lindtner, "The Problem of Precanonical Buddhism," *Buddhist Studies Review* 14:2 (1997): 110. Schayer ("New Contributions," 512) remarks that the *anātman* doctrine is incompatible with a precanonical cosmology in which impermanence (*anitya*, *anicca*) is confined to the *rūpa* category. Admittedly, making the case for the traditional character of Pudgalavāda remains, owing to the extreme paucity of evidence for the formative period of Buddhism as compared to what we have for Christianity, unavoidably speculative and hypothetical.
91. Bauer, *Orthodoxy and Heresy*, xxiii–xxiv and passim.
92. The classic example of this phenomenon would be the fate of various forms of so-called Jewish Christianity.
93. See, for example, Maclean, *Religion and Society in Arab Sind*, 66–77 and passim, on how changes in inter-regional trade during the Arab "conquest" of Sind between the eighth and eleventh centuries (CE)—in particular, competition from the Arabs themselves—led to the erosion of material support for the institutions of Saṃmitīya Buddhism in the region. The reasons for the eventual disappearance of Buddhism and the concomitant survival of Hinduism in this period have little to do with respective beliefs of these two religions.
94. S.iii.25–26.
95. As Collins (*A Pali Grammar*, 11) notes, *saṃvṛti* is a false Sanskritization of a Middle Indic or Pali derivative of *sam* + √*man* ("think together," "agree on"), *sammati* or *sammuti*, not the unlikely but theoretically possible *sam* + √*var*, "cover." The concept of *saṃvṛti*, with its underlying metaphor of covering or concealing another reality, has metaphysical connotations that were likely absent in the original formulation.
96. Tracy, "Kenosis, Sunyata, and Trinity," 150–51.
97. Cf. Collins, *Selfless Persons*, 106–10.
98. Lakatos, "History of Science," 102–3, 118–21.
99. This model encourages a disciplinary separation between, on the one hand, Philosophical Theology, corresponding to Lakatos's internal history, and, on the other, the History of Religions, corresponding to external history.
100. It is noteworthy, in this connection, that the autonomy of an internal history of science is even a matter of debate among philosophers of science. Lakatos, who argues that an internal history of science should be autonomous, argues that his methodology of scientific research programs has a distinct advantage over its inductivist and falsificationist rivals in its ability to recognize what might be called "scientific

dogmatism"—that is, the circumstance that sometimes it is necessary for scientists doggedly to stick with a promising theory even when confronted by data that the theory cannot as of yet explain (Lakatos, "Falsification and the Methodology of Scientific Research Programmes," 87; 89; cf. also Kuhn, "The Function of Dogma in Scientific Research," 347–69)—as a rational process and thus part of the internal history of science ("History of Science," 114, 132–34). Some of his critics, however, have questioned whether his theory is able to deliver on its promise to recognize an objective basis to the judgment that a given research program is "progressive" and thus to be retained in spite of recalcitrant data (see Bloor, "Two Paradigms for Scientific Knowledge?," 106–7).

101. Ricoeur, "The Metaphorical Process," 78–79.

5 “An Interpreter and Not a Judge”: Insights into a Christian-Islamic Comparative Theology

Axel Marc Oaks Takács

The dialogue between Muslims and Christians has a long, rich, and complex history. Long, in that the first extant *theological* encounter between a Christian and a Muslim occurred over 1,200 years ago between Mar Timothy I (728–823), the Catholicos of the Church of the East at the time, and the ruling caliph, al-Mahdi (who ruled from 775–785); this excludes any sort of early exchanges that may have occurred among Muhammad, his companions, and Christian tribes in the Arabian peninsula, possible interreligious engagement among Christian ascetics and proto-ṣūfī's, and statements in the Qur'ān that explicitly address Christian theology, such as Christology, Mariology, religious life (for example, the matter of monks), and the conceptions of God that were intended to redress a certain understanding of a Trinitarian theology of a particular group of Christians. Rich, in that the advent of the Islamic religious tradition resulted in no dearth of confrontation between Christendom and the various Islamic caliphates and communities from Andalusia to the Ottoman world geographically, and from debates, philosophical transmission, crusades, an irenic conversation between St. Francis, and an Ayyūbid Sultan of Egypt, colonialism, and terrorism historically. Complex, in that no extant text can do justice to the variety of interactions “on the ground,” as it were, and no amount of whitewashing can conjure up a broad “theology of religions” to characterize Muslim-Christian interaction without taking into account the social, political, economic, and cultural contexts that surely shaped and were shaped by Islamic and Christian theology. Thus, it would appear that taking this long, rich, and complex history into account when performing a Christian comparative theology with the Islamic religious tradition should be a prerequisite for any project worthy of critical attention.

Or should it? Without arguing for an ahistorical method of comparative theology with the Islamic religious tradition, I aver that the aforementioned history has perhaps slowed progress in the field more than it has facilitated it. Frequently, an abstracted and reified Christian theology is put into conversation with an Islamic one; this is certainly the case when it comes to Christology and Trinitarian theology vis-à-vis the Islamic tradition's uncompromising disavowal of so-called "incarnationalism" (*ḥulūl*) and its doctrine of strict divine oneness. As interesting as it may be to put a Christian theology of Trinitarian relations into conversation with Islamic *kalām*[1] discourse on absolute unity and the Divine Names (*al-asmā' al-ilāhiyya*), these comparisons remain at the level of metaphysical speculation and divorced from theological anthropology, i.e., how these doctrines are reflections of an individual's experience of God, and how these teachings (and, as I will argue later, the texts in which these doctrines are explicated) are transformative of an individual's very being-in-the-world. As a result, Christian comparative theology with the Islamic tradition has been constrained by these debates, and thus has yet to enter the imaginative and creative sphere into which comparative theology with, say, the Buddhist or Hindu religious traditions, have long ago entered (with few exceptions[2]).

I do not thereby intend to claim that such interreligious conversations have been or are to no avail; such a generalization would not reflect some of the more fruitful scholarship, both historical and contemporary, that has indeed been produced. Rather, I contend that in order for Christian comparative theology with the Islamic religious tradition to reach the level of constructive theology that is characteristic of, say, Buddhist and Hindu comparative theology,[3] a certain "break" from the historically received and constructed past may need to occur.[4] This break may be characterized by a certain reading and writing practice and internal spiritual and intellectual disposition I intend to expound below.

To that end, I will proffer some insights regarding the practice of comparative theology, which I have gleaned from my engagement with the texts of one of the most famous and influential thinkers of the Islamic religious tradition: Muḥyiddin Ibn al-ʿArabī, known as *al-Shaykh al-Akbar*, or the Greatest Teacher (d. 1240). I will argue that the concepts of interpretation and liminality are not just central to Ibn al-ʿArabī's rhetoric, but also woven into the very seam of reality at all levels. Consequently, his "rhetoric of realization"[5] has proven fruitful in my own elucidation of the method involved in comparative theology. Furthermore, his later readers developed his cosmology, which is basically a theory of perpetual revelation through three imbricating and intersecting books: the book of God (Qur'ān), the book of the cosmos (nature), and the book of the soul (the human person); this complex theory provides an avenue for understanding how comparative theology may be performed.

Implied in this essay is an appreciation and support for the methods used by such comparative theologians as Francis X. Clooney and Michelle Voss Roberts, to name a couple. However, rather than merely explicating their own implicit methods as I understand them, I intend to expound a method by actually engaging in an exercise of comparative theology that brings the Islamic tradition and the Christian tradition into conversation. This purpose is twofold. The first is to explicate comparative theology *as* and *from within* the Christian theological tradition, thereby arguing that the discipline may be understood as part of this rich tradition, albeit a novel one in that it engages a second tradition. The second purpose is to demonstrate how engagement with the Islamic religious tradition leads to a fruitful encounter with the works of Ibn al-ʿArabī, thereby permitting me to illustrate how comparative theology produces "fresh theological insights that are indebted to the newly encountered tradition/s as well as the home tradition."[6]

To that end, I will offer a close reading of Ibn al-ʿArabī's short prologue to his famous *Fuṣūṣ al-Ḥikam*, or Bezels of Wisdoms, in order to present Ibn al-ʿArabī's hermeneutical principles. I will then compare these principles both to Medieval Christian theology and also to Hans Urs von Balthasar's theological method, and then end with a challenge to the very concept of "method" as it relates to the practice of theology, comparative or otherwise. What I aim to expound is a way of *both* reading texts *and* writing thereafter, a way that has been informed by these three thinkers and challenges *both* much Islamic-Christian interreligious scholarship until now *and* a theology held captive by method.

Ibn Al-ʿArabī's *Khuṭba* (Prologue) to the *Fuṣūṣ al-Ḥikam*

Ibn al-ʿArabī's *Fuṣūṣ al-Ḥikam* is by far his most commented upon text from his œuvre. In this section, I will explicate his cosmology via its prologue, thereby demonstrating how his hermeneutical principles cannot be understood without reference to his entire anthropocosmic, theological vision. Ibn al-ʿArabī himself implies this by the content of his introduction. The comparative theology of "fresh theological insights" will follow.

Ibn al-ʿArabī begins with the following:

> In the name of God, the merciful, the compassionate. Praise be to God, who sends down wisdoms upon the hearts [*qulūb*] of the words [*kalim*] through the unity [*aḥadiyya*] of the manifest-and-clear [*al-ʿamam*] way from the most primordial [*al-aqdam*] station, even though religious creeds [*niḥal*] and religious communities [*al-milal*] differ because of the variety of nations [*umam*].[7]

Perhaps never has anyone been able to elucidate one's own rich hermeneutics, cosmology, and spiritual vision with so few words. Students of Ibn al-ʿArabī know well that one of his favorite interpretative strategies, when expounding upon the Qur'ān or *ḥadīth*, is to utilize all possible etymological, literal meanings of a word, claiming that God intended all meanings allowed by linguistic convention. Applying this method to his own texts is also a fruitful exercise, for this very process is demanded by God's self-disclosure; God has sent down wisdom upon the hearts—the core, the essential reality—of words, also illustrating the transformative nature of the text. This is not just words of language, but also the individual Word connected to each of the twenty-seven prophets, the wisdoms [*ḥikam*] of which Words he explicates in the twenty-seven chapters that follow the prologue. But for Ibn al-ʿArabī in particular, the self-disclosure of God, God's revelation, is not just within the Word of the Qur'ān (and the other various scriptures); he takes seriously the Qur'ānic principle of the threefold revelation: God's self-disclosure is to the Qur'ān, the cosmos, and the heart of the person: "*We will show them our signs*[8] *in the horizons and in their souls so that it may become clear to them that [God] is The Real.*"[9] Thus, the words are the very perpetual self-disclosures of God (*tajalliyāt*) in the world and heart of the servant. The "hearts of the words" are the unending, transforming self-disclosures of the Speech of God, which are all the created things in the phenomenal world—speech, because *kalim* is a collective plural, signifying the unity-in-distinction that is crucial to Ibn al-ʿArabī's cosmology, and to which he turns next.

These wisdoms are revealed, "through the unity [*aḥadiyya*] of the manifest-and-clear [*al-ʿamam*] way from the most primordial [*al-aqdam*] station." This is another dense clause that sums up the cosmological principle of liminal space, i.e., the *barzakh*. For the *Shaykh*, all of Reality is nothing but various levels of interstitial, liminal space—a *barzakh*. The Real—God—is in Essence a *barzakh*, bringing together opposites, for example, the Manifest and Unmanifest, the First and the Last. A *barzakh*, according to the *Shaykh*, is that which brings together two things, yet is not the essential-reality (*ʿayn*) of either of them, but contains the power of each.[10] Ibn al-ʿArabī says as much in this clause: The God at the level of Unity [*aḥadiyya*] brings together the Manifest [*al-ʿamam*] and the Unmanifest (God at the level of his unknown, "most primordial station"). This phenomenal world is also a *barzakh*—a manifestation of the unmanifest Essence, revealing and simultaneously concealing the Real; thus, the cosmos mirrors the liminal reality of God's unity, for God is both fully immanent within, and transcendent from, the cosmos. The cosmos is "*huwa lā huwa*," or "God/not-God," as Ibn al-ʿArabī states so often.[11]

Furthermore, in agreement with many Patristic and medieval Christian theologians, the phenomenal world is scripture, a revelatory text.[12] More explicitly stated, Ibn al-ʿArabī's cosmology offers a hermeneutics that pushes the boundaries of the explicit, inscribed text (the Qur'ān, scripture, or theological texts in general) and the texts that are the cosmos and the self. The later Akbarian tradition called these the Book of God (the Qur'ān), the Book of the Cosmos, and the Book of the Soul (the human person).[13] These boundaries become virtually nonexistent with the proper spiritual perception and hermeneutics, for when one is reading the explicit, inscribed text, it is the self that is actually being read and re-interpreted. Consequently, one's subjectivity is crucial in understanding the text and in achieving self-transformation. Accordingly, we learn to read the Qur'ān, or any sacred text, so that we may read the self and the world; we then return anew to perceive the world, perceive the self, and perceive the text, all as divine self-disclosures. One's cosmological vision is likewise being transformed as a result of interpreting the inscribed text. This calls into question the sharp dichotomy established between ordinary vision and so-called "mystical vision." Without denying moments during a wayfarer's life wherein she experiences "mystical visions," Ibn al-ʿArabī is endeavoring to awaken in his readers the ability to see the world perpetually in this state of mystical vision. The goal is not necessarily a "mystical experience," defined popularly as a psychological, noetic, or affective event undergone by an individual in which one "immediately experiences God" (an inheritance of the Romantic understanding of "mysticism," perhaps). Rather, it is a spiritual perception of the cosmos that leads to transformed practices.[14]

The prologue then turns to the topic of religious traditions. Despite, or rather because of, the Liminal Reality that is God's Unity, "religious creeds [*niḥal*] and religious communities [*al-milal*] differ because of the variety of nations [*umam*]." The word Ibn al-ʿArabī uses for religious creeds has etymological roots with both "gift" and "to narrow, slim, emaciate [of the body]". This complements well one of the first concepts students of the *Shaykh* learn when it comes to his explanation of religious diversity in the world: when people adhere to a "belief" (***iʿtiqād***) they tie (***ʿaqd***) themselves to the "god of their beliefs," making a knot that prevents them from opening their heart (***qalb***) to the infinite self-disclosures of the Real so that they may be transformed (***taqallub***) by them in a never-ending, perpetual process of seeking and finding God. The trilateral root for "belief" is related to "knot," and likewise the root for "heart" is shared with "transformation" or "transmutation"; Ibn al-ʿArabī never tires of pointing this out. The creeds, while narrowing or restricting someone, are also a gift from God, without which individuals would have no starting point from which to begin the path to God. The *umma*, singular of *umam*, is not just nation, but also and more radically a course of life, God's creation, and the beautiful aspect of a face. Thus it must be recalled that, for Ibn al-ʿArabī, the world is a mirror in which God's Face is reflected, for, as it is written in the Qur'ān, "whithersoever you turn, there is the Face of God"[15] and "everything will perish except [God's] Face."[16]

It is already apparent that this turn to Ibn al-ʿArabī's text, as an act of comparative theology, has yielded an insight rarely discovered in traditional sources of Christian theology. Religious creeds are manifold precisely as part of God's cosmological design. This presupposition will be addressed throughout this essay in order to explicate Ibn al-ʿArabī's own reason for studying other religious traditions.

This is an example of the close reading required to unpack the *Shaykh*'s rich language; that is, one must apply his hermeneutical principles to his own texts by seeking out the various levels of meaning within each word. But there is much more to his reading practice than this. Ibn al-ʿArabī, after retelling his vision in which the Prophet Muhammad handed him the book in question,[17] writes:

> I asked God . . . to single me out in all things that I may write with my fingers, and in all things that I may pronounce with my tongue, and in

> all things that may be contained in my heart, through supernal transmission and spiritual inspiration into my soul [*rū'*], and by [God's] preserving support, *so that I may be an interpreter [mutarjim]* and not a judge *[mutaḥakkim]*.[18]

What is a *mutaḥakkim*? It is someone who casts arbitrary, controlling, and dominating judgment, who "has one's own way." Being an interpreter, rather, is the key to Ibn al-ʿArabī's method, for "there is nothing in the world but interpreter/interpreting (*mutarjim*), if it is translated from divine new-Speaking. So understand that!"[19] This is a crucial insight for comparative theology. Not only is the whole world an interpretation or translation *from* God's Unmanifest Essence *into* God's Manifest signs (cosmology), but the heart itself receives the self-disclosures of God (anthropology) so that it may interpret the divine signs—also self-disclosures—in the world and in sacred texts; the threefold revelation creates a liminal space wherein the whole world is nothing but a continual process of interpreting, at least for the individual who is aware of the "real situation" (epistemology). The human person is a *barzakh*, a liminal space, herself interpreting the liminal space of reality through her engagement with the threefold revelation, in order to come to a better understanding of God, who is the Supreme *Barzakh*, or Supreme Liminal Space. Thus, there is nothing static or linear here about hermeneutics or method; it is one perpetual process of interpreting whereby *the individual slips in and out of liminal spaces*,[20] never coming to settle in one state, but rather abiding in variegation. This state leads to a perpetual increase in bewilderment, concerning which the *Shaykh* put in the mouth of the prophet, "O Lord, increase me in my bewilderment in Thee!" Furthermore, Ibn al-ʿArabī linked bewilderment with the state of the believer:

> So consider the bewilderment that pervades every believer. The perfect human being is the one whose bewilderment has intensified and whose regret is continuous—he does not reach his goal because of that which is his Object of worship, for he strives to achieve that which cannot possibly be achieved and he treads the path of Him whose path is not known . . . So if you want your eye to hit the mark, witness Him with every eye, for He pervades all things through self-disclosure. In every form He has a face and in every knower a state. So examine if you will, or do not examine![21]

Once again, Ibn al-ʿArabī offers another compelling reason to turn to other religious traditions in order to discover the various "faces of God."

It is fruitful now to bring the *Shaykh*'s vision, along with his simple prayer seeking to be an *interpreter* rather than a *judge*, into conversation with Christian theology in general, and Hans Urs von Balthasar's own theological method in particular. It is in reading together that this method of comparative theology will be understood.

Putting the Mystical Back into Comparative Theology

In the previous section, Ibn al-ʿArabī's concept of threefold revelation, interpretation, liminality, and religious diversity were briefly explained through a close reading of the prologue to his *Fuṣūṣ al-Ḥikam*, arguably a sound place to find some of his own advice for the purpose of this text, and why and how it should be read. I will now suggest why the *Shaykh*'s advice is so helpful for a modern method in comparative theology. To that end, in this section I will first explain Mark A. McIntosh's argument concerning the development of theology from the twelfth century, and then work my way back to Ibn al-ʿArabī's hermeneutics via Hans Urs von Balthasar. Von Balthasar is an example of a Catholic theologian reading texts in much the same way I am propounding, and thus enables comparative theology to dialogue with, as it were, the Christian tradition.

McIntosh convincingly argues that from the end of the twelfth century, the field of theology began slowly to break from the mystical, resulting in the bifurcation of spirituality and theology: "[at that time,] *spiritualitas* was soon connected with 'the soul' . . . [and thus] began the privatizing tendency in the history of Christianity and the quietist movements" wherein the soul was contrasted with the body.[22] In the end, the "mystical" eventually became fully divorced from the theological: "instead of being considered as the depth dimension of all spirituality, the *mystical* . . . came to be seen either as the revered and chilly reward of grace after untold ascetical struggle or else as a suspect panoply of paranormal experiences and quirky behaviors."[23]

I argue that the practice of comparative theology, especially as informed by Ibn al-ʿArabī's theory of divine self-disclosure, is more akin to theology before this regretful divorce of spirituality from the theological. Many works in comparative theology, such as those by Francis X. Clooney and Michelle Voss Roberts, may in fact reflect theology before this split precisely because of what Ibn al-ʿArabī has to say about the "gods of beliefs." That is, the encounter with another textual religious tradition, another "belief," results in the transmutation of the heart that

Ibn al-ʿArabī deems so essential; comparative theology unties the knots of one's beliefs, as it were, and sets the theologian out onto a creative and imaginative process of theological discovery that is more similar to the "spiritual theology" from before the thirteenth century, and which would have otherwise been precluded.

In addition, just as McIntosh gives the text primary importance in theology, likewise figures in the Akbarian tradition, I argue, viewed the inscribed text to be transformative, effective, and prescriptive of exploratory engagement with the world, rather than explanatory, descriptive, and prescriptive/proscriptive only of orthodoxy and orthopraxy. In other words, the text shapes the interpreter's reality and perception, rather than merely defining or delimiting proper belief or doctrine and religio-legal practices.[24] McIntosh avers that spirituality is oriented toward discovery, toward new perceptions and new understandings of reality, and hence is intimately related to theology.[25] Drawing on Ricœur,[26] McIntosh describes spirituality as the *impression* that the transforming encounter with God makes in people's lives, and theology as the *expression* that this encounter calls forth as people attempt to understand and speak of the encounter.[27] The problem with the separation of the spiritual from the theological is bluntly declared: "Theology without spirituality becomes ever more methodologically refined but unable to know or speak of the very mysteries at the heart of Christianity, and spirituality without theology becomes rootless, easily hijacked by individualistic consumerism."[28] Thus, theology should be the practice of perpetually opening up to the infinite mystery of God as revealed through Christ.[29] The theologian should desire to participate in the world of divine self-disclosure in wonder at the gift from God, rather than inhabit a world of objects that can be sequestered and possessed (as a judge, or *mutaḥakkim*).

Are there modern hermeneutics or theological methods that assist the theologian in creating a framework for doing *comparative* theology? As Marianne Moyaert has pointed out,[30] Ricœur's hermeneutics and translation theory function well as a methodological framework for comparative theology. However, rather than duplicate her remarkable work, I will turn to Hans Urs von Balthasar, a Christian theologian whose hermeneutics and style are both comparable to Ibn al-ʿArabī's and also quite harmonious with the strategies employed by comparative theologians today.

The reading and interpretive strategies of this Swiss theologian reflect the method of textual engagement upon which I am expounding; he, too, explicitly bemoaned the modern rupture between the mystical and the theological, which he understood as the disintegration of theology into the spiritual and the dogmatic.[31] Von Balthasar sought to reintegrate dogmatic theology with spiritual theology and argued that this can be done successfully only through the texts of the great theologians, saints, and mystics of the past. In the following passage, he suggests a reading and writing practice very similar to what I am arguing should be adopted in comparative theology:

> What impedes the reintegration of dogmatic and spiritual theology so disastrously is the loss of the objective spiritual medium of which the old theology was so conscious as it proceeded in its development. Certainly the Fathers had at their disposal all the rational methods of distinguishing and defining for the clarification of concepts; they were used in the fierce controversies with heretics, both by individual theologians and by councils. But the crucial point is that these methods were not the determining factor in the construction of their theology. Even polemical works . . . were embedded in a spiritual, sapiential setting which became more and more pronounced as the decisive element.[32]

For von Balthasar, then, even the most dogmatic texts should be read with practical and spiritual implications. However, he also recognized how theologians had forgotten this spiritual and intellectual disposition required for such a reading and writing practice:

> It may well be harder in our day, when we have come to set so much in store by logical procedure, to bring out this spiritual dimension clearly enough in theology. Yet it is of the utmost importance to see that what is lacking is not just a piece of material that can be easily incorporated into the existing structure, or else a sort of stylistic quality to be reproduced anew . . . The fact is that the spiritual dimension can only be recovered through the soul of man being profoundly moved as a result of his direct encounter with revealed truth, so that it is borne in upon him, once and for all, how the theologian should think and speak, and how he should not.[33]

This passage gestures toward a major point of this chapter, viz., that the modern fascination with logical methods has led many a theologian to forget about the self-disposition, along with a reading and writing practice, required for contributing to a spiritual and sapiential theology. This, I argue, is what comparative theology is aiming to do by breaking from a modern theology held captive by what von Balthasar has called "logical procedure."

But how is this actually performed? The practice I am detailing is more difficult to outline than it is to enact. I can only offer some insight from Ibn al-ʿArabī, put into conversation with von Balthasar; that is, I will *do* comparative theology in order to explain it. Ibn al-ʿArabī frequently mentions "seeing with two eyes," that is, the eye of transcendence/apophasis (*tanzīh*) and the eye of immanence/kataphasis (*tashbīh*).[34] He calls for this simultaneity in order to see the world as a liminal space: "God/not-God." But *how* is this enacted practically? *One way* he offers concerns interpretation; he connects this two-eyed perception with hermeneutics:

> As for the faithful, the truthful, those of steadfastness among the friends [of God], they cross over ["interpret"], taking along with them the outward sense [*al-ẓāhir*], [rather than going] *from* the outward sense *to* the inward sense [*al-bāṭin*]. [They cross over] it [i.e., "interpret it"[35]] through the literal sense ["the letter"] to get to the inner meaning; they do *not* express it [*without* the letter]. Thusly do they see things with two eyes and they witness the two highways with the light of their faith.[36]

Ibn al-ʿArabī here is making reference to the intra-Islamic debate regarding Qurʾānic exegesis, viz., between the "literalist" (*ẓāhirī*) camp and the "esoteric" camp (*bāṭinī*). The former interpreted the Qurʾān as grammatically and linguistically literal as possible, and the latter performed a metaphorical interpretation of the text. Ibn al-ʿArabī, bemoaning the *bāṭinites* for their metaphorical interpretations that very often ignored any literal meaning, often performed a literalist reading of the text that nevertheless took into account the inward meaning through the outward expression. To translate this method for the sake of applying it to the methods and reading practices of comparative theology, one might say that the interpreter of a theological text discovers the spiritually transformative meaning *through* the historically static event (or, the spiritual meaning *via* the literal). The event—an encounter with a heresy, a doctrine requiring explanation, a commentary on an abstruse, mystical text by a ṣūfī—may be the original impetus for writing such a text, while the meaning would be the spiritually practical consequences of encountering the text whereby the interpreter's very being-in-the-world is transformed.

Reading Ibn al-ʿArabī alongside von Balthasar sheds further light on this reading practice. In a paragraph that echoes Ibn al-ʿArabī's own understanding of interpretation and "seeing with two eyes," von Balthasar writes concerning Christology and scriptural hermeneutics:[37]

> The spiritual sense is never to be sought 'behind' the letter but within it, just as the Father is not to be found behind the Son but in and through him. And to stick to the literal sense while spurning the spiritual would be to view the Son as man and nothing more. All that is human in Christ is a revelation of God and speaks to us of him. There is nothing whatever in his life, acts, passion and resurrection that is not an expression and manifestation of God in the language of a created being.[38]

Von Balthasar wishes to theologize from the "expression and manifestation of God," what is revealed from the literal text and the embodied existence of Christ in history. Ibn al-ʿArabī, too, is imploring readers not to abandon the outward for the inward, but to read the two together. Both demand the historical event and perduring meaning of a text to be considered equally crucial in grasping and enacting the significance of the text so that the practices and perceptions of the interpreter may be transformed.[39]

In this section, I have outlined a practice of interpretation informed by Ibn al-ʿArabī and von Balthasar. However, this method is certainly open to critique. To this I turn in the next section, wherein I will also offer my own response via Ibn al-ʿArabī's poem in his prologue, before concluding.

A Theological Method?

Are thinkers like von Balthasar or Ibn al-ʿArabī really offering a method *sensu stricto*? It depends on how one defines "method" in theology. If "method" is defined as a series of steps a subject—the scholar—takes in order to know an unknown object or some aspect of a known object, then these thinkers are offering something perhaps *furthest* from method. However, then *I* would also wish to keep "method" so defined—a product of the modern scientific method[40]—furthest away from the practice of comparative theology. For this definition of "method" presupposes that the subject—the scholar—can be replaced by anyone willing to follow these steps, and that the object is ultimately fully knowable through empirical reasoning: a twofold fallacy!

Let me call forth Ibn al-ʿArabī to explain. Firstly, the so-called object of theology, comparative or otherwise, is ultimately God, and God is the

Supreme *Barzakh*, the *coincidentia oppositorum*, simultaneously knowable and unknowable, and thus no object in the field of objects in the universe, but the ground of all Reality, and the ground for knowing the Real. God cannot be an "object" in a defined method. If anything, God's love, which suffuses reality and the hearts of human beings, is the impetus for our never-ending search for God, Who remains *unknowable* by being *infinitely knowable*. Secondly, the subject is himself a receptacle for the infinite divine self-disclosures, and as Ibn al-ʿArabī never tires of repeating, *the self-disclosures of God never repeat themselves*.[41] Thus, God is only discoverable through these self-disclosures, which simultaneously reveal and conceal God in infinitely unique ways; how we come to know God is based on the self-disclosures to our hearts, each of which are unique. Thus the subject, the comparative theologian, can surely not be replaced by *anybody*, that is, by any other scholar, without altering the product of any given project of comparative theology.[42] The highly personal and autobiographical nature of comparative theology is evident with just a cursory glance at the introductions and prologues to recent books in the field. In this regard, Clooney has elaborated upon the comparative theologian's "spiritual possibility" that stems from a "carefully cultivated intellectual virtue" that opens her up "not only to questions, but also to events, encounters, inclusions, and without protection."[43]

With this in mind, I follow Lonergan, a twentieth-century Catholic theologian who shaped modern method in theology. Once again, the method of comparative theology must not be understood as foreign to theology itself; the "way" comparative theologians encounter texts is not something invented recently. Rather, it can be explained by theologians who never had comparative work in mind.

Lonergan suggests that in religious matters the precedence of knowledge over love is overturned.

> It used to be said, *Nihil amatum nisi praecognitum*, Knowledge precedes love . . . [The] major exception to the Latin tag is God's gift of his love flooding our hearts. Then we are in the dynamic state of being in love. But who it is we love, is *neither given nor as yet understood*. Our capacity for moral self-transcendence has found a fulfillment that brings deep joy and profound peace. Our love reveals to us values we had not appreciated, values of prayer and worship, or repentance and belief. But if we would know what is going on within us, if we would learn to integrate it with the rest of our living, *we have to inquire, investigate, seek counsel*.

> So it is that in religious matters *love precedes knowledge*, and, as that love is God's gift, the very beginning of faith is due to God's grace.[44]

For Lonergan, then, God's gift of love draws forth our own capacity for love; however, the object of our love—God—is revealed as that which is stretching us forward, and not as something wholly understood. Consequently, we seek, investigate, and examine; we "theologize."

Once again to render this essay a comparative project, I bring in Ibn al-ʿArabī, who, along with his predecessors, founds his entire cosmology and theory of divine self-disclosure on the following: "I [God] am hidden treasure, and I loved to be known, so I created the world that I may be known."[45] God's love precedes and is the cause of our knowing him; the divine self-disclosures, which are the signs of God in the world, in the Qur'ān, and in the self, reveal the unknown object of our love, and entice us further "to inquire, investigate, [and] seek counsel." Nevertheless, perfect love implies that we never aim to sequester, dominate, and control the object of our love by assuming that we can know it completely, i.e., by being a judge (*mutaḥakkim*); rather, this love drives us to enter into mystery and to share this experience with others in constructive theology.

Thus, if one were expecting a step-by-step method for *doing* comparative theology, then this essay will have to disappoint; the most I can offer are compelling reasons to engage in comparative theology, and descriptive, theologically refined explanations of the spiritual and intellectual disposition of a comparative theologian. What is offered is not an empirical method, but an encounter with the divine self-disclosure, an opening of the heart toward infinite wisdom. Just as Ibn al-ʿArabī demands, it is a highly personal experience of "divine openings"—and this can be found in the distinction between *ʿaql* (intellect) and *qalb* (heart). The intellect is what binds us into knots;[46] it also ties the object of knowledge into a neatly packaged box. But each person's heart is a unique receptacle of divine self-disclosures, and "can encompass God"[47] in perpetual "transformation." Accordingly, our own *impressions* of our encounters with God are *expressed* in order to open up the hearts of others.[48]

Does this mean that there are no criteria for judging if an exercise in comparative theology has been successfully performed? Are we left with just subjective experience with a text and no objective rubric to assess the success of scholarship? Not quite. Certainly, historical-critical (scientific) methods from area studies fields should be used in the close reading of a text in order to place it in its context. In addition, the comparative theologian should receive and contribute to the cumulative tradition of which she is a part (just like any theologian); this tradition is, to a certain extent, used to assess the work of the theologian. Accordingly, and following Lonergan,[49] the comparative theologian should take seriously the twofold division in method: "harken to the word" and "witness to the word." In the first phase, the theologian performs research and explains history, and in the second phase, she outlines foundations, reconciles doctrines, systematizes, and ultimately communicates. I contend that communication is the most important aspect in this process, and that, unlike Lonergan, the *comparative* theologian has to perform all these functions on two different religious traditions. Furthermore, I would challenge Lonergan on the following:

> Finally, I believe in a theology of encounter, but would not confuse theology and religion. Theology reflects on the religion; it promotes the religion; but it does not constitute religious events. I consider religious conversion a presupposition of moving from the first phase to the second but I hold that that conversion occurs, not in the context of doing theology, but in the context of becoming religious. [. . .] I conceive that coming to understand himself, not as part of his job as an exegete but as an event of a higher order, an event in his own personal development.[50]

According to the understanding of a text as transformative, effective, and prescriptive of exploratory engagement with the world, I argue that it is only if the interpreter undergoes "an event of a higher order" in reading the text that she is thereby able to write fruitfully after her engagement therewith. This may open the comparative theologian up to misappropriation of texts, to *eisegesis*, or to scholarship of a merely affective order. However, methods of the historical-critical kind, training within the field of the study of religion, and a solid grounding in the area studies field should mitigate these concerns. I argue that a theologian who sequesters the "event of a higher order" is the judge (*mutaḥakkim*) who sequesters the text *qua* object of study, dominating it, treating it as dead, rather than the interpreter (*mutarajim*) Ibn al-ʿArabī prays to be.

Conclusion: Islam, Christianity, and Comparative Theology

In the previous section, I questioned what is meant by "method" in theology, comparative or otherwise. Aiming to preserve comparative theology from the accusation that it is *merely* subjective experience and affective reaction to a text (though, it is this, too),[51] I suggested that there are rational and intellectual procedures necessary to begin the *explanation* of a text so that its enduring meaning can be *understood*. However, all that has been said could arguably be applicable merely to theology in general. This is partly intentional, for I view comparative theology as theology, done interreligiously. Notwithstanding, what gives the impetus to do *comparative* theology? This is where the constructive, comparative moment explicitly enters into this essay, and "fresh theological insights . . . indebted to the newly encountered tradition"[52] are disclosed. For Ibn al-ʿArabī proffers a theory that impels readers to do *comparative* theology, and in this way he differs from the aforementioned Catholic theologians. To that end, I will convert the *Shaykh*'s theory of the "gods of beliefs" into practical steps for a Christian comparative theology with the Islamic religious tradition, thereby recalling my introduction on the state of the field, as well as the various places above where I have already drawn from Ibn al-ʿArabī's theory of religious diversity in the world.

Nearly all Islamic-Christian comparative and interreligious work has been tied down by what Ibn al-ʿArabī calls the "gods of beliefs." The *Shaykh*'s rhetoric of realization is aimed at getting readers to untie the knots that are their beliefs and instead turn to the heart in order to seek God. However, most Christian interlocutors, for example, who engage the Islamic religious tradition do so with the predefined goal of figuring out how the doctrine of the Incarnation or Trinity fits into Islam, or whether prophecy after Christ is possible, or how "Islam" fits into the economy of salvation, to name just a few of these overworked topics of discussion. This is because the doctrine of, say, the Trinity is no longer a mystery into which one should enter, but an objectified, reified dogma that one continues to tweak and rephrase in such a way that a Muslim might agree with it ("maybe if I explain what a *hypostasis* is just *one more time*, we'll come to an understanding . . ."). Yet, no matter how inclusive, open, and willing I am to submit my own beliefs to the beliefs of the Islamic religious tradition vis-à-vis the Trinity (to keep the example), I am still at the level of beliefs and thus in a knot, tied down, and trapped by my own reified, static conceptions of what is ultimately a mystery to be encountered in one's quotidian engagements. In other words, rather than being an interpreter (*mutarjim*), one is a judge (*mutaḥakkim*), having one's arbitrary way with the dialogical and interreligious reading process, entering the text already *predominated* by the knot of one's belief and thus *dominating* the text.

I adapt what McIntosh has written concerning interpreting explicitly mystical texts, viz., that a given writer's mystical life is only a part of the ongoing event of meaning-making which "moves *through* (a) textualization to (b) the interaction of text and reader and so on to a new enacted 'textualization' in (c) the transformed practice and perceptions of the reader."[53] Theologians are to "[move] from reading as an event—a moment of confrontation and transformation—to reading as the birth of meaning in the reader's new way of thinking and living."[54] Theological texts of the past, and what I argue comparative theological texts should be today, are more adequately understood not as descriptions of experience, but invitations to shape experience; thus, to engage the meaning of a text is "to allow one's own categories for understanding and experiencing reality to be given over—perhaps broken—certainly to be transformed, by the reality of the other who is always beyond oneself."[55]

Just as Ibn al-ʿArabī's focus on interpreting corresponds to the liminality that is God and the phenomenal world, to the dynamic cosmological process of divine self-disclosures into which one is called to enter, likewise, mystical and theological textualization corresponds, in Christianity, to the Incarnation, and the interpretative process shares in the apophasis of the Cross whereby a "realization of mystical meaning draws one into those new patterns of life and consciousness which have their consummation in the Resurrection and Pentecost."[56] The process can be explained using native Islamic mystical terms: the process of interpreting an Islamic text begins with the very negation of the self in God—*fanāʾ fiʾLlah*—so that one may enter into a renewed vision of the world subsisting in God—*baqāʾ biʾLlah*. Throughout this process, one's religious worldview is challenged and reshaped, and so at times one is left in bewilderment, or *ḥayra*, another mystical station that hovers between *fanāʾ fiʾLlah* and *baqāʾ biʾLlah*. There is no static conclusion, but only a dynamic opening toward new realization—questions, leading to discoveries, and ending in further mystery, to be repeated; for "the ultimate goal in the knowledge of God is bewilderment,"[57] as one of Ibn al-ʿArabī's commentators puts it. Lest someone rebut that such an explorative and ambiguous engagement with the Islamic revelation was neither normative nor valorized, I refer him or her to Shahab Ahmed's *What Is Islam?*, wherein he argues that paradox, ambiguity, exploration, and coherent contradiction were all formative attributes of the hermeneutical engagement with Islamic revelation by a temporal, geographic, and numerical majority of Muslims throughout history.[58] As a Christian comparative theologian, I attempt to enter into the mystery of this Islamic explorative discourse, too.

Ibn al-ʿArabī calls us to transcend our beliefs by exploring the infinite self-disclosures of God to the heart, the cosmos, and the more explicit revelation in scripture. This does not mean forgoing discussion of, for example, the Incarnation in Islamic-Christian comparative theology, much less renouncing it. It does mean, however, removing such sterile understanding of the Incarnation that is the result of the disconnect of the spiritual from the theological (i.e., Incarnation *qua* dogma *alone* rather than Incarnation *qua* how it shapes our experience of being-in-the-world). Theology should be the fruit of the heart's encounter with the infinite mystery of the Incarnation in our daily lives, and not *merely* "one person, two natures."[59]

So what are the criteria for judging whether comparative theology has been properly performed? Let us end with where we left Ibn al-ʿArabī in his prologue, which he closes with a poem.

It is from God, *so listen!*
    And to God do you return.
For when you hear what
    I bring through it, *then put it to heart!*
Then, by understanding, make it clear,
    Treat the speech as a whole and gather it.
Then give it to those
    Who demand it, and do not forbid it!
This is the mercy that
    Encompasses you, *so expand it!*[60]

In this poem, Ibn al-ʿArabī offers his own reading practice that complements well what I have outlined previously. First, you are to *listen* attentively, for this text is one of many means that facilitate your *return* to God. Do not merely (superficially) read it, but take what you understand and *put it to heart* (Arabic: *ʿū*, from *waʿā*), otherwise translated as "become aware of it" or "make it a part of your consciousness." Then, understand and *make it clear* by *setting it forth in detail* (*faṣṣilū*). But do not stop at dissecting the text; *gather it* into its enduring and transformative meaning. Once you have appropriated the meaning, *give it to those who demand it*, i.e., write *from* the text, theologize from the text and offer the meaning to others in your own words. This is, in my view, constructive comparative theology that is the fruit of interreligious reading. Finally, *expand* the *mercy* of God.

Ultimately, the fruit of comparative theology will be judged by its works. The comparative theologian, at least according to this "method," only seeks to expand the mercy of God, or in the words of von Balthasar, objective teaching (part of a uniform *theologia spiritualis*) is "to be realized in practice, in the life of faith, hope and charity."[61] She furthermore strives to awaken others to the infinite self-disclosures of God, and to make others realize—in her own process of realization—the signs in the cosmos, the self, and in her own tradition. She does this by taking Ibn al-ʿArabī's advice seriously:

> So, beware, lest you tie yourself through a particular belief, and thus become veiled [*tukaffar*] by [a belief] other than [your belief], for you would pass over much good, indeed you would pass over knowledge of the situation as it really is. Thus, be in yourself a *prime matter* [*ḥayūla*] for all forms of beliefs, for God is wider and greater than that a certain belief/knot [*ʿaqd*] rather than another one should restrict Him. For God said, "whithersoever you turn, there is the Face of God," (Qur'ān 2:115) . . . and the face of a thing is its reality.[62]

This is Ibn al-ʿArabī's own reason for engaging in what we today call *comparative* theology, a reason not offered by non-comparative, Christian theologians, and thus a "fresh theological insight," in my view. Ignoring comparative theology will result in the fossilization of doctrine and stultification of constructive theology; it will tie us down and keep us in knots, thereby preventing us from seeking the infinite self-disclosures of God in various beliefs or religious traditions. The process of interpreting never ends, neither is it restricted to the text. The practice of comparative theology cannot be reduced to logical procedures, to a static method. Rather, interpreting is a self-transformative "way" of being-in-the-world, and textual interpreting is to be mirrored in interpreting the world and the multiplicity of religious beliefs therein. There is no place for being a judge, if by judging we mean having one's way with the dialogical process, restricting what is otherwise intended to open the heart to divine self-disclosures.

wa'llāhu 'aʿlam!—And God knows best!

Notes

1. That is, *ʿilm al-kalām*, arguably best translated as "dialectical theology."
2. For example, the work of Louis Massignon is avant-garde in the method of his engagement with the Islamic tradition (see Christian S. Krokus, *The Theology of Louis Massignon: Islam, Christ, and the Church*). Furthermore, Dobie's *Logos & Revelation* begins to break from the hold of history; however, he does not offer a systematic or constructive turn for which I will be arguing in this piece.
3. Francis X. Clooney himself has offered constructive insights in his comparative theological projects; however, comparative theologians such as John Thatamanil, Jon Paul Sydnor, Michelle Voss Roberts, and Kristin Beise Kiblinger have explicitly been far more constructive.
4. I am arguing for a break not only from the historically received tradition of interactions, whether textual or personal, between Muslims and Christians, but also from the modern scholarly conception of "Islam" that gives "so much *value* . . . [and ascribes] *meaning* . . . to the *prescriptive* and *restrictive* discourses of Muslims, such as law and creed, and so little *value* . . . and *meaning* . . . to *explorative* and *creative* discourses" (Ahmed, *What Is Islam?*, 303). In other words, part of the problem with scholarship on the comparative study of Islamic and Christian thought is that the field has been hindered by a confining and confined conceptualization of the Islamic religious tradition that is restricted to law and creedal theology, as opposed to the equally, if not more formative, discourses of mysticism, poetry, art, philosophy, and literature. This restrictive conceptualization is thoroughly challenged by Shahab Ahmed in his groundbreaking work, *What Is Islam?*.
5. See Morris, "Ibn ʿArabi's Rhetoric of Realisation," Parts I and II.
6. Clooney, *Comparative Theology*, 10.
7. Ibn al-ʿArabī, *Fuṣūṣ*, 47 (all translations are mine unless otherwise specified).
8. I.e., "*āyāt*," the term also employed for verses in the Qur'ān.
9. Qur'ān *Fuṣṣilat* 41:53 (all translations of the Qur'ān are my adaptations from Nasr et al., *The Study Quran*).
10. Cf. Chapter 63 of Ibn al-ʿArabī's *Futūḥāt al-Makkiyya*.
11. He also refers to this world as an imagination within an imagination, or a dream within a dream. See Ibn al-ʿArabī, *Fuṣūṣ*, 99, 104 (the chapter on Joseph).
12. Recall that the word for "signs" in the world is the same as the word for "verses" in the Qur'ān, i.e., *ayāt*.
13. Respectively, *kitāb Allāh, kitāb* ***āfāqī***, and *kitāb* ***anfusī***. These adjectives are drawn from Qur'ān *Fuṣṣilat* 41:53: "*We will show them our signs in the horizons* [fī'l-**āfāq**] *and in their souls* [fī'l-**anfus**ihim] *so that it may become clear to them that [God] is The Real.*" The Book of God is the inscribed book of the Qur'ān.
14. I am in agreement with Denys Turner's argument that there is a contemporary preoccupation with mysticism as "experience," which he terms "experientialism" (see Denys Turner, *The Darkness of God: Negativity in Christian Mysticism* (New York: Cambridge University Press, 1995), particularly Chapter 11, "From mystical theology to mysticism"). In contradistinction to defining the "mystical" as an event in which one immediately experiences God, I concur with Bernard McGinn's suggestion that there is, rather, a mystical element in Christianity (and, I would argue, in Islam) which is

"that part of its belief and practices that concerns the preparation, the consciousness of, and the reaction to what can be described as the immediate or direct presence of God," (Barnard McGinn, *The Presence of God: A History of Western Christian Mysticism* (New York: Crossroad, 1991), Volume I, xvii). However, I would go further by suggesting that this "awareness of God" is best expressed as perception, which leads to transformed practices; in this case, as Turner suggests, one might even go so far as to say that "theology in so far as it is theology is 'mystical' and in so far as it is 'mystical' it is theology," (Turner, 265). This, in fact, is one of the main arguments of Mark McIntosh's *Mystical Theology*, to which I refer later.

15. Qur'ān *al-Baqarah* 2:115.
16. Qur'ān *al-Qasas* 28:88.
17. Cf., Ibn al-ʿArabī, *Fuṣūṣ*, 46.
18. Ibn al-ʿArabī, *Fuṣūṣ*, 47 [emphasis mine].
19. Ibn al-ʿArabī, *Futūḥāt,* IV 333.11 (all citations from the *Futūḥāt* follow this format: Volume page:line).
20. Clooney, in *Comparative Theology* (particularly 157–62), explicitly alludes to the "insider-outsider" and liminal nature of the comparative theologian.
21. Ibn al-ʿArabī, *Futūḥāt* II 211.29, also in Chittick, *The Sufi Path of Knowledge,* 349. Likewise, "So knowledge of God is bewilderment, and knowledge of creation is bewilderment" (Ibn al-ʿArabī, *Futūḥāt* IV 279.26; Chittick, *The Sufi Path of Knowledge, 380).*
22. McIntosh, *Mystical Theology*, 7. See also 8ff. McIntosh takes his lead from a similar thesis put forth by von Balthasar, particularly in "Spirituality" in *Explorations in Theology*, Volume I, 211–26.
23. McIntosh, *Mystical Theology*, 8.
24. In agreement with Shahab Ahmed, I am in part translating the groundbreaking arguments proffered in his field-changing book, *What Is Islam?* to the field of comparative theology. Ibn al-ʿArabī (as well as the Akbarian tradition) is in fact the subject of one of his six opening questions that guide his study, which reorients the field of Islamic Studies and reconceptualizes what it means to be "Islamic." In brief, Ahmed sheds significant insight into the valorization and meaning-making given to "exploration, ambiguity, ambivalence, wonder, aestheticization, diffusion, differentiation, polyvalence, relativism, and contradiction" (Ahmed, *What Is Islam?*, 303) by an overwhelming majority of Muslims throughout much of Islamic history. The Akbarian tradition is just one example of how these explorative and hermeneutical discourses were valorized and overwhelming influential within the larger Islamic tradition.
25. McIntosh, *Mystical Theology*, 6.
26. See Ricœur, *Interpretation Theory*, 19ff.
27. Along the same lines, Clooney has equated the discipline of comparative theology and comparative religious reading with spiritual practice—for example: "Comparative theology is best conceived of as a particular reading practice, or a series of exercises in close reading. It has to do with the cultivation of knowledge within one or more traditions for the sake of the transformation of the individuals engaged in that study," (Clooney, "Reading as a Way of Disclosing the Truth in a Religiously Diverse World," in *The Wiley Blackwell Companion to Religious Diversity*, edited by Kevin Schilbrack, Chapter 25). My presentation on the transformative nature of the text is also echoed by Clooney in Chapter 9 of *Comparative Theology*, particularly 154–56.

28. McIntosh, 10.
29. Von Balthasar asserted that even spiritual theology is ultimately dogmatic theology at its profoundest level, that of mystery, and that catechetics *should* lead the believer from the exterior to the inner understanding of this mystery (see von Balthasar, *Explorations in Theology*, Volume I, 212–13).
30. See Moyaert, *In Response to the Religious Other.*
31. In particular, see von Balthasar, *Explorations in Theology*, Volume I, 211–26, especially 212–13, from which McIntosh draws his thesis and expands upon it in his *Mystical Theology.*
32. Ibid., 214. See Chapter 2 of McIntosh, *Christology from Within*, wherein he makes a strong case that von Balthasar reads theological texts as offering a practical and constructive Christology.
33. Ibid., 214.
34. For example, "[Humankind] has two visions of The Real, and therefore [God] made him with two eyes. With one eye he sees [God] as being independent from the worlds; he does not see [God] in anything or in himself. With the other eye he sees [God] as the [Divine] Name the Merciful which demands the world and which the world demands; he sees [God] permeating existence in everything" (Ibn al-ʿArabī, *Futūḥāt*, III 151.27).
35. The trilateral root for "interpret" (*ʿayn, bāʾ, rāʾ*) implies a "crossing over" or "traversing."
36. Ibn al-ʿArabī, *Futūḥāt*, III, 257.4.
37. It is hard to separate von Balthasar's Christology from his scriptural hermeneutics, further demonstrating the integrity of spirituality and theology for him. Just as Christ's divinity is only revealed *through* his humanity, likewise the meaning and projected spirituality of a text is revealed *through* its textual body.
38. Von Balthasar, *Explorations in Theology*, Volume I, 20–21. While the Swiss theologian is speaking of scriptural hermeneutics, his understanding of how the saints and mystics manifest Christ in the world via a participation in the economy of the Son would allow one, I argue, to transfer this method to theological texts.
39. See ibid., 20–21, for the way von Balthasar connects scriptural hermeneutics with Christology. In particular, "Faith, the foundation of all our understanding of revelation, *expands our created minds by making them participate in the mind of God, disclosing the inward divine meaning of the words through kind of co-working with God* (1 Cor 2:9, 16); for this reason it is the saint, the man most open to the working of the Spirit, who arrives at the closest understanding," (ibid., 21). My emphasis is intended to highlight the fact that "method" here is more of a spiritual discipline that forms one's reading and writing practice, and not a logical procedure.
40. That is, this is basically the scientific, empiricist method that began to take hold of much, though not all, of theology after Thomas Aquinas. Von Balthasar gestures toward this, too, in *Explorations in Theology*, Volume I, 213–14.
41. The famous ṣūfī axiom, *lā takrār fi'l-tajallī*, "there is no repetition in self-manifestation," is cited often by Muslim thinkers, and it is perhaps based on what Ibn al-ʿArabī ascribes to Abū Ṭālib al-Makkī (d. 996), the author of the ṣūfī manual, *Qūt al-qulūb*: "God never discloses Himself in a single form to two individuals, nor in a single form twice." (Ibn al-ʿArabī, *Futūḥāt*, I 266.9, and also in Chittick, *The Sufi Path of Knowledge*, 103.)

42. One might add, not even by another self. That is, that which was revealed to a reader the first time she reads a text can, and often is, different from what is revealed to her the second or third time she reads the same text. Furthermore, mention should be made of the fact that, within this worldview and epistemology, subject and object ultimately collapse in the process of knowing one's self in order to know one's Lord, as the Prophet demands we do in the famous prophetic narration: "He who knows himself knows his Lord." It should be noted that this so-called *ḥadīth*, or prophetic narration, is cited and commented upon often not only by Ibn al-ʿArabī, but by other authors of the broader Islamic religious and intellectual tradition; however, Ibn al-ʿArabī himself acknowledges that it is "not established (*thābit*) by transmission (*naql*) but considered sound (*saḥīḥ*) on the basis of unveiling." ("Notes on the more than human saying: 'Unless you know yourself you cannot know God,'" http://www.ibnarabisociety.org/articles/notesonsaying.html, accessed September 3, 2016; see also Ibn al-ʿArabī, *Futūḥāt*, II, 399.28).
43. Clooney, *Seeing Through Texts*, 310. He continues, "It is to let slip the careful boundaries between what one thinks, how one feels, what one does, all without certainty about some ultimate coherence. It is letting one's beliefs intrude into scholarship, and risking them there, without having something ready and wise to say in summation. Everything gets included, eventually," (Clooney, *Seeing Through Texts*, 310). In Chapter 5 of this work, Clooney describes his concept of a biblio/biography, which I think is comparable to what I am aiming to develop. "After this [comparative enterprise], other, extended reflections can follow later, elsewhere, by which one can speak beyond the songs, the commentaries, and the features of one's biblio/biography, seeing through them, through oneself. Then one might state more systematically what one has learned, the meaning of one's acts of inclusion, for the sake of those who could neither have seen nor heard in the same way," (Clooney, *Seeing Through Texts*, 311).
44. Lonergan, *Method in Theology*, 122–23.
45. This is a *ḥadīth qudsī*, which is a saying of the prophet in the voice of God.
46. The trilateral root for intellect (*ʿayn, qāf, lām*) originally meant the rope used to tie a camel to a post, or the process whereby a camel is thusly tied.
47. As the famous *ḥadīth* states: "My earth and My heavens do not contain Me, but the heart of My faithful servant does contain me."
48. Cf. Morris, "How to Study the Futûhât," 73–89; see also Morris, "Ibn 'Arabi's Rhetoric of Realisation," 96.
49. See Chapter 5 of Lonergan, *Method in Theology*, 125ff.
50. Ibid., 170.
51. Clooney gestures toward this "intensification of affect" in comparative theology. See Clooney, "Passionate Comparison," 368. This is also one of the main themes of his *Beyond Compare*.
52. Clooney, *Comparative Theology*, 10.
53. McIntosh, *Mystical Theology*, 131.
54. Ibid., 133.
55. Ibid., 135.
56. Ibid., 136.
57. Jāmī, *Naqd al-Nuṣūṣ fī sharḥ Naqsh al-Fuṣūṣ*, 278. Jāmī is commenting on Ibn al-ʿArabī's own summary of the chapter of Muḥammad from the *Fuṣūṣ*. However, Ibn

al-ʿArabī himself has much to say about the role of bewilderment in seeking God, particularly in how the divine self-disclosures increase this bewilderment of the person who possesses the type of heart (*qalb*) I have been describing in this essay. See Chapter 50 of Ibn al-ʿArabī's *Futūḥāt.*

58. As I have mentioned variously throughout this piece, the field of Islamic studies has often focused on legal and creedal discourses as normative, as opposed to other discourses (poetic, mystical, philosophical, artistic, and so on), to such an extent that "when Muslims act and speak *exploratively*—as opposed to *prescriptively*—as they seem to have spent a very great deal of their historical time doing, they are somehow not seen to be acting and speaking in a manner and register that is representative, expressive and constitutive of Islam," (Ahmed, *What Is Islam?*, 303). Furthermore, modern discourse, both popular and academic, tends to reduce the Islamic revelation to the Text of the Qur'ān, whereas in practice various Islamic discursive traditions (for example, the Sufi or the philosophical) have understood the Textual revelation of the Qur'ān as just one of three aspects of revelation: the Pre-Text, Con-Text, and actual Text. The Pre-Text of Revelation is "*ontologically and alethically* [i.e., as regards truth] *prior to the Text*" of the Qur'ān and "*is that upon which the Truth of the Text is contingent*" (ibid., 347; for example, the Pre-Text for Ibn al-ʿArabī and the Sufis is "Existence," and for the philosophers it is "Reason"—see ibid., 347–56). It is *not* chronologically prior to the text, but rather is continuously present in the hermeneutical engagement with reality. This is an explicit conceptualization of what is implied in the Qur'ānic verse cited earlier that refers to the Book of God, of the Cosmos, and of the Soul: All is revelatory of Truth. Furthermore, the Con-Text of Revelation is the "*whole field or complex or vocabulary of meanings of Revelation that have been produced in the course of the human and historical hermeneutical engagement with Revelation*" (ibid., 356). It thus becomes apparent that the Akbarian tradition presented in this piece is both constitutive of, and normative to, "Islam" and not to be regarded as a mere exception to the Islamic tradition of hermeneutical engagement with Revelation.
59. This is the Chalcedonian Christological formula proffered by Pope Leo I. Von Balthasar would argue that even Leo's Tome, properly understood, is ultimately a spiritual theology and not merely a response to a perceived heresy. Indeed, "one person, two nature" has anthropological concomitants that surely prescribe a way of being-in-the-world.
60. Ibn al-ʿArabī, *Fuṣūṣ*, 47–48.
61. Von Balthasar, *Explorations in Theology*, Volume I, 212.
62. Ibn al-ʿArabī, *Fuṣūṣ*, 113.

n Some Suspicions Regarding Comparative Theology

Glenn R. Willis

If theological comparisons do not connect themselves to the concerns of actual religious communities, it is not clear how comparison can be theological at all, given that theologies must implicate the writer in some community of practice. This essay addresses several quiet but sustained suspicions about theological comparison as a religiously relevant project. There seems little reason to deny that comparisons are often subject to an "ingrained resistance,"[1] particularly among theologians.[2] In what follows, I first deepen several fundamental critiques of comparison, emphasizing that theologies must offer more than virtuoso interreligious vision, before suggesting some ways in which comparison can sometimes become more constructive for religious communities themselves. The essay ends by arguing that comparative theology should be an apologetic theology.

In North America, the theologian is sanctioned as a professional not by any religious body, but by the university[3]—a situation that produces some ambiguities of theological purpose. The theologian explicitly serves communities of higher education, where theological commitments are not often central, while implicitly claiming to be relevant in some vague way to religious communities themselves. Comparative theology is implicated in a more general contemporary confusion about the real audiences of professional theology.

One way to resolve this confusion has been to adopt an implicitly pluralist theological perspective from which one's religious scholarship can be presented as support for the equality, and the peace, of global cultures. From this perspective, virtually any interreligious scholarship is worthy, not because it is constructive of religious communities, but because it allows for an imagined ethical globalism.

By the time Jonathan Z. Smith wrote his still-influential 1982 critique of religious comparison, "In Comparison a Magic Dwells,"[4] comparative religious writing had for decades adopted a somewhat naïve form of theological pluralism emphasizing the ultimate equality of religious traditions—a position articulated by several widely read writers, such as Huston Smith, Thomas Merton, and Joseph Campbell.[5] But the recognition of mere religious similarities, J. Z. Smith argued, is almost certain to arise in the process of research in multiple religious traditions: What is not clear is how a single scholar's recognition of similarity can be justified; and similarities themselves do not necessarily imply anything about religious realities:

> Often, at some point along the way, as if unbidden, as a sort of déjà vu, the scholar remembers that he has seen "it" or "something like it" before. . . . This experience, this unintended consequence of research, must then be accorded significance and provided with an explanation. In the vast majority of instances in the history of comparison, this subjective experience is projected as an objective connection through some theory of influence, diffusion, borrowing, or the like. It is a process of working from a psychological association to an historical one . . . [6]

Comparison, in Smith's view, too easily becomes a personalized assertion of whim supporting an implicit historical or theological claim about the ultimate equality of traditions. He concludes by writing that "Comparison requires the postulation of difference as the grounds of its being interesting (rather than tautological) and [also requires] a methodical manipulation of difference . . . in the service of some useful end."[7]

Smith's perceptive criticism of naïve pluralist comparisons has allowed some theologians to presume that such naïveté is intrinsic to theological comparison itself. That dismissiveness is not usually expressed in formal published form, but it is expressed in quite forceful, ironizing terms in many less formal but important professional interactions.

Skeptics of theological comparison have also derived a separate, perhaps more powerful, shorthand denial of comparative viability from the work of George A. Lindbeck, whose cultural-linguistic account of religious doctrine and experience has been used to bolster intense doubt that anyone can inhabit more than one religious grammar or way of being in a given lifetime. Comparative theological work can therefore be nothing but a form of dilettantism, pretending to a deep understanding of multiple traditions that is simply impossible from a cultural-linguistic perspective. I have heard such views expressed by older and younger colleagues alike, offered at times with a slight hint of superior apology, as if their critical sentiment must be somehow surprising or new—or as if their sentiment is not politically correct, and is therefore likely to be heroically true.

A cursory reading of Lindbeck's work does appear to confirm him as a profound skeptic of all comparison. A cultural-linguistic approach to religious study suggests that a "religion" is "similar to an idiom that makes possible the description of realities, the formulation of beliefs, and the experiencing of inner attitudes, feelings, and sentiments. Like a culture or a language, it is a communal phenomenon that shapes the subjectivities of individuals rather than being primarily a manifestation of those subjectivities."[8] It is unlikely, then, that a non-Buddhist, separated from the formative particularity of Buddhist languages and practices, can coherently "say anything true or false about Nirvana, or even meaningfully deny it."[9] For Lindbeck, "different religions and/or philosophies may have incommensurable notions of truth, of experience, and of categorial adequacy, and therefore also of what it would mean for something to be most important (i.e., 'God'). Unlike other perspectives, this approach proposes no common framework . . . within which to compare religions."[10]

Like Jonathan Z. Smith, Lindbeck reserves his highest rebukes for presumed similarities: "Granted that a shrinking world makes it more and more imperative that religions no less than nations learn to communicate—but does it help in doing this to think that their deepest experiences and commitments must somehow be the same?"[11]

The study of other traditions has, in fact, been morally justified for decades through the repeated suggestion that interreligious study allows us to encounter our neighbors with greater empathy in a world of growing proximity to religious difference. And Lindbeck is right to ask whether a global ethic that presumes ultimate religious sameness is more, rather than less, likely to produce violence. This "informed political empathy" justification for interreligious scholarship also implies, wrongly, that empathy for religious others cannot be generated within the study and practice of one's own tradition. "Informed political empathy" justifications for interreligious study have assumed further that neighbors from other traditions are unambiguously devoted participants of those traditions, and can be represented as such. This is a dubious assumption, at best, in North America. Lindbeck and Smith rightly undermine the sort of moralistic pluralism that asserts similitude as a necessary ground for imagined peace, as if political cooperation could ever be achieved through presumed similarities.

Lindbeck himself, like Smith, sees the identification of difference as the key to any constructive dialogue or comparison between traditions:

> Because [traditions] are in their own right comprehensive cultural-linguistic systems . . . different religions are likely to have different warrants for interreligious conversation and cooperation.[12] This lack of a common foundation is a weakness, but it is also a strength. It means, on the one hand, that the partners in dialogue do not start with the conviction that they really basically agree, but it also means that they are not forced into the dilemma of thinking of themselves as representing a superior (or an inferior) articulation of a common experience of which the other religions are inferior (or superior) expressions. They can regard themselves as simply different and can proceed to explore their agreements and disagreements without necessarily engaging in the invidious comparisons that the assumption of a common experiential core [across all traditions] make so tempting.[13]

Smith and Lindbeck are sometimes thought to have said that comparison must always involve self-deception. They insist, instead, that careful comparison, focused on relevant differences in service of identifiable purposes, is difficult. Theological comparativists won't disagree.

However, several important conclusions follow from these arguments for the careful identification of difference, and for epistemic humility about those differences, in any comparison or dialogue between traditions—conclusions that haven't always been taken seriously enough by comparative theologians.

First, if a primary purpose of comparison is to locate new options for religious thought and practice in one's own tradition, in order to "serve some useful [religious] end," it remains unclear to some theologians why interreligious comparison is a better method for recognizing those new options than exploring the history of one's own tradition. Does the turn from Christianity toward Hinduism or Islam or Buddhism reveal a failure to skillfully investigate the diverse richness of Christianity itself? What is the *added* benefit of exploring another tradition, for understanding one's own?

The comparativist might respond, first, that a systematic and historical understanding of their own tradition is an essential foundation for all comparison—not only so that relevant differences can be perceived between traditions, but also so that the re-interpretation of one's own tradition can draw from relevant resources within that tradition. No comparative theology can afford historical or systematic illiteracy, and the comparativist always stands open to the critiques of experts in those areas. Again, then: What is the *added* benefit of exploring another tradition if one's true purpose is to understand one's own tradition?

It is an experiential truth of the comparative process that in the process of exploring another tradition, in recognizing the dynamics of an unfamiliar soteriology or anthropology, the theologian's own tradition is made strange, renewed as an object of mystery and inquiry. That renewal is very likely to produce new insight and curiosity in ways that historical and systematic investigations, on their own, may not.

Consider a Christian living in a psychological culture like that of North America, who may seek to make a distinction between repentance, on the one hand, and damaging self-castigation, on the other—because American psychological culture tends to conflate repentance with destructive shame. The theologian of repentance may find it helpful to study Buddhist practices of critical but compassionate self-evaluation in order to return more skillfully to the study of similar, now largely discarded practices in Christianity. However—and this is a second consequence of the epistemic humility advocated by Lindbeck and Smith—when the Christian theologian turns back toward the confessional and penitential resources within the history of Christianity itself, *there is no longer any clear need, theologically, to refer to Buddhist thought or practices in any way.* In fact, a robustly and communally constructive theological project, intended to support the integrity of its own tradition, may be obliged to actively *obscure* the comparisons it pursues. To the extent that comparisons are openly demonstrated, to the extent that an argument *must* be comparative to succeed, the comparative theologian seems implicitly to imagine a pluralist audience, and therefore, most likely, a university audience.

Further, it is not clear why comparative theology requires any truly accurate understanding of another tradition beyond one's own, if the purpose of comparison is to enrich one's perceptual abilities before returning creatively to the resources of one's own theological home. One can be demonstrably wrong in one's interpretation of another tradition's doctrines or practices, and still be returned creatively and inquisitively back into one's home theological tradition.

So long as these ambiguities of comparison are not addressed, theological comparison will continue to be perceived as depending too thoroughly upon an implicit pluralism that ultimately dissolves formal religious commitments. North American comparative theologians do not often make explicit demands on any religious community, but address readers primarily as individuals. In works such as *Beyond Compare: St. Francis De Sales and Sri Vedanta Desika on Loving Surrender to God* and *His Hiding Place is Darkness: A Hindu-Catholic Theopoetics of Divine Absence*, Francis X. Clooney begins from a close reading of medieval Hindu devotional poetry in order to explore and revivify devotional longing. Though Clooney is Catholic, his core theological problem is not specifically Catholic at all: "[H]ow is one to speak passionately of God after pluralism has seeped deep inside even the most resolute and confident believer?"[14] North American comparative theology sometimes represents itself as an extraordinary search for one's own pluralist commitments, leaving readers to make a further "constructive" movement of their own, choosing the directions of their own devotion.

Not all theologians will accept the terms of Clooney's question: Pluralism, for some, is precisely what appears to prevent a truly passionate engagement with God, in as far as passion involves a skillful limitation of focus—a limitation provided by the boundaries of tradition. Certainly pluralism is now irrevocable and central for many theologically invested human beings. Clooney is right that the problem of coherent devotion has become a serious one. But how can pluralism motivate any common commitments, if the point of pluralism is that individuals may perceive truth across multiple traditions, but in different ways and combinations, so that commonalities of perception, affect, and action are few? Communally constructive theology in a pluralist mode appears to express a contradiction: Pluralism and religious individualism are mutually reinforcing.

Clooney, in *His Hiding Place is Darkness*, writes in passing of "real and necessary religious borders,"[15] and notes that when he does work across those boundaries, he seeks to do so "without letting go of the original love, in my case for Jesus, this beloved."[16] Clooney expresses a hope that his double readings might serve as an invitation to "a new community of readers,"[17] but that almost certainly academic readership is not the same thing as writing for a defined theological community.

The pluralist philosophical formulations of Raimon Panikkar have drawn a dedicated community of North American academic readers, but this readership seems pervaded by interest in the writer as an extraordinary paragon of synthetic vision—a vision that others may find obliquely fascinating but finally uninhabitable, in so far as such a unique interreligious synthesis must be dependent upon a complex set of elite formations to which most persons do not have access.[18] Similarly, Paul Knitter, in *Without Buddha I Could Not Be a Christian*, begins from a perspective that explicitly emphasizes Christian theological and ethical inadequacy[19] and attempts to locate a metaphysics and a set of practices that will give him access to a more robust liberationist ethic than the one that he believes either Christians or Buddhists can marshal on their own terms. The transformation imagined by the pluralist interreligious thinker is often a transformation of the individual self toward new capacities and identities—Knitter rejects any "such thing as a neatly defined, once-and-for-all identity,"[20] a typical pluralist commitment in an epoch marked by a general liquidity of identities.

A number of theologians claim a multiple-religious belonging or participation. John Thatamanil has eloquently advocated for such multiple participation as a marker not of any negative promiscuity, but of a more expansive devotion.[21] My own view is that more definitive forms of religious belonging can better provide focus and discipline in those normal periods of thinness, confusion, or distraction that mark any religious life over the long term. The relational commitments involved in a formal, extended belonging are more likely than episodes of participation to structure both the joys and the difficulties of religious maturation. I agree with Lindbeck that "to become [and remain] religious . . . is to interiorize a set of skills by practice and training. One learns how to feel, act, and think in conformity with a religious tradition that is, in its inner structure, far richer and more subtle than can be explicitly articulated. The primary knowledge is not *about* the religion, nor *that* the religion teaches such and such, but rather *how* to be religious in such and such ways."[22]

If Lindbeck is correct that religious understanding is primarily an understanding of action, pluralist theologians who defend multiple religious participation will need to say more about the virtue of discernment by which such multi-religious persons might come to determine which religious teaching is applicable to which challenge in their lives, at which times. And how would such a skillful prudence be developed? Unbounded vacillations of religious participation and perception may allow persons to *avoid* a more difficult maturation of religious commitment, a commitment that might withstand time and challenge. It may be that theological pluralism will always be better at fostering a proliferation of ingenious conceptuality, or a solitariness of vision, than it will be at clarifying the most important paths of everyday action.

I share a skepticism about the long-term viability of pluralist versions of comparative theology, not because pluralists (implicit and explicit) somehow fail as extraordinary models of cross-cultural investigation, or as careful representatives of passionately ethical, globally engaged argumentation. I just do not see how pluralist comparisons can be constructive for, or questioned by, any specific community of practice: pluralist globalism is rarely talking to anyone in particular.

Nonetheless, comparative theology itself should not be entirely dismissed. The critiques of comparison outlined here may too easily lead toward a kind of superior skepticism that refuses to recognize the very real benefits of comparison for the most disciplined and dedicated theologians. Perceiving one's own home topographies differently, because they have been re-imagined and re-valued after traveling elsewhere, hardly involves any failure of commitment; comparison almost certainly cultivates a greater sense of the particularity of one's own committedness, and thereby sharpens or intensifies that commitment. This intensification of commitment is probably one source of the real pleasure of theological comparison, over against any naïve "discovery" of religious sameness.

Comparisons that identify a relevant difference in the service of such intensified insight are indeed possible. Consider Erich Auerbach's well-known essay "Odysseus' Scar," in which the uncanny depth of character produced in the narratives of *Genesis* is illumined through direct comparison with the Homeric convention of more fully displaying character through extended descriptions of memory, motivation, and affect: for example, the back-narrative of the origins of Odysseus's scar, by which Euryclea, his former nursemaid, recognizes him upon his return to Ithaca. Through comparison with Homer's characterological narrative techniques, Auerbach artfully illumines the very different, counterintuitive effect of Hebrew reticence—the way in which *Genesis*, by refusing at crucial points to name the motivations of human action, induces a heightened characterological intensity: What are Abraham's thoughts as he approaches Mt. Moriah with Isaac? We are not told. Hebrew reticence invites an interpretive multiplicity that Homer does not demand (see, for example, Kierkegaard's *Fear and Trembling* as an illustration of Auerbach's point).

Another example: In Martin Asscher's essay, "The Questionable Problem: On the Logic of Suicide," Asscher compares the cases of Primo Levi and of the Japanese Vice-Admiral Ōnishi Takijirō, a formulator of kamikaze strategy in the Pacific during the Second World War, who committed suicide on August 15, 1945. Asscher begins with an argument that Levi's death, assumed to be a suicide (against the testimony of close friends), is actually much more ambiguous and unknowable than a variety of commentators and biographers have claimed. By offering the reader selected quotations from a suicide note by Ōnishi Takijirō, Asscher himself is able to demonstrate the remarkable cultural formulations and expectations that made Ōnishi's suicide unambiguous: "In a certain sense, Ōnishi's suicide might even be declared 'satisfying,' given that he identified himself completely with 'his' pilots in his farewell letter and in his death."[23] The comparison between the unambiguous suicide of a defeated admiral, on the one hand, and the death of Primo Levi, on the other, helps Asscher to clarify the way in which certitude regarding suicidality is not an appropriate response to Levi's death, and should not be used as a convenient key to the interpretation of his writing. Here, as in Auerbach's essay, we find a manipulation of difference "in the service of some useful end." One might produce arguments about the Hebrew text of *Genesis*, or the supposed suicide of Primo Levi, without offering any comparisons at all—but in each case comparison *clarifies and amplifies* an attempt to change the reader's perception of some concrete concern.

Similarly, creative clarifications very often occur in theological comparison—a truth that critics of theological comparison should be more willing to admit. However, I also wish to suggest that theological comparison is far more likely to become religiously relevant when it not only offers a clarification of one's own tradition but also provides an apologetic argument in favor of that tradition.

Such apologetics may be unwelcome among pluralist theologians, for whom apologetics between traditions can only ever be destructive of a global ethic. Among more tradition-bound theologians, though, constructive theology in a pluralistic age may *need* to be apologetic, if it is to help defend and develop tradition-specific forms of creativity in a cultural atmosphere that devalues the integrity of traditions.

A Christian theologian of repentance might, for example, suggest that Christian forms of repentance are superior to Buddhist confessional practices that aim toward a total purification, precisely because the Christian celebrates imperfection as the necessary, ongoing point of contact between the human and the divine: Augustine's *felix culpa*. Christian repentance has to do, perhaps, with a greater acceptance of ongoing imperfection in a given life than some Buddhists might allow, and may therefore be presented as more anthropologically realistic, from that Christian perspective. For such an apologetic, significant consideration should be given to the possibility that many Buddhists, too, value human imperfection as a creative opportunity, rather than a mere obstacle. But the Christian's confidence in the greater metaphysical and experiential truth of their own anthropological commitments *should* be the direction of Christian argumentation, if the argument is to be concretely constructive at all for Christians, as opposed to an abstract global community. Only in an apologetic mode do religious differences become religiously relevant for persons who are serious about religious belonging.

Apologetic arguments are always risky: Their arguments depend upon accuracy in a way that comparative theology, in its pluralistic modes, does not (see above: our vision can be creatively renewed by another tradition, even if we do not understand that other tradition). It should also be noted, however, that critical apologetics need not involve the wholesale condemnation of other traditions: Apologetics may express more humility than pluralism, in many ways.

John Makransky's essay, "A Buddhist Critique of, and Learning from, Christian Liberation Theology," is a case in point.[24] Makransky writes first to celebrate liberation theology's possible challenge to himself and to other Buddhist practitioners, encouraging them to focus attention more intensively on excluded persons. But he also writes to challenge Christians themselves to avoid the temptation to divide humanity into those worthy of love (the poor, for liberation theologians), and unworthy others: For Makransky, the wealthy should indeed be forcefully challenged, but that challenge should be addressed to their actual capacities for compassion and active care.

Makransky's essay accepts a Christian challenge to his own tradition, but also provides a carefully argued, ethically invested apologetic in return. His perception of mutual challenge does not lead him to condemn Christians; he seeks instead to empower them, and names the way in which they have empowered him. This is confident comparative work that is critical and constructive towards multiple traditions, without lapsing into any naïve pluralism.

Comparison is more likely to be constructive when it is apologetic for the simple reason that apologetics demand genuinely deep learning about another tradition, while also requiring the theologian to discern with great care whatever may be important for the ongoing integrity of their own. A comparative theology should be an apologetic theology if it is to be constructive and vital.

Comparative apologetic arguments are most able to respond to the skepticism of those theologians who, like Lindbeck and Smith, distrust pluralism, often for good reason: What community of actual practice can pluralism sustain? Pluralist interreligious theologies may continue to offer ingenious personal insights generated from an expanding variety of multi-religious sources. Such works may offer extraordinary virtuoso performances of synthetic vision—but without supporting the ongoing integrity and vitality of traditions themselves. A more confident argument for the specific greatness of one's own theological tradition will always stand a better chance at becoming, and remaining, a constructive theology.

Notes

1. Asscher, *Apples and Oranges*, 4.
2. "Religious traditions seem often enough to abhor comparison as almost necessarily superficial, a distraction from true learning . . ." Clooney, *Beyond Compare*, 203.
3. Theologians in Germany submit, for instance, to a process of confirmation by local ecclesial evaluative bodies—a sometimes difficult and fraught process that nonetheless allows the university community a much greater opportunity, and responsibility, to interact in an ongoing way with religious worlds beyond the formal classroom.
4. Smith, *Imagining Religion*.
5. See Prothero, *God Is Not One*, especially "Pretend Pluralism," a section of the book's Introduction. Prothero's apparently principled demarcation of strict religious boundaries ("I know what these men are doing") is at least as questionable as "pretend pluralism" itself.
6. Smith, 22.
7. Ibid., 35.
8. Lindbeck, *The Nature of Doctrine*, 33.
9. Ibid., 48.
10. Ibid., 47–49.
11. Ibid., 54.
12. And interreligious study, one might add.
13. Lindbeck, 55.

14. Clooney, *His Hiding Place Is Darkness*, 39.
15. Ibid., 39.
16. Ibid., 44.
17. Ibid., 64.
18. It might be suggested that pluralism rightly demands that each religious person reflect carefully on their own complex formations. I see such a demand as rooted in an academic context where such reflection is given support and guidance—support and guidance that are arguably unavailable to most persons. Theological pluralism requires intensive long-term education to function at all.
19. I am grateful to Loyola Marymount University Professor Karen Enriquez for clarifying discussion on these issues. Paul Knitter writes, "The Christian tradition and its spirituality is a well that contains waters of deep mystical, non-dualistic experience of the interconnecting Spirit and of the Christ who lives and acts within the community of believers. The Christian mystics attest to the depths of this well. But for many of us . . . the buckets that we have at our disposal to draw up those waters have holes in them" (Knitter, *Without Buddha*, 140).
20. Knitter, *Without Buddha*, 214.
21. Thatamanil, "Binocular Wisdom: The Benefits of Participating in Multiple Religious Traditions."
22. Lindbeck, 35.
23. Asscher, 60.
24. Makransky, "A Buddhist Critique of, and Learning from, Christian Liberation Theology."

PART II

Comparative Theology Is What Comparative Theology Does

7 Embodiment, Anthropology, and Comparison

THINKING-FEELING WITH NON-DUAL SAIVISM

Michelle Voss Roberts

Imagine the constructive theologian as a beachcomber. She attentively picks her way through the landscape of the Christian theological heritage, salvaging treasures that sparkle unexpectedly in the sun of the contemporary moment. From this or that angle, a dusty practice or neglected doctrine takes on new beauty. The theologian's tools of detection sound the alert: There is something relevant here, something useful, something true! The detectors include sensors for scriptural soundness, doctrinal fidelity, rational coherence, and contemporary resonance. Many different tools can be used to look and to dig.

Comparison belongs to the toolkit of constructive theology, although it sometimes goes unnamed as a methodology. Tina Beattie's *Theology After Postmodernity* takes up a project that can be loosely described as comparative: Beattie reads a Christian theologian (Thomas Aquinas) alongside a thinker from another discipline (the psychoanalyst Jacques Lacan) to address contemporary questions. Although she supports postmodernism's abandonment of absolute certainties and embrace of difference, she wants to challenge the postmodern rejection of metaphysics. Through the lens of the comparison, she finds new potential to rescue the metaphysical project:

> There are resources in Thomas's writings to construct a different account of the relationship between God and creation . . . and to imagine a less totalizing but more hopeful vision of the human species earthed in creation and dreaming of heaven, than what postmodernism offers.[1]

Lacan's methodology, and in particular his analysis of human desire, enables Beattie to recover the "repressed otherness in Thomas that awaits an outing."[2]

Lacan helps Beattie to recover desire and materiality in her reading of Thomas Aquinas, and through him, she retrieves the influence of Pseudo-Dionysius, for whom God is *beyond* Form and Being and is instead named as Goodness and Yearning. Beattie celebrates the Aquinas that writes,

> For God brought things into being in order that His goodness might be communicated to creatures, and be represented by them; and because His goodness could not be adequately represented by one creature alone, He produced many and diverse creatures, that what was wanting to one in the representation of the divine goodness might be supplied by another. For goodness, which in God is simple and uniform, in creatures is manifold and divided and hence the whole universe together participates in the divine goodness more perfectly, and represents it better than any single creature whatever.[3]

Beattie reclaims this metaphysic, in which creation proceeds from God and is destined to return to God, to celebrate diversity as the overflow of divine goodness. Although Lacan could never accept such a metaphysic, which he criticizes as a projection that lacks backing in reality, she holds it in Christian hope.

In this essay, I have found myself on the same beach, looking for the same treasure. I am tantalized by the ambiguities in Aquinas's theological anthropology that have never quite left Christian theology, particularly in relation to gender and materiality. Like Beattie and other feminist theologians, I find myself returning to Aquinas to comb through his work for clues to a holistic Christian view of the human person. He invites rereading because his comprehension of the earlier Christian tradition and his influence on the subsequent tradition cannot be ignored, and because his thought contains much subtlety and nuance that can assist the contemporary theological project. For myself, as for Beattie, constructive theology hinges on the point at which I begin to think about and feel the world through a category learned from another tradition or discipline. On one side of that hinge is a question generated by studying historical Christian theology—an irritant, if you will, created by an anthropology that excludes women, children, and persons with mental and intellectual disabilities from fully bearing the image of God. The hinge itself is where a solution to the problem starts to take hold: a new category begins to make sense as a way to organize the image of God in humanity. On the other side of the hinge lies constructive

Christian thought and new ways to acknowledge human dignity amid diversity.

I stroll the same beach as Beattie, but I hold a different comparative detector. Instead of Lacanian psychoanalysis and the scholarly discipline known as comparative literature, I am aided by comparative theology, the interreligious hermeneutic that is the subject of this volume. Study of non-dual Saiva (Hindu) theology helps me to rediscover the depths of the Christian tradition and to select the treasures to pick up and reexamine. One might argue that learning from Lacan is qualitatively different from learning from another religious tradition because he, Aquinas, and Beattie all operate within the same Catholic theological stream. However, this does not necessitate similarity: given Lacan's rejection of metaphysics, certain Hindu theologies are arguably closer to Christian assumptions and commitments. In any case, both comparative literature and comparative theology draw upon theory from disparate realms.

The non-dual Saiva theological system invites Christians to explore, expand, and invert aspects of a metaphysic of procession and return that might again inform theological anthropology. In its procession-return scheme, thirty-six principles (*tattva*s) emanate from Siva in creation and return to him in cosmic dissolution. The thirty-six range from the gross and subtle elements, through capacities for sensation, action, and individual consciousness, to subtle degrees of limitation and union with Siva. This scheme is reflected in the tradition's theological anthropology: The human being reflects all thirty-six principles. This metaphysical system appreciates diversity, multiplicity, and embodiment as reflecting the divine image. Christians have inherited a similar procession-return pattern from centuries of Christian Neoplatonist thinkers, but it has fallen to the wayside in postmodernity. Using the *tattva*s as the hinge in my constructive project, I wager that the procession-return metaphysic is worth another look.

Because this comparison concerns how human beings experience God and the world, it will also shed light on how theologians do comparative theology: Comparative theology is an embodied practice with multiple tiers of understanding. On this account, the *tattva* schema pushes Aquinas's anthropology toward greater appreciation for the epistemological contribution of the body, the senses, and other faculties for theology, so that constructive comparative theology can be seen as a practice of thinking-feeling with the categories and questions of another tradition.

Premodern Interventions in the Body-Soul Paradigm

Much of the appeal of Thomas Aquinas for theological anthropology lies in his positioning as a premodern thinker whose assumptions about the human being break away from well-ingrained habits of thought in the contemporary context. In contrast with certain modern, dualistic reductions of the human being to mind and matter, he follows Aristotle in espousing a theory known as hylomorphism. In this theory, everything that exists participates in both matter and form. Put differently, matter and form are always unified in particular things. Although Aquinas is sometimes tempted to view the human body as an impediment to imaging God fully, for him soul and body are inextricably related.[4] He defines the soul as "the first principle of life in those things which live" (Ia. 75) or "the form of the body" (Ia. 75, 5). The soul is the "substantial form" of the human being, which means that a human being is by definition *informed* by a human soul. The soul unifies the person; it permeates the entire body (Ia. 76, 8). The flip side of this teaching is that the senses and materiality are equally essential to being human. Without a body, a soul is not a human being.[5]

In addition to this deep enmeshment of body and soul, Aquinas resists modern dualisms by breaking down the body-soul complex into a multiplicity of parts. He does this in part because the soul, the essence of which is hidden, can be known only indirectly through its powers or potentialities (Ia. 77, 1). Following Aristotle, Aquinas sorts these powers into five genera: vegetative, sensitive, appetitive, locomotive, and intellectual (Ia. 78, 1). Each contains more parts. The *vegetative* power consists of nutritive, augmentative, and generative parts (Ia. 78, 2). The *sensitive* power names the five exterior senses, each directed to its respective object through the appropriate organ (Ia. 78, 3), and the interior senses, which include common sense, phantasy/imagination, estimation, and memory. The *appetitive* powers are analyzed in terms of the sensitive appetite and the intellectual appetite (Ia. 80, 2). The sensitive appetite, or sensuality, moves toward things apprehended by the physical senses (Ia. 81, 1); and it has two sub-types, one that seeks pleasure (the concupiscible) and one that avoids harm (the irascible) (Ia. 81, 2). The intellectual appetite includes both the will, or simple desire, and free-will, which is the power of choice governed by reason (Ia. 83, 2). The *intellectual* powers have a similar bifurcation: Understanding simply accepts knowledge, but reason moves from knowledge of principles to conclusions (Ia. 83,

4). With this multiplicity, Aquinas models a non-reductive view of the human person that attends to many facets of embodiment.

The distinctions between and within the various powers not only prevent Aquinas from reducing the human being to only two parts, but they also lend his thought to a nuanced treatment of their interrelationship. He identifies sensory and intellectual dimensions within higher powers such as memory, imagination, and desire (Ia. 79, 6). Form and matter are inseparable. The interior senses process external sensations and pivot them toward cognition (Ia. 85, 1).[6] Knowledge and understanding similarly rely on all of the other faculties (cf. Ia. 93, 2). Hylomorphism thus reaches into each of the soul's functions, so that even the basic vegetative and sensitive powers belong to the composite of the body and soul.

THE PRIORITY OF THE INTELLECT

Despite these nuances, Aquinas nevertheless restricts the image of God to the rational soul—specifically the intellect. How does he arrive at this position? And what are its implications for human diversity?

At the beginning of the "Treatise on Man" in the *Summa Theologiae* (Ia. 75–102),[7] Aquinas identifies what he considers as theologically significant about the human being: "Now the theologian considers the nature of man in relation to the soul; but not in relation to the body, except in so far as the body has relation to the soul" (Ia. 75). Soul and body thus remain the major divisions in the human person, and the soul is what matters for theology. Aquinas further pinpoints the intellect as the most theologically significant aspect of the soul. He writes that other than the intellect and will, "the other powers of the soul do not come directly under the consideration of the theologian" (Ia. 84). Therefore, when he discusses the parts of the soul, he dispatches the vegetative, sensitive, and locomotive powers fairly quickly because, for him, they do not yet point to what is essential to being human. After all, animals share many of the same abilities to receive and process information.

Aquinas provides more analysis as he moves into the *appetitive* powers, which have obvious relevance for human moral life. Here humans and animals differ. Animals are governed by a sensual appetite that exhibits a kind of reason ("particular reason"), as when sheep fear wolves because they naturally estimate the threat wolves pose to their lives. In humans, the sensitive appetite is also guided by "universal reason" through the intellectual appetite or will (Ia. 78, 4; Ia. 81, 3). The will and the intellect distinguish humans as properly human. However, they exhibit such a close relationship that the will is nearly eclipsed by the intellect's governance (Ia. 82).[8]

The *intellectual* powers receive the bulk of the Treatise's attention (Ia. 84–89 and passim). Here, the point of comparison shifts from animals to angels, the purely intellectual beings that are closer to God in the hierarchy of creation. Unlike the human intellect, which knows forms by abstracting from material substances by way of the phantasms, the angelic intellect relies on neither corporeal organs nor matter. Aquinas writes that "the human intellect holds a middle place" (Ia. 85, 1) because of its inherent enmeshment with bodies.

Aquinas's fixation on the intellect forfeits many of the merits of his hylomorphic anthropology. When he ties the image of God in humanity to the intellect, his theological anthropology excludes many people from the fullness of the *imago Dei* (Ia. 93, 2). He views differences in intellectual ability primarily along gender lines, with the consequence that women do not possess the image of God in equal measure to men (Ia. 93, 4, ad. 1; and Ia. 92, 1, ad. 2). His androcentric perspective views woman as a "misbegotten male" (Ia. 92, 1). A hierarchy applies to other physical differences as well, for "it is plain that the better the disposition of a body, the better the soul allotted to it" (Ia. 85, 7). Thus, not only women, but anyone whose body is impaired, cannot fully "imitate God in his intellectual nature" (Ia. 93, 4). Beattie draws out Aquinas's underlying discomfort with materiality and embodied difference. Despite the characteristics of his anthropology already described, his "understanding of contemplation is Platonic rather than Aristotelian, and it is implicitly predicated upon a dualistic concept of God as form and body as matter, so that the closer one comes to union with God, the more one rises above one's material condition."[9]

Theologians informed by feminist, disability, and critical race theories view such pronouncements with a strong hermeneutic of suspicion. To return to the beachcomber metaphor, once this anthropology is unearthed, its underside turns up rotten, pecked away by some gull. The link between good bodies and good souls diminishes the dignity and moral agency of persons with mental disabilities and, indeed, anyone whose embodiment is considered inferior to cultural norms. Beyond simply rejecting these ideas as outmoded, these theologians recognize how such assumptions continue to undergird both popular and academic theological perspectives. They continue the search for a better specimen.

Because the dualisms Beattie identifies are entrenched in metaphysics, the theological solution for an inclusive anthropology may require an alternative metaphysic. The non-dual Saiva conception of how humanity reflects the divine is a good candidate. In this view, all parts flow from, return to, and resemble God, allowing differences and multiplicity to become values rather than deficits. I outline its articulated theological anthropology in the next section.

Toward an "Extensible" Concept of Embodiment

This summary follows the discussion of the *tattvas* in an agamic scripture, *The Goddess of the Three* (*Paratrisika*). My reading is informed by two commentaries on this text, the long commentary (*Paratrisika-Vivarana*) by the great tenth/eleventh-century theologian Abhinavagupta, and a short commentary that is attributed to him, but is more likely of later South Indian provenance (*Paratrisikalaghuvrtti*, PTlv).[10] In this essay, I focus on the latter, which I treat as part of Abhinavagupta's tradition: These texts fall within the Trika sub-tradition of non-dual Saivism, of which Abhinavagupta is the most influential exponent. His broader Tantric (i.e., non-Vedic) tradition is sometimes called Kashmir Saivism; but because these traditions must be distinguished from others in Kashmir that name ultimate reality as Siva, and because they are not limited to Kashmir, as the South Indian origin of the short commentary demonstrates, I employ the term *non-dual Saivism* in this essay.[11]

The non-dual Saiva tradition modifies the metaphysical scheme of the Samkhya school, which posits a dualism between spirit (*purusa*) and matter (*prakrti*), the first two of twenty-five metaphysical categories (*tattvas*) in Samkhya metaphysics. In Samkhya, the masculine *purusa* is the uninvolved witness of the feminine *prakrti*, material creation. Liberation is achieved by transcending the constraints of matter and identifying instead with *purusa*. Non-dual Saivism overcomes this dualism by enveloping it in eleven higher levels of Siva's consciousness, for a total of thirty-six *tattvas*. Here, *purusa* is not the transcendent cosmic principle but the individual center of consciousness that, in each person, mirrors the movement of divine consciousness.

In the non-dual Saiva imagination, the first two *tattvas* differentiate Siva from Sakti, his feminine counterpart. Rather than reinscribing the gendered Samkhya dualism between spirit and matter, "Sakti" names Siva's own power or energy. *The Goddess of the Three* is a dialogue between the divine couple. The beginning of the short commentary explains that the questioner, Siva, and the questioned, Sakti, are, in fact, one. This unity applies as well to the remaining *tattvas* that emerge from them: They are all Siva; and, likewise, they are all Sakti. The title, *Paratrisika*, names Sakti "goddess of the three," because she differentiates herself as pure consciousness (*para sakti*, or *siva*), awareness of unity in difference (*parapara sakti*), and created diversity (*apara sakti* or *nara*, lit. "man"). The third category refers broadly to external creation and narrowly to its microcosm in every conscious being, including humans.[12] Each level of reality can be read as masculine (*siva*, *siva*'s *sakti*, *nara*) or feminine (the three *saktis*: *para*, *parapara*, and *apara*).

Together, the thirty-six modifications of divine consciousness are viewed as the divine body, "the body of consciousness or body of light." This body is recapitulated twice: in the macrocosm of the world and in the microcosm of individual beings. Gavin Flood explains, "The idea of the body is therefore extensible and has variable meaning."[13] This extensible concept of embodiment, in which all of the *tattvas* can be viewed as the body of Siva, the body of the cosmos, and the body of every human being, has the potential to expand traditional Christian ways of conceiving of the human person as the image of God.[14]

This extensible body can be approached in two ways: from the "top down," as it were, or the "bottom up." The visual schematic of the *tattvas* is usually arranged vertically, with the unity of divine consciousness (Siva) at the top and the gross elements at the bottom.

Tattvas 1–5	Degrees of Subject-Object Union and Differentiation
Tattvas 6–11	Powers of Limitation
Tattvas 12–16	Capacities for Individual Consciousness
Tattvas 17–21	Capacities for Action
Tattvas 22–26	Capacities for Sensation
Tattvas 27–31	Subtle Elements
Tattvas 32–36	Gross Elements

Read from the top down, this scheme tells a story of how creation emanates outward from the unity of consciousness.

Read from the bottom up, the *tattvas* trace the journey by which a conscious being can return to Siva and realize the divine unity that is the pulsing heart of created diversity. The short commentary on verses 6–8 of *The Goddess of the Three* takes this bottom-up approach. We will follow its treatment of the thirty-six parts in five groups. Although the text esoterically names them using the thirty-six phonemes in the Sanskrit alphabet,[15] I designate the groups more descriptively as the elemental body, the engaged body, the subjective body, the limited body, and the contemplative body.[16]

THE ELEMENTAL BODY

The short commentary explains what each group includes, beginning from the bottom of the hierarchy, with the gross and subtle elements.

> There now occurs the appearance of knowable objects . . . As knowable objects begin to appear, begin to separate themselves, there occur, on the gross level, the five gross elements and, on the subtle level, the five subtle elements. This results in ten principles, namely: earth, water, fire, air, space, smell, taste, form, touch, and sound. This is the manifestation of the knowable objects. (PTlv, 210)

As a general cosmological principle, the parts on the bottom of the hierarchy are the most dense or coagulated. These are the gross elements (*mahabhutas*): space/ether, air, fire, water, and earth. Objects in these *tattvas* can be known and felt.[17]

The gross elements provide the foundation for the rest of the cosmic body. These five correspond to other pentads in the hierarchy, starting with the five subtle elements (*tanmatras*): sound, touch, form, taste, and smell. These correspond in homologous fashion with the gross elements so that sound resonates in space, touch is mediated by air, and so forth. The subtle elements give rise to the gross elements as creation unfolds downward. They also mediate the interaction of the "higher" principles with the physical realm.

In the cosmic body, each *tattva* contains multiple worlds of experience. The human world, along with the worlds of plants, insects, birds, wild animals, and domestic animals, is part of the earth *tattva*.[18] These beings are determined by the gross elements to such an extent that, for many of them, their consciousness extends no further. Flood explains,

> A person's experience or perception of a world depends upon the degree of contraction or revelation of supreme consciousness: the more contracted supreme consciousness is, the more particularized and individualized it becomes and the more limited the world of experience or perception.[19]

Because each part is recapitulated at each level (divine, cosmic, and individual), however, individuals are not bound to one *tattva*. Even though the human world manifests within the lowest realm of creation, liberating awareness is possible. With training, human beings can follow the movements of procession and return, experience all levels of the cosmos, and access them at will.

THE ENGAGED BODY

The next ten parts of the cosmic body engage the "knowable objects" just described. The engaged body consists of the capacities (*indriyas*: "powers" or "organs") for sensation and action. The short commentary explains,

> At the same time [as the appearance of the knowable objects], the sense capacities are being manifested as instruments of cognition. That is to say, the five action-capacities, namely, sexual, excretory, ambulatory, grasping, and speaking, in which the power of action predominates; and the five sense-capacities, smelling, tasting, seeing, touching, and hearing, in which the power of cognition predominates. (PTlv, 210)

The capacities for sense (*buddhindriyas*) and capacities for action (*karmendriyas*) correspond with one another in a manner that parallels the gross and subtle elements, pairing hearing with speaking, touching with grasping, and so on.

Because these parts of the body of consciousness manifest in human beings as the organs that perform these functions, they are sometimes listed as ears, hands, eyes, tongue, nose, and so forth. In the cosmic body, however, the "organs" are principles that make sensation and action possible. Embodied beings participate in these principles insofar as they possess ears and the like, and insofar as they apply them to their respective tasks.

As with the lower group of ten, these capacities both arise from the higher principles of consciousness and provide objects for them. They "manifest as instruments of cognition" (PTlv, 210). Everything we hear, touch, see, taste, and smell, as well as the activities of daily life, becomes data for the next set of faculties to process.

THE SUBJECTIVE BODY

Continuing to climb the cosmic hierarchy, the next five parts of the cosmic body account for an individual's engagement, as a subject, with the twenty principles already enumerated.

> Then, when by gradual degrees, the aspect of the "knowable objects" begins to diminish, the perceiving aspect begins to manifest itself, namely: mind, egoity, intellect, primordial materiality, and individual consciousness. (PTlv, 211)

This set of capacities refracts what many modern thinkers reduce to the rational mind. Four fall within the class of matter (*prakrti*), and only the highest, "individual consciousness," (*purusa*) transcends the material realm.

Materiality (*prakrti*) governs the three principles of inner awareness (*antahkarana*): the intelligence or volition (*buddhi*), the ego or sense of "I" (*ahamkara*), and the mind-heart (*manas*), which is the seat of the emotions as well as the faculty that receives sensory data and forms concepts from it.

Individual consciousness (*purusa*) in the earlier dualistic Samkhya philosophy is utterly separate from the material realm: It neither acts on matter nor causes it to come into existence, but merely witnesses or observes. When non-dual Saivism places additional powers above *purusa*, it too becomes an object for higher divine consciousness: "The individual consciousness, even though it is a limited perceiver, is here reckoned as belonging to the group of knowable objects. For without it, who would perceive the objects of knowledge beginning with 'earth'?" (PTlv, 211). This *tattva* constitutes human beings as individual centers of awareness and subjectivity, or the "who" who perceives.

THE LIMITED BODY

Non-dual Saivism next envelops the preceding twenty-five parts of the body within five more parts, the "sheaths" (*kancukas*). These principles explain *how* universal consciousness can be particularized into individual centers of consciousness. The sheaths are Siva's own powers (*saktis*) of limitation, which give him the ability to contract divine consciousness. Without them, Siva would simply be pure consciousness, unable to apprehend any object. The first limitation is the veil of consciousness (*maya* or *mahamaya*),[20] followed by limited power, limited knowledge, and limited satisfaction (desire). Lists sometimes also include limitation in time and limitation in space (contingency).[21] Continuing the pattern of homology, these powers correlate with the elements. For example, air impels a limited capacity for action, and fire illuminates a limited capacity for knowledge (PTlv, 211).

If these *tattvas* are divine powers for Siva, humans ordinarily experience them as deficits because they veil the unity of reality. The short commentary explains that these powers "maintain the individual soul resting in the middle . . . which otherwise would fall into the condition of complete inertia like a rock, or would ascend into the sky of consciousness like the supreme Lord" (PTlv, 211). In other words, without these limitations as parts of the extended human body, we could neither differentiate ourselves from Siva nor transcend the state of insentient earth.

Because human beings do not experience divine omnipotence, omniscience, satiety, and freedom, we ordinarily cannot recognize our true identity as pure consciousness. Limited power, impure knowledge, desire, and boundedness in time and space form the conditions within which individual centers of consciousness (*purusa*) can arise. All of these limitations are permutations of the cosmic principle of artifice, *maya*, which in turn evolves from the final, and most subtle, set of *tattvas*.

THE CONTEMPLATIVE BODY

All of the body parts described so far, from *maya* to the earth principle, are known as the "impure path" because they smudge the mirror of consciousness and prevent created beings from comprehending the unity amid diversity. With the contemplative body, we arrive at the five remaining principles, the "pure path." Each of these principles marks a subtle degree of differentiation from the pure consciousness of "I" to the gradual apprehension of an object. Again, this group correlates with the elements: "[Suddha]Vidya, Isvara, Sadasiva, Sakti and Siva . . . are formed of the 'subtle' earth, water, fire, air and space" (PTlv, 211).

When a person traces these parts of the cosmic body to their source through contemplation, awareness of objects gradually recedes back into pure consciousness:

> When the aspect of objectivity begins by degrees to be concealed, and the form of consciousness begins to unfold, then to that degree there oc-

> curs a firmness, an increasing fullness of the form of consciousness; a union with its light, a vibration which is characterized by the attainment of supreme freedom. Everything is then thoroughly pervaded by the form of consciousness. (PTlv, 211)

From the perspective of these higher aspects of consciousness, each of the thirty-six parts is non-different from Siva, from whom they emanate and to whom they return.

This process takes place in vast cosmic cycles of creation and dissolution, but it also occurs within every moment. As Paul Muller-Ortega puts it, "the expansive-contractive impulse occurs so rapidly that the manifestation is simultaneously established as gross and fully formed, and at the same time, it is always fully abiding in the undifferentiated unity."[22] Non-dual Saiva contemplative practices attempt to grasp this simultaneity by observing mundane processes, such as breathing, thinking, perceiving, and enjoying food and art. Each of these experiences encapsulates the subtle movement of subject-object union and differentiation that is at the heart of reality.[23]

Comparison

In my search for a holistic and life-giving theology, my theological detector is set for several features that invite comparisons between these traditions. Multiplicity is intrinsic to both theological anthropologies. Neither reduces humanity to a single feature. Rather, they consider diverse human capacities, which they arrange on a spectrum from the subtle to the gross (non-dual Saivism) or the relatively simple to the relatively complex (Neoplatonism). Their detailed analyses of the parts or powers of the human being can prevent any single faculty from monopolizing theological anthropology. For all his emphasis on the rational intellect, Aquinas does not conflate intellect with the soul, which remains the "form" of the human body and "principle" of the intellect and other powers.[24]

Both insist that the faculties are interrelated. The commentaries on *The Goddess of the Three* trace homologies, in which the pattern of the gross elements replicates itself in each successive set. For Aquinas the body is so essential to being human that the "separated soul," which exists between death and the life to come (Ia. 89), is not truly a human being until reunited with a body at the resurrection.[25] Furthermore, even though Aquinas teaches that the intellect belongs not to the body but to the soul alone (Ia. 77, 5), he is explicit that the higher capacities rely upon the lower capacities, and that numerous bridge faculties, such as the imagination, process and mediate the flow of information.

Both traditions recognize natural and legitimate limits for created beings. Non-dual Saivism makes this explicit through the inclusion of limitations within the divine reflection in creation. Readers of Aquinas might not notice it without comparison with Abhinavagupta's tradition, but for Aquinas, the location of the embodied human intellect in the hierarchy of beings denotes its limits. Because the soul is "the form of the body," its powers exhibit particular capabilities and limitations related to embodiment (Ia. 85, 1). Furthermore, just as the human intellect cannot rival that of the angels, angels in turn are limited through the lack of bodies.

Finally, both traditions also dignify the human being by speaking of humanity as the reflection or image of the divine. While Christians identify humanity as the image of God, non-dualist Saivas see the entire cosmos, replicated in the human being, as the reflection of divine consciousness. An Aristotelian Thomist might worry that this emanationist view obliterates important distinctions between human beings and other creatures. However, because different species have different degrees of access to the thirty-six grades of this reflection, the non-dual Saiva view does not call into question the fact of human distinctiveness. Instead, it reframes the nature and content of this distinctiveness. Christian interpretations of the *imago Dei* often focus on individual capacities, such as when Aquinas locates the image in rationality. Because feminist, queer, disabilities, and critical race theories have proven that this approach is not as helpful or accurate as it might be, Christians can learn to think about the full range of faculties within the human being, which are not separate from the rest of creation, as mirroring the divine image. The implications of this comparison require a much larger project.[26]

In order to clear the way for this constructive work at the level of theological anthropology, obstacles in Aquinas's metaphysics, which provide the foundation for his anthropology, must be addressed.

ANTHROPOLOGY AND METAPHYSICS

Abhinavagupta's tradition links anthropology to metaphysics: The human being mirrors both the cosmos and divinity itself. This metaphysic consistently reads the pattern of creation's unfolding through every conscious being. Each of the thirty-six parts of the divine body is replicated in individual beings.

Aquinas writes in a period of competing metaphysical systems; and although he achieves a unique synthesis of Platonist, Aristotelian, and Neoplatonist systems that proved influential for many theologians after him, his anthropology maps inconsistently onto these systems. The following paragraphs observe how, when disconnected from Neoplatonist elements, his Platonist and Aristotelian leanings lead to distortions in theological anthropology. Although this inconsistency is the point at which his theological anthropology breaks down, it is also the opening to develop the helpful dimensions of his thought. In particular, Christian theological anthropology would benefit from reconnecting with the Neoplatonist metaphysics of procession and return, which is both important for Aquinas and much of the broader Christian tradition and also creates space to learn from its resemblances to non-dual Saiva metaphysics.

The combination of Platonist, Aristotelian, and Neoplatonist philosophical elements in Aquinas's thought contributes to the inconsistency. We have seen that Beattie faults his Platonist notion of contemplation for his repression of the body and desire. In this view, human beings participate in divinity primarily through the intellect, which is also the central dimension of the image and likeness of God. Human beings possess an "intellectual light . . . [which] is nothing else than a participated likeness of the uncreated light" (Ia. 84, 5). As pure intellect, angels reside closest to God in the created hierarchy. Human souls are below angels and "hold the lowest place among intellectual substances" (Ia. 89, 1). Irrational creatures fall short of God's image because of a lesser degree of participation (Ia. 93, 2, ad. 1). The likeness to God sufficient to call a being created "in the image" of God occurs only in beings with the capacity for intellect, and most of all in those who imitate God's example via understanding. If we hold up this model of the *imago Dei* next to the thirty-six *tattvas*, we see that Aquinas cuts off at least twenty-two of the *tattvas* (everything "below" intelligence or *buddhi*) from reflecting the divine image.[27]

Even as readers can locate Platonist assumptions in Aquinas, he joined the medieval revival of Aristotle so enthusiastically that references to "the Philosopher" abound in his work. Just as Aristotle, in his rejection of the forms, preferred to think from particular things (substances) to larger categories, Aquinas discusses the various classes of beings in terms of substance. He describes human beings, for example, as "composed of a spiritual and corporeal substance" (Ia. 75). He also borrows a robust theory of causality from Aristotle.

Aquinas does not follow Aristotle's rejection of the forms so far as to reject the possibility of an idea of the Good, a self-subsistent form that "could be regarded as identical with the universal principle of all things, which is God."[28] Like many of his contemporaries, including Bonaventure, Mechthild of Magdeburg, and Meister Eckhart, he teaches that because created things *exist*, they participate in *being*. They also participate in *goodness* insofar as they exist.[29] They inherited this less-dichotomous version of the form-matter relationship from a Neoplatonist Christian tradition stemming from the second century, which was passed on especially through Pseudo-Dionysius. A Neoplatonist notion of participation, in which finite things participate imperfectly in a realm of eternal, immaterial forms, encouraged these early and medieval Christians to develop a theory of creation in which all things emanate from, return to, and participate to various degrees in God. As we have seen, however, Aquinas chooses not to follow his Neoplatonist predecessors and peers in imagining the soul's ascent to God via a continuum between matter and form; instead, his ideal of the contemplative life returns to the earlier, more dichotomous Platonist model.

Contemporary theologians including Beattie emphasize that Pseudo-Dionysius is a significant source for Aquinas, which creates tantalizing possibilities for developing his thought.[30] However, despite vestiges of an emanation-return movement in his thought, his understanding of God's causality (borrowed from Aristotle) effectively breaks up the continuum of participation in the Christian Neoplatonist imagination. For him, God imparts a likeness to creatures as their *efficient cause*. Beings may then accrue an additional degree of likeness when they imitate God as their *exemplary cause*, but they retain a distinct, non-divine substance.[31] Created things disclose a "likeness (similitude)" to God that differs from God's essence, which "remains 'unparticipated and uncommunicated.'"[32] Aquinas thus develops a Neoplatonist vocabulary of participation within an Aristotelian notion of causality. With these distinctions, Aquinas guards against the idea that created things can be or become divine, as might be inferred from both Neoplatonist and non-dual Saiva emanation models. From this angle, the continuity of participation is cut off at the very beginning: created substances participate in *no part* of God's essence, but can only imitate and become like God.

On the question of whether and how created beings participate in God, then, Aquinas is not entirely consistent. By contrast, Abhinavagupta's tradition tethers divinity to every type of embodiment. In this metaphysic, every degree of creation manifests divine power (*sakti*). It consistently replicates the pattern of divine embodiment in the human being; and multilayered homologies within the pattern (as when the "pentad of brahman" reflects the five gross elements) keep the "lower" enmeshed with the "higher" at every stage.

CONSTRUCTIVE REFLECTIONS

Exclusions of entire classes of people from the *imago Dei* persist in Christian theology today.[33] In light of this troubling pattern, and in light of the inconsistent metaphysics that has at various times undergirded it, Christian theologians might reinvigorate the metaphor of emanation and return. If this model was already beginning to fall out of favor in Aquinas, who preferred Aristotle's empiricism, it was nearly erased when Enlightenment science met the iconoclasm of the Protestant Reformations. The gulf between Creator and creation widened, with only the more mystical and ecological strands of Christianity retaining a continuum of being between them. Though the emanation-return rhythm has waned in modern thought, the history of Christian interpretation does provide a clear Christian precedent from which to retrieve such a metaphysics. If contemporary Christian theologians would not only recognize the flux of religious and philosophical influence as a historical fact but also take it up as the source of constructive possibility, the framework of the *tattvas* might inspire a creative new take on this metaphysical pattern.[34]

I am not suggesting that Christians adopt this particular schema as the definitive map of reality, much less return to earlier philosophical worldviews such as Neoplatonism. All maps of reality, including scientific explanations, are metaphorical: They use words and images to make sense of the world, and in turn they shape how we interact with the world. However, this rubric does open new routes through problems that haunt Christian theological anthropology. It offers novel ways to imagine the relationship of human beings with the rest of material creation. It gives a framework for cognizing the dignity of human beings amid our diversity. Thinking-feeling with the *tattvas* allows the comparativist to try on a metaphysical framework that houses a robust and holistic anthropology.

A constructive theological anthropology in conversation with non-dual Saivism can reinvigorate the theological language of participation. Although Aquinas seizes upon the intellect as the means of human participation in God, his wider theological commitments—God as the Good and existence as participation in the Good—leave the door open for other modes of participation that involve a full range of faculties within the human being.

It will also be helpful to view all dimensions of existence not only as "powers" or "faculties" but as parts of the body as non-dual Saivism does. The *tattva*s represent an internally diverse "body." They also direct attention to the many grades of physicality, providing a theological impetus to think more holistically about the human person. Rather than separating body and soul, matter and spirit, Christian theologians may view all of the human capacities as a spectrum of divine and human embodiment and, therefore, as theologically significant.

Most importantly, perhaps, a constructive Christian theology in light of the *tattva*s will acknowledge multiple dimensions to the image of God. Because Aquinas focuses on the intellect and will, which are conceptualized under *buddhi*/intellect-volition and *manas*/mind-heart in Indian thought, Aquinas's analysis may aid in further constructive work on these faculties. However, Aquinas diminishes the importance of the vegetative, locomotive, and sensory powers. Not only does he devote a relatively tiny amount of space to them, but he also draws negative contrasts with other beings (animals, angels) in relation to them. Abhinavagupta's categories offer correctives to prevalent assumptions about the status of the rational mind in Christian theological anthropology. Re-reading Aquinas through the extensible body of non-dual Saiva metaphysics, Christians can reclaim parts of the human that Aquinas acknowledges but does not develop. The holistic reach of the *tattva*s can inspire Christian theologians toward a more robust and inclusive anthropology that reincorporates the powers Aquinas names as theologically insignificant (the elements, the senses and organs of action, and limitations) as well as individual mental abilities.

Thinking-Feeling as a Comparative Theologian

The intellect takes up the lion's share of attention, not only in theological anthropology, but also in epistemology and discussions of theological method. If the constructive anthropology I have sketched is valid, then comparative methodology might attend to multiple, embodied ways of knowing. My analogy with the beach comber has already implied as much: what one treasures depends on sensory, emotional, and aesthetic ways of knowing, as well as rational notions of what is useful, good, or beautiful. Theology does not stop with the rational mind but relates to many facets of engagement.[35] The non-dual Saiva view of the extensible body can help to name how comparative theology performs this work.

In this map of the human being, a basic pattern replicates itself at each level. I venture to extend this homological manner of thinking one step further by suggesting that the *tattva*s correspond to a range of methodological approaches in comparative theology. The *tattva*s suggest that we not only *think* but *feel* with other traditions, in every sense of the word. Each group—the elemental body consisting of the gross and subtle elements, the engaged body of sensation and action, the subjective body with its capacities for individual consciousness, the limited body, and the contemplative body's subtle degrees of unity in differentiation—belongs to the corpus of this discipline. To demonstrate this thesis, I focus on the subset of comparative theology's growing canon with which I am most familiar: Hindu-Christian studies.

THE CONTEMPLATIVE BODY

Comparative theology has been presented as an alternative to an "impasse" in the theology of religions, in which the classic theories posit either complete difference between religious systems (exclusivism), basic sameness (pluralism), or some mechanism by which one tradition participates imperfectly in the truth best represented by another (inclusivism).[36] Non-dualist Saivas might say we cannot resolve this discussion because the answers lie in the contemplative body. One must pass beyond the veils of *maya* to ascertain the subtle relations between subject and object, unity and difference. Most mortals can hope only to glimpse this level of reality because their particular limitations of history, culture, and religious tradition prevent them from gaining a clear understanding of the whole. However, with attention to the contemplative body, the practitioner can hold religious difference in tension with these insights, which transcend human cognition.

The place of unknowing, beyond the reach of ordinary human faculties, can also become a space for comparison: This is where Francis X.

Clooney locates his recent book, *His Hiding Place Is Darkness*.[37] His interlocutors in both the Hindu and Christian traditions dwell in unknowing, rupture, and the dark night of the soul; and the comparativist sometimes dwells there as well.

THE LIMITED BODY

The first principle of the limited body of consciousness is *maya*, which veils the relationship of creation with the Absolute. Here, people not only perceive particular beings that are delimited in time and space; but they also perceive *as* particular, limited beings. The contingency of knowledge, which dawned as something of a revelation in the study of religion, lies behind the discipline of comparative theology. Hugh Nicholson describes this "new comparativism," as "interested and placed," with a commitment to "openly acknowledging the comparativist's own theological and political commitments."[38] As comparative theologians have become aware of the political realities and often hegemonic tendencies of their discipline, they have become more adept at identifying the limitations of their work. Particularity, both of scholars and the religious traditions they study, has become a watchword of comparison.

The sheaths of *maya* provide categories for locating limitations: power, knowledge, satisfaction, time, and place. Each houses a set of questions about contingency and method. Power: On one side, what professional and institutional constraints do comparativists experience on their scholarship? On the other side, many of the shells on the beach are homes to living things; indeed they *are* living things. The beachcomber risks doing harm when she handles them. In what ways does comparison itself exert power in the post-colonial/neo-colonial setting? Knowledge: Scholars in a postmodern world can no longer pretend omniscience. What lies beyond the scholar's knowledge, either because of insufficient preparation or the particularities of one's training? Satisfaction: What desires drive comparative inquiry? A lack in one's own tradition? Something that beckons from another tradition? Time: How does historical positioning affect this work? Place: How do travel and geographical point of origin shape comparative inquiry? Just as the list of limitations varies between non-dual Saiva sources, comparativists might theorize other factors, perhaps particular to themselves, that set parameters around their work.

THE SUBJECTIVE BODY

It almost goes without saying that the capacities of the subjective body, particularly thinking, are central to scholarship. This is the realm of subject and object, *purusa* and *prakrti*, where the sense of self (*ahamkara*), the intelligence-volition (*buddhi*), and the mind-heart (*manas*) flex their muscles in exercises of writing, thinking, and evaluating. Clooney examines reason's usefulness in comparative theology on topics such as the existence and nature of God in *Hindu God-Christian God: How Reason Helps Break Down the Boundaries Between Religions*.[39]

Reason does not encompass the full spectrum of the subjective body. In accordance with the resonances of *manas* as mind-heart, Clooney also demonstrates the affective dimensions of comparative reading when he describes being "won over by the text and to the purposes of its author and community . . . [and] surrendering in love," as he encounters Srivaisnava devotional texts.[40] Tracy Sayuki Tiemeier's work on the Tamil poet saint Andal explicitly calls for sensitivity to the mind-heart that blurs distinctions between intellectual and affective approaches.[41] So, too, Jeannine Hill Fletcher observes that the affective disposition of wonder often attends interreligious encounter.[42] Each of these studies expands the capacities of cognition and awareness deemed relevant for comparison.

THE ENGAGED BODY

Human bodies permit various degrees of hearing, touching, seeing, tasting, smelling, speaking, grasping, walking, excreting, and sexual intimacy. These ten capacities for sensation and action constitute the engaged body. Beyond hearing and speaking, how might these be relevant to theological method? Metaphorically, Clooney's *Seeing Through Texts* uses visual terminology, and my book *Tastes of the Divine* employs the Indian notion of aesthetic tasting (*rasa*) to comprehend interreligious encounter.[43] A strictly metaphorical approach to sensation and action, however, would again place comparison within reason's grasp, i.e., *thinking about* senses rather than engaging in sensation and action.

Comparative theology is an embodied activity with embodied effects. Clooney excels at showing readers how to cultivate the dispositions and habits modeled in religious texts. With him, we learn styles of being in the world such as how to read like a Vedantin and to surrender to God like a Srivaisnava.[44] Similarly, Reid Locklin describes his work on the performative aspects of Sankara's texts as aspiring "not merely to read the *Upadesasahasri* as a sacred text, but to participate in its scripts as a privileged, sacred practice closely akin to liturgical performance: a *liturgy of liberation*, enacted through oral performance."[45] Jon Paul Sydnor's experiments with aesthetic vision likewise demonstrate how senses and sensitivities do comparative work.[46] Looking ahead, ethnography provides clues to a fully embodied comparative theological method. Its promise for the discipline is only beginning to emerge.[47]

THE ELEMENTAL BODY

The elemental body represents the foundation upon which embodiment depends: sound and space, touch and air, form and fire, taste and water, smell and earth. As with sensation, language treats these metaphorically; but, as I have demonstrated elsewhere, elements are more than metaphors. Because nearly every embodied being has some experience of them, they provide a level of shared experience upon which comparisons can be constructed.[48] Furthermore, as strife increases over the allocation of water, land, and air, concerns of ecological justice will likely become an important site of comparative theological inquiry in relation to the elements.

The method of homology, in which the five gross elements have resonances at each of the "higher" realms of discourse, invites theology to remain grounded. Homology calls into question the vertical, hierarchical arrangement of the *tattvas*. Instead, the vertical descent into matter can be flipped on its side so that divine awareness of diversity and materiality unfolds horizontally. In this vein, Beattie proposes that "the idea of creation as hierarchical emanation from the divine being yields to a more horizontal celebration of diversity as a good in itself, a diversity in which God is revealed and worshipped." She continues,

> Our capacity to understand something of God is enriched by our ability to see something unique of God in every species and individual that we encounter. Not only does Thomas argue that "God is in all things," he also argues that "as the soul is whole in every part of the body, so is God whole in all things and in each one." This is an astonishing insight that opens into a mystical sense of being beyond all human comprehension.[49]

The non-dual Saiva metaphysic of emanation, when reclaimed alongside the mystical, Neoplatonist strands in Aquinas, can help contemporary theologians find divine presence in every corner of creation.

The elemental body may present the largest challenge for the method of comparative theology. The "language" of the things closest at hand is difficult to incorporate, even more than the subtleties of the contemplative body, in part because it has been so undervalued. We are only beginning to ascertain whether and how cultural and other differences affect the basic, elemental means of knowledge. By proposing a horizontal trajectory for theological knowledge, however, we remember that human beings belong to the earth *tattva*, where all of our comparative and theological activity begins.

Still on the Beach

I have laid out the treasures of my comparative theological beachcombing. They sparkle in the presence of one another; their possibilities leap into view when placed side by side in this morning's light. But what has been accomplished, really? Have I produced any real and replicable knowledge?

Comparative studies have been accused of being more art than science, magic rather than scholarship, figments of the individual imagination rather than rational discovery.[50] The accusations point to an unavoidable truth about the humanities in general and comparison in particular. There are good historical, structural, and topical warrants for comparing Aquinas and Abhinavagupta, but in order to move from many potential comparisons to an actual event of comparison, scholars rely just as much upon the quirks of formation that impel them to pick up certain things, and not others, on the beaches where they like to stroll.

To elaborate: This comparison has activated memories of my own tradition along with the affects and aversions I associate with them. Indeed, the misogyny and patriarchy embedded in Aquinas's Treatise have been a nagging presence in my mind ever since I began studying theology, even as Aquinas's dialogical way of engaging diverse sources gives me hope for the theological task. Given my posture toward these aspects of the Christian tradition, non-dual Saiva thought captures my imagination and kindles my creativity. These affective responses derive from the particularities of my embodiment, not least my gender, my positioning within higher education, and my various limitations.

The comparison also stems from desire, especially insofar as it leans toward constructive theology. I long for a coherent and life-giving worldview, a hospitable and responsible way to engage religious neighbors, and so forth. Thus, I have not merely lined up the non-dual Saiva map of the human person alongside that of Thomas Aquinas. Being imaginatively caught up in its creative movement of emanation and return, I have rediscovered how this motion has felt, and might again feel, as a Christian idiom in the contemporary moment. Because I am committed to the flourishing of persons who have been marginalized by doctrines of the human person, I have focused on positive opportunities for a holistic and inclusive anthropology.

In thinking-feeling with the *tattva*s about comparison, I hope to have thought in a new style about the methods comparative theologians already employ. Comparative work is certainly not devoid of reason or method, but this should not be emphasized at the expense of the affects and desires that are important parts of all human inquiry, whether acknowledged or not. This comparison opens new ways to recognize these faculties and to employ them attentively. Like any metaphor, the *tattva*s are a limited and imperfect construct: they reveal only what they are deployed to help us to think, feel, and perceive. Nevertheless, these categories may offer helpful modifications to assumptions about the status of the rational mind—not only in theological anthropology, but in comparative theological method as well.

Notes

1. Beattie, *Theology After Postmodernity*, 90.
2. Ibid.
3. *ST* Ia. 47, 1, cited in Beattie, *Theology After Postmodernity*, 316. Unless otherwise noted, citations follow the Benziger Brothers translation of Aquinas, *Summa Theologica*. I reference the first part (Ia.), the question number, and the number of the article or reply to an objection (ad.) within that question.
4. Although Christians sometimes speak of the human being as body, soul, and spirit, Aquinas describes spirit as a subcategory of the soul: "The rational soul is both soul and spirit. It is called a soul by reason of what it possesses in common with other souls—that is, as giving life to the body. . . . But the soul is called a spirit according to what properly belongs to itself, and not to other souls, as possessing an intellectual immaterial power" (Ia. 97, 3).
5. Pasnau, *Thomas Aquinas on Human Nature*, 44, 73.
6. Cf. Pasnau, *Thomas Aquinas on Human Nature*, 237.

7. Although his term for "human being" is the generic *homo* (rather than *vir*, "male"), when Aquinas writes of human beings in general, he has a male norm in mind, as becomes clear shortly.
8. One commentator writes that the will, directed by and subsumed by reason, seems "trivial, almost superfluous" in comparison. Pasnau, *Thomas Aquinas on Human Nature*, 225.
9. Beattie, *Theology after Postmodernity*, 127–28.
10. Cf. Abhinavagupta, *Paratrisika-Vivarana*. Quotations from the short commentary, the *Paratrisikalaghuvrittih* (PTlv), follow Muller-Ortega's translation, Abhinavagupta, "The Short Gloss on the Supreme," which is the translation available to me at the time of writing. On authorship of PTlv, see Bäumer, *Abhinavagupta's Hermeneutics of the Absolute*, 33–35.
11. For an introduction to the various groups within this tradition, see Sanderson, "Saivism and the Tantric Traditions."
12. Singh, *Pratyabhijnahrdayam*, 13.
13. Flood, *Body and Cosmology in Kashmir Saivism*, 3.
14. I have not found in non-dual Saiva texts any evidence of a distinction between male and female in terms of their reflection of the thirty-six *tattvas*. Although some theologians might lift up the equality of Siva and Sakti as the solution to Aquinas's gendered exclusions, this is not the primary reason I find the *tattvas* helpful. Aquinas does not diminish women primarily on the grounds of God's figurative or literal maleness, but because of an assumption that a singular capacity, the intellect, is the most divine thing about humanity. For this reason, I take my inspiration for a holistic anthropology from the multiplicity of capacities and body parts that image God in non-dual Saiva thought.
15. Siva explains the principles to the Goddess using a phoneme mysticism that correlates the emergence of creation with the utterance of the letters of the Sanskrit alphabet: "O virtuous One, within the five classes of phonemes from *K* to *M* stand in order the twenty-five principles from 'earth' to the 'Self.' / Above that group of twenty-five is the tetrad of supports—namely the wind, fire, water and Indra. Higher than that are the phonemes beginning with *Ś*, generally known as the pentad of *brahman*. / The process of manifestation whose root is *A* and whose end is *KṢA* has thus been declared. Its course is to be known" (*Paratrisika* vv. 6–8 in PTlv, 208).
16. The following explanation is somewhat simplified because various texts number the *tattvas* in different ways, depending on the correspondences they wish to emphasize.
17. Readers should avoid the temptation to call these the "material" elements because "matter" encompasses a total of twenty-four *tattvas*, beginning with *prakrti*.
18. Flood, *Body and Cosmology in Kashmir Saivism*, 67.
19. Ibid., 34.
20. Non-dualist Saivas sometimes list the great divine power to create and delude (*mahamaya*) as one of the *tattvas*, either alongside or without *maya* as a separate power of limitation. Hindu traditions treat *maya* or *mahamaya* (feminine) as a goddess. Non-dual Saivism adds to this imagery by maintaining that each of the sheaths of *maya* is one of Siva's "powers," i.e., a *sakti* in its own right (PTlv, 211).

21. This passage mentions four powers of limitation, but in other places Abhinavagupta alludes to more.
22. Muller-Ortega, *The Triadic Heart of Siva*, 139.
23. Many of the practices are described in Singh, *Vijnanabhairava or Divine Consciousness.*
24. Pasnau, *Thomas Aquinas on Human Nature*, 164; cf. Ia. 77, 5, ad. 1.
25. Pasnau, *Thomas Aquinas on Human Nature*, 361–62. This intermediary state makes the soul anomalous as a subsistent form, which ordinarily only "subsists" in matter. For Aquinas, the soul can be unique in this way only because it is also immortal and incorruptible.
26. See Voss Roberts, *Body Parts.*
27. Among the "higher" principles, he would also be unlikely to recognize materiality (*prakrti*) or any of the principles of limitation as belonging to divinity.
28. te Velde, *Participation and Substantiality in Thomas Aquinas*, 25.
29. Ibid., 44.
30. See, for example, Padilla, *Divine Enjoyment.*
31. te Velde, *Participation and Substantiality in Thomas Aquinas*, 259.
32. Ibid., 93.
33. Cf. Haslam, *A Constructive Theology of Intellectual Disability.*
34. For example, David Lawrence sees in the non-dual Saiva notion of divine self-recognition a type of *logos* theology resonant with the work of Karl Rahner, David Tracy, and Bernard Lonergan. Lawrence, *Rediscovering God with Transcendental Argument*, 22.
35. In a similar vein, Michael Barnes has encouraged Christian theologies of religious pluralism to move away from the pluralist project of "progress toward ever more 'reasonable' accounts of Christian faith" and "reconciliation of 'family resemblances'" with other traditions and to base theological reflection on "the actual engagement with the other and on the whole complex process of inter-personal communication which is represented by the term inter-religious dialogue." Barnes, *Theology and the Dialogue of Religions*, 13.
36. Fredericks, *Faith Among Faiths.*
37. Clooney, *His Hiding Place Is Darkness.* For other recent contemplative Hindu-Christian comparisons, see issue 27 of the *Journal of Hindu-Christian Studies*, particularly Bannon, "Thou, That, and An/Other"; and Clooney, "On the Scholar's Contribution to the Contemplative Work of Hindu-Christian Studies."
38. Nicholson, *Comparative Theology and the Problem of Religious Rivalry*, 42.
39. Clooney, *Hindu God-Christian God.*
40. Clooney, *Beyond Compare*, 2.
41. Tiemeier, "Engendering the 'Mysticism' of the Alvars," 348. Also see Hillgardner, *Longing and Letting Go.*
42. Hill Fletcher, "As Long as We Wonder: Possibilities in the Impossibility of Interreligious Dialogue."
43. Clooney, *Seeing Through Texts*; Voss Roberts, *Tastes of the Divine.*
44. Clooney, *Theology After Vedanta*; and Clooney, *Beyond Compare.*
45. Locklin, *Liturgy of Liberation*, 32.
46. Sydnor, "Shaivism's *Nataraja* and Picasso's *Crucifixion.*"

47. Jeannine Hill Fletcher engages in constructive comparative work via ethnography in *Motherhood as Metaphor*, Chapters 5 and 6.
48. Voss Roberts, *Dualities*, 14–16.
49. Beattie, *Theology After Postmodernity*, 316, quoting *ST* Ia. 8, ad. 1 and Ia. 8, ad. 2.
50. Smith, *Imagining Religion: From Babylon to Jonestown*, 19–35.

mparative Theology er the Shoah

RISKS, PIVOTS, AND OPPORTUNITIES OF COMPARING TRADITIONS

Marianne Moyaert

The Shoah, insofar as it forms the climax of a longstanding tradition of anti-Jewish discrimination, contains one of the most important inducements for the revolutionary change in the Church's attitude vis-à-vis Israel. After the Shoah, the Second Vatican Council (1962–65), and in particular the promulgation of the document *Nostra Aetate*, brought about a turning point in Jewish-Christian relationships. Later such documents as the *Guidelines* (1974), *Notes* (1985), *We Remember* (1998), and *The Jewish People and their Sacred Scriptures in the Christian Bible* (2001), together with various dialogical initiatives, affirmed the Church's determination to break away from the "teaching of contempt" (Isaac 1964). This determination was once again affirmed in the recently released document *The Gifts and the Calling of God Are Irrevocable* (2015). Today, fifty years after *Nostra Aetate*, we can say that of all interreligious dialogues, Christian-Jewish dialogue is probably the most advanced.

From a Christian perspective, the greatest challenge is to formulate a non-supersessionist theology that recognizes the intrinsic and lasting significance of Judaism (von Stosch 2003) in God's plan of salvation. In this area, a lot of work has already been done by post-Shoah theologians who are intent on freeing Christian theology from its anti-Jewish ideology (Williamson 1998: 46). Most theological discussions have focused on doctrinal questions related to both Christology and ecclesiology. In effect, one could say that the dialogue between Christians and Jews has become a *locus theologicus* to reconsider some of the central Christian beliefs.

In this chapter, I argue that comparative theology—understood as the "the rereading of one's home theological tradition . . . after serious engagement in the reading of another tradition" (Clooney 1993: 3)—may also contribute to the formulation of a non-supersessionist theology. Comparative theology not only resolves to break with the hegemonic past of Christianity (Moyaert 2016b) but also makes this resolution concrete in how it brings different traditions together, i.e., through practices of cross-reading (Nicholson 2011). Comparative theology makes room for the complex (and often internally diverse) self-understanding of different traditions by engaging in a comparative praxis of close reading of religious texts and their commentaries. This comparative scriptural focus holds a great deal of potential especially when considering that throughout history, Christians have basically denied Jews the right to self-definition.

Comparative Theology's Disinterest in Judaism

It is my finding, however, that there are not many comparative theologians who actually compare texts from Jewish traditions with texts from Christian traditions and go on to formulate constructive theological reflections after this comparison. I also do not know any post-Shoah theologians who would call themselves comparative theologians.[1] Though there are many theologians who reread the (Hebrew) Bible after the Holocaust (Linafelt 2000), comparative theology, as distinct from biblical theology, is not common in the field of post-Shoah theology (Joslyn-Siemiatkoski 2010). If Christian scholars do study—for example, rabbinic sources—they often do so from a more historical-critical perspective, but without formulating theological conclusions. In brief, post-Shoah theology (which is usually also intertwined with Christian-Jewish dialogue) and comparative theology have not yet joined forces in an effort to overcome supersessionist theologies. As a post-Shoah theologian myself (Moyaert 2016) who also describes herself as a comparative theologian (Moyaert 2014), I wonder why that is. Could it be that post-Shoah theologians want to avoid new comparative violence at any cost?

Jewish-Christian encounter, perhaps more than any other interreligious encounter, happens in a fragile hermeneutical and theological space (Moyaert 2011a: 277). This space is anything but neutral; it is a space marked by collective memories and trauma, but also by collective responsibility and guilt. No matter how one looks at the relationship between Judaism and Christianity, it remains a fact that this relationship has been marked by a tremendous power imbalance, and this both impacts the way Christians engage Judaism and explains why Jews may react negatively to certain Christian theological interpretations of Judaism (even when they are—from a Christian perspective—viewed as open, dialogical and progressive). Post-holocaust Jewish theologians Alan Berger and David Patterson explain this cogently as follows:

> While many Jews have hated and feared many Christians, associating the cross not with salvation but with annihilation, Christians have never had any reason to associate the Star of David with the same sort of butchery and brutality . . . . Christians bear a far greater heritage of guilt for the atrocities committed against the Jews than the Jews bear vis-à-vis Christians (Berger and Patterson 2008: 177, 181).

Moreover, both communities dispute and deny each other's religious self-understanding; and they do so based on a different theological hermeneutics of the "same" scriptures. Implicated in this conflict is a tremendous rivalry over which community is the true heir of God's blessing, who may rightfully claim to be God's covenanted people, and who has fulfilled the prophecies that may be found in the Hebrew Scriptures. Throughout most of Church history, Christian claims to fulfillment have given the impression that "God's faithfulness and presence are not experienced in their fullness among Jews and Judaism" (Klein 2007: 47). This has, moreover, given way to the more exclusivist claim that Judaism after the coming of Christ is obsolete, a claim that in turn has been used to legitimize pogroms, expulsions, and even murder.

In light of their violent history, both Jews and Christians know that a theologically committed comparison of religious texts may be a deeply ambiguous endeavor. Some Jews may be rather skeptical about the success of this novel comparative theological project. Consider why. Comparative theology, understood as a "rereading of one's own tradition in light of other traditions" (Nicholson 2005: 191), is theological throughout. The "intention is to inscribe within one's own theological tradition theological texts from outside it, and to (begin to) write Christian theology only out of that newly composed context" (Clooney 1993: 7). I am trying to picture how this particular project of faith seeking understanding might be received in light of the history of tense Jewish-Christian relations. I can imagine that some would argue that this is not new at all! For is this not exactly the story of Christianity's dealing with Jewish tradition, a re-reading of Jewish tradition in light of the Christ-event and a reading of the Christ-event in light of the Jewish tradition?

Comparisons, the history of Jewish-Christian relations shows, may lead to distortions. Although I am well aware of the fact that the preceding definition of comparative theology is usually complemented with a series of caveats precisely to avoid distortions, and although I am also aware that there are many intellectual safeguards built into the process of cross-reading to avoid the pitfalls of grave misunderstanding, nevertheless, in view of the history of Christian anti-Judaism, it becomes understandable that some Jews would be somewhat suspicious vis-à-vis this comparative endeavor, and that Christian theologians devoted to establishing friendly relations with Jewish others may refrain from engaging in such a potentially ambiguous practice.

Furthermore, when Christians comment on Jewish scriptures, finding the right balance between distanciation and nearness, continuity and discontinuity, and similarity and dissimilarity, can be very challenging. If anything, the history of Jewish-Christian relations shows how difficult it is to engage in a comparative reading without falling prey to supersessionist typological readings which depreciate Judaism. At the same time, the recent turn to dialogue and the Christian willingness to express solidarity and to strengthen the bonds between church and synagogue is sometimes rejected by Jews (and sometimes also by Christians) as a form of undue philosemitism that neglects the real differences that exist between both communities (Sandmel 2010: 417). Exclusion and inclusion can both be problematic.

To conclude the first part of this contribution, I suggest that the history of Jewish-Christian relations makes the risks of comparative theology very tangible. If so, then the reason why Judaism is not often engaged in comparative theological projects is because there is a sense among theologians that to engage in a comparative theological reading of Jewish and Christian scriptures is to enter into a minefield where misunderstanding and misrecognition are difficult to avoid, even with the best intentions.

In the remainder of this chapter, I propose to bring to light the potentially violent nature of comparisons between Jewish and Christian scriptures by means of one concrete example that has been at the heart of Jewish-Christian disputes over scripture, namely the story of sibling rivalry between Jacob and Esau. After exploring some of the classical Christian (and anti-Jewish) readings of this story, I will formulate some ground rules for Christians who wish to engage Jewish scriptures in a way that avoids new comparative violence. Next, I will turn to classical rabbinic interpretations of this same story taken from Genesis Rabbah (the midrash on Genesis), followed by a more contemporary reading by rabbi Jonathan Sacks. With each step, I will develop theological reflections on what this story means for the relationship between Esau and Jacob, Church and Synagogue, and Christians and Jews, and I will showcase how comparative theology can contribute to the formulation of a non-supersessionist theology.

Early Christian Commentaries on Jacob and Esau

From the very beginning of the Christian era, synagogue and church have related to each other as sibling rivals, competing for the same paternal love and blessing. Striving for the same exclusive love of God and the same inherited entitlement, both Jews and Christians have denied each other's claim to being God's elected people. What is more, the way Christianity has read the Christ-event in light of the Old Testament and vice versa is a form of (problematic) comparative theology.

TYPOLOGY

In the still prevailing Christian hermeneutic that converges with replacement theology, Christ's life, suffering, and resurrection function as the hermeneutical key for understanding the Old Testament.[2] The underlying idea is that the "Old Testament" must be read as prophecy about the coming of Jesus the Christ, understood as the Messiah. This understanding has been translated in a very specific form of comparative theology—i.e. typology. It is probably more nuanced to state that typology, certainly when placed in a supersessionist theological framework, exemplifies what Hugh Nicholson (2010), Paul Hedges (2013), and others have called the old comparative theology. The old comparative theology intends to affirm the superiority of Christian tradition while disregarding the self-understanding of the other tradition (in this case Judaism). It is a form of comparing that knows in advance what insights (truths) the comparison will yield. A confrontation with this typological comparison is necessary if we are to point out the dangers to which comparative theology is liable.

Starting from the Christian assumption that Christ is the pivot and climax of God's plan of salvation, a Christian typological exegesis claims that events, figures, and even statements from the Old Testament prefigure or foreshadow events, figures, and statements from the New Testament. In such a typological framework, the New Testament takes theological priority over the Old because the Old has meaning only in light of the New, which fulfils and supersedes the Old (Pollefeyt 2001: 232). Typological interpretations often imply that Hebrew Scriptures undergo devaluation—they are interpreted as a "spiritually inferior prefiguration of an event in the life of Jesus" (Gellma 2005:36). Such typological readings almost always build on a process of othering: The more Jews are othered, the more Christian identity is enhanced. Throughout the history of Jewish-Christian relations, this exegetical approach has contributed greatly to the teaching of contempt.

In what follows, I want to illustrate the violent potential of typological readings that are set in a supersessionist framework, and I will do so by turning to the story of Esau and Jacob. As I will show, this tale about the two brothers' fighting for the blessing of their father intersects with the conflict between Judaism and Christianity from its inception to our own day—a conflict between chosen and rejected and between persecuted and persecutor (Yuval 2006:3). It is precisely their consanguinity that explains the harsh and often violent conflicts between Esau and Jacob and between Synagogue and Church.

JACOB AND ESAU

Jacob is the son of Isaac and Rebecca and the twin brother of Esau. Genesis recounts how the two brothers were already struggling with one another even before their birth. Owing to this, Rebekah seeks out God's counsel, who informs her of the following:

> The LORD said to her, "Two nations are in your womb, and two peoples from within you will be separated; one people will be stronger than the other, and the older will serve the younger." (Gen. 25:23)

This prophecy follows the recurrent pattern in the Old Testament, according to which the younger son receives the blessing from the father (Cain and Abel, Isaac and Ishmael, Judah and Reuben . . .). Jacob—incited by his mother Rebekah, who plays a key role in this story—swindles Esau out of his rights as firstborn, by means of a bowl of lentils (Gen. 25:34); deceiving his father, he receives the blessing Isaac had reserved for Esau. A great hatred against his brother is stirred within Esau upon discovering how Jacob has deceived him and his father, and Esau swears to kill him.

This story plays a key role in the ecclesial interpretation of the relation between Jews and Christians. Early in Christian history, building on Paul's Letter to the Romans, Church Fathers placed this story in an anti-Jewish typological supersessionist framework, according to which the Church usurps the Jew's place in God's salvific plan. Crucial to the Fathers' interpretation is the identification of Esau (the older brother) with Israel and Jacob (the younger brother) with the Church. Irenaeus of Lyon (140–202) ponders the significance of Jacob's name. In Hebrew, there is the wordplay between the name *ya'aqov*, "Jacob," and the verb *'aqav*, "to take a hold of and supplant," as this passage shows:

> If anyone, again, will look into Jacob's actions, he shall find them not destitute of meaning, but full of import with regard to the dispensations. Thus, in the first place, at his birth, since he laid hold on his brother's heel, he was called Jacob, that is, the supplanter—one who holds, but is not held; binding the feet, but not being bound; striving and conquering; grasping in his hand his adversary's heel, that is, victory. For this end was the Lord born, the type of whose birth he set forth beforehand, of whom also John says in the Apocalypse: "He went forth conquering, that He should conquer." (Adv. Haer. 4.21.3)

Ireneaus's typological reading of this story legitimizes the ecclesiological claim according to which the Church, as the new people of God, has superseded Israel, the old people of God. Thus Esau became the archetype of the Jew, the elder brother who lost his birthright to his younger brother; and Jacob, the younger brother, became the prototype of the Church. Some early Christian thinkers even traced the charge of deicide—the most vehement charge ever brought against the Jews (cf. Melito of Sardis)—to this story, which relates that Esau held a grudge against Jacob because of the blessing his father had given him. He said to himself, "The days of mourning for my father are near; then I will kill my brother Jacob." Esau's wrath on Jacob is said to prefigure the Jews' hatred for Jesus and their desire to kill him. This passage from Genesis 27:41 is sometimes read as a prophecy not only of the passion of Christ, but also of the Jews as murderers of Christ, Son of God (for example, Hyppolyte of Rome). Ambrose of Milan (339–97) also commented on the rivalry between the two brothers. In his interpretation the clothes of Jacob and Esau are central:

> Accordingly, Jacob received his brother's clothing, because he excelled the elder in wisdom . . . Rebekah . . . gave to the younger son the clothing of the Old Testament, the prophetic and priestly clothing of the Kings of Solomon and Ezekiel and Josiah, and she gave it to the Christian people, who would know how to use the garment they had received, since the Jewish people kept it without using it and did not know its proper adornments. This clothing was lying in the shadow, cast off and forgotten . . . . The Christian people put it on, and it shone brightly. (Ambrosius quoted in Yuval 2006: 19)

The fact that the prophecy declares that the elder will serve the younger was used to legitimate, throughout Christian history, the dominance of the Church over the Synagogue. The harsh saying written down in Malachi 1:2–3 according to which God is said to love Jacob but hate Esau, only adds to the antagonism between both communities. With the Church's eagerness to translate religious convictions into reality, this replacement theology, together with the idea that Esau (Israel) was to serve Jacob (the Church), became a political reality made concrete in a variety of repressive laws (Cohen 1991: 254–55).

Rules of Engagement

The complex history of anti-Judaism was fostered by a supersessionist theology, a Christology of discontinuity, and an exclusivist typological exegesis. Hermeneutical distortion is incited by theological convictions that have led to unethical violent behavior. Clearly, theologies are not innocent but impact the way people belonging to different faith traditions relate to one another. After the Shoah we must ask, what are the rules of engagement when engaging Judaism from a comparative theological perspective?[3]

HERMENEUTICAL OBLIGATIONS: DOING JUSTICE TO JEWISH SELF-UNDERSTANDING

If the old comparative theology takes root in a strategy of othering—enhancing one's own identity by means of a negative stereotyping of the other—the new comparative theology, as developed by Francis Clooney, James Fredericks, Catherine Cornille, and others, aims at articulating "a viable understanding of the other in which the encountered other is not manufactured to the comparativist's prejudices" (Clooney 1993: 7). Its starting point is hermeneutical openness, i.e., the willingness to understand the other in his or her otherness and to avoid reading one's own presuppositions into the religious world of the other (Moyaert 2012). Not meeting this request for hermeneutical openness is an expression of misrecognition. Put more forcefully, a lack of willingness to take the other seriously in his or her otherness is a form of closedness. Before judging, before assessing, before appreciating—either positively or negatively—the religious other deserves to be heard and understood (Moyaert 2012a). This requires humility and empathy (Cornille 2013).

Christians as a rule have denied the Jews the right to self-definition (cf. Frank Littell). Indeed, typological readings placed in a supersessionist theological framework led to a distorted Christian understanding of the lived religious experience of Jewish people. This history of distortion points to the responsibility of comparative theologians to do justice to the self-understanding of the Jewish other and his/her religious community and tradition.

This implies first of all recognizing that Judaism is a living tradition. Throughout most of its history, the Church was unable to relate to Judaism as a vibrant tradition, with its own symbolic practices and textual hermeneutics. To the question of why Judaism continued to exist after the destruction of the Temple and the establishment of the Church, Christians as a rule gave two responses: first, because Jewish scriptures prophesy about the coming of Christ and thereby affirm the truthfulness of Christianity, and second, because Jewish scriptures testify to what happens to people who do not recognize Christ.

Of all forms of "interreligious dialogue," Jewish-Christian dialogue stands out because both communities affirm the authority of the Hebrew Bible (what Jews call "Tanakh" and Christians call the "Old Testament") (see Emet 2002). Nevertheless, the first challenge for Christian comparative theologians when engaging Jewish texts is not to focus solely on the relationship between Old and New Testament, but to acknowledge that even the so-called shared Jewish and Christian scriptures do not completely overlap with one another as canon, and that rabbinic interpretations of the Hebrew Scriptures and Christian interpretations of the "Old Testament" developed "in parallel and interaction, both based on their own presuppositions" (Kasper, 2011: xv).

Doing justice to "Jewish" self-definition also implies accepting *the asymmetry* that exists between the traditions. From a supersessionist theology, Judaism *needs* Christianity to understand the deeper-lying meaning of its own scriptures. From the perspective of fulfillment theology, Christ fulfills the prophecies that may be found in the Old Testament. In any case, Judaism is incomplete without Christianity. When engaging Judaism as a living tradition, comparative theologians after the Shoah, however, should acknowledge that while Christians heavily rely on certain aspects of Jewish tradition, theologically speaking, Jews (in their own self-understanding) do not need Christianity. As far as the Jews are concerned, Judaism is self-sufficient. Clearly, it is quite *difficult to reconcile Christian self-understanding* (Christianity supersedes/fulfills Judaism) and *Jewish self-understanding* (Judaism does not need Christianity).

UNLEARNING FINAL READINGS

Typological exegesis, understood as an expression of old comparative theology, is Christocentric and exclusivist and may lead to a denial of the intrinsic value of the Hebrew scriptures. Such Christian interpretations of the Hebrew Scriptures have had fatal consequences for the Jewish people. Therefore, it is particularly important to develop a Christian hermeneutic that does not end in triumphalism. For comparative theologians, this means acknowledging that there is not just one valid way of reading texts from the Hebrew scriptures and that these texts do not all point in the same *Christological direction.* Certainly, exclusivist typological readings that wrongfully give the impression that the Hebrew prophecies only have meaning as *predictions of the Coming of Christ* are to be avoided.

Comparative theology after the Shoah must at least admit that the Christological interpretation of the Hebrew scriptures is not the only valid interpretation. In this perspective, the following passage from the document of the Pontifical Biblical Commission released in 2002 is of tremendous importance: "It may be asked whether Christians should be blamed for having monopolized the Jewish Bible and reading there what no Jew has found . . . Christians can and ought to admit that the Jewish reading of the Bible is a possible one, in continuity with the Jewish Sacred Scriptures from the Second Temple period, a reading analogous to the Christian reading which developed in parallel fashion. Both readings are bound up with the vision of their respective faiths, of which the readings are the result and expression. Consequently, both are irreducible," (§22). Put differently, Christian theologians need to unlearn their focus on "final readings" which, according to Brueggeman, unfortunately have contributed to "final solutions" (Brueggeman 2000: 64).

To my mind, comparative theology after the Shoah has a lot to learn from hermeneutical philosopher Paul Ricoeur. In his text hermeneutics, he explains that texts (and this also upholds for religious texts) are always open to multiple conflicting interpretations. To his mind, this points to their "surplus of meaning." Because of its plurivocity, no one reading can exhaust a text. To attend to the plurivocity of a text requires not only an unlearning of triumphalist readings, but especially a close reading and comparing of texts, making use of a variety of critical methodologies. Ricoeur strongly believes in the creative power texts have to challenge, interrupt, and transform readers that engage in a close reading (Moyaert 2014).

I also think that the unlearning of final readings, which often become triumphalist, may be informed by Talmudic tradition itself, which is not aimed at formulating definite and conclusive interpretations. As Susan Handelman explains, "the infinity of meaning and plurality of interpretation are the cardinal virtues and even divine imperatives for Rabbinic thought" (Handelman 1982: 21). As a consequence, there is no attempt to determine the final meaning of a passage or the most original or correct interpretation. The understanding is rather that many interpretations are possible. When these interpretations come into conflict with one another, this is seen as a celebration of the greatness of God, whose thoughts are greater than ours. Jewish hermeneutics is pluralistic hermeneutics. As the sages put it: "Just as a hammer splits a rock into many pieces, so a verse of Scripture may yield a number of arguments" (BT Sanhedrin 34a). Maybe this pluralistic hermeneutics can be injected in a comparative theology after the Shoah that is intended to unlearn the ambition of final readings?

THEOLOGICAL OBLIGATIONS: CONSTRUCTIVE THEOLOGICAL REFLECTIONS

According to comparative theologian James Fredericks, one of the purposes of comparative theology is to forge new forms of solidarity and to overcome old patterns of hegemonic theological discourse (Fredericks 2004: 100–2). Indeed, this comparative project may not be reduced to a mere hermeneutical project; this venture is a theological one through and through. Francis Clooney rightly remarks that it is a form of constructive theology that resists closed systematic frameworks and favors more open-ended reflections. Indeed, it is often said that comparative theology values asking questions above formulating definitive and final answers (Moyaert 2012b).

To a certain extent, I would agree that constructive theological reflections should always retain their preliminary character; it is, after all, precisely the claim to final and absolute answers that has strengthened the hegemonic inclination of Christianity in the past. What is more, after the Shoah, age-old certainties were shattered, and the ground on which Christians stand has become shaky at best. Asking questions and postponing the formulation of definite answers matches the experience of fragmentation. I am, however, a little bit concerned that this open-endedness of comparative theology may weaken its potential to contribute to the formulation of a non-supersessionist theology. Though I value the virtue of humility and theological prudence, too much prudence may not be to the benefit of Jewish-Christian relations. If constructive theological formulations remain too fragmented, I am afraid they will not really impact mainstream theologies (christologies and ecclesiologies). Theological conclusions can be premature, no doubt, but is it not the case that they can also be too cautious?

To my mind, Christianity needs to revise its theology of Judaism and comparative theology may help to contribute to this larger theological project. So, though I share many of the concerns comparative theologians formulate with regard to systematic theologies of religions, my particular involvement in post-Shoah theology and Jewish-Christian dialogue has made me realize how important it is for comparative theology to contribute to a larger theology of Judaism. The relationship between Church (Christianity) and Israel (Judaism) is of another nature than that between, for example, Christianity and Hinduism. If a distorted theology of Judaism has affected negatively the relations between Christians and Jews, I believe a constructive theological approach intent on reconsidering this distorted theology is needed to open up a new future. This theology should be informed by a comparative reasoning focused on undoing final readings.

To make this rule more concrete, let me return to the story of Esau and Jacob and learn from what rabbinic tradition teaches about the rivalry between the brothers.

Midrashim on Jacob and Esau

Stories about the rivalry between Jacob and Esau not only figure in Christian tradition, but play a central role in Jewish tradition, too. Indeed, they are included in the weekly Torah portions (*Parashat ha-Shavua*) read in the Synagogue: *parsha Toledot*—"generations" (Gen. 25:28–28:9) and *parsha Vayislakh*—"and he sent" (Gen. 32:4–36:43). There are also numerous *midrashim* on the relationship between the two brothers, the most important of which can be found in Genesis Rabbah, a collection of ancient homiletical interpretations of the book Genesis.[4] Genesis Rabbah is aggadic: It is a narrative exposition expanding on, recomposing, and recontextualizing the stories found in the book Genesis. It takes the form of a line by line commentary. Typical of aggadic Midrashim is that they are not that concerned with bringing forth the literary or original meaning of the biblical texts they comment on, but rather an interpretation that is rather independent of *p'shat*, the close literal reading of the biblical narrative. The midrash wants to address issues lying deeper in the text.

Genesis Rabbah, compiled in the land of Israel, is dated between 400 and 650 CE, a time in which the Jewish people saw the transition from pagan rule to Christian dominance. The parting of the ways was a fact, and the Jewish people saw itself increasingly confronted with a triumphalist Church that adopted a politics of repression vis-à-vis them. This novel religious-political situation challenged the Jewish people. As Jacob Neusner puts it in his introduction to *Genesis Rabbah*: "The issue confronting Israel in the land of Israel therefore proved immediate: the meaning of the new and ominous turn of history, the implications of Christ's worldly triumph for the other-worldly and supernatural people, Israel, whom God chooses and loves" (Neusner, 1985a, ix). In view of this crisis, the numerous *midrashim* on Jacob and Esau are particularly illuminating because they function as a kind of counter-narrative to the Christian typological reading.

THE STORY OF JACOB AND ESAU IN RABBINIC LITERATURE

From the very beginning, the story of the twin brothers does not bode well. We are told that the twins are already fighting in the womb of their mother, Rebekah, even to such an extent that she asks "If it is thus, then why do I live?" According the sages, this struggle already points to the very different nature between both brothers:

> R. Yochanan said: each ran to slay the other, and Resh Lakish: each annulled the laws of the other. (Gen. Rabbah 63:6)[5]

If R. Yochanan points to the physical hostility between both brothers, Resh Lakish alludes to the way the brothers embody very different virtues and ideals. If Jacob appreciates spiritual power, Esau strives after physical power. This discussion between R. Yochanan and Resh Lakish illustrates the general understanding of the sages that Jacob shows exemplary behavior. Rabbinic literature generally speaking has not been very nice to Esau. In quite an anachronistic manner, the sages comment (Genesis Rabbah 63:6) that when Rebekah "stood near synagogues and schools, Jacob struggled to come out; hence it is written, *Before I formed thee in the belly I knew thee* (Jer. 1:5). While when she passed idolatrous temples, Esau eagerly struggled to come out; hence it is written, *The wicked are estranged from the womb* (PS 58:4)." Jacob (Israel) is eager to serve God by dedicating himself to the Torah; according to the sages, however, Esau's idolatrous mind stands out.

When the boys grow up, the differences in their characters become increasingly clear. Esau is a skillful hunter, an outdoor man who dwells in the fields. Jacob is quieter and dwells in tents (Gen. 25:27). If Esau is Isaac's favorite, Rebekah loves Jacob. Indeed the sages say "the more she heard his voice, the more she loved him" (Gen. Rabbah 63:10). Later, the sages argue, we learn that Esau, the older brother, does not care about the things that really matter; this is also borne out by the fact that Esau would later sell his birthright to Jacob for lentil stew, an act that already prefigures the loss of his father's blessing. Clearly, Esau is driven by earthly passions and has no sense of what is really important. The comments of the sages on this passage are quite harsh. They link Esau's behavior not only to that of a brute, an uneducated man, but also to murder and idolatry (Gen. Rabbah 65:20).[6] This rabbinic characterization, which contrasts Jacob to Esau, justifies the dramatic events that will partake in their life: Jacob "steals" Esau's blessing under Rebekah's direction. Instead of depicting Jacob as one who deceives his brother (and father), the general understanding amongst the sages seems to be that Jacob, who rules by the study of the Torah, deserves the blessing of the father.[7] Following the line of reasoning, Jacob did nothing wrong when he tricked Isaac into blessing him rather than Esau.[8] Jacob takes only what is lawful; he is *entitled to* Isaac's blessing:

> May God give you of the dew of heaven [and of the fatness of the earth, and plenty of grain and wine. Let peoples serve you and nations bow

down to you. Be lord over your brothers and you mother's sons bow down to you. Cursed be everyone who curses you, and blessed be everyone who blesses you]. (Gen. 27:27–29)

The drama between the two brothers continues. When Esau heard what Jacob did, he went to his father and "cried out with an exceedingly great and bitter cry [and said to his father, 'Bless me, even me also, O my father']. And Isaac answered him 'Your brother came with guile and he has taken away your blessing.'" Rabbi Yochanan comments on this passage, legitimizing both Jacob's and Isaac's actions: "[He came] with the wisdom of his knowledge of the Torah." Esau is outraged and out to kill Jacob, which brings Rebekah to the following exclamation: "Behold your Brother Esau comforts himself by planning to kill you. Now therefore my son . . . flee to Laban my brother in Haran, and stay with him a while until he forgets what you have done to him; then I will send and fetch you from there. Why should I be bereft of you both in one day?" (Gen. 27:42–45).

Jacob spends twenty years with his uncle Laban. There he marries the sisters Leah and Rachel and fathers twelve children. When his youngest-but-one, Joseph, is born, Jacob expresses his longing to return to the land of his birth, Canaan. He knows not what awaits him, only that his lot lies in Canaan. Jacob is incredibly afraid of the encounter with his brother Esau. Nevertheless, when the story reaches its climax and the brothers finally meet again, the text says: "And Esau ran towards him, and embraced him, and fell on his neck, and kissed him, and they wept" (Gen. 33:4). Though the text seems to point at a reconciliatory moment between the two brothers, the sages are not convinced. There is great discussion about the exact interpretation of the word kissed (*vayishakeihu*). This word has a line of dots above it, which is the torah's way of saying that there is something peculiar going on: this kiss was not a normal kiss. But what then was abnormal about it?

The Midrash gives us two interpretations. Some sages argue that the kiss was wholehearted. R. Shimon b. Elazar and R. Shimon Bar Yohai argue that Esau pitied his brother and kissed him sincerely (cf. Gen. Rabbah 78:9), which was abnormal in the sense that Esau actually hates Jacob. However, other sages take another stance, arguing that the kiss was not a real kiss, but rather a bite, an act of aggression rather than of reconciliation; that would moreover better befit Esau's general character as an untrustworthy person. Most explicit is R. Yannai who said, ". . . he didn't come to kiss him but rather to bite him, but Yaakov Avinu's neck turned to marble; and thus the teeth of that wicked one were blunted. Thus, when the text says 'and they cried'—this one cried over his neck and this one cried over his teeth."[9] These broken teeth are predicted in Psalm 3: "You have broken the teeth of the wicked."

ESAU/EDOM/ROME

The sages perceived in the story of the two brothers "a pattern of behavior between two nations and two worldviews" (Tamari 2011: 47).[10] According to them, the contrary characterization of both brothers tallies with God's prophecy that two nations are in Rebekah's womb, two nations with different ideals and desires (Gen. 25:23). Elaborating on the two nations, it becomes clear that Esau is regarded as the forefather of Edom (for example, Jeremiah 49: 7–22; Ezekiel 26:12–14), once the fierce enemy of the Israelites.[11] The Israelites and Edomites were not only involved in an ongoing struggle about land; it is also said that the Edomites at the time of the destruction of the First Temple took advantage of the situation and seized control of parts of Judah. Some biblical texts allude to Edom as co-responsible for the destruction of Jerusalem (Psalm 137:7, Obadiah 11), and that they were even involved in the destruction of the first Temple (Obadiah 16). For that reason, they are called the eternal enemies of Israel (Amos 1:11; Ezekiel 35:5). One of the reasons for this identification is probably that Esau was red—"all his body was like a hairy mantle"—and Edom means red. This is reaffirmed in the commentaries of Rabbi Yochanan and Rabbi Lakish on Esau who sells his birthright for red pottage. Rabbi Yochanan said: "he wanted his own and his master's [namely what belonged to Edom, for *edom* is the word red, hence the red pottage of Edom] while Rabbi Lakish said, "He wanted what belonged to him and people like him" (Gen. Rabbah 63:12). Commenting on this narrative in his book *Two Nations in Your Womb*, Israel Yuval argues that a territorial dispute is projected into this narrative:

> Jacob and his descendants are described as destined to be lords of the land, while Esau and Ishmael are to serve as their subjects—a reality fulfilled at the time of the First Temple after the subjugation of Edom by David. At the end of the First Temple period, during the Babylonian rule over the kingdom of Judaea, Edom took advantage of this opportunity and ruled over the border regions of Judaea in the northern Negev and

> thereafter was considered a treacherous brother deserving of the harshest revenge and punishment. (Yuval 2006: 9)

For the sages, Esau, by being connected to Edom, becomes the symbol of evil and foreign oppressors. In a later historical phase, when the threat of the Edomites was no longer real, the sages came to identify Edom with the massive political power of Rome. The colonial empire Rome not only oppressed Israel but was also held responsible for the destruction of the second Temple (70 CE) and the expulsion of the Jews from Jerusalem (a divine punishment according to the Church). This connection between Rome and Edom seems to have emerged around 135 CE, after the failed rebellion of Bar Kokhba against the Roman oppressors. In light of these dramatic events, we can understand the midrashic comment: "Two nations are in thy womb: they are two proud nations in thy womb, each taking pride in his world, and each in his kingdom. There are two rulers of nations in thy womb, Hadrian of the gentiles and Solomon of Israel." There is no greater contradiction possible, it seems: On the one hand, Solomon, king of Israel, builder of the first temple and son of David, and on the other hand Hadrian, ruler of Rome, who built a temple for Jupiter in Jerusalem (!), which led to the Jewish uprising under Bar Kokhba. There even exists a (later) midrash that legitimizes this connection by claiming that Rome was actually established by a grandson of Esau/Edom. Again a clear anachronism, but that is not the point. The point is that the sages "sought to trace the real spiritual source of the power and so the connection was made with Esau" (Tamari 46). In even later tradition, during the Middle Ages, the sages connect Esau/Edom to Christianity, which was not only based in the Roman Empire, but also developed into a mighty worldly power oppressing the Jewish people (Cohen 1991). The conflict between Jacob and Esau is less about territorial claims, and more a conflict between worldviews, a cultural-religious conflict (Kessler 2005: 222). While the Christians claimed to be Jacob, the New Israel, it is clear that the Jewish people, identifying with Jacob, saw the Church as Esau, with all the implied negative connotations. In his article, "Esau as a symbol in early medieval thought," Gerson Cohen notes that the transition from identifying Edom/Rome with the Church was not a great leap in Jewish minds:

> The official establishment of the Christian Church as the religion of the empire made no discernible impression on the Jews of the fourth century, for by that time the chasm between Judaism and Christianity had grown so deep and wide that the alignment of the machinery state

> with the Church was of no greater moment than the succession of one emperor by another. To the Jew, it was a shift from one idolatry to another, one more aggressive and openly hostile, but not a change in kind. Thus, it required no effort on the part of Jewish homilists to extend the name of Edom to Christendom. Esau might exchange his eagle for a cross, but he was Esau nonetheless. (Cohen 1991: 249)

In this identification of Christian Rome with Esau, the Christian *claim* to being heir of Abraham's blessing is implicitly acknowledged. The underlying charge is that Christian Rome is "Israel's brother, counterpart and Nemesis" (Neusner 2004: 106).[12] According to this interpretation, the Church (Esau) is a fraud and this will become obvious at the End of Times. The story enabled the Jewish people to make sense of their current situation (they are being oppressed by Esau (Edom/Rome/the Church) while at the same time projecting a messianic future in which Jacob (Israel) will rule and Esau (Edom/Rome/the Church) will serve him.

THEOLOGICAL REFLECTIONS

We have seen in the first part of this chapter that Christianity reinforced its identity by means of a typological reading of Hebrew scriptures, which nourished a negative stereotyping of the Jewish people as the old people of God. This typological approach, which identifies the Church with Jacob and the Synagogue with Esau, contradicts (or even perverts) Jewish self-understanding, according to which Jacob is Israel. In the case of the conflicts between Jacob and Esau, the sages seem to turn the Church's christological reading around, arguing not only that Jacob points to Israel but also that Esau stands for the Church as an embodiment of Edom. The misdrashic interpretation not only brings to the surface the violence of triumphalist ecclesiastic theology, but also the perverse and fraudulent nature of the Church, which unduly claims to be Jacob, the rightful heir of the divine blessing. Placed in an eschatological framework, the expectation of the sages is that at the end of time the real nature of the Church will become blindingly obvious. Israel may be suffering at the hands of his brother in the present, but keeps God's prophecy and promise alive: "in the future the persecuting brother" will lose his powerful position and "become a slave to Jacob" (Yuval 2006: 19). Consider in this regard the following midrash: "Rabbi Aha said in the name of Rabbi Huna: Esau, the evil one is destined to put on his cloak and dwell with the righteous in the Garden of Eden in the Time to Come. But the Holy One Blessed be He will drag him out and throw him out of there" (Neusner 1985b: 66 quoted in Yuval).

The sages, it can hardly be denied, hold a mirror up to the Church's face. The mirror image is not a nice image: It is that of a triumphalist church that has oppressed its younger brother, which is awaiting the eschatological times when God will reveal that Israel and not the Church is the rightful heir of God's blessing. This interpretation leaves little room for dialogue and reconciliation: Even what promises to be a moment of rapprochement (the kiss) turns out to be the opposite. Esau cannot be trusted, and without trust there is no dialogue. After the kiss, which is another act of deception, both brothers go their own way without any expectation of reconciliation. It is unclear, from this perspective, if the suspicion of Israel vis-à-vis the Church will ever be lifted. Nevertheless, if any reconciliation is to take place, it will at the very least presuppose the willingness of the Church to confront its anti-Jewish legacy and seek ways to root out supersessionist theologies. Although I am sure Nostra Aetate (§4) and the subsequent documents are sincere symbols of the Church's desire to establish friendly relations with the Jewish people—the Church's kiss is real and sincere—nevertheless Esau and Jacob still have a long way to travel. Perhaps it is a good thing for comparative theologians to be mindful of the profound distrust (some) Jews may still have of Christians because expressions of solidarity and reconciliation that come too soon can become blind and oppressive again.

A Contemporary Reconciliatory Reading

Contemporary rabbinic interpretations of the Esau and Jacob saga are more nuanced and pay ample attention to the complexities of the interactions between the brothers. Esau is being depicted with greater sympathy, while Jacob's role in this drama is being looked upon more critically. In the last part of this chapter, I want to consider one more recent interpretation by rabbi Jonathan Sacks, and explore what his interpretation may entail for a Christian theology of Jewish-Christian relations.

JACOB WHO LONGS TO BE LIKE ESAU

Rabbi Jonathan Sacks draws on biblical passages that are much more critical of Jacob's behavior. To Sacks's mind, the rivalry between the two brothers is a classic case of mimetic rivalry, with Jacob playing the leading part. Instead of arguing, as did most of the sages, that Jacob took what he was entitled to when he tricked Isaac into blessing him, Rabbi Sacks argues that this dramatic passage is the climax of a life filled with envy: Jacob wants to be the firstborn, he wants Esau's birth right and Isaac's blessing—a blessing pertaining to land and power. Esau's anger is justified, for Jacob did not take what was his own. He deceitfully took what rightfully belonged to his brother.

When, after twenty years, Jacob is about to meet his brother again, Jacob is terribly scared. According to the biblical tradition, time does not appear to heal all wounds. In expectation of the following day, Jacob withdraws alone nearby the river Jabbok. And it is here that he is surprised by a strange man who comes to fight him. Jacob fights as if his life depends on it. Only after he has been wounded and blessed with a new name (Israel) does the struggle end, but without any clear winner.

After this night-time encounter, Jacob is ready to meet his brother face to face. His nightly exploits have changed him—he who has just wrestled with God now finds the strength to confront his brother. And, in fact, the confrontation runs very differently from what Jacob's earlier preparations would have portended. Jacob walks on ahead, "bowing himself to the ground seven times, until he came near his brother" (Gen. 33:3). Esau rushes to meet him, embraces and kisses him (Gen. 33:4). Jacob's fears were unfounded. Esau is not intending to kill his brother as he once threatened to do. And likewise, Jacob is not hiding behind diplomacy or seeking recourse in military strategies. The reconciliation, so it seems, is real. Esau's kiss is authentic and Jacob's tears are also authentic.

Jacob's behavior is noteworthy—he bows seven times—as is his communication. When meeting Esau, he is full of humility: He calls himself Esau's servant. Jacob's eagerness to oblige goes further. He offers Esau gifts:

> But Esau said, "I have enough, my brother; keep what you have for yourself." Jacob said, "No, please; if I find favor with you, then accept my present [Heb. *minchah*] from my hand; for truly to see your face is like seeing the face of God—since you have received me with such favor. Please accept my gift [lit. "my blessing," Heb. *birkhati*] that is brought to you, because God has dealt graciously with me, and because I have everything I want [Heb. *yesh li khol*]." So he urged him, and he took it. (Gen. 33:9–11)

According to Sacks, the key word in this passage is "blessing." Sacks reminds us of the fact that just before Jacob flees to his uncle Laban, Isaac blesses Jacob a *second time.* Isaac, who now *knows* who is before him, grants Jacob another blessing, i.e., the blessing that has been reserved for the patriarchs:

> May he give to you the blessing of Abraham, to you and to your offspring with you, so that you may take possession of the land where you now live as an alien—land that God gave to Abraham. (Gen. 28:4)

This is a very different blessing than the one that Jacob stole from his brother. It deals with children and land, two things that God had promised to Abraham much earlier. These are the blessings of the covenant. They have nothing to do with the blessing of power and riches that was meant for Esau. God never promised Abraham any power, neither did he speak of the fatness of the earth. Instead, God promised Abraham children, who would continue to keep the covenant, and a land where they would live. It is this covenant blessing that Isaac gives to Jacob when he leaves to go to Laban: Jacob is the one chosen to continue the covenant. That is the blessing meant for him. Only after the nocturnal wrestling does that realization dawn on Jacob. He seems to have finally understood that the blessing he stole from his brother was never his blessing. He comprehends that he cannot truly be himself by trying to be his brother. That is why, Sacks argues, Jacob returns to Esau the blessing that he has stolen in the form of a gift: goats, camels, ewes and rams. He also calls Esau "my Lord" and acknowledges by this that power belongs to Esau. Jacob no longer needs these things. He is not reliant on them. No longer does he yearn to be like Esau. He already has everything (*yesh li khol*): He has been blessed by the God with whom he has wrestled.

WHAT HAPPENED DURING THAT NIGHT OF WRESTLING?

According to Sacks, this night-time wrestling is the final stage in the long journey that Jacob travels from deceit to responsibility—a journey that began when he left Laban and that now reaches its climax at the border to the promised land. The moment when Jacob acknowledges what he has done and who he has been up to that point is also the moment when he is ready to take on his own destiny. That is why Jacob does not let God go until he is blessed. It is as though Jacob asks: "What then do You want from me? What is my lot? Who then am I? Where is my place in the story that You began with Abraham?" Jacob's new name, Israel, is God's answer to Jacob's question. It is as though God responds to him: "In the past you strove to be like your brother Esau. In the future you shall wrestle not in order to be Esau, but instead to be yourself. Before you held fast to Esau's heel. In the future you shall hold fast to God. You will not let him go, and He will not let go of you. Let go of Esau now so that you can hold onto God."[13] That is precisely what Jacob does the next day: He lets go of Esau and returns to him his blessing. Riches and power are not the lot of Israel, and even though he maintains a permanent injury from his encounter with God, according to the story Jacob arrived safely in Canaan (Gen. 33:18; Heb. *vayavo Ya'aqov shalem*). He enters the land as a changed man. This is now symbolized through his changed name: He is no longer Jacob who clasps the heel of his brother. He is now Israel who has striven with God. That is the truth that Jacob has discovered in the midst of his wrestling.[14]

THEOLOGICAL REFLECTIONS

The narrative concludes that the lot of Israel is different from the lot of Esau. Esau, who is also called Edom, is the ancestor of the Edomites. Esau not only symbolizes worldly power, but is later identified with world powers such as Babylon and Rome. That is not the lot of Israel. Israel is not called to might, but to responsibility.

What does this reading mean for the relation between Church and Synagogue? There is, so it seems to me, more than one possible answer. Indeed, the way one answers this question, really depends on another question: with which character in the story does the Church identify itself? If we identify the Church with Esau, we identify her calling with power and property. Although it is correct to say that the Church has certainly tended to attire itself in such earthly garments, this is not the way those who follow Christ understand the Church's calling on earth. Certainly, since the Second Vatican Council and the promulgation of the dogmatic constitution *Lumen Gentium*, a different ecclesial understanding has emerged which moves beyond ecclesiological triumphalism.

Another reading is possible, too. As is the case with the two brothers, we could say that the conflict between Church and Synagogue originated in the younger brother's desire to take the place of the older brother. In this reading, we would have to say that the Church wanted to become Jacob/Israel. The harsh conflict between both communities also took root in mimetic rivalry. Listening to Sacks, and learning from his commentary, we could argue that the Church, too, has to pass through a nocturnal struggle (certainly after the Shoah—facing her responsibility in this tragedy) and has to discover and ask anew who she really is. What is her calling; what is her role in God's plan for humanity? Who is she to be or to become, and should she really define herself by taking the blessing God has given to Israel—or does God have more than one blessing (Boys 2000)? The problem, so it seems,

> . . . is not in God but in our own failure to understand that God loves different peoples equally. Learning how to be mature and healthy siblings celebrates the unique ways in which love is bestowed from above. Perhaps, as in Genesis, this new understanding can only come after sibling rivalries degenerate into fratricide, exclusion, or abandonment. But after the Shoah, are we not ready to reconceptualize our broader family through a more loving paradigm. Can we afford not to? (Lander and Lehman quoted in Boys)

For comparative theology after the Shoah, guided by the rules of engagement laid out earlier, the real challenge will be to formulate a non-supersessionist theology, in which the relation between Church and Synagogue is revisited. This chapter cannot do that. It has only formulated fragmentary theological questions and reflections. But doing so, I hope it does contribute to a process of theological revision that has already begun in Jewish-Christian dialogue after the Second Vatican Council.

Notes

1. An exception is Klaus van Stosch 2010: 113–36.
2. The notion "Old Testament" is problematic in view of Jewish-Christian relations. It does not do justice to the self-understanding of Judaism as a vivid tradition. This notion fits in a supersessionist framework. E. Levinas questions this notion in *Difficult Freedom*: "Thus it is that voice of a precursor, as the voice of the Old Testament which—to use a phrase from Buber—the rest of us who are Jews have no reason to consider either a testament or old, or something to be situated in the perspective of a new" (Levinas 1990: 13).
3. It is my contention that these ground rules are also significant for comparative theologians engaging other traditions.
4. The linguistic root of the Hebrew word Midrash is *derash*, which means sermon.
5. Jacob Neuwner, *Genesis Rabbah: The Judaic Commentary to the Book of Genesis, a New American Translation* (Atlanta: Scholars Press, 1985). Resh Lakish (200–275 CE), a Palestinian amora of the second generation: It is sometimes said that before becoming

a sage, Resh Lakish worked as a gladiator, until one day he encountered Rabbi Yochanan, founder of the Academy of Yavneh. He challenged Resh Lakish to devote his strength to the study of the Torah. Later, Resh Lakish even married the sister of Rabbi Yochanan. They maintained a close relationship and together they become known as great authorities in the land Israel.

6. It is said that "Esau came from the field." According to one of the sages, this means that "he had sexual relations with a betrothed girl, in line with the verse: 'But if the man find the damsel that is betrothed in the field and the man take hold of her and lie with her' (Deut. 22: 25)," (Gen. Rabbah 63:12).
7. As we know from the story, Isaac is by then almost blind. According to R. Eleazar b. Azariah, he was blind, "so that he could not see the wickedness of the wicked person," (Gen. Rabbah 65:10).
8. According to the narrative, Isaac loved Esau and thinks him to be great. The sages pondered this. Why is Esau called great? The explanation some of the sages give is that Isaac, as a parent, cannot but think highly of his son. See Gen. Rabbah 65:11: R. Eleazar b. R. Simeon: "The matter may be compared to the case of a town that was seeking a bodyguard for the king. There was a woman there, whose son was a dwarf. She called him 'Tallswift.' She said, 'My son is "Tallshwift," so why do you not take him?' They said to her: 'In your eyes he is "Tallswift," in our eyes he is a dwarf.'"
9. R. Joseph Pazanovski, author of the Pardes Yosef (a commentary on Pentateuch) tells us that Esau was believed to have said: "I won't kill Jacob with bows and arrows, but with my mouth and teeth."
10. Tamari, 47.
11. According to Yuval, the story about the two brothers may be read as a mythic history that legitimizes "a contemporary political reality . . . Jacob and his descendants are described as destined to be lords of the land, while Esau and Ishmael are to serve as their subjects—a reality fulfilled at the time of the First Temple after the subjugation of Edom by David. At the end of the First Temple period, during the Babylonian rule over the kingdom of Judaea, Edom took advantage of this opportunity and ruled over the border regions of Judaea in the northern Negev and thereafter was considered a treacherous brother deserving of the harshest revenge and punishment," (Yuval, 9).
12. Jacob Neusner, in contrast to Cohen, locates the identification of Esau with Christianity already in post-Constantine Rome, but this is not the dominant interpretation.
13. Jonathan Sacks, *Vayishlach 5768—Leah's tears*; http:www.chiefrabbi.org/thoughts/vayishlach5768.html.
14. For a more extensive reading of Jacob's nocturnal struggle, see Moyaert, "Abraham's Strangers."

9 Using Comparative Insights in Developing Kalām

A PERSONAL REFLECTION ON BEING TRAINED IN COMPARATIVE THEOLOGY

Muna Tatari

Starting Points

When I started working on my dissertation in Paderborn in 2010, I was already quite familiar with Islamic theology.[1] I had graduated University with a degree in Islamic studies, a subject quite separate and apart from Islamic theology. I was also a visiting student at an Islamic theological faculty in Jordan for three semesters, and finally studied Islamic theology at a private institute in Hamburg for six semesters. From 1996 to 2010, I worked as a freelance facilitator in the field of inter-religious dialogue. I regularly trained teachers and vicars and co-developed teaching materials with groups of Muslims, Christians, Buddhists, and Jews. I was qualified to contribute basic introductions on a variety of themes in Islamic theology. However, although I thoroughly enjoyed my job, I was keen to avoid becoming just a run-of-the-mill Islamic theologian lacking more profound theological insights.

As such, and in order to improve my theological skills, I decided to apply for a position as a Research Assistant and Ph.D. student at the University of Paderborn in 2010. Because my potential employment at the University was to be within the Centre of Comparative Theology and Cultural Studies, I set out to understand what my role might entail by reading several articles in advance. But, as is often the case, later practice was more effective in imparting a true impression of what it means to engage in comparative theology.[2]

My initial theological research and my proposal for my dissertation, with which I applied to the University of Paderborn, focused on several approaches in Islamic liberation theology. Because of the specific connection between faith and action, I was concerned with how concepts of God and the imperative of ethical responsibility could be convincingly interconnected.

In accordance with my knowledge at the time, I deemed the Muʿtazilite school of thought a particularly fruitful focus for my field of research, based on the idea that the school has a strong focus on rationality, which has over and again proved relevant to contemporary Islamic reform movements.[3] It seemed that by following the Muʿtazilite school, by means of reason, a free space for new theological beginnings could be possible. At the same time, I viewed the Ašʿarite school through a slightly more skeptical lens, not because of its reservations against rationality, but rather because of its stern emphasis on the texts of the tradition as more authoritative than reason.[4] I also had the intuition that the panentheistic worldview approach of the Islamic mystical Philosopher Ibn ʿArabī had a certain potential to moderate the concept of an untouchable and distant God, which was, and still is, widespread in Islamic scholastic theology. I assumed that within his framework, God could be understood more as a God present in history, concerned about his creation and in a dialogical relationship with humans. In terms of ethical questions, the idea of a tangible God could better be recognized as theological grounds for human responsibility.

Areas of Influence

As I began my Ph.D. program at the Centre of Comparative Theology and Cultural Studies, I took nine courses in Christian theology at the University of Paderborn, many of which focused on Catholic theology. I took classes on Christian systematic theology, reason and revelation, Christian theology of the twentieth century, the philosophical framework of doing theology in late modernity, and biblical sciences (hermeneutics). Alongside my own and individual Islam-focused studies, I also attended advanced seminars covering scholars such as Plato, Aristotle, Ibn Rushd, Immanuel Kant, Abū Ḥāmid al-Ġazālī, Fazlur Rahman, Ludwig Wittgenstein, and Friedrich Nietzsche, as well as several contemporary approaches to Trinitarian theology, including those of George Essen, Bernhard Nitsche, Thomas Schärtl, and Karl-Heinz Menke. During the advanced seminars, all Ph.D. students and students (both

Muslim and Christian) spent a weekend together each semester, hosted by a Catholic academy. Here, we discussed all these approaches, confronting complexities such as how to respond theologically to the radical critique of religiosity by Nietzsche. I encountered different interpretations of the aforementioned philosophical and theological approaches that were clearly influenced by differences in the theological backgrounds of the students. This, in turn, facilitated a general sensitivity to the question of epistemic limitations and possibilities. In keeping with Kant's insight that truth is always mediated through humans, the theory of a linguistic turn formulates the relational character of truth more precisely. I noted the latter point within the Christian-Muslim mixed group of Ph.D. students and students; points of view were framed by our individual biographical and scientific backgrounds. Such consonances in theological insights sometimes happened to cross the religious border. Nevertheless, what also became clear to me was that each contextual theological approach ought to be challenged to show its universal meaningfulness.

Another important point of influence during the process of writing my dissertation was my experience of co-teaching with my Christian colleagues on topics such as liberty in Christianity and Islam, liberation theological approaches in Christianity and Islam, salvation as a problem in Christianity and Islam, and introduction to Islamic systematic theology. As an outsider teaching an unfamiliar religious tradition to its own members, I faced many challenges, but my confidence in my knowledge grew over time. Misunderstandings were corrected *coram publico*, a technique that also proved useful for the students. As time unfolded, it became obvious to me that I needed the religious other to clarify whether my understanding of his/her texts was overlaid by my assumptions and pre-understandings as a Muslim. This framework of co-teaching ultimately benefited our search for a normative truth and often led to fruitful arguments and discussions. We were thereby all aware that no one can claim to own the normative truth, and we were convinced that each theological approach should never stop its effort to come as close as possible to that truth, in a never ending process. The questions coming from another religious tradition can help us to rethink our own theological presuppositions and to give a clear and distinct meaning to our own assumptions about theological thinking. The experience of finding and delving deeply together in theologically meaningful argumentation, each colleague speaking for his/her respective theological tradition, was, and still is, enriching and exhausting. Because terms like mercy, justice, salvation, obligation, and nature are settled in different language-games that frame meaning differently, no theological sentence remains self-explanatory to me anymore.

Thus, at the beginning of my encounter with comparative theology, I came to realize that I had not only a quantitative lack of knowledge, but also a qualitative lack of knowledge related to my own religious tradition. Regarding current philosophical discourses and theories of knowledge, I was not well equipped and therefore faced the challenge to catch-up with those academic discourses in Germany that are crucial to any theology, including Islamic theology, if it desires to be part of an academic and public discourse community rather than a *sui generis* or isolated science.

By way of practice—doing—comparative theology, I consciously decided to delve into late modern scientific insights and modes of discourse, trying to open my mind as far as possible. Alongside my analyses and insights within Islamic theology, this helps to foster a rich debate with my dialogue partners, and it is a process that is very much on-going.

My engagement with a comparative approach to theology has influenced my theological thinking in several ways. For example, it was my initial engagement with Christian approaches to the nature of God and God's relation to creation in Trinitarian structures that awakened my enthusiasm for systematic theology in general. Consequently, I changed my plan for my dissertation dramatically and departed from an approach that emphasizes the contextuality of each theological approach to an attempt that commits itself to a systematic normative concept in the search for Islamic concepts of God—in which God could be understood as graspable in concrete historical dimensions.

In the then-modified concepts of my original dissertation proposal, which was then entitled "God and Humans in Relation to Justice and Mercy: An Attempt to Clarify an Islamic Position," I therefore dealt with two central issues. On the one hand, I wanted to clarify the relation between two concepts of substantial importance in the Qur'ānic text: justice and mercy. On the other hand, still inspired by and convinced of the importance of the impulses that liberation theology provides, I wanted to focus on ethical questions by trying to explore the possibility of an anthropological turn in Islamic theology. The language of an anthropological turn is widespread in current Christian theology in Germany; it says that theology has to start with anthropology, as Karl Rahner starts his foundations of Christian belief with a chapter on the nature of human beings.[5] The correlation of theological subjects with anthropological questions wants to be a framework for theology that addresses the critique of enlightenment thinkers and helps theological investigations to be existentially relevant. In my own theology I try to show whether such an approach makes sense as a framework for Islamic theology. This would help me to understand the categories of justice and mercy not only in a transcendent dimension, but as concrete qualities that can be experienced in daily life.

In what follows, I will discuss five major topics within my dissertation that were inspired by comparative theology. I hope to show how I used tools and insights developed by Christian theology and by the philosophy of late modernity to reconstruct Islamic thought on a specific subject.

Metaphysical Approaches and Their Inherent Difficulties

The first of my chosen topics that was at the heart of my dissertation pertains to the issue of Islamic theology and Islamic philosophy in scholastic frames. Both have traditionally applied almost identical methods and have dealt with almost identical subjects. Both sciences blossomed through the reception of Greek philosophy and its further development by Muslim thinkers. The works of Aristotle, Plato, and Plotinus, who were some of the most important thinkers relative to classical Islamic thought, have almost never been questioned by the majority of Muslim thinkers, even until today. They are still highly influential in the construction of ideas and concepts within Islamic theology. However, the means of explaining reality itself, either by empirical or rational approaches, which is characteristic of metaphysical approaches and therefore of scholastic Islamic theology, is, in most Western scholarly traditions (at least in continental Europe), generally considered out of date since the times of Immanuel Kant and the impact of his insights on humanities.

One important section of my dissertation dealt with the Muʿtazilite theologian ʿAbd al-Ǧabbār (d. 1024), whose approach is framed dominantly by the category of (God's) justice, and the Ašʿarite theologian Abū Ḥāmid al-Ġazālī (d. 1111), who was keen to argue against the Muʿtazilites and in favor of the category of God's omnipotence and (though not in the same obvious manner) for God's mercy. Representatives of their time, they acted within a metaphysical frame of reference, and both are still considered to be unquestioned authorities in their field. Sensitized by my doctoral studies, however, I was able to contextualize the apodictic nature of their thinking and to classify both scholars as representatives of a certain, and until today, influential period.

It was one thing for me to reconstruct the philosophical-historical development in Europe on a theoretical level, without any influence on my personal belief. It was quite a different thing, however, to apply this theoretical reconstruction to my own theological tradition in practice. In my struggle with the theological arguments of both scholars, I was not able to find answers to late modern theological questions that focus on concepts of freedom, a dialogical human-God-relationship, and new approaches to concepts of God. This is because ʿAbd al-Ǧabbār and al-Ġazālī lived in a different time period, were driven by other pressing questions, and worked within different frames of reference. Recognizing this changed my relationship to these scholars of the past. I remain far from claiming that the insights of ʿAbd al-Ǧabbār and al-Ġazālī are outdated; I was, and still am, able to recognize the value of their works for present day issues. But because I am able to contextualize their ideas and claims, I am now able to pose my theological concerns in a more deliberate relationship to them. Without being obliged to think like ʿAbd al-Ǧabbar, I can nevertheless still honor his great emancipatory achievements in regard to his trust in the epistemic skills of human beings and their ability to fructify this insight in regard to current issues.[6] And without adapting the same philosophical system for my theological thinking, I am still inspired by the intellectual curiosity of al-Ġazālī, which has opened new and creative ways of reasoning that are relevant up to the present time.[7] Without great reservations, al-Ġazālī used the philosophical systems of Neoplatonic and Aristotelian thinking to frame his theological convictions, which were the systems of reasoning in his days Thus, I found that delving into contemporary Christian and philosophical thinking today must be seen neither as an alien movement nor as a threat to Islamic theology. Al-Ġazālī is a key witness to the fact that every scholarly approach grapples with the methodologies of its time. Ebrahim Moosa, for example, is aware of the dependence on context of every insight and every methodology used. Therefore, he describes his relationship to al-Ġazālī not as one of uncritical adaption but as one of friendship.[8] Humans take the opinion of a good friend seriously, but not uncritically. Through my comparative education, I learned to gain distance from the authorities of the scholastic tradition by becoming aware how much their reasoning was influenced by Greek philosophy. But at the same time, I learned how to take them seriously in a new way by using insights of the anthropological turn for the sake of rereading my own tradition.

AN ANTHROPOLOGICAL TURN IN ISLAMIC THEOLOGY

The task of getting a fresh insight into my own tradition by following the anthropological turn was a second challenge for my Ph.D. project. I had to explore whether anthropological ideas and insights of transcendental philosophy can become relevant for Islamic theology. Is it possible that there could be an Islamic equivalent to the anthropological turn that was prominently introduced into Catholic Christian theology by theologians such as Karl Rahner?

Studying Immanuel Kant and Karl Rahner helped me to shed new light on the Islamic tradition and to explore new ways of thinking within Islam. Stepping back from proclaimed and believed metaphysical certainties leaves room for further developments and enables one to appreciate the interpretations of theological concepts in the past—partly, although not wholly, as mirrors of their times. Therefore, I wanted to examine an Islamic approach that begins with creation itself and, thus, with the human being itself. This hermeneutical shift enables one to argue for a deeper appreciation of the whole of creation and of human beings and their particular needs. Such new theological thinking can then, I suggest, be reconnected to the teachings in the Islamic tradition in general.

From the perspective of contemporary challenges, formulated by philosophers and theologians of other religious beliefs and convictions, I argue that the richness of the Islamic tradition can be rediscovered. Isolated and unconnected fragments and methods of the past, when combined, can provide grounds for a new and consistent approach—for example, that of an anthropological turn. In this way, the subsequent tradition gains importance because it seems to deal with the fact that knowledge has always to do with the presuppositions of concrete persons. You cannot gain insights without looking at how humans perceive it, and even the Qur'ān cannot be understood without looking at how humans perceive it. Insight in the need for a mediation process between a text and its understanding is already reflected in some sense in a prominent text written at the very beginning of Islamic scholarship:

> . . . Members of the Khawarij accused ʿAli of accepting the judgment and dominion (*hakimiyya*) of human beings instead of abiding by the dominion of God's law. Upon hearing of this accusation, ʿAli called upon the people to gather around him and bring a large copy of the Qur'ān. ʿAli touched the Qur'ān while instructing it to speak to the people and inform them about God's law. Surprised, the people gathered around ʿAli exclaimed, "What are you doing? The Qur'ān cannot speak, for it is not a human being!" Upon hearing this, ʿAli exclaimed that this was exactly his point. The Qur'ān, ʿAli explained, is but ink and paper, and it does not speak for itself. Instead, it is human beings who give effect to it according to their limited personal judgments and opinions [. . .].[9]

This teaching from ʿAli makes clear that there cannot be knowledge of the Qur'ān without humans dealing with it. This can be seen as a first move toward an anthropological turn in Islam. When looking further into possibilities of such a turn in Islamic theology, I discovered promising methods and theories external to the theological arena in the discipline of Islamic law, jurisprudence, and ethics (*fiqh*). Consequently, I engaged in the discipline of discovering the roots of Islamic law, jurisprudence, and ethics (*uṣūl al-fiqh*), by a methodology that predominantly discusses the epistemic capacities[10] of humans.

The question of the importance of human judgment was predominant in Islamic jurisprudential discourses, and this resulted in two main movements.[11] On one hand, the Muḫaṭṭīʾa school assumed that there is only one fixed truth decreed by God. All efforts that do not comply with or reflect this truth are thus wrong (*ḫaṭṭaʾan*). On the other hand, the Muṣawwiba school held that in the area of unsolved questions (*al-masāʾil al-fiqhīya aẓ-ẓannīya*) every *muǧtahid* who exerts the utmost effort in his/her endeavor to extract a right ruling and reach a conclusion or judgment is deemed correct because it is assumed here that there is not only one definite commandment of God. This opinion is valid for most of the members of this school (the majority of them belonging to the Ašʿarīya school). This argumentation, however, does not apply to areas of definitive and clear formulations (*al-qaṭʿīyāt*). Interestingly, this claim was not left uncontested among the scholars of the classical time. Some of them also assumed that every honest human effort, even in regard to the *qatʿīyāt*, is right, even if, as a consequence, different views of God's essence and attributes arise. The underlying notion here is that God simply cannot punish humans for what they cannot do even if they try their best, namely to approach a problem in an objective manner to gain a single objective truth.[12]

Thus, based on the approach of the Muṣawwiba school, we can see that awareness of the influence of context on knowledge, whether it be biographical, historical, or methodological, can be found in classical Islamic tradition. This can even be said to enlarge Kant's approach because of an acceptance of different results in reasoning. This acceptance is based on the conviction that all people cannot be assumed to have the same subject-structure, as Kant seemed to assume. Rather, by a perspective initiated by Nietzsche and spelled-out in the linguistic turn in late modernity, the diversity of subjects was acknowledged, based on their respective contexts, such as were already present within Islamic tradition. So, prompted by a European discourse, I was able to figure out in which ways Muslim scholars dealt with the fact that due to diversity, people come to different conclusions. Especially within the school of the Muṣawwiba, one can recognize an acceptance and appreciation of a diversity of results and a discourse based on the development of arguments.[13]

Anver Emon takes the theological implications of both schools (*muḫaṭṭiʾa* and *muṣawwiba*) into consideration. With regard to the Muḫaṭṭiʾa school he, alongside Khaled Abou el-Fadl, understands the process of recognizing that the fixed truth of God is a process that will remain forever unfinished. Because no human being can claim to be able to assess God's thoughts, no one can have an authoritative legitimacy to terminate this process of searching for divine truth. However, Emon criticizes the approach of the Muḫaṭṭiʾa school, arguing that no space is left for human creativity if one insists that God has already stipulated one specific truth. In matters of anthropology, it is important to recognize the difference between the schools: whether humans are said to be only able to discover what was already decreed by God, or whether they are said to be able to create and discover new insights, as the Muṣawwiba school taught. Accordingly, Emon finds in the latter attempt a greater degree of creative freedom, due to the fact that God has not established any fixed contents, and that humans, therefore, have to find their own way.[14]

Additionally, I discovered several other anthropological approaches within classical Islamic law discourse that can be interpreted as greatly appreciating human beings as rational subjects with their own perspective which should usually be taken into account. Contrary to mainstream classical theological propositions that hold humans to be defined exclusively by their dependency on God, there were very early discussions in the Islamic legal tradition dealing with the rights of God (*ḥuqūq allāh*) and the rights of human beings (*ḥuqūq al-ʿibād*). Through studying these discussions, I found, additional steps can be taken toward a more differentiated positioning of God and human beings.

The rights of God and the rights of human beings have frequently been discussed in criminal law, but the meanings of these as specified in past historical contexts can hardly be adopted directly in current times.[15] The paralleling of the rights of God with the interests of the public good is a crucial matter that is very controversial today. But for the purpose of this paper, it seems to me important to focus on the relational structure between *the rights of God and the rights of human beings*. The main point here for my research interest was that the reciprocal claims of God on the one side and humans on the other were negotiated in the practice of legal scholars. Sometimes the decision by lawyers to implement a private law for the human was done at the expense of God's right.[16]

It seems to be obviously anachronistic to try to recognize in this discussion the idea of the autonomy of the subject as discussed in modernity. Indeed, from a religious-theological perspective, complete autonomy of the subject is simply unthinkable. Ultimate dependence of the human being on God is a structural element essential also to Islamic theology. However, it would be a mistake to neglect the emancipatory features of the discussion that was outlined earlier wherein jurists of Islamic Law decided that human beings were given rights distinct from God's right, such that these rights were sometimes esteemed as of more value than God's right.

This classic discussion regarding where God's rights and human rights have their respective domains, and how the latter is to be respected as distinct from God and God's perspective, can be used as a bridge to modern concepts and theories that attribute to the human perspective its own value. Thus, the distinction between the perspective of God and the perspective of human beings, along with an appreciation of both, does not need to be perceived as alien to the Islamic tradition. To summarize the benefits of those insights by using the method of comparative theology: It can be said that I gained fresh insight into my own religious tradition through questions arising from my comparative work. I discovered the importance of discourses in Islamic jurisprudence, leading to a new approach in Islamic systematic theology. Comparative work thus makes you more sensitive to the richness of your own tradition, and it helps you to discover tools for a better structure within your own thinking.

It confronts you with new questions, but also affords you new capacities for looking into your own tradition.

Ibn ʿArabī's Substance-Ontological Approach and the Question of Freedom

The views of the mystical philosopher Ibn ʿArabī (d. 1240) formed the third topic in my dissertation This engagement has been less helpful in leading to the solution of my theological questions than I had expected; indeed, it has aggravated them. As an Ašʿarī theologian with strong neoplatonic imprints, Ibn ʿArabī tried to cope with both the idea of the total independence of God and the conviction that God is present in, and as, creation (*tağallī*); this resembles a panentheistic position. Panentheism is most often understood as the belief that the divine interpenetrates every part of the universe yet also exists beyond time and space. Panentheism in my understanding maintains therefore a distinction between the divine and non-divine, but at the same time maintains also the presence of the divine in all reality.

Ibn ʿArabī explicated his reasoning consistently in an ontological framework that thinks of God as a being, and which sees a link between God's being and human's being in the very substance of being. I call this kind of ontology, which thinks of God and creation in terms of being and substance, a "substance-ontological framework" in philosophy. It is quite common in the Greek tradition in metaphysics, and it is criticized by thinkers who insist that it is not being or substance that is the ultimate foundation of reality, but relation and process. In the light of this distinction, Ibn ʿArabī is using a substance-ontological framework instead of using relational ontology, positing God as the supreme being and creation as a relative being. Here Ibn ʿArabī is concerned with the question of *how* creation is possible; within a substance-ontological framework, he concentrated on the cause of creation.[17] However, his approach does not fit into modern frameworks when he tries to close the gap between the unconditional (God) and the conditional (God's creation) by claiming that they consist of the same substance, but in a different degree of purity. According to my understanding of the critique of the metaphysical tradition in transcendental philosophy, such claims of a sameness of substance in God and human cannot be defended coherently. Moreover, scholars like Daniel A. Madigan have rightly pointed out that in the context of revelation—which is an important aspect of the question of the relationship of God and creation—the idea of a gradual transition from an unconditioned being to conditioned beings does not really solve the problem of how creation and God's relation to it can be imagined. In my view, such a Neoplatonic perspective just distributes the speculative problems into many small ones without allowing us to conceive a real relationship between God and human.[18] Nevertheless, I am still struggling with the idea of accessing the God-human relationship from a panentheistic perspective, and for that reason I try still to learn from Ibn ʿArabī, yet without buying into his metaphysical system.

In my view, the approach of ʿArabī can be reframed with correlative insights arising in modern process theology. Taken together, these have the potential to allow for an understanding of God as the ground of being, and thus an understanding of creation as a consequence of God's being.[19] Accordingly, a God-creation relationship determined on substance-ontological terms must be put aside in order to strengthen the idea of the otherness that exists between God and the human, and in that way to give more space to the categories of freedom, autonomy, and, consequently, human responsibility. From a panentheistic perspective, difference is part of the very being of God and, therefore, God's creation can be considered to be part of this difference within God. However, it is important to note that I am aware of the great theological implications this will have in regard to God's nature. I will address this concern in very brief notes in the section that follows.

Regarding the question of the freedom of the human being, which is crucial in a panentheistic approach, Jürgen Werbick, a Catholic fundamental theologian, holds that freedom can be understood as the full and willing agreement of a person to what his/her nature created by God already provides.[20] Similarly, freedom in Islamic thinking can be understood in reliance on the work of Ibn ʿArabī, as saying "yes" to God's plan, which then becomes a reality through human freedom. This understanding of freedom also ties in with the idea of aš-Šṭibīs (d. 1388), who pointed out that the objective of the *Šarīʿā* (the way to God) lies in "free[ing] human from his vain wishful thinking so that man can become a servant of God by choice, as he is already a servant without choice."[21]

Future Theological Challenges

All the challenges that I have discussed thus far are located primarily in the realm of philosophy, thus showing the huge impact of philosophical insights on theological reasoning. They show that the philosophical frame of Christian theological concepts in the Western tradition in modernity can be fruitful for Muslim thought as well. In my concluding paragraphs, I want to focus more explicitly on theological subjects and on my way of struggling with theological challenges arising due to my comparative education. In general, it can be said that dealing with comparative theology has led me to a new and better understanding of theological problems in general. Looking back, I now understand that my dissertation was an effort that provided me with an important basis for my current and upcoming theological work. Throughout my thesis, I dealt with the key categories of mercy and justice, and tried to show that there is a reciprocal relationship. Now, based on the issues raised by my late modern analysis of the approach of Ibn ʿArabī, I tend rather to focus on the principle of *tauḥīd* (oneness of God) in relation to the ninety-nine names of God. This helps me to elaborate a concept of God that includes movement and difference and that also includes His relation to creation. Accordingly, I am trying now to develop a new theological concept that allows me to combine the insistence on the oneness and unity of God with a deep respect for difference and diversity. The tool for doing this is my insight that *tauḥīd* has to be conceived as a dynamic category pointing to the process of unification, and not to a substance or a closed state of affairs.

By focusing on *tauḥīd* and the names of God, I indirectly examine the historic classification of the seven main attributes of God (life, power, will, knowledge, speech, hearing, vision), which have remained relevant from the time of Islamic scholasticism to the present day, but which suffer from the fact that they have undergone no redefinitions in regard to their conception or content. At this point, I think it will be fruitful cautiously to question the usefulness of strictly holding onto these categorizations, especially when contemporary Islamic theology does not act within the limitations of a scholastic framework and when relevant key categories such as justice and mercy are not included therein. So, the key question will be to ask: To what extent does it still remain necessary to attribute seven main attributes to God, and to what extent does this attribution need to be reconsidered? Through reconsidering this attribution, a space can be opened up for new responses to the challenges of late modernity, as, for example, its option for a greater appreciation of difference and diversity.

A New Framework: Critical Traditionalism

Reflecting on the broader frames of my theological thinking as a fifth topic within my dissertation, my views have significantly changed and my working methods have grown more precise. While arguing for the same theological insights as before my dissertation, I have utilized different frames of reference according to the challenges of modernity and I have also distanced myself from certain theological ideas concerning the concept of *tauḥīd*, for example, as explained previously.[22] My encounter as a Muslim with Christian thought in the pattern of comparative theology was helpful in this regard. In practice, I experienced the usefulness of the theoretical claim that there is no Islam as such and no Christianity as such; rather, there are different views in each tradition regarding how to understand and practice the tradition. Engaging in discussions and theological arguments from a specific, clearly defined perspective, as is characteristic of comparative theology, deepens and intensifies the search for truth and relieves one of the unrealistic claim that one should be able to value tradition all at once, as a totality. This thematic deep drilling is able to provide insights into other theological traditions in a very focused way. It enables each partner in the dialogue to walk for a while in the shoes of the other and to understand that person within his/her context. The focus on concrete theological attempts neither forecloses the question of truth nor implies relativism. Rather, it places each result in relation to specific contexts. On this basis, an honest appreciation of the religious other is possible, without covering over theological differences.

Seeing my tradition through the eyes of the religious other and being challenged by the arguments and methods of late modernity have led me to question my own convictions. The fruitfulness of maintaining a distance from what is dear and valuable to a person is also a Qur'ānic insight. The reader of the Qur'ān is encouraged to ponder the Qur'ān; indeed, the Arabic expression *tadabbur* means to reflect, to ponder, to turn one's back to somebody or something.[23] The combination of meanings here suggests that a temporal distance from the subject of study can increase insight. This, too, is what comparative theology is about.

All of this leads me to the following considerations. My presumption that the methods of the Muʿtazilite school may be especially useful for theological departures because of their emphasis on rationality has proven to be only partially true. The confidence of Abd al-Ǧabbār in the epistemic capacities of human beings has great potential to connect with certain humanistic ideas. He was driven by his effort to understand human beings as able to reason to the highest degree in regard to the creation and its creator. Nevertheless he, unlike al-Ġazālī, failed to consider the conditioned nature of the cognitive ability of humans. He bought too fully into a metaphysical system that was not always helpful to understand what the Qur'ān wants to say. For example, ʿAbd al-Ǧabbār understood God as bound by the same ethical principles as humans, which can be an important corrective to the notion of an arbitrary unpredictable and ultimately untrustworthy God. But he paid a high price for this from a theological perspective. I now see that he left no room for the ultimately incomprehensible greatness of God, which is expressed in Islamic theology by the term *allāhu akbar* (God is greater). This important insight also has its Christian equivalent in the term *deus semper major* (God is always greater), as scholars in the Latin tradition put it.

Although the Ašʿarīya school emphasizes the *bi-lā kaif* ("without asking how") doctrine, which seems to be at odds with the search for understanding in science, this school also provides a framework which seems more adequate to the complexity of current theological challenges. Scholars of the Ašʿarīya school did not try to solve a problem from the perspective of a single primary category. Pace the Muʿtazilites who always use the category of justice and pace some modern approaches of Christian theology, which use the category of free will to solve all problems, Ašʿarites are flexible in their ways of dealing with problems. Rather, they approach the subject in terms of different categories, and this approach seems to be more adequate for theology today. Theological thinking cannot be restricted to a specific one-way perspective. As Jürgen Werbick suggests, theological thinking cannot finally resolve theological problems, but it can and should stabilize tensions.[24]

In my theological work I dealt intensively with exemplary Islamic theological positions of the scholastic era and strove to grasp its deep insights and evident context-given limitations. This work has led me to seek a foundation for my theological thinking. If one takes Martin Heidegger's insights seriously, then an engagement with a text of the past for the purpose of seeking an answer to today's questions in the works of the classical scholars is fruitless: They cannot give answers to questions of another time.[25] If, according to Heidegger, understanding is based on the context of individual circumstances, then every person is only able to act and think according to his/her current context and for her/his current context. What, therefore, can be the purpose of studying the texts of famous and honored scholars of the past? In my opinion, Moosa gives an appropriate answer to this. He points out that texts of the tradition have no independent status. They are intertwined with past and current interpretative efforts. As Gadamer puts it, every tradition itself forms prejudices that influence the interpretation of a text.[26] And according to Moosa, tradition is more than the text itself; it is an attitude inscribed in the body and mind.[27] Therefore, reconstructing tradition means keeping in touch with the past in a specific way, by critically reflecting upon and choosing consciously those impulses by which one wants to frame oneself in relation to current debates. This process implies the possibility of active and critical self-reconstruction. Through my comparative work I have gained many insights that were helpful in this process.

Concluding Remarks

As will now be clear, I had an exciting and challenging time during my Ph.D. research. My results thus far, like every theology, must undergo further reconstruction and re-examination. I am very much convinced of the dialectical structure of gaining knowledge. No insight can be taken for granted; certainty and doubt alternate continuously.[28] This is the source of an ongoing struggle to deepen one's knowledge of God and God's vision for creation.

Engaging in comparative theology has very much stretched the boundaries of my theological framework. Without comparison and scholarly exchange there is a danger of staying with an approach from a single perspective that does not take challenges and impulses from other traditions into account. Facing the dangers of monolithic tendencies in theology I became aware of a Qur'ānic expression. For a long time, I struggled with the Qur'ānic notion of Muslims building up a "median" community (*ummatan wusatan*),[29] a community with balanced structures and points of view. Yet I always suspected that searching for a median community is consequently followed by a "mediocre" theology, unable to engage people. But if one takes the idea of a dialectical structure of knowledge acquisition into account, this Qur'ānic expression can be understood as encouraging always to struggle to travel a balanced middle way as an ongoing process. This includes stretching oneself to the edges. This is the way I have interpreted my probing of new ways of doing theology within the framework of comparative theology: Finding a middle way, a balanced way, requires comprehensive studies at the edges.

Notes

1. This paper presents my personal and subjective encounter with comparative theology and how it influenced the process of writing my Ph.D. dissertation. This speaks to the question of how to do comparative theology because I was one of the first two Muslim student to go through a special Ph.D. program in comparative theology at Paderborn University. Part of the program was a deep encounter with Christian theologies.
2. For a detailed introduction to comparative theology in a German context, see von Stosch, *Komparative Theologie als Wegweiser*, vol. 6.
3. See Martin, *Defenders of Reason.*
4. Both schools, Mu'tazila and Ašʿarīya, emerged in the eighth and ninth century and belonged for a long time to the major theological schools in Islam. The school of the Muʿtazilites dissolved in the fourteenth century and its main ideas were integrated in Schiʿi Islam, while Ašʿarite theology remains influential to Sunni Islam until today.
5. Cf. Rahner, *Grundkurs des Glaubens.*
6. For a Muʿtazilī understanding of reason, see Reinhart, *Before Revelation*, 151–57, 159, and for a definition of the relation between reason and revelation in the thought of ʿAbd al-Ǧabbār, ibid. 151–54, 157–60.
7. Moosa, *Ghazālī and the Poetics*, 28, 57.
8. Ibid., 29.
9. Abou el-Fadl, "Islam and Democracy."
10. The notion of "epistemic capacities" points to the "Kategorien und Anschauungsformen," which are so important in Kant's critique of pure reason. Thus, it shows that every human has a noetic structure that forms her knowledge and her understanding of reality. To take into consideration those capacities and structures in the analysis of how humans understand reality is the first step toward including anthropological insights in theology.
11. For a general introduction to this subject, see Kevin Reinhardt, *Before Revelation*. The following passages are a translation from my dissertation, *Gott und Mensch.*
12. For those different schools of thought, see Poya, "'*Iǧtihād*' und Glaubensfreiheit," 244–56.
13. Ibid.
14. See Emon, *Religious Pluralism and Islamic Law*, 201–2.
15. For a definition of those terms and their application in praxis, see Emon, "Ḥuqūq Allāh and Ḥuqūq al-ʿIbād."
16. Ibid.
17. For a general introduction, see Chittick, *The Self-Disclosure of God* and for the god-creation relation see Izutsu, *Sufism and Taoism*, 49–57.
18. See Madigan, "Revelation and Inspiration."
19. See Faber, *Gott als Poet der Welt*; Alpyagil, "Trying to Understand Whitehead in the Context of Ibn ʿArabi," and Whittemore, "The Process Philosophy of Sir Muhammad Iqbal," 113–30.
20. See Werbick, "Zur Freiheit hat uns Christus befreit," 68–69.

21. See aš-Šāṭibī, al-Muwāfaqāt, vol 2, 469. In Arabic: *Al-maq(odot)sad aš-šarʿī min waḍʿ aš-šarīʿa iḫrāj al-mukallif min dāʿīya hawāhu ḥatā yakūn ʿabdan li-llāh iḫtīyaran kamā huwa ʿabd li-llāh iḍṭrāran.* See also those Quranic verses dealing with willing and unwilling submission to God's vision of creation: Qur'ān 3:83, 13:15, and 41:11.
22. For another example, i.e., my conviction on theodicy, see my paper "Plädoyer für die Klage vor Gott" ["Plea for a Complaint to God"], 279–85.
23. See Lane, *Arabic-English Lexicon*, vol. 3, 844–48.
24. See Werbick, *Theologische Methodenlehre*, 23–31.
25. See Harvey, "Hermeneutics," 3930–36.
26. See Gadamer, *Wahrheit und Methode* [Truth and Method], 301.
27. See Moosa, "Transitions in the 'Progress' of Civilization," 15–130.
28. See Abu Zaid, "Was bedeutet der Begriff Gewissheit?" ["What connotes the term Certainty?"], 89–106.
29. See Qur'ān 2:143.

10 Difficult Remainders

SEEKING COMPARATIVE THEOLOGY'S REALLY DIFFICULT OTHER

Francis X. Clooney, S.J.

Seeking a True Other for Christian Comparative Theology

The Christian comparative theological engagement with other faith traditions is most often driven by attention to select themes, images, and practices already somewhat familiar, even if inexactly, in Christian tradition. This approach makes sense and is fruitful. The preference for the familiar risks an evasion of the more difficult realm of the unfamiliar, and reducing the great texts of other traditions to compendia of ideas available for selective consideration as desired. Comparisons are often asymmetrical, too. Christian comparativists at their best work with a rich sense of the completeness of Christian faith, and of the organic coherence of Christian doctrine and practice. But often enough we do not match this sensitivity with a corresponding appreciation and appropriation of the wealth and depth and integral order of other traditions, explained on their own terms and not simply by methods and theological measures already familiar to us.[1] We overlook their overall coherence, and render them impotent, even as they are received into a very well-meaning Christian theological project. To do better as Christian theologians hoping to learn interreligiously, we need to reconsider what we read, and learn to attend to whole texts and how things are said, and not just to themes. Style is key here, given the discipline and precision with which texts were written, and their expectation of careful readers.

If Christian comparativists do take the texts of other theological traditions seriously as integral wholes and as works of literature that require holistic and respectful reading, we will be confronted with the resistance that integral wholes pose to those seeking merely one or another useful idea. Complex and systematic texts proceed by a technical vocabulary and in accord with architectonic structures that regulate how they are to be received and read. Readers respectful of their rather obvious structures and ranking of terms will be more reluctant merely to mine them for insights into one or another topic. Granting that the overall intentions of whole Hindu theological texts may resemble those already familiar to the Christian theologian—the defense of the faith, the careful use of reasoning in support of faith, the coherence of scriptural statements, and the coherence of text and practice—nevertheless, the insistence on a certain completeness and even perfection in a given, refined statement of traditional beliefs places a formidable whole before the theologian who can no longer pick and choose items of interest out of context.

I therefore propose in this essay that the next great test for comparative theology is to engage these difficult, near-complete systems to see how comparison works in the face of an intensely rationalized other that is difficult because it requires intense thinking, engagement as a whole, in a difference that is not a matter of experience or the apophatic, but straightforward, different language. My example is the Mīmāṁsā ritual thinking of the Vedic and Hindu traditions. One of the most important and distinctive Indian ways of thinking, it overwhelms us not by its rarity or inaccessibility, but rather by its utter lucidity and completeness—and difference.

What is Mīmāṁsā? This ancient Indian mode of ritual analysis is characterized at the start of the Mīmāṁsā Sūtras, the oldest text of this tradition, as the "inquiry into dharma" (the right order and ordering of nature and society, rituals, and ways of thinking). This inquiry may be elaborated as "the desire and effort to know in proper measure," "the effort to intense reflection," and "enquiry, theoretical discussion (sometimes as opposed to practice)."[2] The goal is to analyze and understand the deep harmony of the ritual texts and practices of the Veda, the primary oral body of revelation pertaining to rituals and their cultural and social frame. Mīmāṁsā is considered one of the key and ancient supporting disciplines (*veda-aṅga*) of the Veda, and as essential to it, the Veda's own fundamental reasoning, *veda-tarka*. The approximately 900 cases debated in Mīmāṁsā comprise the set of ritual acts and ritual texts determined by Jaimini (300–200 BCE) to be open to dispute. These cases form the substance of the 2700 sūtras (brief statements, often part of arguments) of his Mīmāṁsā Sūtras. These were elaborated by generations of Mīmāṃsā scholars.

Mīmāṁsā analyses are grounded in the material detail of simple and elaborate Vedic rituals and the texts governing those rituals. As analytic and oriented to the clarification of interpretive rules, Mīmāṁsā does not directly offer guidance on how actually to do rituals,[3] and it does not venture any overall interpretation of the Veda or the Vedic rituals. It focuses simply on the difficult cases where it is interestingly uncertain how to read and apply one or another text, and accordingly understand the web of rituals properly performed and their texts properly read. It did so for the sake of clarity regarding principles about performance and, it seems, for the sake of the purest, simplest understanding of the rules governing and therefore facilitating ritual and textual coherence and synergy, texts and actions in perfect harmony: the complexity and confusion of traditional practices and discrepant texts are only apparent, given the deep underlying cohesion of the rules enunciated and enacted.

It is hard to define or quantify what the Sūtras are about, but we can draw a general estimate by noticing the themes traditionally taken to characterize each book (*adhyāya*): the authority (*pramāṇa*) in the form of injunctions, commendatory statements, and so on (Book I); distinction (*karma-bheda*) among actions, sacrifices, gifts, and so on (Book II); the accessory status (*śeṣatva*) of the fore-sacrifices, and so on, as for the sake of the new and full moon sacrifices, and so on (Book III); decisions regarding aptness (*prayukti*), sorting out which actions are done for the sake of the ritual, and which are for the sake of the person, as ritual performer or more generally in his ordinary life (Book IV); constraint in terms of order or succession (*krama*), even if this is mentioned and not explicitly enjoined (Book V); the fact that there is ritual eligibility (*adhikāra*), competence for agents in general, but not of those ineligible due to various deficiencies, plus other cases related to ritual eligibility and competence (Book VI); transfer in general (*sāmānya-atideśa*) of details from an amply described ritual to another ritual incompletely sketched or merely named, by explicit statements and by statements inferred with reference to the names of various sacrifices, and so on (Book VII); special cases of transfer (*viśiṣṭa-atideśa*), dependent on which mode of procedure is followed, which deities or materials are substituted, and so on (Book VIII); modification of rituals (*ūha*) in their adapted forms, by the changing of the name of deities receiving the offering, materials offered, and so on (Book IX), the cancellation (*bādha*) of no longer relevant details in adapted rituals, as when threshing, appropriate to the preparation of rice, is recognized as inapplicable to gold coins taking the place of rice in an adapted ritual, and so on (Book X); the common performance (*tantra*) of subordinate helps, such as the fore-sacrifices, performed once but serving multiple rituals (Book XI); the incidental help (*prasaṅga*) of subordinate rituals, such as the fore-sacrifices, brought in to help the primary animal ritual, but also contributing to related rituals (Book XII). Every one of these interpretive categories organizes differing perspectives on ritual practice, in accord with deep reverence for that practice. Each category then occasions rigorous analysis aimed at articulating rules that can govern the actual practices of rituals, without pushing aside the actual practices for the sake of inner meanings or wider generalizations. It is in the relatedness that the intellectual core and theological heart of the Mīmāṁsā lies.[4] These are the categories in terms of which one must think, if one is to think in accord with Mīmāṁsā.

Mīmāṁsā is a large and complex system, difficult in its details and organized by categories other than those ordinarily familiar to Christian theologians. Mīmāṁsā is rational, clear, and systematic, and the Sūtras, among close study, yield layers of reasoned inquiry. Yet at the same time, Mīmāṁsā is strikingly different in its content, resistant to efforts at generalization, and even dismissive of appeals to the transcendent and experiential such as those that drive much of Christian theology. It is accessible as a whole only after a great deal of prolonged and patient study, and even the basic commentaries are often too long and too detailed to enable intelligent apprehension of them as wholes. To appreciate the vast bulk of the Mīmāṁsā inquiry without disparaging ritual reasoning as an older and largely irrelevant stratum of Hindu tradition, we need to go deeper, and for this, we need an economical point of entry, a text dealing with that material in a manageable fashion.[5] We can hardly expect to be ready for the very long course of study that would make us masters of the Mīmāṁsā.

Luckily, there are texts that, either as straightforward summations or under the guise of introductions, present long and complex Hindu traditions in a relatively simple form that nevertheless does justice to the traditions distilled and compressed. Here I propose just one for our consideration: the *Jaiminīya Nyāya Mālā* (*Garland of Jaimini's Reasons*; henceforth *Garland*) of Mādhava (1297–1388).[6] This is a teaching text of the medieval Mīmāṁsā tradition, comprising about 1400 two-line verses (*śloka*). Composed at a time when traditional learning was being consolidated and rendered pedagogically more accessible, it aims to resolve as simply and elegantly as possible classic problematic cases in ritual interpretation, a set numbered at about 900 since the time of Jaimini (first century BC through first century CE), the first great Mīmāṁsā author known to us. Like much of Mīmāṁsā, the *Garland* is a difficult, dry, detail-driven treatise, seemingly devoid of sentiment and mysticism.[7]

The *Garland* becomes relevant to the comparative theologian because it encapsulates the nuances of each of Jaimini's cases in one or several verses each. It is brilliant in the economy of what it says and also in what it leaves out; deciding on inclusions and omissions requires a decision about what matters most in the tradition. An adornment, a garland, for one of the greatest of human intellectual systems, the *Garland* is also one of the very best introductions to Mīmāṁsā in its completeness and actual practice.[8] It makes possible a comprehensive engagement with Mīmāṁsā in a way no other text does, and thus enables and then challenges the Christian theologian to think about the whole of Mīmāṁsā as an integral tradition. The *Garland* is written in such a way that a reader can learn its reasoning through the words of its finely honed verses and thus, in case after case, detect the reasons or rationales (*nyāya, ratio*) constituting the intelligibility of the Veda at those intersections of text and practice that are the most complicated and unclear due to ritual or textual ambiguities. The *Garland*, though by no means an easy text, is a promising place to begin for both the amateur and the expert. Thus, Mādhava himself says that he composed the *Garland* for the ease of beginners and the deep satisfaction of experts.

But is the Mīmāṁsā, even when made available as a whole and in a concise way in the *Garland*, possibly relevant to Christian theology so as to become a productive site for comparative theological study? Various approaches are possible if one seeks to draw Mīmāṁsā into comparative theological reflection. For example, in a recent study,[9] I approached the challenge of the *Garland*'s aptness to Christian theological expectations and possibilities, particularly with respect to the question of the divine. I asked how the gods and possibly God are handled in Mīmāṁsā reasoning as presented in the *Garland*. I showed the difficulty of any straightforward comparison, and thus necessarily detoured in the rather complex issue of whether there are Christian texts similar in certain respects to the *Garland*. Seeking at least plausible analogues in Christian practice, I proposed three formative treatises of the Catholic tradition that succinctly distill and organize large amounts of commentarial literature, older classics, and the varied practices of the Catholic community: Gratian's *Decretum*, Lombard's *Sentences*, and Peter Canisius's (Catholic Reformation) *Catechism* as analogues that to an extent begin to enable us to locate the *Garland* on our intellectual maps. In that essay,

I was looking to establish some slender links between the *Garland* and Christian theology based on an instance of content and an instance of style. I thereby hoped to convince the Western reader that the *Garland* in certain ways resembles what is familiar in Western theology.[10]

Here, by contrast, I propose another beginning for the work of comparative theology. I propose that Mīmāṁsā, as represented by the *Garland*, is also relevant precisely in the difficult challenges it poses to the comparative theologian. I begin with the logic and vocabulary of Mīmāṁsā as grounded in ritual detail, as sharpened in the *Garland*. I seek to theologize, or move toward theology, on grounds measured by its terms. For the experiment that constitutes this essay—as another demonstration of comparative theology in practice—I have chosen III.5, a section that includes twenty of the nine hundred cases in the Sūtras of Jaimini. It is all about sacrificial remainders, largely liquid left in cups, which are to be consumed (or not) by the relevant priests. The problems are small and fine-tuned, and the quest is to show that each has a clear resolution according to rules honed and honored by tradition. It is a section that lends little support to generalizations or philosophical detours. My goal here is to think through what is learned when one is instructed by III.5, as it is in all its difficult yet extreme rationality, and without too quickly seeking similar texts to compare it to. The first challenge is simply to read the text; what follows hereafter is my translation of III.5 of the *Garland*, on remainders.

The Text of III.5: Remainders and the Questions They Raise

Verse 15 of the introduction to the *Garland* places III.5 in the whole of the Third Adhyāya of Jaimini's Sūtras: "All of this covered in the eight chapters: explicit meanings (III.1) and indirect meanings (III.2), conflicts among sentences and other measures of knowledge (III.3, 4), *the disposal of remainders* (III.5), statements without context (III.6), statements with multiple meanings (III.7), the concerns of the lord of a sacrifice (III.8)." III.5 thus treats "the disposal of remainders," just one among eight topics raising complicated matters that are ordered in this way so as to cluster sequentially various warrants for right knowledge.

Mādhava, as is typical, does not tell us much about the context of III.5 and the Vedic ritual treatment of remainders. Other commentators[11] usefully point out that III.5 seems to be occasioned by III.4, case 15:

> When it says, "With the remainder, the remainder ritual must be done," is this remainder taken from all the sacrifices, or from just one? If the remainder ritual is done with just one remainder, the requirement that it be done is satisfied.
>
> No. It should be taken from all the preparatory rituals, since all have equal status.

Because there are no grounds to select a remainder from just one of the rituals, it makes sense to put together a remainder drawn cumulatively from all of them. This is the simpler and more elegant solution. III.5 extends this rule from III.4 to a whole set of complications, in a series of directly or indirectly related cases that deal with remainders. With agility, Mādhava leads the reader through exceptions and variants and through related side issues. III.5, dedicated to such questions, keeps posing problem cases that ask when there are remainders such as merit or require remainder rituals, whether they have other uses, and who it is that consumes the remainders. III.5 admits exceptions to the basic rule—all the remainders are potentially subject to ritual consumption—and faces up to complications related to those exceptions. It presents the exceptions and ascertains the underlying reasons governing the accepted right practice.[12]

The *Garland* is faithful in reporting the conclusions passed down in its tradition; the debated practices are not thought to be symbolic nor taken to stand in for matters of greater portent, rather, the problems and their solutions are grounded in the actual practice of ritual performers, habitual ways of acting that are now defended as consistent, harmonious with precedent, and in keeping with rational analysis. The opposing views first presented are never foolish or merely wrong. In the *Garland*, Mādhava distills a tradition that sees itself in practice simply as detecting underlying reasons already there.

In III.5, as throughout the Sūtra system, lavish attention to particularities is unrelieved by myth and allegory; the reader is left no escape from the details, except by way of discovering the intelligibility of the Vedic whole woven of such details. There is no distance here from the complicated and (to us) tedious matters of cups and remainders, deciding whether this or that priest is a drinker of remainders; such is the material site wherein Mīmāṁsā's Vedic thinking occurs. By the Mīmāṁsā account, and plausibly so, here we are glimpsing the reasoning in and of the Veda, in a set of twenty concrete cases essentially and in detail grounded in the practice of sacrifice—the Veda as enacted in the sacrifice, in its particular detail. The *Garland*, as Mīmāṁsā, privileges the reasoning manifest in Vedic problems, while describing no performance in wholly or in a linear fashion; but it is only in those problems that it is manifest at all. And so, as a Mīmāṁsā intellectual ambitioning a comprehension of the whole of Mīmāṁsā, Mādhava avoids abstractions that would distract from the work of disclosing the fuller intelligibility of Vedic utterance and performance.[13]

Here, then, is *Garland* III.5, comprising twenty cases, in my translation and with my section titles:[14]

Whether a remainder ritual is to be performed

1. Is a remainder ritual to be done with material left over from the whispered sacrifice, or not? It is to be done, due to the statement, "This is done for all rituals with these characteristic remainders."

No. The remainder of the mentioned melted-butter material will be used in another oblation and other acts that are still to be done. Hence, there will be no remainder needing disposal. So how could a remainder ritual be done?

2. Does the instruction "He steps forward with the pots (at the *sākaṁprasthāyīya*)" signal a remainder ritual or not? Yes, because, as at the original ritual, here too there is a dividing with the spoon, and so here too a remainder ritual is appropriate.

No. Because there is no completing of a remainder ritual with the pots at the original ritual, neither is there such action at the derivative *sākaṁprasthāyīya* ritual. So the remainder ritual is not to be done. Rather, the spoons are given to the fire-lighter.

3. As for the cup offering at the *sautrāmaṇī* ritual, is there a remainder ritual, and so forth, or not? There are, because there is a remainder.
No, since the remaining *soma* juice and milk are to be used elsewhere.

Single or multiple remainder rituals

4. The ritual deities known as "Indras" are distributed in accord with the respective *rathantara* verses, etc., but their cake is not thus distributed. In this case then, is the remainder ritual distributed, or not? It is distributed, because distribution occurs in the rituals, as is signaled individually by implied injunctions.

No. Because the remainder is common to all those deities, that ritual is to be offered only once.

5. Is the consumption of the remainders of the Indra and Vāyu ritual offerings done just once or separately for each deity? Because of the preceding rule, only once, for the sake of completion.
No. There is a statement on this, so let there be two consumptions, one for each ritual offering.

One remainder ritual or none

6. At the *soma* juice oblations, is there no consumption of a remainder, or is there consumption? There is no consumption, since the cup oblations leave behind no remainder.

No. Because there is mention of "a little," there is a remainder, and there is consumption of that. This is an instruction about something already unknown.

7. In the same context, "Let the oblation-offerer's cup come forward," is there no consumption or is there consumption? There is no consumption, since none is mentioned.

No. Simply by reason of name—mention of the "oblation-offerer's cup"—consumption is to take place.

Multiple consumers of remainders

8. Where it says, "Let the chanters' cup come forward," should just one chanter consume remainders from that cup? Or all the chanters? Or all the *sāma*-chanters who are named as "*subrahmaṇya* priests"? Or all the priests, altogether? Because they are "together with him," the first option. Because of the explicit mention of chanters, the second option, the chanters. Because of the plural, by connection with the chanting, the third option, all the *sāma*-chanters.

Since the restrictive root meaning ("chanters") is blocked by the conventional inclusive meaning ("*subrahmaṇya* priests"), then because of the name mentioned in that connection, by the maxim of "the one holding a staff," the fourth view (indicating all those who chant) is correct. This is the view of the Commentator (Śabara). The third view is held by the author of the Verses (Kumārila) because there is no entering into the seat (where the consumption would occur).

9. Is the "consumption of the *hāriyojana* cup" undertaken only by those actually holding such a cup, or by all? The former, since these are mentioned in the context of the pertinent preceding statement.

No. In the context of the *hāriyojana* cup ritual, it says, "All are anointed," so all, even the *grāvastut* priest, should consume. Whether he is a cupholder or not is not decisive.

10. Does the injunction, "The first-consumption is done by the *vaṣaṭ!*-utterer,"[15] indicate simply that he goes first, or does it rather limit consumption to him, since his *vaṣaṭ!*-uttering is the occasion for consumption? Because there is no determination of his being-first on other grounds, the former.

No, because it is not feasible to render the compound that way ("the first among the consumptions is his"). Therefore, the injunction ("the first-consumption is entirely his") indicates that his consumption is qualified by the fact that the first-consumption is his. "*Vaṣaṭ!*-uttering" occasions that consumption.

Identifying the consumer of remainders

11. Is the *vaṣaṭ!*-uttering expressed in the name ("*vaṣaṭ!*-utterer") the sufficient condition to prompt the consumption, or are the sprinkling and oblation requisite too? Here let it be the former, by way of explicit instruction.

No. It is said, "After pressing (the *soma juice*) in the oblation-holder, after offering the oblation, then let him consume, in his seat." Since this is explicit, these are two supplementary reasons for consumption, along with the others.

12. When there is a cluster of reasons potentially distinguishing the consumption, is there an option among them, or does one rule out the others, or is there a combination of reasons? Because the reasons are equal, option. Let the other options, even if they have opportunity, be ruled out by what is named.

No. What is expressly stated cannot be set aside. Since in this case the consumption is completed by way of the dividing, option is not proper. Hence combination is to be accepted.

The order of consumption

13. When there is just one cup, should the *adhvara*-ritual priest consume first, or the other priest? Because the cup is set in his hand, his is the first consumption.

No. By the mantra, "Let just the oblation-offerer first protect us," the *vaṣaṭ!*-utterer (oblation-offerer) goes first. This is mentioned; here, too, what is stated is not to be set aside by reasoning.

Permissions and invitations

14. Is consumption not preceded by permission, or is it? Here, for the sake of simplicity, the former: it is not preceded by permission.
No. Due to what is said—"Therefore it is not to be drunk by one who is not invited"—the latter: it is preceded by permission.

15. Is this permission an ordinary statement or a Vedic statement? It can be either, because there is no difference.

No. Due to a textual clue found in the invitation mantra, it is Vedic.

16. Should "Invite me" and "You are invited" apply to both priests without distinction, or are they distinguished with respect to permission and permitting? Because there is a lack of an instrument to mark such a distinction, it applies to both priests without exception.

No. Due to a textual clue, the act of permitting is marked by "Invite me." The other, "You are invited," therefore pertains to the permission.

17. Does this invitation apply to all of the priests without exception, or only to those holding a cup? Let it be the former, for the sake of some unseen result.

No. Because of an abundance of explicit clues, the latter.

Substitutions

18. When the oblation-offerer's sacrificing-verse is omitted, is there also omission of his *vaṣaṭ!*-uttering and his consumption, or is there only the omission of the verse? There are no additional omissions, since these are all different cases.

No. It says, "It must be sacrificed by the sacrificer;" accordingly because there is no sacrifice without *vaṣaṭ!*-uttering, and because *vaṣaṭ!*-uttering belongs with the sacrificing-verse and hence, too, with the consumption, all three are omitted.

19. Should the substitution—instead of *soma* juice, banyan seeds are consumed by those of the *kṣatriya* class and those of the *vaiśya* class[16]—occur just at that consumption, or also at the related *soma* juice sacrifice? The statement at the beginning and the end, "Let him consume," marks the intention to consume, so the modification pertains only to the consumption in this case.

No. Since it says explicitly, "Let him sacrifice with the result-cup," the modification applies also to what is offered at the *soma* juice sacrifice. Similarly, the preparation of the consumption is for the *soma* juice sacrifice too.

20. At the princely coronation ritual, there is consumption from the agent's cup, by the men in tens. Are the princes the consumers, or the brahmins? The former because it is evident by way of number that the reference is just to a single birth class (that of the princes).

No. Since it is the hundred brahmins who are referred to by the statement "ten to each cup," the princely cup goes to the brahmins.

Thus III.5 of the *Garland*: twenty interconnected problems related to ritual remainders and the consumption of them by specific ritual performers. A range of rituals, primary and derivative, are at issue; we are not dealing with any single sacrifice, to which the consumption of remainders is an appended section, nor a separate section of a ritual handbook "on remainders." Several different contexts are adduced, in order that similar problems can be stated, standing as examples and counterexamples to one another. We are left, after the chapter, not with any vision of a single ritual properly performed, but with twenty instances where doubts were cleared, plausible but ultimately wrong alternatives put aside, and the best practices validated. All this happens for reasons that can be respected within the traditions of performers and ritual analysts.

Admittedly, because it is a set of arguments and reasons that begin from ritual examples, it would indeed be useful to know something at least about Vedic rituals, even if not the specifics of these cases. But the concision of the *Garland* makes it possible to learn what is most important even without that desired ritual knowledge. It is the reasoning that matters, and so even the novice reader may explore the logic of the cases without becoming detained by the quest to explain the background ritual detail. But before returning to the direct work of a Christian comparative theology, let us step back for a moment and consider what it is we are reading when we read *Garland* III.5.

On the Meaning of *Garland* III.5—and What It Does Not Mean

Even insiders and practitioners would not strongly defend the notion that the details of remainder-rituals might be of real significance outside the Vedic sacrificial context. Remainders and their ritual consumption are strictly local matters; but intelligibility and coherence do matter, and the right, most apt handling of the remainders is a small step in securing the harmony and intelligibility of the Vedic ritual whole. It is the thinking through of the harmony and reasonability of details and action regarding them, as well as the actual ritual details themselves, that matters. This is a thinking inseparable from the practice, but not entirely subordinate to practice. It is in this thinking through and from ritual detail that the rationality of and in the Veda is manifest. It is a simple, real, unencumbered thinking that appeals to our intelligence even if we do not understand the ritual context.

This is why Mādhava's reasoning in III.5 is compact and concise, each case reduced to the minimum required for an adequate statement of the matter and interpretive process involved. The structure of argument is clear even when we do not entirely understand the details of the cases before us. Mādhava may assume readers who know the details, but his primary audience is not practitioners but those who want to learn how to think like a Mīmāṁsā intellectual. He is not filling in the details for his readers, and neither does his own commentary (the Vistara, *Elaboration*) provide all that needs to be known. Learned readers can go back to the older and very ample commentaries of Śabara and Kumārila, if they wish. In any case, Mādhava's presentation of the cases reduces them to the essential elements of reasoning at issue; he wants us to think through the reasons. III.5 asks when remainders are or are not consumed, whence they are derived, and by whom they are to be consumed. As a whole, the chapter seeks to state clearly the minimal adequate set of rules by which such decisions about remainders are made, and in that way to show the coherence of the Veda in its details. When we study problems in the Vedic rituals and ritual texts in accord with the *Garland* within the realm of Mīmāṁsā, we are dealing with the challenges arising with respect to the literal meaning of a text distant from us in time and culture.

Key to understanding III.5, then, is that the section is clearly and resolutely about understanding certain Vedic actions that pertain to remainders—including the limits on such action, when such actions are not to be done—and consequently showing that everything proceeds in good order, the complications of performance and non-performance all in accord with identifiable rules which, even if complex, can be shown to be in harmony. Each case is decided by an appeal to a rule, but seemingly pertinent rules accumulate (right here, and in light of all 900 cases) and must constantly be sorted out with respect to one another.

No general theories can be lifted out of III.5, but we can tease out some plausibly useful rules of reasoned interpretation. For example, here are some generalized rules, gleaned from the cases:

1. Common sense has weight in construing the meaning of statements.
2. What is known due to familiarity with actual practice is decisive.
5. Explicit statements take precedence over merely plausible extensions of rules.
6–7. Verbal clues are decisive in determining what is to be done or not; what is genuinely new is to be preferred.
9. Explicit statements take precedence over interpretations dependent on context.
12. What is explicit cannot be set aside; it is certain and cannot be rendered optional.
13. What is stated is not to be set aside solely by reasoning.
14. Explicit statements take precedence over even a predilection for simplicity.
15. What can be construed from the mantras recited in a ritual takes precedence over common sense.
17. What is explicit in a ritual context is more authoritative than conjectures of unseen results.
18. Actual ritual connections take precedence over verbal distinctions.

These are context-grounded generalizations of a kind that may be of interest quite apart from the specifics of the problems of remainders, in helping us to interpret difficult ritual texts in any tradition. We can think about such claims and think them through, even if we do not know the specific case contexts whence the claims were generated. Our thinking is intensely focused, in a process by which we are educated in the details and rules of right ritual.

Thus we find our way into a fruitful engagement with the *Garland*'s Mīmāṁsā if we successfully think in deference to the rules identified and applicable to the instances of ritual practice under discussion. What we have in the *Garland* is a workbook for scholars and students, such as instructs its beginning and expert readers on how the Veda's rationality plays out harmoniously in practice, despite apparent uncertainties and contradictions. The subtle but eventually discernible links among the cases constitute a web of meaning that overlays the ritual/revelation, yet without having any enduring significance apart from that underlying ritual/revelation. If we recognize this reasoning-grounded-in-the-revelation, we will have made some progress in our encounter with one of comparative theology's difficult others. From the outside in, from the cases as formulated in the *Garland* but also in other, more cumbersome, texts, we find our way into the reasoning of the Mīmāṁsā, by way of the ordered set of cases raising specific problems in a particular order. Only weakly do the cases stand on their own, and we ought not in the long run think them through without attention to the details of their implementation in actual rituals. The reasons, once distinguished, are clear and sharp, but we need to be careful not to generalize those reasons in a way the core Mīmāṁsā tradition seemed hesitant to do, lest it seem the Veda was merely the occasion for a manner of reasoning more interesting and relevant than the Veda itself. If this is thinking that finds its way through the cases in their fixed matrix, then thinking-into this set of cases is a legitimate way into the whole of the Vedic ritual context. It is, as mentioned earlier, the reasoning of the Veda, the *Veda-tarka*. At this point, we begin to respond theologically to the revelation, not by thinking about it, but by thinking on its own terms.

Can *Garland* III.5 Be Engaged from a Christian Theological Perspective?

181

We can now return now to the primary question of this essay, the theological one. How does a Christian theologian learn from Mīmāṁsā, so complete and coherent, rational and practical, traditional of a community's deeper understanding of its ritual practice? What is the Christian theologian to do with *Garland* III.5, a small and difficult example of that Mīmāṁsā reasoning, a remnant of the tradition, as it were, yet one that turns out to be highly significant? Given the specificity of the ritual analysis, such as resists generalization, allegory, and so on, it is not easy to find a common ground.

Most avenues of expected comparison are closed. Certainly, general comparisons with Christian liturgical theology will not be apt because *Garland* III.5 is hardly an example of what Christians mean by liturgical theology. Though inherently and intimately tied to ritual, Mīmāṁsā does not theorize the meaning and purpose of ritual in light of cosmic or divine realities. It is rather, as we have seen, a kind of legal reasoning dedicated to particular cases, liturgical law that dwells on particulars. How we must proceed is in one sense simple and clear: Study the *Garland*. The purpose of that study, and the theological accommodation it might promise, is our matter of inquiry in these last pages.

I mentioned earlier in this essay that in a recent essay,[17] I sought to work out a rapprochement between instances of Mīmāṁsā thinking and Christian systematic thinking, so as to bring Mīmāṁsā into conversation with Christian theology. For that purpose, I pointed to imperfect but useful parallels with religious/legal texts (such as Gratian's *Decretum*), early efforts to systematize theological literature (such as Lombard's *Sentences*), and pedagogically motivated distillations of complex material (such as Reformation catechisms). In that essay, I thus drew the *Garland* onto the familiar ground of Christian theology.

Here, as likewise indicated earlier, my intention has been rather to draw the Christian theologian onto the terrain of technical Mīmāṁsā discourse, the technical religious reasoning of another tradition, in at least a provisional, experimental manner. It is bewildering at first, and a bit overwhelming, to try to think in the categories and by the rules of authority (*pramāṇa*), distinction (*karma-bheda*), accessory status (*śeṣatva*), aptness (*prayukti*), order (*krama*), ritual eligibility (*adhikāra*), transfer in general (*sāmānya-atideśa*), special cases of transfer (*viśiṣṭa-atideśa*), modification of rituals (*ūha*), cancellation (*bādha*), common performance (*tantra*), or incidental help (*prasaṅga*). Taken in this context, III.5 is but an example of the arduous work of thinking through new categories. These will not lead up to or answer established and familiar Christian theological questions such as existed even before the Mīmāṁsā tradition was encountered. Therefore, much of this essay has been about the difficult (and at first glance so difficult as not to merit our attention) cases treated in III.5—how to read them and make sense of them without erasing their necessary ritual context and without minimizing real differences.

not
many
Sentences

Rather than stepping away from the discrete, matter-of-fact "surface" reality of III.5—it really is about remainders, understood properly—we can decide to stay on the surface, with the literal. We know by now that while Mīmāṁsā is a superlative system of interpretation, it is also literalist to the extreme, proceeding only in terms of the particular. Mīmāṁsā rules out a shift to symbolic meanings, deeper meanings, generalizable rules or theories. It is a rather unexpected suggestion that we turn to the literal meaning as a point of reference in engaging a difficult, very different, religious other, because our every instinct pushes us to generalize and turn to symbolic meanings removed from the literal, the specific, and concrete detail.

In Mīmāṁsā, the literal resides not in historical detail but in ritual enactment. It pertains to the actual details of actual rituals that are taking place; such rituals are entirely visible and audible. This detail cannot be surrendered or quickly transcended. In the Mīmāṁsā view of it, revelation plays out in the details, in clusters of subtle problems, such as we see in III.5. Revelation is not general, universal, or susceptible to signification apart from what happens. Mīmāṁsā's attention to literal meaning, adherent to ritual practice, does not reduce to the audible and visible phenomena of ritual, but never leaves the ritual behind. It becomes accessible to critical reasoning in terms of problems, reasons, and counter-reasons that arise in resolving uncertainties while leaving what is seen and heard intact. This is the reasoning protective of specific words and actual deeds, and in understanding that fine-tuned reasoning, we have access to the revelation itself.[18]

This Vedic reasoning, inscribed in discussions such as that regarding sacrificial remainders, may guide Christian theologians to think differently about revelation in the Christian context. From the Mīmāṁsā perspective manifest in *Garland* III.5 (and everywhere else among the 900 cases), revelation is manifest in ritual acts, performed properly and understood in sufficient depth so as to perceive their deep harmony such as subsists in the details of worship, even small details pertaining to remainders. Here is a *lex orandi* that generates but is never replaced by the *lex credendi* and *res credendi*. The revelation subsists in a perfect practice, words as part of the practice and not superior to it; the revelation would be the tangible, visible, audible ritual enacted over time, without a retreat to inner meaning or a spiritualized substitution for the perceptible. The prospect of this whole, in all its parts, is where we have to begin rethinking Christian theological reasoning after Mīmāṁsā reasoning.

If we stay with literal meaning—not losing sight of the fact that the problems are exactly what they seem to be—this is also a strategic and intelligent defense of the text before us, the one we are asked to read. Attending patiently to what it says, resisting a hasty turn to secondary meanings, is a prudent step in interpretation that forecloses asides and avenues of curiosity that threaten to betray particular, definite matters of Vedic import.

But is not the literal meaning often taken to be most resistant to exchange with the Other? This seems hardly a promising path to travel, and indeed it is the proverbial road less traveled. I suggest that taking the literal seriously opens a narrow pathway back to a certain kind of Christian theological disposition, one that is willing to take seriously the literal meaning of scripture and practice, even while deferring metaphorical and spiritual readings.

Mīmāṁsā does not welcome allegorical interpretations, and its closest allies may be Christian theologies that are similarly disposed. It stays, in a strongly reasoned fashion, on the surface of texts, with an eye toward what makes sense in performance. How to think properly about literal meanings is, of course, no simple task. We know, of course, that literal meaning is honored in the tradition of Christian Biblical interpretation; unless the literal meaning is taken seriously, other levels and dimensions of meaning do not stand. Henri de Lubac famously explicated for modern readers the fourfold meaning of scripture, necessarily beginning with the literal meaning as the narrow gate of access to other layers of meaning; there is more than the literal meaning, but without it, further elaborations lack foundations. De Lubac closely linked the literal meaning to the historical, after recognition of which, one can move to the spiritual and allegorical. Spiritual meanings will not be made accessible apart from the continuing presence of the literal, which is never entirely done with. The literal and historical remain deeply theological in significance, as the ground for all further interpretations. We therefore need a theological perspective that enables the literal/historical to open into the spiritual in a way that non-theological historiography does not; and by analogy we need a way to take seriously the Mīmāṁsā's commitment to details and things, as the necessary ground for whatever meanings we might thereafter wish to construe.[19]

A further incentive to this onerous and patient concern for the literal is that respect for it opens a door on how a community reads, by its own priorities. Of course, even a discovered meaning that seems simply "there," remaining on the surface of texts, is really an event, the fruition of a community's long history of interpretation, such as is itself imbedded in that community's habitual practice and solution to problems over time. The literal remains a word read/practiced in community. This is why attention to a consensus view on the literal meaning draws the interpreter into a community of discourse curious to outsiders who might otherwise want merely to "look in." A close reading of III.5 thus shows us how Mādhava and others in the Mīmāṁsā community of scholars thought about the Veda in its inherent intelligibility.

The specificity of literal meaning, that which one reads on a page yet which is always much more than mere words and merely obvious meanings, does not constitute itself automatically but requires of the reader consent, even participation. The price of understanding religiously is therefore to forego safe distance and enter, rather, into an intellectual community and its habits of practice and interpretation. As Hans Frei puts it in *Types of Christian Theology*, "The literal meaning of the text is precisely that meaning which finds the greatest degree of agreement in the use of the text in the religious community. If there is agreement in that use, then take that to be the literal sense." And so, the literal meaning is in a way evident in the words, provided one reads in accord with what the early community thought: "No wonder, then, that if [the person of Jesus] was the focus of agreement, it became a kind of center for the literal sense from which literal reading radiated outward to other parts of the New Testament, all of it stemming from the use of the text in the Church."[20]

There is no larger significance that excuses us from the specificity of Jesus, no meaning apart from or behind the narrative about him.[21] The particular does not give way to more general meanings. The stories about Jesus of Nazareth constitute, rather than refer to, what is significant and thus worthy of preservation in the community. By turning to the literal as affirmed and passed down in tradition, we are confronted with Jesus as the Gospel's deep, literal, and indispensable meaning. His is a specificity that cannot be diminished or generalized; and yet, because he stands at the core of meaning in the early Christian community, Jesus embodies a significance accessible to cognitive assent, moral imitation, spiritual response, and constructive theological reasoning. Similarly, Mīmāṁsā judgments on particular Vedic acts and meanings, including its practical wisdom about remainders, is a truth that is the fruition of the age-long reflection on word and deed by a particular community of believers and practitioners.

Attention to the literal, surface meaning of texts, such as is constituted by traditions' habits of reading and determining meanings, has the beneficial effect of making possible more difficult comparisons, as juxtapositions for the sake of theological reflection. From this perspective, the raw particularity of the *Garland*'s Vedic thinking, and more particularly the unrelieved particularity of a chapter such as III.5, can now be taken to stand as parallel to the story of Jesus. Yes, the story of Jesus opens up into the whole array of Christological and soteriological claims later on made about him; so, too, the particular density of any given section of the *Garland* serves as the thread guiding us to the interwoven whole that is the totality of the Vedic ritual complex. These great particularities resist and ultimately thwart any turn to merely symbolic or merely generalized thoughts about "the Christ," or of "ritual" and "sacrifice" or even "Veda." Jesus remains at the core of any interpretation of Christ; chapters such as III.5 remain inherent in the dharma. While juxtaposing such singularities forms an odd pairing that does not easily yield generalizable insights of wider application, it is the right place for us to stand: the singular alongside the singular, intensified and not lost sight of in the comparison. Direct meaning, use, and the community's habitual signification, are intertwined in a rich literal sense. Dense specificity, such as cannot be evaded, stands in the face of the outsider but eludes the spectator, remaining almost tauntingly inaccessible in its presence. The unique, irreplaceable specificity of Christ in Christian community and known through the sacred text now has parallels in another tradition that in terms of content is strikingly different: a matter of remainders that can neither be neglected nor merely disposed of.

Conclusion

In the preceding pages, I have set forth and examined an instance of difficult comparative theological study. This was no easy example of a Hinduism similar to Christianity, or even different simply by obviously contrasting themes. This Mīmāṁsā way of thinking is studiously and deeply grounded in ritual, steadfastly literal, pluralistic, rationalist to the extreme, and is accentuated and distilled in the *Garland*. By design, I chose a chapter, III.5, that deals with matters of remainders, designedly, in the Mīmāṁsā plan of things, bereft of symbolic meanings and unlikely to be of interest to the modern reader expecting to encounter the familiar and already-meaningful in interreligious learning. Because the

Garland comprises the whole of Mīmāṁsā reasoning in the small space of about 1500 verses, and III.5 makes sense as a part of that whole, it is not possible to read it and understand it, and still easily subsume it into any dominant, governing Christian theological frame. It catches hold of us and demands that we revise our thinking so as to see the importance of what had, at first sight, surely seemed simply an odd chapter on remainders, but which, upon analysis, turns out to manifest intense and subtle reasoning aimed at discovering harmony and detail in every detail of revelation.

This singular and small Christian encounter with the *Garland* stands as a specific instance of comparative theological work as a most difficult case. It offers a true encounter with an Other: not an apophatic Other, nor an Other accessible only in deep experience or through a negation of logic, but a transparent, logical, self-evident Other. It is resistant to easy cooptation precisely because it is integral, coherent in whole and part, different and unexpected, yet still perfectly rational. It stands on a communal foundation that allows and then requires that one become an insider to that way of thinking, thinking rationally with the community. While this novel proximity of particulars to one another remains difficult, it is no small achievement for a Christian comparative theology to encounter and take seriously a particularity that resists subsumption into a system constructed in Christian terms, for Christian reasons.

Notes

1. We fortunately find exemplary instances of engagement with whole texts in the series edited by Catherine Cornille, *Christian Commentary on Non-Christian Sacred Texts.*
2. See Clooney, " Mīmāṃsā as Introspective Literature and as Philosophy."
3. It is not likely that the points debated in Mīmāṃsā would actually have needed to be resolved one way or the other, as if the community of ritualists was awaiting a decision before proceeding with the ambiguous ritual activity. Clarity on the reasons for settled practice is rather what is at stake, along with the perfection of a simplest statement of those reasons. On the lack of novelty and lack of practical urgency in the Mīmāṃsā debates, see Krishna, "The Mīmāṁsaka vs. the Yājñika."
4. As summarized in the explanatory Vistara (henceforth Elaboration) accompanying the *Garland of Jaimini's Reasons* (*Jaiminīya Nyāya Mālā*) of Mādhava, but drawing on a tradition in this regard dating back to Śabara (200 CE) the first commentator on the Sūtras that has come down to us. Regarding Mādhava's Garland, see the next paragraphs.
5. See Clooney, "Mādhava's Garland of Jaimini's Reasons as Exemplary Mīmāṃsā Philosophy."
6. Regarding issues related to the dating of Mādhava and the extent of his writings, see Clooney, "Mīmāṃsā for the Mīmāṃsaka-s." Mādhava wrote an auto-commentary on his work, a paragraph or two in prose on each set of verses. I do not deal with the prose

Elaboration in this essay. I note also that the Garland is the most important of the works of Mādhava who is an influential fourteenth-century scholar. In addition to the Garland, Mādhava wrote also the *Parāśara-Mādhava*, a commentary on the *Parāśara Smṛti*, which includes a novel, long appendix known at the *Vyavahāra-Mādhava*; a text on ritually relevant calendric issues and time, the *Kāla-Mādhava*; and, possibly, the famed *Jīvanmuktiviveka*, on the life of the renunciant, freed from ritual obligations. The Garland shares with these works a commitment to the details of practical and prescriptive texts, a respect for the complexity and plurality of realities to be taken into account, and a determination to explain with extreme economy what is at the heart of any given vexed case.

7. In every case, Mīmāṃsā and then, too, Mādhava presuppose, usually without description: acts of sacrifice, texts (*mantras*) recited in the course of those acts, texts (*brāhmaṇas*) ruling over right acts and right recitation. Three further points distinguish the domain of Mīmāṃsā: the identification of interestingly problematic texts and practices, a set of cases usually numbered around 900; groups of particular cases, such as the questions related to remainders, which we will discuss in this essay, as gathered in the fifth chapter of the third book; the ordering of these questions/problems in any given chapter, so that an instructive learning process occurs by taking them up in this specific order.
8. See Clooney, "The Contribution and Challenge of Mīmāmsā to the Dream of a Global Hermeneutics," and "Mīmāmsā as Introspective Literature and as Philosophy."
9. Clooney, "Discerning Comparison." Some of the cases found in III.4, the immediately preceding chapter, were dealt with in Clooney, "Toward a Complete and Integral Mīmāmsā Ethics."
10. See also my recent efforts to engage the text in terms of issues in philosophy and in ethics: Clooney, "Mādhava's Garland of Jaimini's Reasons as Exemplary Mīmāmsā Philosophy," and the above mentioned "Toward a Complete and Integral Mīmāmsā Ethics."
11. Pārthasārathi Miśra in the *Śāstra Dīpikā*, and Somanātha in the *Mayūkhamālikā*.
12. We know from Śabara's *Bhāṣya* on the original *Jaimini Sūtras* that the cases in III.5 have largely to do with matters described and ritually disambiguated in the *Taittirīya Saṃhitā* and *Taittirīya Brāhmaṇa*. Mādhava's verses do not advert to those contexts, and even his auto-commentary, the Elaboration, does little more than occasionally expand the cited words to a fuller verse, and usually, as is the custom, without naming the source.
13. Some Mīmāṃsā thinkers did generalize and take up larger theoretical issues related to metaphysics and epistemology, grammar and theology, for instance. The contributions of figures like Kumārila Bhaṭṭa to the larger, pan-Indian conversations need not be denied. But in fact, more intimately and evidently characteristic of Mīmāṃsā on its own ground is the Garland, which barely touches on larger philosophical issues, but remains dedicated to the reasons ensuring the coherence of the details of ritual performance.
14. I have included the full translation here, to make available the text I am reading in this comparative theological experiment, and to invite the theological reader into the comparative process of receiving the Mīmāṃsā analysis into a contemporary theological context by studying this translation carefully.

15. "*vaṣaṭ*" is an exclamation uttered by a specific priest.
16. *Kṣatriyas* (warriors, princes) and *vaiśyas* (merchants, farmers) are the second and third among the four religious classes (*varṇa*) of ancient India. These classes are sometimes loosely referred to as castes, though the latter categories are best reserved for a much broader set of birth groups (*jāti*).
17. See Clooney, "Discerning Comparison."
18. Certainly, there is an abundance of instances in Indian religious literature where rituals are allegorized, transsignified by mythic meanings, and interiorized as activities taking place within the self. But Mīmāṃsā largely eschews allegory, myth, and the construction of meaning through acts of spiritualization.
19. For a fine overview of de Lubac on the literal meaning and its theological grounding, see Wright, "The Literal Sense of Scripture According to Henri De Lubac."
20. Frei, *Types of Christian Theology*, 15. How the Gospels communicate to us the meaning of Jesus, a meaning that is Jesus, depends on the text, to be sure, but also the text as received in accord with the consensus of a community. Hans Frei, for instance, highlighted literal meaning as a reality that directs us to the text-read-in-community. With reference to the Gospel narratives, Frei observes that "the community has generally read the 'surface' of the story, rather than seeking some real meaning 'behind' it." Frei finds in Karl Barth's theology the model of a plausible literalist theology, a model which "does not propose a correlation between heterogeneous equals." Rather, such a theology reverses the priority we are used to, instead giving precedence to the practical and the regulatory: "the practical discipline of Christian self-description governs and limits the applicability of general critualria of meaning in theology, rather than vice versa . . ." As a result, theological statements have "a status similar to that of grammatical rules implicit in discourse," while "their relation to the broader or even universal linguistic or conceptual context within which they are generated remains only fragmentarily—perhaps at times negatively—specifiable." Intention and enactment are to be thought of as a single continuous process, so that "you cannot for this purpose go behind the written text to ask separately about what the author meant or what he or she was really trying to say." (*Types*, 15–16)
21. Thus Charles Campbell on the determinative role of Jesus: "The worship of the unsubstitutable person, Jesus Christ, shaped the community's reading of Scripture; the rules governing the *sensus literalis* were embodied in the worship of the church—for example, the Eucharist, where the church continually re-enacts the story about Jesus. In short, the piety and worship of the church not only shaped the form of the canon, but also gave rise to the *regula fidei* for interpreting it. That worship is finally more important than any abstract rules for training Christians in the ascriptive logic of the gospel narratives. It is thus not surprising, as George Lindbeck has noted, that 'the interpretive rules imbedded in liturgy or worship have partially protected some communities against loss of canonical patterns of interpretation . . .'" (Campbell, *Preaching Jesus*, 95). As Mādhava and other Mīmāṃsā thinkers knew well, right practice serves to protect right meanings, and even the community's identity.

11 *Sagi Nahor*—Enough Light

DIALECTIC TENSION BETWEEN LUMINESCENT RESONANCE AND BLIND ASSUMPTION IN COMPARATIVE THEOLOGY

Shoshana Razel Gordon-Guedalia

This essay, titled, "*Sagi Nahor*[1]—Enough Light: Dialectic Tension Between Luminescent Resonance[2] and Blind Assumption in Comparative Theology," engages in comparative theological examination of two ritual-legal systems, *Mīmāṃsaka* and *Rabbinic*, which, *prima facie*, share "measures" of hermeneutic reasoning—tools for culling ritual law from respective Urtext, each expanding into vast commentarial corpora, each yielding distillation into terse legal codes in the medieval period. Proper comparison yields illumination, while sheer conflation blinds. Even as we study test cases, seeking to delineate each system-specific matrix with regards to ritual efficacy and agency, concerns loom: Can one suspend current sensibilities when exploring cosmologies of old—and if so, should one? Can one nimbly leap from one's home tradition to an*other* and return with system-specific integrity intact—and if so, towards what end?

Eleventh-century St. Anselm defines theology as "faith seeking understanding." This call is aim and spirit to Francis X. Clooney, S.J., who explains his use of the word "theology" as,

> A mode of inquiry that engages a wide range of issues with full intellectual force, but ordinarily does so within the constraints of a commitment to a religious community, respect for its scriptures, traditions, and practices, and a willingness to affirm the truth and values of that tradition. More deeply, and to echo more simply an ancient characterization of theology, it is faith seeking understanding, a practice in which all three words—the faith, the search, the intellectual goal—have their full force and remain in fruitful tension with one another.[3]

Clooney's vast, luminary comparative theological scholarship is rooted in his Catholic faith, and expressed in embrace of hermeneutic mining of Catholic text (in my case, rabbinic) with tools found in *other* text, granting fresh lens on return to text of home. Comparison is *in itself* a hermeneutic act. Juxtaposed reading applies pressure from a system-specific case to one resonant in an*other*, probes one with tools of an*other*, unveils treasures hidden in system-specific corners beneath cobwebs woven of our blind spots, what Clooney calls "an exercise in intensifying religious reading across traditions."[4] Choosing material to compare calls for balance between a thrilling *sense* of inter-traditional similarity and measured critical study, which may yield myriad claims—be they trans-historical or cross-cultural—due to influence, or to the stuff of our joint humanity; unique, or typical of similar traditional evolutionary stages of development; common primordial needs; recognizable rubrics of logic and ethics; resonant writerly conceit; familiar polemic style; or kinship in praxis. Rigorous empathic comparison may yield any, all, or none of these. We must be willing and ready to be surprised.

My focus is oft on ritual law—gesturing toward the "liturgical turn" discussed recently in comparative theology—on religio-legal theory, on ethics, on performative theology, on praxis. Much as comparative method spans myriad forms, theology, too, manifests variously, as: practical, systematic, feminist, liberation, ethical, liturgical, hermeneutic, moral theology, and even as law—ritual, religious, or otherwise. "Law," says Donald Davis, "is the theology of ordinary life. When the theological is brought to bear on ordinary life, the result is law."[5] Both law *and* theology profit from such terminological generosity. Theological influence on law should not be viewed as tainting,[6] or as counter to the spirit of justice. Says Davis:

> Associations of theology with religion bring out the sense of higher purpose involved whenever law is invoked . . . challenge all-too-easy understandings of religion *itself* as mere belief . . . if law is the theology of ordinary life then religion is not a phenomenon directed solely at otherworldly ends, at God or gods, or at escaping or circumventing the practices of ordinary life . . . transcendence does not have to imply denial of or disengagement from the world. Law is both a means and an end for giving ordinary life meaning and value through worldly transcendence. This is why law is often connected with other human goods such as order and justice.[7]

By framing law as theology, the jurisprudential system, oft accused or even manifest as spirit-crushing imposition of rubric, is seen as a semiotic vehicle for *worldly transcendence*. Thus, both law *and* theology attain new respect. Much as law ought not function as spiritless grid, void of ethical encounter *anew* in each singular case, neither ought theology be seen as mere belief, severed from quotidian impact, transcendent *from* ethical imperative.

The comparative theological journey is *sui generis*. Such study hails from *singular* paths of "faith seeking understanding," as woman of faith ventures from her *own* cosmology into that of an*other* faith, seeking deeper insight into her *own* faith, reading her *own* sacred text and/or praxis in light of an*other*, perhaps even yielding *mutual* insight. Before I begin my experiment in which the twelfth-century ritual legal code of Moses Maimonides meets that of thirteenth-century Mādhava—in which *Rabbinic* and *Mīmāṃsaka* lenses probe ritual efficacy and agency—I will share my journey.

Journey

My engagement in comparative theology *qua* religio-legal theory is driven by lifelong focus on the relationship between theology, praxis, and law. Raised halakhically[8] observant in Jerusalem, steeped in Rabbinics,[9] I observed with keen interest as religio-legal disputes float off the talmudic[10] page, coming to visceral fruition in the fractious air of the holy city. From neighbors kicking our snowman to slush, yelling, "Idol!";[11] to teachers banning female public singing;[12] male mobs shouting, "Loose woman!" as I walked by in short sleeves;[13] my testing a Talmudic ban on passing between two women, two dogs, two palm trees,[14] standing opposite a friend on a narrow path to see if *haredi*[15] men would walk through (they would not); some eating rice on Passover,[16] others avoiding even wet *matzah*, lest errant flour specks leaven;[17] Zionist-messianic settlers of barren bethistled biblical hilltops and those calling Zionism, "devil's work"[18]—all Jews, all waving rabbinic text.[19] Were these polemics hermeneutic, personal, societal, all of the above? Times change, societies change, people change. How is the divine Word expressed in the quotidian realm, in what laws, what customs, what norms? How elastic is the system? Who are ethical decisors[20] of integrity, attuned to singularity *and* casuistic precedence, whose keen hermeneutics allow sifting of enduring law from temporal lore?[21] Who, amidst clang and clatter, has agency, whose voice holds sway? Whose not?

While researching the matter of female agency pertaining to Orthodox Jewish ordination, I stumbled upon John Meier's[22] critique of Catholic magisterial hermeneutic selectivity vis-à-vis fixed versus evolving praxis. He claims that hermeneutic tools used to mine apostolic tradition, etched in creedal stone—to glean possible valid adaptations to new norms—vanish or seem inoperable when it comes to female agency. This thrilled me. I marveled at my sense of having just read a *rabbinic* hermeneutic polemic on this topic—so close to my heart. I felt a need to study Canon law, as I wondered what theological jurisprudential parallels I might find to my own rabbinic tradition, how magisterial polemics might compare in text and praxis. My doctoral studies began with a sense of kinship, as I found in Francis Clooney a deeply committed scholar practitioner, whose love of God drives his empathic yearning for understanding of humanity in its myriad singular faces, as he immerses in other systemic cosmologies, illumining his *own* faith by light of divine sparks found in *other* praxis, in texts penned by *other* souls, as did my rabbinic father,[23] rest his soul.

Mīmāṃsaka reasoning, as taught to me by Clooney, meshed with my lifelong study of rabbinic reasoning. My early reflection papers for his course gushed with declarations of familiarity *ad* identity. Margins of my notebooks from Catholic Canon law and sacramental theology at St. John's Seminary that semester were filled with exclamations of kinship born of first cursory exposure, crossing lines, at times, to blind assumption, yet yielding parallels more worthy and satisfying when I allowed their *distinctions* to challenge my understanding of rabbinic texts, read anew in light of juxtaposed reading with thematically similar texts of an*other* tradition.

While rewarding, such endeavors carry risk. The more I study, the more terms and systemic ways of thinking of other cosmologies permeate my rabbinic parlance and thinking. While I believe that such expansion of mind and spirit is positive, while my rabbinic father—professor of philosophy and ethics[24]—encouraged my comparison-born insights, woven into synagogue sermons and discussions with co-religionists, I felt caught off guard when some asked that I refrain from addressing the congregation if I quote other faiths. Banter, which I took to be mere idle teasing—such as, "Why dabble in foreign worship?"—donned gravitas, as I was increasingly "othered" by my kin.

The Talmudic tractate *Hagigah* tells of four sages, who ventured into "the orchard," who got too close to a realm of esoteric knowledge that proved dangerous:

> Said the rabbis: Four entered into the orchard, and these are, Ben Azai, Ben Zoma, *Acher* [the other], and Rabbi Akiva . . . Ben Azai peeked, and died . . . . Ben Zoma peeked and was smitten . . . *Acher* severed saplings. Rabbi Akiva emerged in peace.[25]

This passage is said to depict an instance of risky straying into the realm of "esoteric" or "other" knowledge—the type of contact that is best avoided. As to Ben Azai, commentaries explain that he peered *directly* at God and died as a result. Ben Zoma is said to have peered at the *side* of the divine flow and was thus smitten. "*Nifga*," which I translate as "smitten," has several possible meanings, such as, "touched," or "encountered." I choose "smitten" so as to express the *double entendre*. We are in murky territory here. Was Ben Zoma mesmerized? Was he hurt? Was he paralyzed? Can one escape such a gaze as the gaze of Ben Zoma upon the side of the divine flow? By avoiding a *direct* gaze upon the Infinite—peering, as he did, on the side—he was spared death. But having gazed upon the divine flow, perhaps he experienced a paralysis, akin to the *tremendum*, which Rudolph Otto describes as eclipsing *mysterium*.[26] Awe-stricken, in the faced of the Ultimate, a human being can experience paralysis due to the sense that in the face of the ineffable, all human action is futile—an experience, a cognizance, if you will, from which there is no return to functioning in the quotidian realm, and alas, no remaining capacity to heed the Levinasian ethical call of the "other."[27]

Acher (meaning, "the other") "severed saplings." Through his particular manner and experience of this fraught trespass, Rav Elisha Ben Avuya became the quintessential "*Other*"—*Acher*—due to his irreversible gaze upon the *other*. Some say that he was entranced by an*other* belief system—that his sojourn into an*other* realm implicated him to such an extent that he became alien to his people and even to himself. And furthermore, in an experience, which may well have been his projection of his own inner turmoil unto God, the All-merciful, *Acher* seems to hear a heavenly voice: "Return to me, O wayward sons, All, save for *Acher*." Rav Elisha Ben Avuya—"Acher"—is forever lost—stripped of his identity. Having "severed saplings," he has lost his roots.

And what of the fourth orchard sage? How did Rabbi Akiva manage to emerge unscathed? Given his particular biography—the first half of Akiva's life depicted as steeped in the quotidian realm, until he began to immerse himself in Torah study, at age forty—it seems fair to venture that his equilibrium, born of having lived in harmony with the visceral thrum of the universe, served to keep him anchored.

"To truly make an impact on 'the other,'" says David Grossman, "on our society, on humanity, we must willingly accept some of the other's 'symptoms' on ourselves."[28] Such a goal conjures Levinas, as he bids us not to forsake the face. Face-to-face encounter with the *other* entails risk, and yet, it is *just this risk* that a comparative theologian must assume if her faith truly seeks understanding. Some say that an Orthodox Jew who delves in *other* traditions risks being lost like *Acher*. True encounter leaves none untouched, none stagnant. If I am careless, I may say the wrong thing in my community, or to my friends at St. John's Seminary. However, by not forsaking the clerical collar as *other*, I gained mutually nourishing relationships with my canon law and sacramental theology teachers as with my seminarian classmates as we forged our own joint language. To remain cloistered in one's own box, individual or cultural, is to turn a deaf ear to the ethical call of the *other*. The mandate to engage the *other*, to don her cosmology, *while* preserving one's rooted self, is the call to comparative theology.

Experiment: Rabbinic and Mīmāṃsaka Lenses on Ritual Efficacy and Agency

What follows is a comparative reading of rabbinic and mīmāṃsaka texts pertaining to ritual efficacy and agency. The rabbinic source texts for analysis here are sections from the Talmud as well as from Maimonides' twelfth-century code of law *Mishneh Torah* and *Sefer* (book of) *Mitzvot*. The mīmāṃsaka source texts are from Clooney's translation of and thoughts on Mādhava's thirteenth-century code of law, *Garland of Jaimini's Reasons*, and his elaboration on VI.1 (Book 6, Chapter 1) pertaining to conditions governing eligibility to perform sacrificial rites.

To set the cosmological stage, we begin with historical background, with what I call, "the codification era," in which both scholars—Maimonides and Mādhava—wrote, as with systemic commentarial evolution of the rabbinic and mīmāṃsaka traditions of which both scholars are a part. The "codification era" was the stage upon which codifications surfaced and flourished across myriad traditions in response to growing concern among scholars and institutions that widespread variance in tradition-specific praxis must be distilled. The eleventh to thirteenth centuries were a jurisprudential collation era in several legal systems, in addition to those Hindu and Jewish. In Islam, this era saw the crystallization of four Sunni jurisprudential *madhahib* (schools)—*Shafi'i, Maliki, Hanafi,* and *Hanbali.*[29] In Christianity, customs and praxis were gathered from minutes of disparate local councils across the empire, where decrees were issued over years—and collated into the *Concordance of Discordant Canons* by a monk named Gratian, who later obtained papal blessing for his contribution. Thus began the classical period of Canon law, aided by this structured and vetted matrix of laws, granting the papacy a full-fledged legal system—providing verisimilitude and gravitas to the coalescing institution.[30]

Rabbinic Judaism considered Maimonides' collation, *Mishneh Torah* and *Sefer Hamitzvot,* which he declared *the* last word on all religio-legal matters, meant to replace all disputes, to serve as *the* guide for proper practice. Maimonides' stated impetus for his terse collation of commandments was his frustration with digests in verse—an all too popular form in his time—which he found ill-sourced and unsystematic, prioritizing poetic conceit *over* scholarship. Says Maimonides,

> Whenever I heard the many *Azharot* . . . composed among us in the land of Spain, "My pangs have come writhing upon me," since I saw how popular and disseminated they were. True, these authors are not to be criticized; they are poets, not rabbis, and as far as their art is concerned—namely, well-balanced expressions and beauty of rhyme—they have performed with perfection. Yet in the context of their poems they have followed the author of *Halakhot Gedolot* and some other later rabbis . . . Such is, unfortunately, the mentality of even elect in our times—they do not test the veracity of an opinion upon the merit of its own content but upon its agreement with the words of some preceding authority, without troubling to examine that preceding source itself, and if this is true of the elect, how much more so of the populace.[31]

We note that while Maimonides' work did indeed receive wide acclaim, he did not avoid the condemnation of detractors who found his endeavor presumptuous, near heretically so. Yet given the broader context of the "codification era," his project should not be shocking.[32]

Keeping in mind Maimonides' aforementioned concern with the flourishing of digests around him, and his own response in systematic scholarly codification, our foray into the Hindu realm of the codification era should spark recognition. Says Lawrence McCrea,

> Beginning around the twelfth century, there is a marked shift in *Dharmaśāstra* literature, as commentary ceases to be the dominant mode of textual production and more and more *dharma* authors choose . . . *nibandhas* or "digests," topically organized compilations of quotations from various *smṛtis* (. . . from *Purāṇic* sources as well) (Lingat 1973: 115ff.). The earlier works of this genre . . . are, if anything, less concerned than the commentators were with *Mīmāṃsā*-derived debates over authority of *smṛti* or with demonstrating authenticity of specific *smṛti* texts. Their method of composition is basically additive, simply assembling all the passages concerning a particular topic from as many putatively authoritative sources as possible, and seldom, if ever, pointing out potential conflicts between them or seeking to weigh their relative authority against one another.[33]

Given the spirit of the era and Maimonides' disdain for *Azharot*, it would be no surprise if a thirteenth-century *mīmāṃsaka* scholar like Mādhava considered the flourishing of unsystematic assemblages of cherry-picked quotations from one source or another, as depicted by McCrea, a risk to traditional integrity. Mādhava may have been just as worried about loss of systemic integrity in this atmosphere as was Maimonides with Andalusian *Azharot*, leading Mādhava to craft the *Jaiminīya Nyāya Mālā*, as did Maimonides, *Sefer HaMitzvot*. Says Clooney of Mādhava,

> Over the centuries the commentarial discussions around the Sutras and the 900 problematic cases grew voluminous, too vast and complex for students to understand, and too unwieldy for experts to be satisfied with . . . The *Garland of Jaimini's Reasons* (*Jaiminīya Nyāya Mālā*) by Mādhava (1297–1388) is a distillation of the 900 cases to about 1500 two-line verses (*ślokas*). Each case includes context, a first view, and then a rejection of that view with a statement of the reasons for that rejection. The format thus models the old debate-style of reasoning in such matters. Mādhava composed the verses of the Garland at the behest of his king, for the sake of beginners and to edify experts by the concision of his summation. Upon receiving it, the king praised it, and also complained that it was too difficult, and ordered Mādhava to write the "Elaboration" (*Vistara*) in prose, to explain the verses . . . Mādhava is author of the verses and the elaboration.[34]

Mādhava's Garland, then, was written in response to a royal decree. This could have been expression of political concern with the dissipation of systemic tradition. It is oft in a king's interest to centralize and organize dissemination of knowledge. He may also have wished to seem wise and scholarly by having this work emerge per his decree. This may also explain his wish for elaboration, lest he feel unlearned. And finally, concerns of the *Mīmāṃsaka* intelligentsia in general may themselves have served as motivator for the king.

Having sketched out the codification era as macro-comparative backdrop for the codes of Maimonides and Mādhava, we continue to both scholars, their works and their traditions of origin, before our micro-comparison upon specific thematic parallel reading—as each relates to matters of ritual efficacy and agency.

To enter the cosmology of rabbinic study is to encounter the energy, logic, humor, and terminology of the vast ocean of Talmud—the religio-legal argumentative commentarial elaboration of Jewish Law. The Talmud[35] depicts hermeneutical commentarial adventures of several generations of rabbinic scholars, "*Amoraim*," whose aim it was to flesh out the Mishnah—the terse religio-legal code of the *Tannaim*. The *Tannaim* used hermeneutic measures, *mīdot*, to glean praxis rules from the prescriptive and proscriptive Pentateuch, replete with its precedential accounts, and from those in the narrative swath of the Bible at large. This process articulated an imitable system of acts—248 prescriptive,[36] and 365 proscriptive[37]—613 commandments in all. The *tannaitic* measures were then used by *Amoraim*, followed by an ongoing commentarial tradition post the "sealing" of the Talmud, circa fifth century.[38] As rabbinic commentarial literature expanded and proliferated, need arose for a coherent code of conduct. In the twelfth century, Moses Maimonides—rabbi, rabbinic judge, philosopher, doctor in the royal court of *Andalus*—distilled the commentarial corpus down to a code of law, organized by topic, into chapters, and the latter into terse paragraphs, easy for all to grasp, remember, and follow. His *Book of Mitzvot* also served as an antidote to what he deemed problematic, poorly sourced and erroneously enumerated *Azharot*[39] of his time.

Shifting from Maimonides to Mādhava, we note some biographical similarities between the two scholars. Clooney shares the following about Mādhava:

> He lived in the south Indian Vijayanagar kingdom and was a councilor in the royal court. Mādhava wrote several other texts on legal and religious law (including the *Parāśara-Mādhava*, which includes a long

appendix known as the *Vyavahāra-Mādhava*, and the *Kāla-Mādhava*, a text on calendric issues). Late in life he may also have written the famed *Jīvanmuktiviveka*, on rules and regulations governing individual who had reached liberation even while still living.[40]

Mādhava was Maimonides' junior by one century. The former lived in South India, while the latter lived in Andalus. Both were councilors in the royal court. Both were prolific writers across disciplines. Both wrote in the realm of law and religious law. Maimonides wrote on medicine and policy as well, and in his philosophical work, *Guide to the Perplexed*, he illumines, among other things, what it would mean to attain "prophecy," which he defines as a form of philosopher king status, such that it seems to resonate with Mādhava's *Jīvanmuktiviveka* as to rules and regulations governing individuals who have attained *mokṣa* while still alive.

To enter the cosmology of *Mīmāṃsaka* reasoning is to encounter energetic religio-legal argumentation revolving around intricacies of ritual matters in a debate style reminiscent of the rabbinic style. To appreciate this, one must be aware of and able to temporarily set aside theological distinctions vis-à-vis "divinity," for example, or certain ritual aspects of each system, identifiable as antithetical to the other system, among other distinctions. Among the resonances are style of reasoning and debate and approaches to efficacy and agency in ritual praxis.

Providing commentarial traditional context for Mādhava's *Garland of Jaimini's Reasons*, Clooney describes the *Mīmāṃsā* ritual reasoning system, which yielded Mādhava.

> The *Mīmāṃsā* school of Hindu ritual exegesis traces back to the Sūtras of Jaimini (c. 2nd century BCE). The Sūtras are comprised of about 2700 short, often obscure statements—sutras—too often lacking in clear context, each ranging from one or two words to ten or fifteen. Though unclearly demarcated, they were interpreted apparently in oral tradition and then by Śabara (2nd c. CE) and later commentators as encapsulating 900 problem cases in the exegesis of ritual texts and ritual acts, problems that required subtle interpretive strategies in order to know how best to resolve problems in reading and acting. From the Sūtras to the Garland and until today, *Mīmāṃsā* stands forth as a school of religious legal reasoning, and many of its principles were extended to deal with other texts, philosophical or legal, and even into British and post-Independence India.[41]

In Clooney's description of Madhava's methodological approach, stylistic conceits, and motivations for writing the Garland, he provides us with an invaluable lens upon this argumentative reasoning culture, for which the *Mīmāṃsā* tradition is known. The vast intricate world of the scholastic *mīmāṃsaka* reasoning system, as gestured to here, and as meticulously analyzed by Clooney in *Thinking Ritually: Rediscovering the Purva Mimamsa of Jaimini*,[42] evokes Talmudic resonance. The energy, logic, and humor, the hauntingly familiar terminology, down to the very exegetical "measures" of the Talmud,[43] almost beg comparative investigation into *Mīmāṃsā*'s seemingly rabbinic religio-legal theory and system.

Mulling over kindred, near parallel, strata of legal sources in each system, one begins to ask: What is Veda, but Torah, *śruti* but *d'Oraita*—each highest in their system-specific strata. What is *smṛti* but *d'Rabbanan*; *Pūrva Mīmāṃsā* but *Mishnah; Śabara-bhāṣya* but *Talmud*; *Kumārila Bhaṭṭa* and *Prabhākara* but variant *Savoraic* and *Geonic* schools? And finally, what is Mādhava's *Jaiminīya Nyāya Mālā* but Maimonides' *Mishneh Torah* and *Sefer HaMitzvot*? Did both scholars not seek to distill vast commentarial corpora in each scholastic tradition for coherence, for ease of transmission, to facilitate appropriate practice?

As mentioned, resonance must be balanced with distinction. Yes, both Mādhava and Maimonides strove to create concise palatable codes out of commentarial oceans. Mādhava strove to explicate the *nyāya* behind each case, and Maimonides, the *ta'am* for commandments—both providing meaning and contours for praxis, thus facilitating proper intent. Both responded similarly to needs of their era. However, despite these examples of kinship, and others, it would be a grave error to utterly conflate motivations or literary styles, much as it would be to equate the spirit of each tradition distilled by these scholars.

While Mādhava presents variant ritual-legal stances and the hermeneutics that yielded them in as terse a manner possible, while remaining comprehensible, Maimonides by and large eliminated dispute and variance, declaring his position singular and ultimate. While Mādhava, as a Mīmāṃsaka, highlights out-of-the-box cases for system-delineating hermeneutic analysis, Maimonides presents *all* commandments, stating how each must be performed. While Mādhava wrote in the literary conceit of *ślokas*, couplet verses, one per case, typical of ancient sacred Hindu literature, Maimonides wrote in prose, by topic, by chapter, by terse numbered paragraphs. Stylistics aside, *śloka* or terse prose, each strove to facilitate systemic preservation and praxis.

Variances between these traditional systems, cosmologies, prohibit *pat* comparisons of *Mīmāṃsā* and *Rabbinics.* Intricacies of theological worldviews, of scriptural authorship, of legal source stratification, are debated inter- as well as intra-systemically. Even as we use a term such as "scripture," we must articulate our intent to subsume the Vedic *Urtext* under this broad tent, *not* in a manner which might negate or flummox traditional queries or understandings of Vedic origin or authorship by claiming *Divine* source, but perhaps in ecumenical spirit akin to that of Chakravarthi Ram Prasad, which Clooney depicts as a bold bidding, as he cites:

> It takes no great effort but only goodwill to see that "Biblical" can be replaced by "Vedantic" or other qualifiers, in order that we may come to a comparativist and cross-traditional understanding of what theology can mean, generously conceived.[44]

On examination, we *do* find hermeneutic resonance between *śruti,*[45] law anchored in explicit vedic text, highest on the legal source stratum articulated by mīmāṃsakas, and parallel rabbinic tools for gleaning legal rulings from scripture,[46] but we do well to keep in mind the generosity inherent in our extension of the term scripture lest we erroneously superimpose notions of a Sinaitic God having revealed scripture in *both* cases, for example, certainly an inappropriate prototype for Veda. Furthermore, *Mīmāṃsā* depictions of sacrificial rites—while resonant with *rabbinic* discussion of Temple matters, such as priestly need for purity maintenance, or precise mandates of ritual form to ensure efficacy—vary vastly from the latter, given *vedic* emphasis on *familial* sacred fires, rather than Temple-centric sacrifice in the latter—even as this sacrificial matrix ended abruptly with the destruction of the Jewish Temple in 70 AD. While we might be tempted to equate the Brahmanical renunciant move of rendering his familial sacrificial fire an internal fire, as he leaves the ritual realm, with the Jewish ritual shift from visceral sacrifices to prayers and to ritual symbolic representations of the sacrifices of old, we must, again, pay as careful attention to distinctions, as to the pleasing sense of resonance.

Caution noted, we proceed to examine both texts and their hermeneutic tools, one, for deciphering the 900 ritual cases described by Clooney, the second, of the 613 *Torah* commandments, as we compare these systemic scholastics—mīmāṃsaka and rabbinic.

We begin our experiment—the juxtaposed reading of rabbinic and mīmāṃsaka texts pertaining to ritual efficacy and agency for ritual performance—by fleshing out terminology, and by delineating probing questions for which we seek answers in each case. In discussing ritual efficacy, we focus on the goal of successful ritual outcome—ontological change attained by proper manipulation of designated objects, in strict accordance with delineated ritual rules. If a school child hooks wire to battery to light-bulb and there is light, her experiment was successful. If there is no light, it was not. Here we see that both ingredients and manner of their manipulation are critical to proper outcome, since the ritual is obligatory. It must be done. Incumbent upon whom, however, is this obligation to ritual performance? Here we gesture toward sub-questions: A. Who is the actor *required* to initiate and bring ritual to concrete fruition? B. Does one who is *not required* have agency to perform said ritual as a voluntary act? C. If one who is *not required* performs said ritual, will the act succeed, will ontological change come about? D. If the answer to the latter is "no," then might we say that he, the individual who is *not required*, is an improper *material ingredient* for ritual fruition? E. Is there an actor-centric goal to ritual whereby, setting aside efficacy for a moment (efficacy defined as unseen ontological change achieved by following the ritual "recipe" to a T), there are fruit to be gained by an individual engaging in ritual performance, personal benefit that all might want access to? F. If the latter is true, how, in each system-specific case, are competing oughts of ritual efficacy and equity of fruit-yielding-agency for ritual performance, balanced?

Both liturgical systems—rabbinic and mīmāṃsaka—tend to analyze the focal point or goal of each ritual and each portion of ritual through this lens of somewhat competing, while at times complementary, oughts: object/act-centric versus actor-centric. In rabbinic terms, in Aramaic, we call this "*cheftza*," from "object" or "act," versus "*gavra*," from "man."[47] In mīmāṃsaka terms, in Sanskrit, we call this, "*kratvartha*," from "act/sacrifice as goal," versus "*puruṣārtha*," from man, as in "man-centered," or focus upon "phalam," fruit or reward for the man—how the actor is benefited by performing said act.[48]

Speaking of section VI.1 in Mādhava's *Garland of Jaimini's Reasons*,[49] the section that spells out conditions governing eligibility to perform sacrifices, Clooney says:

> It deals . . . with *adhikāra*, with the right harmony of persons and things, words and actions, actions and results . . . with the right fit of persons to sacrificial performance: who is eligible to perform the sacrifices, who is

> ineligible for what reasons, and which exceptions can be made. The thirteen cases cover specific instances related to humans in general, to people who are in some way disabled, to women, to the low caste community known as *Śudras*, and to several exceptions to established rules. The cases are specific, but also educative, instructing the student on how harmony works, who and what fits appropriately into the matrix that is an act of sacrifice.[50]

By speaking of "the right harmony of persons and things, words and actions, actions and results, etc.," Clooney fleshes out the parameters of what is at stake within the Mīmāṃsā ritual rubric. He unpacks the competing oughts quandary through this systemic lens. Is the prime focus on ontological fruition of rite or on one's *right* to perform the rite; on efficaciousness or on satisfaction of actor. As seen earlier, this dichotomy of oughts, in line with our introductory questions, resonates in both *rabbinic* and *mīmāṃsaka* ritual reasoning.

As we examine ritual cases in both traditions in parallel, we note that the rabbinic sources chosen for our comparison tend not to be as viscerally sacrificial in nature as we might expect, given the *mīmāṃsaka* context, as well as the Jewish Temple rite context.

"The prayers were instituted according to the daily offerings," says the Babylonian Talmud.[51] Jewish Temple rites morphed into prayer, into liturgical analysis, into less visceral ritual—post Temple destruction. Thus, not all rabbinic texts below display sacrificial motif. To the post-Temple rabbis, it was not sacrificial rite that sustained the world, but Torah study.[52] This preface is apt background for the following passage from the Babylonian[53] Talmud, tractate *Avoda Zara* (foreign worship), with which we begin our comparative examination:

> Rabbi Meir: Where do we learn that even a non-Jew who studies Torah is rewarded like a high priest? As it says,[54] "That man may perform them and (through their merit) live." Since it says "man" in general, and not, Priests, Levites or Israelites, we learn that even a non-Jew who studies Torah is rewarded like a high priest.[55]

Up to this point in the passage, we see that close examination of the language used in the injunction—the general term, "man"—yields the understanding that all may study Torah—that all are eligible—since all men deserve to live through the merit of the words of Torah. Based on this position, we seem to be focused on the *gavra* or *puruṣārtha*—on the person and his right to attain fruit. This section is the initial, or, interim position. Next, the qualifier:

> However, we must understand that, while worthy of reward, they do not reap the same reward as those who were commanded and (therefore) perform. Rather (they are rewarded) less: as per the measure of those who perform an act, though *not* commanded. As Rabbi Hanina said: Greater is he who is commanded and performs (an act), than he who is *not* commanded and performs (an act).[56]

What has shifted in this second section is not the focus on *gavra* or *puruṣārtha.* We are still speaking of the individual and the priority given to his want or need of fruit for his actions. What is introduced, however, is the idea that a ritual act done out of obedience, rooted in the need for adherence to something *required,* yields *greater* fruit for the person required than for the person who acts voluntarily, though not required. Here we pause and wonder as to the efficacy of the rite performed by one who was not required, in terms of efficacy of rite itself, namely, from a *cheftza* or *kratvartha* perspective, centered on object of act, of rite. Did the light go on? The debate here pertains to why it is that one obligated in a ritual—one with capacity, agency and obligation to perform this ritual—reaps a greater reward.

In this vein, we find the following passage from the Maimonidean code, in the section relating to Torah study:

> A woman who studies Torah reaps reward, yet her reward does not equal that of a man, since she is not commanded [to study Torah], and all who perform an act in which they are not commanded, do not reap a reward commensurate with the reward reaped by one who is indeed commanded to perform the act, but a lesser reward.[57]

Maimonides is very clear as to priorities regarding *reward* for performance. In this particular passage about Torah study, he echoes the Talmudic passage above, both factoring in reward for the performer as well as stressing the prevailing value of an act by *commanded* actor, whose status attains for him, in his performance, the added fruit for *obedience* in and of itself.

We now shift from Rabbinics to Mīmāṃsā—to Garland VI.1. Case 1 opens the section discussing conditions governing eligibility to perform sacrifices:[58]

Case 1: What renders a person eligible to perform a sacrifice?

> 1 Does everyone have eligibility (*adhikāra*) for sacrifice, or not? No, because the word is explicit, | And it is evident from the verb that there is an obligation to act. This rules out enjoyment of results (as a factor). ||[59]

Case 1 begins by referring to the matter of obligation upon the particular actor, akin to what we just discussed with regarded to our second rabbinic section. The case opens by focusing upon the verb connoting one called upon to adhere to the dictates of a command. Fruit desired by the person is a secondary matter. While the obligation is upon the person, his individual desire for fruit is *not* the focus. Do all have agency for sacrificial performance? As per the opening of this case—no. With a legal reasoning move similar to the rabbinic one above, Mādhava closely examines the injunctive language. The explicit nature of the verb form teaches us that eligibility, as in wanting to have the *right* to do something so as to reap fruit, is *not* the priority. The *obligation to act* is the priority. This, as seen earlier, though in thematic inverse, is the *initial/interim* stance. Next—the qualifier:

> By the stronger explicit injunction, the process (of fulfilling the obligation) comes second. Here, what is to be brought about is heaven (the state of happiness desired by all). Because it is for the man's sake, it is connected to him as performer. So here there is (eligibility for all). ||[60]

This concluding stance is reasoned like the *initial* stance in the rabbinic passage above, where the crux of the matter, the prevailing ought, the priority, seems to be heaven, what *all* men desire, namely—actor over act, *gavra* or *puruṣārtha* over *cheftza* or *kratvartha*. Says Clooney:

> Sacrifice may be seen as obligatory for everyone, or for certain persons eligible due to learning, caste, etc. If sacrifice is for the sake of heaven, and heaven is happiness, then perhaps sacrifice is for everyone who wants to be happy. But if sacrifice is a duty, and heaven just a place, the action takes precedence over rewards, incentives. Much of this case has to do with parsing "let him sacrifice," the Sanskrit *yajeta*, and whether the adjective "desirous of heaven" is important or not. Since it is determined to be important, then the scope of sacrifice includes everyone who wishes to be happy, and that wide scope must be narrowed.[61]

As we see, these competing oughts, actor or act, *gavra/puruṣārtha* or *cheftza/kratvartha*, found in both traditions, manifest as tension between rite as obligation, implying that it can only be fulfilled by those who have capacity to fulfill it, on the one hand, and on the other, its being of profound benefit to all, and thus, unfair to restrict. In both traditions, the actor-centric position views respective rituals as gift to humanity, and thus, take an expansive view of agency. On the other hand, we have ritual efficacy, a lens through which human desire is *irrelevant*, given that man is *but one material ingredient* ensuring proper ritual completion.

We segue now to a specific case within our general theme of ritual efficacy and agency, as applies to the status of the blind.

> Rav Yehuda exempted [the blind] from all Torah [level] laws. Said Rav Sheysha son of Rav Idi: What is Rav Yehuda's reasoning? "These are the commandments, the statutes, and the ordinances,"[62] says the verse, to teach us that all those subject to ordinances, are subject to commandments and statutes, and all those not subject to ordinances [like the blind] are not subject to commandments and statutes.[63]

This opening passage supplies us with injunctive reasoning pertaining to obligation, to exemption, and even gestures towards permissibility or prohibition against ritual performance by those not ordained as ritual actor—as ritual *gavra*—as ritual *kartṛ*. This takes us deeper into the hermeneutic woods of agency.

According to this first section, those, such as the blind, who cannot be obligated in certain ordinances due to an incapacity of some type of significance in the realm of ritual performance, are *not subject to* commandments and statutes *en general*. This section seems to represent the latter category, which we discussed, the object/act-centered perspective—that of *cheftza* or *kratvartha*. We turn now to the next section on this Talmudic page, in which we meet a great scholar, who is blind *himself*:

> Said Rav Yosef [who was blind] "First I was wont to say: If the ruling were like Rav Yehuda, who exempted the blind from all commandments, I would prepare a festive feast, and pour drinks for the scholars. Why? Since although I am not obligated, I still perform all commandments."[64]

Rav Yosef relates to the opinion of Rav Yehuda with joyous optimism, as an individual, from the first perspective—that of *gavra* or *puruṣārtha*. He rejoices because his intent to perform the commandments while not obligated, seems to him to be voluntary or altruistic, and therefore, ironically, of greater satisfaction.

However, Rav Yosef then hears of another stance regarding the ritual agency or obligation of the blind, and in his characteristic positive attitude, he says the following:

> "But now I heard Rabbi Hanina, who said, Great(er) is he who is commanded to perform an act, and thus performs this act as one who is obligated, than one who is not commanded, but nevertheless performs the act. Therefore, were anyone to tell me that the ruling is *not* like Rabbi Yehuda, *then* I would prepare festivities for the scholars. Why? Because when I perform acts for which I am commanded, I reap a greater reward for these acts."[65]

Rav Yosef's concern, then, is for his capacity to attain the highest spiritual fruit *qua* merit for his devotional acts. Given the question of whether or not the blind are exempt from all commandments, given his response as both devoted man of faith and learned scholar, we see clearly that the matter at hand is not *solely* one of ritual efficacy. While some might rejoice at being *exempt* from ritual obligation, Rav Yosef is eager to perform these rituals even *sans* obligation. And since this discussion revolves around *gradations* of heavenly reward, depending on whether or not one is commanded, we see that at least in this passage, we are not dealing with a zero sum game of ritual efficacy or none at all. One *may indeed* participate for the sake of heaven—even though he *need not*.

We move now to particular cases in which visual impairment may indeed inhibit ritual efficacy, where the question of agency comes into sharper focus. These cases help delineate the parameters of our competing oughts—ritual efficacy and performer fruit.

In the following passage, the rabbis ask whether or not the blind are eligible to recite a particular prayer and certain blessings:

> The blind may recite the introductory prayers and blessing before *Shema* [Hear O Israel . . .] and may translate The Torah portion into Aramaic. Says Rav Yehuda: He who has never seen the luminaries, may not recite the first blessing before *Shema*—the blessing over the luminaries [sun and moon] . . . [It was] said to Rav Yehuda: Many have seen enough with their mind to expound on the divine chariot, though they have never *seen* it. So too, even one who never saw the luminaries may recite the blessing.[66]

The debate in this section highlights the question of what lacks or deficiencies inhibit efficaciousness of rite—in this case, that of the recitation of the *shma* blessing—namely, *meakev*, as one who holds one back from progress, and what lacks are minor and do not inhibit successful/efficacious performance of ritual. Rav Yehuda seems to indicate that one who is blind, and therefore never saw the luminaries for which the *shma* blessing expresses gratitude, may not articulate this expression of gratitude, since he does not really know what he's thankful for. The oppositional view counters him by citing esoteric visions that one cannot "see" with his physiological sense of sight, and yet about which mystics, for example, expound. Why then, challenges the counter stance, should the blind, who have not seen the luminaries with their eyes, not be able to express gratitude for them in a manner relating to the blind's individual type of appreciation for the luminaries, as per his capacity?

> And how does Rabbi Yehuda counter this argument? He can say, as to the Chariot: this depends on the heart's grasp. One can focus his mind and comprehend the Chariot even while never having seen it. As to the luminaries, however, recitation of the blessing is linked to one's derivation of benefit from them. Since the blind derive no benefit from them, they may not recite a blessing over them.[67]

Rav Yehuda responds to the counter claim by saying that grasp of esoteric matter is dependent on the individual's singular grasp, and can span a range of perceptions as per an individual's heart. The luminaries, however, as per Rav Yehuda, either benefit you, because you are sighted, or do not, because you are blind. In the following section, the rabbis in the counter position prevail with the provision of a narrative proof text:

> The rabbis hold that even a blind man derives benefit from the luminaries, per Rabbi Yosei, who said: All my life I was troubled by this verse, which I did not understand: "And you shall grope at noon as blind grope in the darkness."[68] I was perplexed: What does dark or light matter to the blind? They cannot see either way, so why speak of the blind in darkness? I continued to ponder this, until this incident: I was walking in sheer darkness of night, and I saw a blind man walking with torch in hand. "My son," I said, "why do you need a torch if you are blind?" Said he: "If I have a torch, people save me from pits, thorns and thistles." Even the blind derive at least indirect benefit from light. Therefore, they may recite the blessing over the heavenly luminaries.[69]

Note that their counter argument does not refute the necessity of benefit to the proper intent of the individual reciting the ritual blessing. One must indeed avoid reciting this blessing on what might be deemed false pretenses. The anecdote which serves as prooftext, however, shows that there are myriad ways by which one may derive benefit from the luminaries—from light. In the case discussed, the benefit to the man who was blind was direct, via the indirect gaze of the others—the sighted—who are able to see the blind man, and thus guide him to safety if he is found in peril. Practicality and context, as we see, have more than ample place in ritual reasoning.

This passage is illuminating on several levels. Until now, we have been discussing human benefit and obligation *qua* ritual efficacy as dichotomous. In the above passage, we are introduced to what seems like a new category—it seems that in order to be eligible *qua* obligated, one must, in fact, gain enjoyment from the fruit. In fact, in a case where one cannot gain benefit from the fruit, that person would not have agency to perform the ritual act, the efficacy of which is dependent upon person's enjoyment of the fruit! Much as in *mīmāṃsaka* ritual reasoning, accuracy of utterances is critical. How can one bless God for the luminaries she has not seen? The first answer to this query is quite fascinating. One utters blessings regarding the mystical heavenly chariot, even though one has never seen it, since one can conjure its image with proper focus, (meditation, perhaps?), vision, therefore, can have myriad meanings, as can the grasping of an image or an idea. And finally, this passage then illumines another facet for our inquiry, namely, how does one define fruit? What is construed as benefit? In this case, there can be benefit to one in what the other sees.

Let us return to Mādhava's Garland, to Case number two in VI.1, which discusses "Why the blind and others are not eligible to perform sacrifices."

> 2 Do the blind and others have (eligibility) or not? Because they too desire heaven, they do. | In accord with the mention of the primary sacrifice, let him do the subsidiary rites insofar as able. ||[70]

The first stance of this *mīmāṃsaka* case emphasizes the equitable access to the fruit side of the equation—namely, the human-centric side—that of *gavra/puruṣārtha* over *cheftza/kratvartha*. Through this lens, the priority is not upon optimal performance, or upon success in terms of efficaciousness, but upon the individual doing as best as she can, given her capacity, so that she too can perform, so that she too can glean reward, to which all should have access. And now to the counter stance:

> The injunction to "gaze upon the melted butter," etc. does not pertain merely to the man, | But as such it is an injunction regarding the rite. Therefore, there is no eligibility for the one unable. ||[71]

This case emphasizes the ritual efficacy side of our competing oughts discussion—*cheftza/ kratvartha* over *gavra/puruṣārtha*. If the matter was merely one of fruit for the performer—as per everyone's desire for heaven—then the blind would be just as eligible to perform this sacrifice. However, injunction of this specific rite calls for the act of *gazing* upon the melted butter. This is a critical step in the ritual process, without which the butter will not undergo ontological change. Unless the performer is capable of carrying out the gaze upon the ghee, the ritual will fail—it will not be efficacious. In rabbinic terms, we may say that the gazing upon the ghee is *meakev*, namely, prevents the rite from progressing—from reaching successful completion. Therefore, one who lacks gazing capacity is not eligible to perform—to be a ritual *kartṛ* in this case. Try as he may, desire as he may—with him as actor, as "ingredient," the act will fail. *Cheftza/kratvartha* trumps *gavra/puruṣārtha* in this case.

We end with a passage from Maimonides code, in the section pertaining to the laws of *tzitzit*, the ritual strands, which must be attached to the four corners of a garment:[72]

> The commandment (to wear) *tzitzit* [strings when wearing a four—cornered garment], is by day, not by night, as it says, "And thou shalt see it,"[73] at the time of seeing. And the *suma*, the blind, is obligated in (wearing) *tzitzit* (strings), even though he cannot see, (since) others see him.[74]

The first thing this passage tells us is that *tzitzit* strings must be worn by day and not by night. Next, we hear that this proviso is based on Pentateuchal prooftext: The strings must be seen—meaning that, much like the gazing upon the ghee in Mādhava's aforementioned verse, a critical performatory component of this rite is a properly functioning gaze. And yet, we hear that the blind are indeed obligated in this rite. Why? Did we not hear that sight is needed for proper rite completion? Well, yes. However, the last line in Maimonides, "even though he cannot see, (since) others see him," clarifies that while seeing must be done, it can be done by anyone, and is therefore, not dependent on the *performer*'s capacity for sight.

Conclusion

This last passage in Maimonides provides us with a good finish line, in that we were asked to evaluate what "ingredient" is essential, and which is "inessential" to efficaciousness of ritual. We understand from the verse about "seeing the strings" that sight is a necessary component. If the commandment to wear these strings is linked to being able to see them, then, strictly speaking, wearing them unseen would seem to accomplish nothing. Recall the story of the blind man carrying a light. If the strings must be seen, the question becomes: seen by whom? If the answer is that they must be seen by the *wearer*—that would gesture toward a form of *kartṛ*-centric thinking—doer, actor, human—*gavra* or *puruṣārtha*. Whereas if the essential need is for the strings to *be seen*, then as long as they are seen *by anyone*, the ritual is efficacious. Based on the latter, we are object/act focused, namely, *cheftza/kratvartha* trumps *gavra* or *puruṣārtha*—specificity of *kartṛ*.

This rabbinic case articulation, in that it takes the "seeing" component further—to the question of whose seeing is essential, is greatly enhanced by the mīmāṃsaka discussion as to the ghee. The latter discussion put pressure on the ritual string discussion, in that it poses a third paradigm of thought. The idea that the strings must *be seen*, and not necessarily by the ritual *gavra* or *kartṛ*, makes deeper sense now that the idea of ontological change needed to effect the ghee is considered. Although the prevailing stance in the case of the ghee is that inability to gaze bars agency to perform, (and there does not seem to be a suggestion of an*other* gaze as sufficient), while in the *tzitzit* string case, the prevailing stance is that of *as long as they are seen by anyone*—the "gaze" upon the ghee and strings cases in conjunction, illumined new layers of comprehension and possibility, worthy of future study, as we may ask of the rabbinic case, for example: Are we saying that a gaze—any gaze—ontologically changes the strings? And we may ask of the mīmāṃsaka case, for example: Are we suggesting that there might be a way to tag team ritual performance, whereby an*other* gazer may complete that final stage, thus enabling ritual completion for the blind actor? And might that final gaze, made by *other* acting in his stead, be conceptually similar to the categorization of priestly acts expressed in alternate Sanskrit verb types: *parasmaipada* connoting acts on behalf of others, and *ātmanepada* on behalf of self? And how might the latter relate to Jewish Temple priestly acts on behalf of others, or on behalf of themselves and their own families, as per careful Rabbinic linguistic parsing of prooftexts from Leviticus?[75]

Our micro comparative theological experiment in juxtaposed reading of mīmāṃsaka and rabbinic legal reasoning cases—dovetailing off of our macro or mezzo comparative theological cross systemic introductions—yielded, in addition to validation of resonant ritual-legal hermeneutics, luminescent discovery of new categorical possibilities, born of pressure applied from parameters of one system-specific case to that of another. Our experiment showed how such close reading in tandem can provide fertile soil for "conversation," enriching the grasp of shared themes and terms, as well as each, further dimensions of self and other. Such parallel reading promises further opportunities for mutual text examination, through newly generative lenses, allowing deeper riches of legal reasoning to arise, as pressure is applied to each case from angles not yet attempted, even as neither tradition is forced into inappropriate labels or general antithetical categories. As a scholar with a passion for comparative ritual hermeneutical reasoning, as a woman of faith seeking understanding, this is how I propose to do comparative theology.

Notes

1. See Talmud B. *Brachot* 58a, where "*sagi nahor*" is used as a polite euphemism for "blind," using semiotic inversion. *Sagi* means "enough," or "much," and *nahor*—"light." (Talmud translations are my own. Standard Talmud references indicate B. for the Babylonian Talmud or J. for the Jerusalem Talmud; the name of the tractate, which goes back to the underlying Mishnaic ordering; and the folio number, which has been standardized since the first printed edition about seventy years after Gutenberg.)
2. I use the term "luminescent resonance"—a mixed metaphor to be sure—to somewhat playfully allude to Midrashic discussion of the Sinaitic moment of revelation, expanding upon the verse in Exodus, which describes the people as *seeing* the *sounds* . . . So intense was the experience of Divine revelation that its impact defied the boundaries and delineations of the senses—traversing systems, as it were—traversing systems, much as comparative theology aims to do, in search of deeper meaning—of faith seeking understanding.
3. See Clooney, *Comparative Theology: Deep Learning Across Religious Borders*, 6–7.
4. Clooney, "Methodological Aspects of Comparative Theology."
5. Davis, *The Spirit of Hindu Law*, 1.
6. To some modern secular religio-phobic sensibilities.
7. Davis, 1–6.
8. *Halakhah*, Jewish law, from the root word *halakh*, walking the path, thus, religious law as way of life, which, as per Jewish theology, permeates every step on her life's ethico-religio journey, akin to Hindu *dharma*, to *Dharmaśāstra*, Hindu law, *dharma*, the way one ought to walk/the path one ought to follow.

9. The study, analysis, and praxis of the intricacies of traditional and ongoing hermeneutic debate within centuries of rabbinic literature about Jewish law—debates that continue still today—as to religio-legal theory and applicability to each new case on the temporal horizon.
10. The Talmud, written in discursive argumentative style, similar to that of Mīmāṃsaka ritual-legal texts, is the expansive rabbinic elaboration on the mishnaic code, which was itself collated as a system of imitable rules, thereby unpacking the Pentateuch itself, given the latter's terseness, among other reasons.
11. Based on overly literal reading of Exodus 20:3, "Thou shalt make for you neither statue nor image."
12. See Talmud B. *Pesachim* 48a, translation by author, on *kol b'isha erva*, the voice of a woman is nakedness (*erva* in Hebrew is similar to *awra* in Arabic, serving a similar purpose in discussions of modesty rules in Islamic law).
13. See Talmud B. *Pesachim* 48a, where female arms, legs, hair, and voice are discussed with regards to whether or not there are specific measure of concealment or exposure that can be seen as objectively causing licentiousness.
14. See Talmud B. *Pesachim* 109b–12a.
15. This term, from the root *hared*, anxious, trembling, terrified, refers to the black-clad Ultra-Orthodox, whose nomenclature bespeaks their self-perception as *the* most meticulous or stringent in *halakhic* observance.
16. Ashkenazi Jews do not eat rice on Passover—concerned, given the *gravitas* of not consuming leaven on Passover, with rice sacks being sold beside wheat sacks—lest wheat kernels got mixed in. Sephardic Jews *do* eat rice on Passover, and avoid risk, by sifting all rice in advance of the Passover holiday.
17. Hassidic Jews do not allow matzah—the unleavened bread specially baked for Passover—to come into contact with any liquid whatsoever (no dipping it in soup, for example) lest some errant bubble in the matzah, which inadvertently contained a speck of flower, come in contact with liquid and leaven.
18. See Aviner, et al., *Torat Eretz Yisrael of HaRav Tzvi Yehuda HaCohen Kook*, and Teitelbaum, *Vayoel Moshe*. Tzvi Yehuda Kook vs. Joel Teitelbaum—Zionism as mystically redemptive, versus Zionism as brazen defiance, seeking to hasten the messianic age, prior to God's initiative, thus, ironically, delaying the messianic age as per the latter.
19. See Gordon Guedalia, "Jerusalem Is Burning."
20. The term used for one who issues religio-legal rulings, such as a *poseq* in Hebrew. See Gordon Guedalia, "The 'Pesaqratic Oath.'"
21. See Gordon Guedalia, "Lethal Wives and Impure Widows."
22. Meier, "On the veiling of hermeneutics," 212–26.
23. Gordon, *Studies in Modern Orthodoxy.*
24. See ibid.
25. See Talmud B. *Hagigah* 14b.
26. See Otto, *The Idea of the Holy.*
27. See Levinas, *Ethics and Infinity.*
28. From a lecture by David Grossman at the Harvard Science Center 2013.
29. However, whether or not these established eponyms and specific codifications of authenticated decrees into *Mukhtasar* manuals spelled the closing of the gates of *ijtihad*,

of maverick scholarly creative analysis of sources, yielding rulings or ended prior jurisprudential fluidity, is up for debate.

30. See for example, Berman, *Law and Revolution: The Formation of the Western Legal Tradition*; Coriden, *An Introduction to Canon Law*; Helmholz, *The Spirit of Classical Canon Law*.
31. Maimonides, "Introduction to the Book of Mitzvot," 428–29.
32. See for example, Maimonides, "Introduction to the Book of Mitzvot," and, Twersky, *Introduction to the Code of Maimonides*.
33. McCrea, "Hindu jurisprudence and scriptural hermeneutics," 123.
34. Clooney, "Mādhava's *Garland of Jaimini's Reasons* and his Elaboration VI.1, on conditions governing eligibility to perform sacrifices," Presentation handout. See also, Clooney, "Toward a Complete and Integral Mīmāṃsā Ethics: Learning with Mādhava's Garland of Jaimini's Reasons," in *The Bloomsbury Research Handbook of Indian Ethics*, edited by Shyam Ranganathan (New York: Bloomsbury Academic, 2016).
35. In this study we encounter its more widely studied version, the *Babylonian* rather than the *Jerusalem* Talmud.
36. Said to correlate with the number of parts of the body.
37. Said to correlate with the number of days of the solar year.
38. Or later—widely debated.
39. *Azharot* means "warnings" and was the term used for popular lists of commandments put to verse in that era.
40. Clooney, "Mādhava's *Garland of Jaimini's Reasons* and his Elaboration VI.1, on conditions governing eligibility to perform sacrifices," Presentation handout. See also, Clooney, "Toward a Complete and Integral Mīmāṃsā Ethics: Learning with Mādhava's Garland of Jaimini's Reasons," in *The Bloomsbury Research Handbook of Indian Ethics*, edited by Shyam Ranganathan (New York: Bloomsbury Academic, 2016).
41. Ibid.
42. Ibid.
43. The *mīdot* by which the Torah is explicated, as parallel to Mīmāṃsā hermeneutic measures—*mā* being the Sanskrit root for measure. See Whitney, *The Roots, Verb-Forms and Primary Derivatives of the Sanskrit Language*, 119.
44. See Clooney, "Introduction to the Role of *Śruti* in Hindu Theology," 1–5.
45. See Clooney, *Thinking Ritually*, 20–24, 88–94, and 120, where he is careful to stress how tightly linked to apt execution of each stage and step of sacrificial rite hermeneutical tools like *Śruti* are, or at least to the Mīmāṃsakas—scholar of the Mīmāṃsā school, whose focus is assuring accurate understanding to bring about correct ritual action, because thus must it be done.
46. See Elon, et al., "Interpretation," 814–27 for an articulation of the Jewish hermeneutical system, and Clooney, *Thinking Ritually*, 20–24 and 88–94 for Mīmāṃsaka articulation of Vedic hermeneutics and comparison with modern legal reasoning, and Holdrege, *Veda and Torah*, 351–53, 361–73, and 400–1 for her view of both hermeneutical systems in juxtaposition.
47. These concepts: Man vs. Object, or Actor vs. Act, feature heavily in the legal reasoning of the rabbinic school of Brisk, whose legal rulings hail from Maimonides more than those of most rabbinic schools.

48. See Clooney, *Thinking Ritually*, Chapter 5, "Jaimini's 'Decentering' of the Human," 163.
49. See for example, Clooney, "Toward a Complete and Integral Mīmāṃsā Ethics: Learning with Mādhava's Garland of Jaimini's Reasons," in *The Bloomsbury Research Handbook of Indian Ethics*, edited by Shyam Ranganathan (New York: Bloomsbury Academic, 2016); "Pragmatism and Anti-Essentialism in the Construction of Dharma in Mīmāṃsā Sūtras 7.1.1–12," *Journal of Indian Philosophy* 32, no. 5 (2004): 751–68; "Difficult Remainders: Seeking Comparative Theology's Really Difficult Other," in this volume.
50. Clooney, "Mādhava's Garland of Jaimini's Reasons and his Elaboration VI.1, on conditions governing eligibility to perform sacrifices." Presentation handout. See also, Clooney, "Toward a Complete and Integral Mīmāṃsā Ethics: Learning with Mādhava's Garland of Jaimini's Reasons," in *The Bloomsbury Research Handbook of Indian Ethics*, edited by Shyam Ranganathan (New York: Bloomsbury Academic, 2016).
51. See Talmud B. *Brachot*, 26B.
52. Referring to study of the Bible, "written Torah," while chiefly to rabbinic teachings, referred to as "oral Torah."
53. "Babylonian," or "Bavli," comes as a distinction from the "Yerushalmi," or "Palestinian" Talmud.
54. Hebrew Bible, Leviticus 18:5.
55. Talmud B. *Avoda Zara*, 3a.
56. Ibid.
57. Maimonides, *Mishneh Torah*, Book of Mada, Laws of Torah Study, 1:13, translation by author (as are the rest of the quotes from Maimonides).
58. Clooney, "Mādhava's Garland of Jaimini's Reasons and his Elaboration VI.1, on conditions governing eligibility to perform sacrifices." Presentation handout. This translation of Francis X. Clooney, S.J., is the very first translation of the Garland into English. Section VI.1 is the first complete section that Clooney translated fully, both verses and elaboration. See also, Clooney, "Toward a Complete and Integral Mīmāṃsā Ethics: Learning with Mādhava's Garland of Jaimini's Reasons," in *The Bloomsbury Research Handbook of Indian Ethics*, edited by Shyam Ranganathan (New York: Bloomsbury Academic, 2016).
59. Ibid.
60. Ibid.
61. Ibid.
62. Hebrew Bible, Deuteronomy 6:1.
63. Talmud B. *Bava Kama* 87a.
64. Ibid.
65. Ibid.
66. Ibid.
67. Ibid.
68. Hebrew Bible, Deuteronomy 28:29.
69. Talmud B. *Megillah* 24a.
70. Clooney, "Mādhava's Garland of Jaimini's Reasons and his Elaboration VI.1, on conditions governing eligibility to perform sacrifices." Presentation handout. See also, Clooney, "Toward a Complete and Integral Mīmāṃsā Ethics: Learning with Mādhava's

Garland of Jaimini's Reasons," in *The Bloomsbury Research Handbook of Indian Ethics*, edited by Shyam Ranganathan (New York: Bloomsbury Academic, 2016).

71. Ibid.
72. Strictly speaking, this only applies to a four-cornered garment.
73. Hebrew Bible, Numbers 15:39.
74. Maimonides, *The Book of Mitzvot*, Laws of Tzitzit, Chapter 3:7.
75. I expand upon the latter in my dissertation, which deals, among other cases, with proper or improper intent in specific priestly practice, as discussed in tractates Yoma and Zevachim, to name two, and as discussed in related sections in Maimonides' aforementioned code.

PART III

Recognizing Comparative Theology by Its Fruits

12 Methodological Considerations on the Role of Experience in Comparative Theology

Emma O'Donnell

The still relatively new field of comparative theology has made great strides in the past few decades, growing into an internationally recognized field with departments in major universities. Throughout this growth, comparative theology has engaged a wide range of religious traditions and has addressed a similarly diverse range of topics within religious thought and practice. Yet, reflecting a wider phenomenon in theology more broadly defined, comparative theology has consistently remained a largely textual venture, based in the comparative reading of religious texts.

It is not a stretch to argue that comparative theology has defined itself as a practice of the comparative reading of religious texts, in which a scholar rooted in one religious tradition reads and contemplates the texts of another tradition, seeking insight that can be reflected back into the home tradition. Indeed, many of the most important and formative works of comparative theology to date have been textual studies. These textual studies offer invaluable insights into religious texts and the traditions related to the texts, and have laid the foundation of comparative theology.

However, while the textual basis of comparative theology has yielded many important insights, and has established the foundation of the field, the vast range of elements of religion that fall outside of the textual has received less attention. The dominance of the textual basis points to what has been pushed by default to the margins: the ritual, the performed, and, above all, the experiential. To be clear, it must be noted that the textual focus of comparative theology has not intentionally marginalized the non-textual elements of religion. It has not hindered comparative theological works that look beyond the textual, and as I argue here, it has in fact paved the way for these studies, for the textual focus points toward the next step—i.e., toward studies that depart from the textual.

If comparative theology wishes to continue to develop as an innovative field relevant to theological scholarship and to religious studies more broadly defined, it must develop further ways to address religions as living traditions, lived and experienced by individuals and communities in today's world. In other words, it must continue to develop new ways to take into account the ritual, performed, and experiential nature of religion. These elements have much to reveal to comparative theological projects, and within the general category of the ritual elements of religion, the way that ritual is *experienced* is a particularly rich resource. The comparative study of religious experience can shed light on nuances of interreligious relationships that might not be evident through a study of the texts of each tradition, and on points of convergence and divergence between religions that occur in the experience of religious practice, which may elude purely textual studies.

Studies of ritual experience have not been entirely absent from comparative theology, however, and a number of publications have explored the role of ritual, experience, and emotion in comparative theology and interreligious dialogue.[1] In addition, despite the predominantly textual focus of comparative theology, the relevance and importance of nontextual foci in comparative theology is widely recognized amongst comparative theologians, even amongst those whose work is primarily or entirely textual. This is exemplified by Francis X. Clooney, whose work is intensely focused on the practice of comparative theological reading. Although Clooney states that, in his view, "the foremost prospect for a fruitful comparative theology is the reading of texts, preferably scriptural and theological texts that have endured over centuries and millennia, and that have guided communities in their understandings of God, self, and other," he also acknowledges the potential of other modes of comparative theology.[2] He concedes that the education and resources required for the practice of comparative theological reading may make it elite, and that it may "seem to run counter to the current turn toward popular religion, the legitimate concern for lived and unwritten dimensions of religion." He agrees "that alternative ways of studying religions can be a solid basis for comparative theology."[3] Clooney explains his decision to focus exclusively on texts by pointing out that a "narrow focus in the face of diverse possibilities is a feature of all academic disciplines."[4] Seconding the latter observation, yet inverting the application, I argue here for the necessity of a narrow focus on the unwritten ritual elements of religion contained beyond the text, and within this focus, for increased attention to the way that ritual is experienced.

While a number of comparative studies of religious ritual address aspects of the experiential element of religion, those that use textual and historical sources as their foundation often remain within that focus. The study that begins with the textual tends to end with the textual, and these elements alone are unable to communicate the layers of meaning that arise from the experience of religious practice and ritual. A similar view is expressed by Jewish liturgical theologian Lawrence A. Hoffman, who criticizes the textual bias of most scholarship on liturgy and challenges liturgists to find a way to handle "prayer qua prayer, not just prayer qua literature."[5] Prayer is of a different order than texts, and is inherently performed and experiential.

Referring to the preference for the textual in studies of Jewish liturgy in particular, Uri Erlich follows a similar line of thought:

> But this primary focus on liturgical formulas, notwithstanding the variety of methods used to study them (literary, historical, conceptual, linguistic, etc.), ultimately leads to the neglect of additional aspects of prayer. A tacit assumption shared by these studies is that the main aspect of the prayer phenomenon, and in many instances its totality, lies in textual formulas. Whether explicit or implicit, this assumption narrows the scope of research and, in some respects, even distorts the research topic itself.[6]

Prayer and other forms of religious ritual, whether spontaneous or scripted, are human, experiential phenomena; they exist in time, and in the human body. As Hoffman explains, texts are readily accessible, and while they are sources of endless interpretation, the less accessible elements of religion—the experiential, performed, human aspects of religious practice—call out to be addressed. Referring to Jewish liturgical practices of the past, he points out, "The essential unknown, that which cries out for clarification, after all, is not the texts; what little we know of them, they are at least before us and are amenable to restoration in more or less accurate facsimile by virtue of manuscript evidence. It is the people about whom we know virtually nothing . . ."[7] Yet even Hoffman returns in the end to the primacy of the text. In the next sentence, he continues, "We ought not to argue from the people to the text, but from the texts to the people."[8] The return to the textual made here by

Hoffman, recognized as a staunch supporter of moving "beyond the text," reflected in the title of his book, indicates the extent to which the textual focus is deeply ingrained.

Texts are, it must be noted, not unrelated to the experiential elements of religion. Texts are always sense linked with experience through the act of reading. In the first place, reading is itself an experiential phenomenon. In addition, the reader inescapably brings his or her experience into the interpretation of the text. And conversely, texts can at times intensify experience. Furthermore, religious texts come in many forms, and while many are narrative, philosophical, or doctrinal, others are ritual. They may be guidelines for ritual, or may be intended to be recited or performed in specific ritual contexts. Thus, the full spectrum of meaning of some of these texts may be completely realized only in their ritual performance.

Another instance of the experiential aspects of texts arises in the processes of secondary reflection and gradual absorption of the texts into the religious tradition. In this less direct, although still significant process, a text becomes experiential as its narratives or philosophies are first incorporated into the religious tradition, and then performed in religious practice and ritual. In these cases, the human body performs the textual tradition. Gavin Flood refers to one form of this process as the "entextualization" of the body, in which "the body becomes the text and is inscribed by the text."[9] In these ways, texts can be intrinsically tied to ritual experience.

The experiential elements and associations of reading texts, while significant, comprise only a very small aspect of the full range of ritual and experiential elements of religion. Only a fraction of religious faith as it is experienced by practitioners is communicated by religious texts. Religious faith is experienced less on the page than it is in the body, in ritual practice, in symbols, and in communities.

The ritual and experiential aspects of religion often involve spoken verbal elements as well, and even the nonverbal elements are often intrinsically connected to textual traditions. However, the verbal and textual aspects are often an undercurrent to the primarily performed and experiential elements. In short, religion is experienced and enacted more than it is written and read, and this points to the great need for a comparative theology that addresses the experiential elements of religion.[10]

Noting the tendency to conceive of religion in interreligious studies as "primarily a matter of teachings and belief in teachings" in which

"teachings are formulated and handed down in texts, or at lea
can be so formulated," John T. Maraldo offers this conclusio

> Insofar as religions include nontextual practices, underst
> gions requires an approach quite different from the kind of
> ing usually conceived in hermeneutics. That approach is through a bodily (re)enactment of the practices rather than a discursive reading of texts and teachings. If interreligious hermeneutics is to account for the full range of religious life, it must articulate an alternative notion of understanding that gives access to religious practices as they are lived.[12]

Marianne Moyaert brings this line of argument into the ongoing discussion on the methodological foundations and practices of comparative theology. She notes the characteristically Western academic lens through which religions are interpreted when they are studied as primarily textual phenomena.

> In particular, I want to examine if the textual focus of comparative theology does not unduly limit this project and does not from the outset misconstrue religious others. In particular, I wonder if comparative theology, because it privileges interest in religious texts, does not remain stuck in the typical Western cognitive approach to religion, focusing on comparable beliefs and containable convictions. Is its underlying understanding of religion not too elitist or even intellectualist, and therefore too narrow?[13]

Moyaert identifies a legitimately serious issue connected to the textual focus of comparative theology. Comparative theologians must remain—and most have, indeed, been quite diligent in this regard—sensitively attuned to the hermeneutical lens through which the texts of another tradition are read, and to the implications of a conceptualization of religion that informs the reading of the text. Yet, comparative theology is also uniquely positioned to address this concern, as it incorporates a self-conscious self-referentiality.

This is found in the theologian's openness about his or her cultural and religious perspectives. Most comparative theologians insist that the discipline of comparative theology must involve a confessional starting point.[14] In this view, the theologian must be rooted in a particular faith tradition, and must openly take account of the hermeneutical lens of that tradition, as it brings the home tradition into dialogue with another tradition. Some comparative theologians argue, however, that a hybrid religious identity, or even a stance that abstains from claiming religious faith, is equally at home in comparative theology.[15] A comparative theologian's religious identity is not always static or firmly bounded, but shifts and develops with time, and can entail forays into other traditions. And for some, the concept of a home tradition may be better described as a place between traditions. The phenomenon of multiple religious belonging, which "may equally range from a selective identification with certain teachings and practices of another religion all the way to the experience of initiation in various religions and the attempt to live in the tension between two entirely different religious traditions," has been mapped by Catherine Cornille, who observes that "profound dialogue with other religious traditions often leads to identification with some of their teachings and/or practices and thus to some form of multiple belonging on the part of the dialogically engaged individual."[16]

Whether comparative theology is engaged in from a place of firm and singular identity, or from a shifting or hybrid identity, it is inherently in touch with first-person experience; it takes into account the experiences, reflections, biases, memories, and hopes of the person involved in the comparative process. In this way, comparative theology is rooted in human experience, and thus has the unique capacity to address the experiential.

The self-referential nature of comparative theology equips it to address a number of concerns. First, it invites a hermeneutical transparency through which the theologian may make clear his or her starting point and interpretive lens. This addresses the concern raised earlier about the typically Western cognitive approach to religion, associated with the privileging of the textual. Second, the self-referential qualities of comparative theology make it intrinsically related to the experiential. If comparative theology is rooted in the experience of participation in a religious tradition—whether the theologian's religious identity is static, fluid, hybrid, or otherwise—then comparative theology is inherently about experience. Comparative theology is, therefore, perfectly positioned to address the ritual, experiential, embodied elements of religion.

This conversation necessitates a clarification of the term "experience," and the concept of religious experience. What is experience, and may it be observed or studied objectively? And if not, how we are to take stock of the subjectivity of the study of experience? According to Clifford Geertz, experience is never "mere experience." Experience categorically cannot be raw or uninterpreted, but is always an "interpretive replay [of an experienced event] as we recollect it to ourselves and recount it to others."[17] This concept is applied to religious experience, specifically mystical experience, by Steven Katz, who proposes that "there are no pure (i.e. unmediated) experiences. Neither mystical experience nor more ordinary forms of experience gives any indication, or any grounds for believing, that they are unmediated. That is to say, all experience is processed through, organized by, and makes itself available to us in extremely complex epistemological ways."[18]

Embedded within experience is an inescapable interpretive activity, as "all experience is construed experience, and the symbolic forms in terms of which it is construed thus determine . . . its intrinsic nature."[19] Experience thus always passes through the filter of perception and interpretation, and it may be argued that this is heightened in religious experience. This is because religious experience is shaped by traditions, narratives, practices, materials, and communities, each of which acts as another filter, shaping the way that religious experience is understood.

Geertz suggests that religious experience in the context of ritual allows that which is experienced firsthand and that which is religiously "imagined" to intersect, together forming one's perception of reality:

> For it is in ritual—that is, consecrated behavior—that this conviction that religious conceptions are veridical and that religious directives are sound is somehow generated. It is in some sort of ceremonial form—even if that form be hardly more than the recitation of a myth, the consultation of an oracle, or the decoration of a grave—that the moods and motivations which sacred symbols induce in men and the general conceptions of the order of existence which they formulate for men meet and reinforce one another. In a ritual, the world as lived and the world as imagined, fused under the agency of a single set of symbolic forms, turn out to be the same world, producing thus that idiosyncratic transformation in one's sense of reality.[20]

This suggests the ways in which aspects of experience can be shared communally. In a religious context, experience fuses the shared "imagined" realm of a religious world-view and narrative with the "world as lived." In the context of religious ritual, the participants practice sets of actions which are intrinsically tied to the religious world-view, binding through their actions a shared religious vision with the world in which they live.

Ritual actions do not simply repeat or enact a set of beliefs formulated textually, but rather, they perform and navigate the intersection of an individual human life with the tradition in which it is imbedded. As ritual theorist Catherine Bell describes, "The performative dimension does not mean an enactment of beliefs and theological ideas; it is not a matter of more didactic recitation or more sitting and standing routines. Rather, the performative plays out—physically, verbally, musically—all the issues of the human condition that concentrate at these moments in life."[21]

Religious experience is thus, to a certain extent, shared, and reflecting the interpretive lenses of the religious tradition from which it arises, can be considered collective. And yet, it is also individual, for experience is filtered, first and foremost, through the individual human subject; each person's experience is ultimately unique. The simultaneously individual and collective natures of experience influence its role in comparative theology: The individual aspect of religious experience allows it to speak of the particularity of religious practice, which cannot be properly understood in the abstract, but must be lodged in the concrete, in a specific practice within a specific person or community. It speaks also of the very human, intimate nature of religious experience, which arises uniquely in each person. The collective aspect of religious experience, on the other hand, allows it to have a greater relevance. An experience that is shared carries a more substantial weight than an experience that is purely individual, and it can be said to reflect elements of a religious tradition that may not be otherwise visible. A collective religious experience communicates an element of the religious tradition that has been absorbed, reflected upon, practiced or acted upon, reflected upon again, and expressed in experiential terms.[22]

The experience of the self in dialogue with the religious other may be explored in both the individual and collective senses. In the individual sense, it is the experience of one person in dialogue with the experience of another. Studies of this nature certainly have much to yield, for they acknowledge the particularity of each person's negotiation of religious tradition and individual identity. Yet it may also be investigated in the collective sense, for inherent in a religious tradition is the understanding that something is collectively transmitted, received, and experienced. This latter sense is perhaps even more promising, for the study of collective aspects of religious experience has the capacity to reveal underlying experiential elements of religious traditions and practices, even if those elements are manifested differently in each individual case.

The phenomenon of collective ritual experience can be seen, for example, in the Passover Seder, the ritual meal of Passover. In the Seder, the participants engage in a ritual, collective remembrance of the narrative of the Exodus from Egypt, with the goal not of simply recollecting the narrative, but of experiencing it as if it were in the present. As an active, participatory remembrance of the events of the Exodus from Egypt, it offers a way of participating in the journey out of Egypt and experiencing the transition from slavery to freedom. The experiential remembrance of the escape from Egypt is considered to be an obligation, as made explicit in the Haggadah, the ritual text of the Seder.[23]

Here, the interaction between text and experience is specified, as the text mandates that a particular internal state be reached. In other words, the experiential element of the ritual is brought to the forefront, and the text serves to clarify the obligatory nature of that experience, and to guide the participant into the experience. The crucial point, then, is not the recitation of the text or the actions of the ritual meal, but the internal experience itself. Rabbi Joseph Soloveitchik addresses the complex nature of this commandment to experience a subjective state: "However, *Be-khol dor va-dor* ["in every generation"] is not a *mizvah* [commandment] of eating; it is one of an emotion, a state of mind. It is the involvement of a modern person who nevertheless lives within ancient events—a very complicated *mizvah*."[24] And, notably, this is a commandment for an experience that is communal. The participants are required to identify with a collective history, and through this ritual experience to exchange their individual identities for one that is communal. Here, the ritual text directs the participants' engagement of memory and emotion, but the text defers to the ritual experience itself, which takes center stage.

While the study of religious experience has much to offer comparative theology, experience is elusive. It slips beneath the radar of objective study and is not readily accessible through the standard textual methods of scholarly investigation. For comparative theology, the study of experience involves the experience of both the self and the other, and while it is legitimately challenging to identify and express one's own experience, it is even more challenging to understand the subjective experience of the "other," particularly when that experience is of a religious life inaccessible in its fullness to those outside of the religious tradition.[25]

Yet if comparative theology is to address religion as it is embodied, performed, and experienced, it must find a way to work within the parameters set by the subjective, elusive nature of experience.

These challenges are grappled with in my own *Remembering the Future: The Experience of Time in Jewish and Christian Liturgy*, which engages in an extended study of ritual experience.[26] Exploring both the limitations and potentials of the comparative study of religious experience, it considers the ultimate untranslatability of religious experience from one person to another, and from the embodied mode of religious ritual into the textual mode of a secondary theological reflection. To address this, the book puts to work an experimental methodology weaving together ritual and performance theories, oral testimonies about religious experience, contemporary liturgical theology, and discussions of traditional Jewish and Christian visions of time, to reach a partial understanding of a subject that is ultimately elusive. It finds that, despite the sizeable challenges in writing about an experience that is beyond the verbal, and the obstacles raised by the subjectivity of experience, the comparative exploration of experience is indeed fruitful. In this particular context, the intimacy and commonality of the experience of time grants it the particular gift of communicating across the boundaries of religious traditions, subtly transgressing obstacles to interreligious understanding.

In the end, however, the academic study of religious experience may be only provisional, for experience ultimately evades objective observation, and even first-person accounts of experience are shaped by the subject's own outlook on life and religious experience, and by the hermeneutical lenses of the reader. Experience can only be known in fullness by the experiencing subject. It cannot be fully understood by others except through the mediation of language, and experience is largely immediate rather than mediated, even given the inescapable processes of formulation and interpretation of which Geertz writes. Religious experience is thus uniquely known by the experiencing subject, and shaped by the narratives and practices of the religious tradition in which it occurs.

Yet this should not be seen as an insurmountable obstacle to comparative theologians. While experience remains impenetrable to a degree, it also brings into focus the layers of cultural and religious formation and interpretation through which the experience is filtered. A religious experience, as known and communicated by the experiencing subject, is not simply individual. When viewed hermeneutically, it reflects the collective shaping of religious tradition, culture, practices, memory, and community. These interpretive filters may be a rich resource for comparative theology, for this is where the heart of lived religion lies, in the embodied practices and experiences of people.

Notes

1. See Gort, *On Sharing Religious Experience: Possibilities of Interfaith Mutuality*; Moyaert, "Inappropriate Behavior? On the Ritual Core of Religion and its Challenges to Interreligious Hospitality"; Moyaert and Geldhof, *Ritual Participation and Interreligious Dialogue*; Voss Roberts, "Beyond Beauty: Aesthetics and Emotion in Interreligious Dialogue;" Voss Roberts, *Tastes of the Divine: Hindu and Christian Theologies of Emotion*; Wynn, "Religion and the Revelation of Value: The Emotions as Sources for Religious Understanding."
2. Clooney, *Comparative Theology: Deep Learning Across Religious Borders*, 58.
3. Ibid., 67.
4. Ibid., 67–68.
5. Hoffman, *Beyond the Text: A Holistic Approach to Liturgy*, 6.
6. Ehrlich, *The Nonverbal Language of Prayer*, 2–3.
7. Hoffman, 8.
8. Ibid.
9. Flood, *The Ascetic Self: Subjectivity, Memory, and Tradition*, 212.
10. While the term "experience" in theological studies may immediately suggest a Schleiermacherian understanding of experience as the source and essence of religion, this is certainly not a necessary theoretical underpinning of the study of religious experience. Giving preference to religious experience does not necessitate the experiential-expressive approach to religion, to use George Lindbeck's categories. The reasoning at work in this essay approaches religious experience as it arises from the context of religious practice and tradition. In this way, it more closely aligns—albeit with reservations and emendations—to the cultural-linguistic approach, in which "religions are seen as comprehensive interpretive schemes, usually embodied in myths or narratives and heavily ritualized, which structure human experience and understanding of self and world." Lindbeck, *The Nature of Doctrine: Religion and Theology in a Postliberal Age*, 32.
11. Maraldo, "A Call for an Alternative Notion of Understanding in Interreligious Hermeneutics," 89.
12. Ibid., 115.
13. Moyaert, "Materializing Theologies of Religions."
14. James L. Fredericks offers a formal definition of comparative theology as "the attempt to understand the meaning of Christian faith by exploring it in the light of the teachings of other religious traditions." Cited in Knitter, *Introducing Theologies of Religions*, 205. Clooney builds on this by offering a definition that departs the specific designation of a Christian starting point but remains firm regarding the confessional nature of comparative theology: "Comparative theology—comparative and theological beginning to end—marks acts of faith seeking understanding which are rooted in

a particular faith tradition but which, from that foundation, venture into learning from one or more other faith traditions. This learning is sought for the sake of fresh theological insights that are indebted to the newly encountered tradition/s as well as the home tradition." Clooney, *Comparative Theology: Deep Learning Across Religious Borders*, 10.

15. The hybridity of religious identity has been explored in depth by Jeannine Hill Fletcher. See Hill Fletcher, "Shifting Identity: The Contribution of Feminist Thought to Theologies of Religious Pluralism."
16. Cornille, "Multiple Religious Belonging," 338, 324.
17. Geertz, "Making Experience, Authoring Selves," 380.
18. Katz, "The 'Conservative' Character of Mystical Experience," 4.
19. Geertz, "Person, Time, and Conduct in Bali," 405.
20. Ibid., 112.
21. Bell, "Ritual Tensions: Tribal and Catholic," 27.
22. The concept of collective experience is indebted to Maurice Halbwachs's study of collective memory, in which he observes, "Often we deem ourselves the originators of thoughts and ideas, feelings and passions, actually inspired by some group. Our agreement with those about us is so complete that we vibrate in unison, ignorant of the real source of the vibrations. How often do we present, as deeply held convictions, thoughts borrowed from a newspaper, book, or conversation? . . . We are unaware that we are but an echo." Halbwachs, *The Collective Memory*, 45.
23. Located in the *maggid* section of the Haggadah, the passage reads, "In every generation a person is obligated to regard himself as if he had come out of Egypt, as it is said: 'You shall tell your child on that day, it is because of this that the Lord did for me when I left Egypt.' (Ex. 13:8) The Holy One, blessed be He, redeemed not only our ancestors from Egypt, but He redeemed also us with him, as it is said: 'It was us that He brought out from there, so that He might bring us to give us the land that He swore to our ancestors.'" Translation from Soloveitchik, *The Seder Night: An Exalted Evening: The Passover Haggadah*, 101.
24. Soloveitchik, 102.
25. This issue is addressed directly by Hendrik M. Vroom in his essay "Can Religious Experience Be Shared? Introduction to the Theme 'Sharing Religious Experience.'" In Gort, *On Sharing Religious Experience: Possibilities of Interfaith Mutuality.*
26. O'Donnell, *Remembering the Future: The Experience of Time in Jewish and Christian Liturgy.*

13 Incarnational Speech

COMPARATIVE THEOLOGY AS LEARNING TO HEAR AND PREACH

Brad Bannon

Formulating the Questions

How—and why—does one do comparative theology? As the essays in this volume demonstrate, there are as many answers to these questions as there are comparative theologians. One's method and purpose even tends to vary from one project to the next.[1] In part, this is because theology is often driven by questions. Differing questions require differing methods of inquiry. Because comparative theologians delve deeply into more than one religious tradition, we are often compelled by more than one question at a time. Because this anthology addresses *how to do comparative theology*, I begin by reflecting on how I formulate the questions driving this particular project. Disparate questions may initially seem disconnected, but begin to fruitfully coalesce as one journeys back-and-forth between religious traditions, transgressing boundaries and founding pathways whereupon faith seeks understanding.

I begin with a simple but profound question concerning the Gospel of John posed a half-century ago by Lutheran theologian, Rudolf Bultmann. John's Gospel narrates the revelation of Christ as the Word-become-flesh: "In the beginning was the Word . . . And the Word became flesh and lived among us."[2] And yet, the very etymology of the word "scripture" connotes *written* words. For the reader of John's scripture, the Word-become-flesh has become text. Thus, Bultmann asked: Can *written* words reveal the Word-become-*flesh*?[3]

Answering "no," Bultmann argued that "[John's] Gospel presents only the fact (*das Dass*) of the Revelation without describing its content (*ihr Was*)."[4] But what does that mean? To better grasp Bultmann's abstract conclusion, it is helpful to focus on a concrete example. In John 4, the

Evangelist narrates an encounter between Jesus and an unnamed Samaritan woman beside Jacob's well. It becomes necessary, from Bultmann's perspective, to distinguish between two different revelations: a revelation to the Samaritan woman, and a revelation to the reader of John's Gospel *about* that revelation. In this episode, the Word-become-flesh was revealed to the woman, sensually: She *saw* and *heard* the incarnate Word. John's scripture reveals (to *us*, as readers) the *fact* that this sensual revelation occurred (to *her*), but John's written words cannot reveal (to *us*) the *content* of that revelation since "what" was revealed (to *her*) was the Word-become-flesh.[5]

Like fellow Congregationalist theologian Gail O'Day, I find Bultmann's conclusion dissatisfying but remain compelled by the question he raised: Can the written word reveal the Word-become-flesh? In order to answer "yes," we must be able to explain *how* such a revelation might occur. In her narrative analysis of John 4, O'Day offers a critique of Bultmann's *that/what* (*Dass/Was*) paradigm by considering "how" (*Wie*) John requires his readers to participate in the revelatory process. O'Day's approach is insightful because it shifts our attention to how one might *participate* in scriptural revelation. Her critique enables us to reformulate Bultmann's question: *How* can scripture reveal its truth beyond the paradigm of writing and reading?

Comparative theology enables us to approach questions like this one from fresh perspectives. That is not to say that one poses a question, *a priori*, in hopes of plundering or (mis)appropriating an answer from this or that religious "other." Such an orientalist approach would be destined to fail because different traditions operate within differing modes of thought. This is both the challenge and the promise of comparative theology; it both requires and enables us to alter *how* we think. Francis X. Clooney's chapter in this volume, for example, demonstrates that studying Mīmāṃsā entails learning "*how to think* like a Mīmāṃsā intellectual," which then enables one to think in a similar way about the particularity of Jesus as "the Gospel's deep, literal, and indispensable meaning."[6] The singularity of each tradition remains uncompromised, but reading them together enables (and requires) "Christian theologians to think differently about revelation in the Christian context."[7] Similarly, my essay strives to think differently about *how* scriptural revelation takes place.

Having reformulated Bultmann's question, this essay turns to Advaita Vedānta to examine how a prominent theologian within that tradition thinks about scriptural revelation. Vedānta cannot answer Bultmann's question for us, but it can change how we think about his question. The goal of this experiment in comparative theology, therefore, is to reconsider *how* scriptural revelation might occur—beyond the activity of reading.

Methodology

Vedānta is one of six classical, orthodox schools of Hindu theology.[8] It is considered "orthodox" because it regards the Veda as an authoritative source of revelation. The term Vedānta literally means "end of the Veda," referring to the upaniṣads, which are a collection of texts comprising the final section of the Veda. Advaita Vedānta refers to a theological tradition within Vedānta that interprets the upaniṣads such that Brahman (Ultimate Reality) and Ātman (Self) are considered to be non-dual (*a-dvaita*). This essay examines a commentary on the Māṇḍūkya Upaniṣad authored by the eighth-century theologian Śaṅkara, who is perhaps the best-known teacher within the Advaita Vedānta tradition.

Comparative theology is a praxis of reading back-and-forth between two or more religious traditions. While this essay purports to rethink Bultmann's question regarding Johannine revelation in light of Śaṅkara's Vedānta, comparative theology rarely (if ever) operates in a strictly chronological fashion. My interest in Bultmann's question arose after and in light of my study of Śaṅkara's writings over the last decade. For Śaṅkara, Vedic revelation entails *hearing* rather than *reading*. By reading Śaṅkara's commentaries, one prepares for the Veda's revelation by learning how to hear. Strictly speaking, the Veda is not referred to as *scripture* (sacred writing) but as *śruti* (literally: that which is *heard*). I argue that Śaṅkara's way of thinking about revelation bears important implications regarding Bultmann's paradox of Johannine revelation. That is to say: While the content (*Was*) of John's revelation (that is, the Word-become-flesh) cannot be revealed by *reading* John's written words, perhaps it can be *heard* when those words are embodied by a living teacher, as is the case in Śaṅkara's Vedānta.

Because Vedānta's teacher-student relationship is unique, without any direct corollary in the Christian tradition, it invites a fresh perspective on Christian homiletics. Like a *guru*, a preacher gives voice to scripture, enabling it to be heard by her congregation. Even if the incarnate Word cannot be revealed through John's *written* word (as Bultmann avers), perhaps it can be revealed through a preacher's incarnational speech.

Giving credence to this hypothesis, I reflect on a sermon on John 4 delivered in 1457 by German theologian and cardinal Nicholas of Cusa.

Focusing on his rhetoric, I emphasize how Cusa embodies John's Gospel, breathing life into the written word. Analogous to a *guru* who embodies *śruti*, Cusa (re)incarnates the Word-become-flesh-become-text for his Brixen congregation. Because his sermon emulates the how (*Wie*) of John's revelatory dynamic, he conveys the fact (*das Dass*) of John's revelation but also its content (*ihr Was*). This interpretation is possible because Vedānta's embodied pedagogy enables us to reconsider the Christian doctrine of *theosis* in terms of homiletics. Hence, this experiment in comparative theology invites us to rethink preaching as a form of incarnational speech wherein the Word-become-flesh is not merely announced, but is revealed.

Mapping the Quest

Because comparative theology entails reading texts closely, back-and-forth between traditions, it is well understood as a journey: a quest of faith seeking understanding (*fides quaerens intellectum*).[9] As a Protestant theologian in the Congregationalist tradition, my inquiry is first drawn to scripture and commentaries within my tradition. I begin with a reading of John 4, informed by Rudolf Bultmann and Gail O'Day. Journeying from Samaria to India, I examine the Māṇḍūkya Upaniṣad, a text that teaches its reader *how to hear.* Informed by insights from contemporary advaitin Anantanand Rambachan, I then focus on Śaṅkara's commentary on the Māṇḍūkya Upaniṣad regarding *how to teach* Vedānta's great sentence (*mahāvākya*), "This Self is Brahman." I then return to John 4 through Cusa's sermon entitled "Speak to the Rock in Their Presence."[10] Coming full circle, I argue that comparative theology enables us to navigate Bultmann's paradox of Word-become-flesh-become-text by regarding Christian homiletics as a performance of incarnational speech, neither altogether the same as nor altogether different from Vedānta's embodied pedagogy. Given the aims of this anthology, I pause at various points along this journey to reflect on my own method of doing comparative theology.

Shared Thirst, Shared Vessels

Hungry and fatigued, Jesus sits alone by Jacob's well, his disciples having gone to search for food (John 4:6, 8). Though thirsty, he lacks a vessel for drawing water (4:11). A woman arrives. He asks her for a drink (4:7). She responds with a question. Her words reduce their identities, prejudging their relationship through socially and religiously constructed essentialisms:

> The Samaritan woman said to him, "How is it that you, a Jew, ask a drink of me, a woman of Samaria?" (Jews do not share things in common [*sugchrōntai*] with Samaritans.) (4:9)

Variations of the word "Samaritan" occur thrice in this verse alone, demarcating tribal and religious differences.[11] *My people are from Samaria; your people are from Judea. My ancestors worship God at Mt. Gerizim; your ancestors worship God in Jerusalem. I am a woman; you are a man.* They "do not share things in common" because reified categorical differences (gender, tribe, and religion) divide them.

At issue is not the water he longs to drink, but the material vessel he longs to share. As David Daube observes, the word *sugchrōntai* means "sharing" in the sense of "*using* together" (not lending or giving) and has long been interpreted as implying close familiarity or intimacy.[12] Only those who know one another well—family or close friends—share the same cup. Jesus wants to drink from her vessel (4:7). He wants to share it together (4:9), because he has no bucket (4:11). Having become familiar with him, she leaves her jar (4:28) so that Jesus, "wearied from his journey" (4:6) might drink from it.[13]

How has this familiarity come about? While the woman's question reduces their identities to essentialisms, Gail O'Day emphasizes that Jesus responds "in terms *specific* to the woman's present situation."[14] He tells her everything *she* has ever done (4:29). He supplants reductive categories of identity (gender, tribe, and religion) with highly particularized identities unique to *this* man and *this* woman. They become familiar because he speaks specifically and particularly *to her*. He does not address her generically or impersonally, like an author writing to an ideal reader. Jesus sees *her* and speaks *to her*.

Despite his absence, the Evangelist depicts the scene for us. His written words (*scripture*) enable us to observe their intimate dialogue. In John's script, the two sit, beneath the noonday sun, in the liminal space between the town and the wilderness, at the edge of Jacob's well (4:5–6). Like Jacob, who has "seen God face-to-face,"[15] Jesus and the Samaritan woman gaze at one another. Their words cut through (*dia-logue*) labels that reduce identity to categories. No longer Jew and Samaritan, no longer male and female,[16] they become familiar enough to share vessels, quenching their respective thirsts.

O'Day observes that John's narrative effects a "dramatic role reversal" through this shift from general, social categories to specific, personal identities.[17] The dialogue functions on two levels, simultaneously. On one level, their discourse pertains to *his* physical thirst, to Jacob's water, and to *her* vessel: the water-pot. On another level, the discourse addresses *her* spiritual thirst, the Father's Living Water, and the vessel that is *his* very body: the Word-become-flesh.

Word-Become-Glesh-Become-Text (*Dass*/*Was*)

Because comparative theology entails close readings of texts, I have initiated this particular experiment with a close look at John 4. While it offers many possible topics for reflection, our focus here is limited to *how* the Word-become-flesh is revealed in this episode. Two questions are at issue: *How* is the incarnate Word revealed *to the Samaritan woman*? *How* is the incarnate Word revealed *to the reader of John's Gospel*?

Rudolf Bultmann argues that the sensual nature of this revelation of the Word-become-flesh presents us, as *readers* of a text (*scripture*), with a problem. He notes that John's announcement, "the Word became flesh," is immediately followed by a *seeing*: "and we beheld His glory."[18] Like Bultmann, Dorothy Lee highlights the fact that John's revelation is thoroughly *sensual*.[19] Throughout John's narrative, the incarnate Word is revealed directly to the human senses. The first epistle underscores the importance of this sensuality for the Johannine community: "We declare to you what was from the beginning, what we have heard, what we have seen with our eyes, what we have looked at and touched with our hands, concerning the Word of life" (1 John 1:1). According to Bultmann, the gospel and epistle writers intend to link *hearing* the Word (*Logos*) with the recurrent phrase, "God said" in Genesis 1.[20] In the sensual theophany at Jacob's well, the incarnate Word is literally seen and heard by the Samaritan woman in and through their intimate and highly specific dialogue.

As *readers* of John's *text*, however, this sensual revelation is unavailable to us. The Word-become-flesh has become text. Like a garment (*textile*), the written word covers the Word-become-flesh even as those words announce the incarnation. Paradoxically, John 4 reveals to us that the incarnate Word was not revealed *to us*, but uniquely and particularly *to her* in a specific context (around noon, beside Jacob's well).

Bultmann responds to this paradox by asserting that John's Jesus is the "Revealer of God [who] reveals nothing but that he is the Revealer."[21] John's Gospel, Bultmann explains, "presents only the fact (*das Dass*) of the Revelation without describing its content (*ihr Was*)."[22] It is simply a revelation *to faith*.[23] As evidence, Bultmann notes that while many people in John's narrative *see* Jesus, some of them lack faith and thus fail to "see" the Word-become-flesh (for example, 14:8f). According to Bultmann, John's language of "seeing" does not refer to bodily sensation (eyes, ears, and so on) but to a spiritual sensation that he terms "faith's perception." Somewhat paradoxically, Bultmann maintains that "faith proceeds from *hearing*."[24]

From Bultmann's perspective, the episode beside Jacob's well narrates the procedure of revelation, whereby the woman *learns to see* the Word-become-flesh. It models *how* the revelation occurred though a process: (1) failing to see, (2) faith proceeding from hearing, and (3) faith's perception.

1. The woman from Samaria *sees* a thirsty man from Judea, but fails to see the Word-become-flesh. She reduces identity to generic categories (gender, tribe, religion).
2. Jesus speaks to her "in terms specific to the woman's present situation."[25] Cutting through constructed categories of identity, he tells her "everything about herself" (4:29). He *sees* her spiritual thirst, making it visible to her, as well. Her faith proceeds from hearing him address her personally and particularly.
3. Her faith enables her to *see* the Word-become-flesh, the vessel by which to quench her spiritual thirst with living water.

However, John's narrative attests to Bultmann's paradox even more strongly than Bultmann himself. After their conversation beside Jacob's well, the Samaritan woman returns to the city and tells the people there to "come and see" (4:28–29). While other Samaritans hear *her* account of the revelation, their faith does not proceed from hearing her witness, but is ultimately grounded in the fact that they have directly and sensually perceived Christ for themselves (4:42). Like her, their thirst is not quenched by testimony but through a direct encounter with the Word-become-flesh. Her words reveal to her neighbors the fact (*das Dass*) of

in a manner that also responds to the paradox of incarnational revelation captured by Bultmann's *Dass/Was* distinction. Rather than circumnavigating this paradox, one might emphasize it all the more: Perhaps the need for an incarnate revelation and the text's inability to reveal the Word-become-flesh is not an academic aporia but is actually John's Good News.

Consider again the two questions posed previously: (1) *How* is the incarnate Word revealed to the Samaritan woman? She directly and sensually perceives the Word-become-flesh through a personal, highly specific dialogue. (2) *How* is the incarnate Word revealed to the reader of John's Gospel? From Bultmann's perspective, it is not. From O'Day's perspective, the incarnate Word is revealed when the engaged reader participates in the revelatory dynamic by attending to John's narrative irony. However, while O'Day's theology of participatory revelation is promising, it continues to think about revelation under the paradigm of reading scripture. Its pitfall, once again, is Bultmann's paradox of Word-become-flesh-become-written-word.

Comparative theology enables us to think through these questions from a fresh perspective. Following an exodus to and sojourn in a theological tradition much farther from Judea, perhaps we might return to Samaria equipped with an alternative way of thinking about scripture, revelation, and incarnate speech. I argue that Śaṅkara's Vedānta enables us to think about the second question more simply, consistent with our answer to the first question, edified with new know-how (*Wie*) for participating in John's revelatory dynamic.

Reading Śaṅkara, Hearing *Śruti*

Śaṅkarācārya (Śaṅkara the great teacher) was an eighth-century Hindu theologian who composed commentaries on sacred texts as well as a text pertaining to teaching Advaita Vedānta.[34] As Anantanand Rambachan states, Śaṅkara "regards himself as offering an exposition of the [Advaita] tradition according to the lineage of teachers who preceded him."[35] While his commentaries explicate and defend interpretations important to his tradition, his writings also equip his readers with hermeneutic tools, passed through generations of teachers, necessary to grasp the truth revealed directly by *śruti* (defined below).

Śaṅkara is appropriately described as a theologian, explains Rambachan, if "theology" is understood to be "the ascertainment and defense of the meaning of revelation."[36] Śaṅkara frequently asserts that *śruti* is the only valid means of realizing truth.[37] However, his understanding of *śruti* (literally: "that which is *heard*") is subtly but critically different from typical understandings of *scripture* (literally: "sacred writings") in Christian theological traditions. By highlighting and expounding the significant distinction between *reading scripture* and *hearing śruti*, this brief sojourn in Vedānta seeks to open a more sensual praxis for participating in John's revelatory dynamic. In other words, the fruit of this experiment in comparative theology is born from the seeds of distinction between *reading scripture* and *hearing śruti*.

To that end, it is helpful to distinguish between *śruti* and written texts. According to Śaṅkara's tradition, the words and meanings of *śruti* are eternal and unauthored.[38] These words and meanings were heard (*śruti*) by great sages long ago and have been passed down orally from teacher to student for millennia. While written documents containing these words may be referred to as *śruti*, the term primarily and properly refers to the eternal words which are *heard* by sage and student alike as this revelation is passed from generation to generation.[39]

Subsidiary to *śruti*, the Vedānta tradition regards certain logical/systematic texts as authoritative. Among these are Jaimini's *Pūrva Mīmāṃsā Sūtra*, which Francis X. Clooney discusses in his chapter in the current volume, and Bādarāyaṇa's *Uttara Mīmāṃsā Sūtra*. While these texts are outside the scope of this particular experiment in comparative theology, it is important to understand their purpose and function within Śaṅkara's tradition. The laconic verses recorded in these texts found a hermeneutics through which the *śruti* is understood and interpreted by the tradition. As Clooney emphasizes, these texts and their commentaries train readers to think in accordance with the tradition. By training readers to think in a particular way, commentaries and logical/systematic texts prepare readers to *hear* the *śruti*.

Drawing from the advaitin commentator Amalānanda, Clooney elsewhere offers a helpful analogy, likening *śruti* to a musical score: "the musical notes are already being played distinctly even when one still lacks the capacity to distinguish them."[40] Just as one gradually cultivates a "refined ear for music," one learns how to hear *śruti* and "notices what was previously unheard."[41] By reading Śaṅkara's commentaries and similar texts, one prepares for the sensual event of *hearing* the revelation of what is heard (*śruti*).

For this experiment in comparative theology to bear fruit, one must ask: *How* does reading a text prepare one to hear? Comparative theology eschews abstract generalizations in favor of close readings of particular texts. Hence, I turn now to the Māṇḍūkya Upaniṣad as a concrete example of *how* texts prepare readers to hear *śruti's* revelation.

Harmonizing Revelation: The Māṇḍūkya Upaniṣad

The Māṇḍūkya Upaniṣad (MU) is a short text, consisting of just twelve prose verses which are interspersed in a longer text, the Māṇḍūkya Kārika, traditionally attributed to the teacher of Śaṅkara's teacher, Gauḍapāda.[42] While these verses were eventually considered to be *śruti* (hence, Māṇḍūkya *Upaniṣad*), it seems clear that Śaṅkara did not regard them as such.[43] He describes the text as "a synopsis (*saṅgraha*) of the essence of the meaning of Vedānta."[44] It draws diverse teachings together, training students to hear them in harmony with one another.

Somewhat like a musical score, the twelve verses of the MU may be divided into three movements sharing a similar cadence, structure, and theme in fugal variation. Individually and collectively, the three movements model a theological practice called "coordination" (*upasaṃhāra*) and cultivate a skill called "harmonization" (*samanvaya*).[45] Simply put, because there are multiple teachings on similar topics spread throughout the *śruti*, one can better grasp the meaning of these teachings by coordinating them with one another. While each teaching must be understood on its own, in its original context, coordination enables Vedāntins to rule out possible misinterpretations. Each teaching must have a unique meaning and purpose because no passage in *śruti* is superfluous. However, if the teachings *seem* to contradict one another, then one's interpretation must be wrong because *śruti* does not contradict itself.

Coordination, however, is more than a hermeneutic tool; it is also a spiritual and ethical practice. Each time one coordinates various teachings, one learns to make decisions in a particular way.[46] Through repeated practice, one begins to think differently. Starting small, one begins with *śruti* teachings that are obviously similar to one another, learning *how* to coordinate similar teachings. Through practice, one learns to coordinate increasingly dissimilar teachings, steadily cultivating the skill of harmonization. In other words, by learning to read and re-read in a particular way, one learns how to *hear* diverse teachings in harmony with one another.

The twelve verses of the Māṇḍūkya Upaniṣad model this theological practice. In the first movement (MU 1), various teachings on the sacred syllable AUM are drawn together from the Chāndogya and Taittirīya Upaniṣads. The similarities and connections between these teachings are relatively easy to see, if only because they use similar vocabulary (for example, the word "AUM"). Likewise, the second movement (MU 2–7) collects teachings on consciousness, spread throughout the Bṛhadāraṇyaka Upaniṣad. Here, the connections are slightly less obvious and the coordination is relatively more difficult.[47] Through careful study and diligent practice, however, one learns how the pieces fit together, so to speak. Finally, the third movement (MU 8–12) coordinates the teachings on AUM with the teachings on consciousness. Here, the connections are far from obvious, requiring a deeper understanding of each teaching in light of the others. Through sustained reading and re-reading, one begins to coordinate increasingly disparate teachings, learning how to hear each teaching, harmoniously.

Amalānanda's analogy, mentioned earlier, of cultivating a refined musical ear is especially poignant.[48] Some students require more "ear-training" than others and, thus, should practice coordination aided by a gracious teacher and commentaries.[49] However, final realization, according to Śaṅkara, only dawns in a moment of grace, devoid of all effort, agency, and action, upon *hearing* the *śruti*.[50] Revelation begins and ends with hearing *śruti*. Everything else is ear-training. The Māṇḍūkya Upaniṣad, from Śaṅkara's perspective, conveys neither the fact (*das Dass*) of revelation nor its content (*ihr Was*), but is paradigmatic of how (*Wie*) revelation can be *heard*.

Coordination is not synthesis. While the MU asserts the underlying identity of that which is signified by "AUM," "Ātman," and "Brahman," these names are not synonymous. For example, in one context I am called "Brad," in another I am called "dad," and in another, "son." If one is to grasp who I am, these terms must be coordinated, without obviating distinctions between these names, which are not synonymous. Each name signifies the same person while indicating distinct relationships. In the praxis of *upasaṃhāra*, differences between "AUM," "Ātman," and "Brahman" are retained, but are heard concordantly. Particular teachings are harmonized without reducing differences to monistic unison.[51] Each passage coordinated by the MU must be understood in its own right, in its own context. And yet, the text trains one to hear these distinct teachings coordinately: a symphony of distinct voices, harmoniously heard.

Embodied Pedagogy

This experiment in comparative theology is beginning to take shape. As we have seen, Gail O'Day's critique of Bultmann encourages us to consider *how* John's Gospel requires readers to participate in scripture's revelatory dynamic. For Śaṅkara, however, one does not participate in *śruti*'s graceful revelation by reading, but only by hearing. For this revelation to arise, one must learn to hear in a unique way. The MU, from Śaṅkara's perspective, prepares one for the revelatory event of hearing *śruti*.

This implies an obvious point, now stated explicitly: Only that which is audible can be heard; once a student has cultivated the skill of hearing harmoniously (*samanvaya*), a teacher must give voice to the scripture if it is to be heard. As discussed earlier, the revelation of Christ, according to John's Gospel, is thoroughly sensual. This point centrally founds Bultmann's paradox of the Word-become-flesh-become-text. Bultmann's solution entails distinguishing between physical sensuality and spiritual sensuality ("faith's perception").[52] As we will see next, Śaṅkara's embodied pedagogy offers a different possibility.

Śaṅkara frequently asserts the necessity of learning Advaita Vedānta from a qualified teacher. As Anantanand Rambachan emphasizes, even the Upaniṣads themselves "are structured in the form of dialogues between students and their teachers."[53] The Muṇḍaka Upaniṣad instructs its reader to "go, with twigs in hand, to a teacher who is learned in the scriptures and who is steadfast in the knowledge of himself."[54] One "should not seek for knowledge of Brahman independently," Śaṅkara avers, but only under the guidance of a teacher.[55]

Being well-versed in the Veda, on its own, does not qualify one to be a teacher. Such a person, explains Rambachan, "can teach what she has heard, but not what she *is*."[56] In addition to knowing the Veda well, a qualified teacher is one who is established in Brahman (*brahmaniṣṭham*) and who is trained in the pedagogical methods passed in the flow of teaching (*sampradāya*) from teacher to student (*guru śiṣya paramparā*).[57] In other words, a teacher is one who knows the Vedas, has grasped their revelatory truth, and has been trained in traditional teaching methods. As Rambachan elucidates, "Advaita is essentially a teaching tradition that seeks to communicate a direct knowledge about oneself, and the teacher *who embodies this wisdom* is the best instructor for the communication of this teaching."[58] A *guru*, he adds, communicates "with a directness and conviction," and also "with the immediacy and power of personal example that will be liberating for her student."[59]

From Śaṅkara's perspective, learning from a traditional teacher is not only valuable, it is also *necessary* because *śruti* is both the means and agent of revelation. This marks a significant difference between Śaṅkara's understanding of scriptural revelation and that of the Christian thinkers discussed earlier. When one reads scripture, scripture is the means of revelation, but the reader is the active agent. From Śaṅkara's perspective, however, if *śruti* is to be the true agent of revelation, then the student must cede all agency and effort. *Śruti*'s truth is revealed in a moment of grace when a student (having learned to hear) refrains from all activities—including reading—in order to receive *śruti's* graceful revelation uttered by a trusted, compassionate teacher.[60]

Comparative theology enables us to alter how we think through theological issues. The reformed Protestant tradition, of which I am a part, emphasizes that divine revelation arises through grace; it is not the result of human effort.[61] While this comparison to Śaṅkara's theology highlights significant commonalities, it also exposes a significant difference. For Śaṅkara, the acts of reading and interpreting require human effort and agency. While reading and interpreting are indispensible practices that teach students *how to hear*, even these human efforts must be relinquished if *śruti*'s graceful revelation is *to be heard*.[62]

Bultmann's paradox of the Word-become-flesh-become-written-word persists so long as scriptural revelation is conceived under the paradigm of reading John's sacred text. Śaṅkara's embodied pedagogy offers a different paradigm—an alternative way of thinking about the relationship between scripture and revelation. For this experiment in comparative theology to be successful, however, it must also address the issue of incarnation. To that end, we turn once more to Śaṅkara's commentary on the Māṇḍūkya Upaniṣad for a concrete example of *how* a *guru* embodies the *śruti*.

Incarnate Words and Pointed Speech (*Wie*)

Due to the nature and content of Vedānta's revelation, the relationship between each particular teacher and student is necessarily unique. The eternal Veda's script does not change, but each incarnation of its words emerges in a new and different context, enabling it to be heard. The relationship between a *guru*, who embodies the scripture, and the *śiṣya* who hears the revelation "about oneself," cannot be replicated or textually inscribed. It can only be (re)incarnated.

The Upaniṣads, once again, "are structured in the form of dialogues between students and their teachers."[63] Just as John 4 narrates a dialogue between Jesus and a Samaritan woman, the Upaniṣads narrate dialogues between teachers and students. In many cases, these episodes are particularly intimate: between father and son (Chāndogya Upaniṣad) or husband and wife (Bṛhadāraṇyaka Upaniṣad). When a student *reads* these dialogues, the fact (*das Dass*) of this revelation is observed, but not its content (*ihr Was*). Reading *about* an intimate dialogue between father and child, for example, is quite distinct from participating in a dialogue with one's own father or one's own child. From Śaṅkara's perspective, however, these dialogues model *how* (*Wie*) Vedānta's truth is revealed. The scripture is, in some sense, much like a script. For example, what Uddālaka says to his son, Śvetaketu, in the Chāndogya Upaniṣad is important—but this dialogue only becomes an event of revelation when that dialogue is *performed* in the embodied context of teacher and student. This need not imply, of course, that the teacher and student must also be parent and child, but could imply that the student must trust and have faith in the teacher, much as a child has trust and faith in his/her parent. The *guru* embodies both the words and the pedagogy, as if reincarnating the Upaniṣadic teachers.

As discussed, the first of the MU's three movements coordinates various scriptural teachings on AUM. The second movement begins with what the Advaita tradition regards as one of four "great sentences" (*mahāvākya*-s), "This Self is Brahman" (MU 2).[64] Coordinating these teachings, Śaṅkara comments:

> The Brahman that was expressed indirectly [by scriptural teachings on AUM] is revealed perceptibly and distinctly as "This Self is Brahman." By means of a [teacher's] gesture, [the word] "This" points out the innermost self . . . [emphasizing] "*This* Self."[65]

Two aspects of Śaṅkara's commentary are especially pertinent to this experiment in comparative theology. First, Brahman is expressed indirectly (*parokṣābhihita*) through texts. Scriptures employ the word "Brahman" to name the unnamable, infinite, non-dual reality. To grasp the content of the revelation, a student must first understand the name itself.[66] The only means of knowing "Brahman," from Śaṅkara's perspective, is the Vedānta scriptures. However, even if one has understood the name

"Brahman" in the great sentence "This Self is *Brahman*," one has still not grasped Advaita's truth.[67] While Brahman cannot be known without scripture, texts can only express Brahman indirectly. At the feet of a teacher, however, this same Brahman can be "pointed out perceptibly and distinctly as '*This Self* is Brahman.'"[68]

Second, Śaṅkara's commentary offers further insight into how (*Wie*) Vedānta's truth is revealed. In his subcommentary, Ānandagiri explains that Śaṅkara's word "gesture" (*abhinaya*) instructs teachers to literally point a finger at the student's body in the region containing the heart.[69] As if offering a stage cue, Śaṅkara indicates *how* the script should be performed if its content (*ihr Was*) is to be revealed. The words are the agent of revelation, but they require mediation if they are to communicate. Physically embodying Vedānta's wisdom, the teacher points to the student, gives voice to the text, and reveals "*This* Self is Brahman." Through this pointed speech, the *guru* (re)incarnates these words, revealing "perceptibly and distinctly" what the written texts express indirectly. The student understands that the words point to him/her, directly and particularly. The teacher becomes a vessel for the Veda's eternal words.[70]

Revealing Vessels

Doing comparative theology requires patience and sustained attention. By delving deeply into particular texts, one learns to think along with the sacred traditions of which they are a part. Each side poses its own questions and presents its own challenges. Like Vedānta's practice of *upasaṃhāra*, each teaching has its own integrity and must be grasped in its own context before these can be coordinated with one another. Contextualized readings, however, remain provisional, inviting fresh re-readings as dissimilar passages are read after and in light of one another. The texts do not change, but the comparative theologian does change as she or he is inscribed into an increasingly complex context.[71]

My method in this comparative experiment intentionally mimics the method modeled by the Māṇḍūkya Upaniṣad. As we have seen, the MU may be divided into three thematic units: coordination of various teachings on one topic (AUM), coordination of various teachings on a second topic (consciousness), and coordination of the first unit with the second unit. Similarly, this experiment in comparative theology involves three movements, two of which have been completed: an analysis of John 4, coordinating readings of that text by Bultmann and O'Day, and an analysis of the Māṇḍūkya Upaniṣad, coordinating insights by Śaṅkara and Rambachan. We now begin the third movement, wherein these teachings are coordinated with one another. Like *upasaṃhāra*, the goal is not to deny the distinctiveness of the Christian and Vedānta teachings, reducing concordant harmonies to monistic unison. Rather, we endeavor to learn how to hear these distinct teachings harmoniously, after and in light of one another, in this third, comparative context.

Śruti, as noted, is both the means and the agent of revelation, according to Śaṅkara's Vedānta. Black ink on a dead page (or palm leaf) cannot mediate *śruti's* truth because its content (*ihr Was*) pertains to one's very Self. It does not speak to a generic audience or address an ideal reader. Only when embodied by a living teacher does *śruti* become the agent of graceful revelation, aided, says Śaṅkara, by a pointing finger and pointed speech: "*This* Self is Brahman." *Śruti* is the agent of revelation, but the teacher is the medium—the *vessel*—incarnating *śruti*, enabling it to be *heard*.

Like the material water in Jacob's well (for which Jesus thirsts), and like the eternal, living water (for which the Samaritan woman thirsts), the eternal words of *śruti* are already "there," so to speak. Nevertheless, each—Jacob's water, the Father's living water, and the words of *śruti*—requires a vessel. While they are "there," im-mediately, they must be mediated. The Samaritan woman shares (*sugchrōntai*) her vessel so that Jesus's physical thirst may be quenched. Jesus shares his vessel, the Word-become-flesh, so that her spiritual thirst may be quenched. Similarly, if *śruti* is to be heard, a revealing vessel is needed. To reveal its truth, *śruti* must be given voice by a teacher. It requires incarnation. A body is necessary.

Comparative theology enables us to read these diverse teachings together, changing how we hear each, but is it also able to change how we think about Bultmann's paradox of the Word-become-flesh-become-text? Śaṅkara insists that a living *guru* is necessary in order that one may *hear* the *śruti*. While there is no direct corollary to Vedānta's unique *guru-śiṣya* relationship in the Christian tradition (not, at least, in my own Congregationalist tradition), I argue that Śaṅkara's emphasis on embodied pedagogy can change how we think about Christian homiletics.

Thirst for Justice

To that end, this experiment in comparative theology now journeys once again. Rather than return to Samaria, it leaps to a (re)incarnation of that scriptural episode on March 25, 1457 in Brixen, Germany. At that particular time and place, Nicholas of Cusa gave voice to John's text in a sermon entitled "Speak to the Rock in Their Presence."[72] Adopting and modifying O'Day's critique of Bultmann's *Dass/Was* distinction, my attention here is drawn to how (*Wie*) Cusa's homily enables his congregation to participate in John's revelatory dynamic. Like a *guru* in Śaṅkara's Vedānta, Cusa embodies both the words and the "how" of John's scripture.

Cusa structures his sermon as many preachers do: He reads the text aloud, line-by-line, adding commentary along the way. Through his recorded words, we observe the flow of teaching (*sampradāya*) from teacher to student (*guru śiṣya paramparā*), neither altogether the same nor altogether different from Vedānta's embodied pedagogy. He reads the script, as it were, enabling John's scripture to be heard. The pastor's comments breathe life into the text, embody its wisdom, paint its scene, and imaginatively lead his flock to drink at Jacob's well.

Cusa enables his congregation to identify with this tired man, thirsting beneath the sun's heat. He preaches: "The fact that Jesus was wearied from the journey shows that He was a real human being who carried around a burdensome body as do other human beings."[73] He describes the scene in sensually vivid terms. No stranger to homiletic genre and its cadence of repetition, his rhetoric raises the temperature on that Friday afternoon, as if cultivating a thirst: "Around noon, when the air grows hot . . . Christ appeared in the middle of the day in the heat of the sun . . . wearied from his journey."[74]

As if practicing *upasaṃhāra*, Cusa coordinates the sweltering heat of Samaria's noonday sun with the torrid oven that scorches evil in Malachi 4.[75] Refusing to divorce the symbolic from the material, he enables his congregation to hear John 4 in harmony with Malachi's Sun of Justice, "with healing in its wings."[76] As Cusa explains to his listeners, Jesus asks the woman to share her water vessel, "in order to excite [her] reception" (*ut excitet ad recipiendum*).[77] Just as the midday sun, shining upon the Son, stimulating his physical thirst for water, Jesus's words shine the Sun of Justice upon this unnamed woman, stimulating her thirst for justice. Likewise, Cusa's pointed speech stimulates his congregation's thirst.

Giving voice to the woman's words, Cusa performs John's script: "Sir, you have no vessel with which to draw [water], and the well is deep."[78] "Since 'the well is deep' for every person," he exhorts his Brixen congregation to "*pay attention to how* [*attende quomodo*] it is necessary to draw any water"; it must be done "with effort and with ingenuity."[79] Like an untapped well, the living water of which Jesus speaks languishes within Cusa's hearers, awaiting their thirst.

Through his spoken words, Cusa enables his hearer to participate in John's revelatory dynamic. As discussed, Gail O'Day argues that John requires his readers to "participate in the revelatory dynamic"[80] because the narrative simultaneously operates on two different levels. In his sermon celebrating the Feast of the Annunciation (announcing the Incarnation), Cusa points to a third level of meaning. He gestures to a third vessel, imperceptible to a reader but poignantly indexed through spoken word.

Like Śaṅkara's gesture to "*This* Self," Cusa points neither to the Samaritan's water pot nor to the Word-become-flesh-become-text, but to each body congregated before him. He gestures to living wells, present in that Brixen cathedral, ready to gush forth and quench a thirst for Justice. Like Moses before a thirsty crowd in Kadesh, Cusa "speak[s] to the rock in their presence."[81] Akin to the Samaritan woman, Cusa's hearers lack neither physical water nor the eternal water; rather, they lack a particular kind of thirst. Embodying scripture's wisdom as a *guru* embodies *śruti*, Cusa gives voice to the Word-become-flesh-become-text. He speaks in order to excite his hearer to receive (*ut excitet ad recipiendum*) a thirst for Justice.[82]

With effort, one can drink water from a vessel and "quench bodily thirst for a time, but after that time has elapsed, one will be thirsty again."[83] Although the "fount that springs up is a living . . . [and] unfailing Fount," it is only "infused into the one who thirsts for it."[84] The eternal words of *śruti*, "are already being played distinctly even when one still lacks the capacity to distinguish them."[85] With effort, one learns how to hear *śruti* and "notices what was previously unheard."[86] Likewise, the living water of which Christ speaks is always already there, waiting to gush forth to quench one's thirst for Justice. The "effort and ingenuity" of which Cusa speaks is not required to draw from the "unfailing Fount," but to cultivate a thirst for it.[87] Unlike this water, our *thirst* for justice is ephemeral; it evaporates as we grow weary.

Cusa offers a second explanation for Jesus's exhaustion. He previously attributed Jesus's fatigue to his burdensome body and Samaria's midday sun.[88] Now, he explains that the Living Well "grows weary when it does not find one who is seeking the water of life."[89] Though tired, thirsty, and hungry prior to his conversation with the woman, their dialogue rejuvenates Jesus, satisfying a different hunger and thirst.[90] Like wisdom and righteousness, the living well is not depleted by sharing its waters; to the contrary, it grows weary through stagnation. Though *śruti* is eternal, it is a gift gracefully bestowed (*sampradāya*) flowing from teacher to student (*guru śiṣya paramparā*). Similarly, the Father's eternal Living Water needs to flow. It is reinvigorated, reanimated, and (re)incarnated when it springs forth in a person thirsting for justice. Its divine outpouring (*kenosis*) requires a space (*khôra*), a vessel, a *body*.[91] Reading the Word will not suffice. As pastor, Cusa embodies the Gospel, leads his flock to Jacob's well, stimulates a thirst for justice, and gestures to *this self* as a bodily vessel for sharing (*sugchrōntai*) Living Water.

Theosis and Theopoiesis: Becoming and Begetting

This experiment in comparative theology has suggested a certain similarity between "how" a *guru* embodies *śruti* in Śaṅkara's Vedānta and "how" Cusa embodies the words of John's Gospel through preaching. Some will understandably object here, insisting that embodying scriptural words is quite different from incarnating the Word. I am not claiming that Bultmann's paradox of the Word-become-flesh-become-text is circumvented by lively preaching.

Comparative theology, as I have stated, seeks neither to plunder nor (mis)appropriate insights from other traditions. Rather, having sojourned in another tradition's way of thinking, it enables us to reclaim, rediscover, and reconsider elements within our own tradition. Returning once more to look briefly, but more closely, at Vedānta's pedagogy will enable us to reconsider Johannine incarnation in light of ancient Christian understandings of *theosis* ("becoming divine") and *theopoiesis* ("making divine").

As discussed, a qualified Advaitin teacher must know the Veda well and model traditional pedagogy, but must also be "established in Brahman" (*brahmaniṣṭham*).[92] Simply stated, a *brahmaniṣṭham* is one who has realized one's non-dual identity with Brahman. While each person, from Śaṅkara's perspective, always already *is* Brahman (ontologically), a *guru* is a person who has *become* Brahman (psychologically, spiritually, and so on). When such a teacher reveals to a student "*This* Self is Brahman," the student also *becomes* Brahman, psychologically and spiritually (provided that the student has understood). Clearly, this exchange involves far more than speaking the words of *śruti* aloud. While the teacher is the vessel mediating revelation, *śruti* is the agent that "makes" the student Brahman (*theopoiesis*) because the student realizes her inherent identity with Brahman (*theosis*).

Similarly, Cusa did not merely read John's Gospel aloud; he became a vessel enabling his hearer to participate in John's sensual revelatory dynamic. As Cusa discusses elsewhere (including his sermon two days later), John conveys the Good News that the power to *become* daughters and sons of God is given to all who receive Christ (1:12).[93] Those who receive the *Father's*[94] living water become daughters and sons of God (*theosis*). As Catherine Keller reminds us, Athanasius articulated "the ancient formula of theopoiesis" in terms of the Johannine incarnation: "[The Word] became human that the human might become God."[95] From Cusa's perspective, because Christ is the incarnation of the Word, those who receive Christ *become* incarnations of the Word. Through his homiletic praxis, Cusa embodies the Gospel's wisdom together with the pedagogy modeled in Jesus's intimate dialogue with the Samaritan woman.

This experiment in comparative theology enables us to reclaim and reconsider the ancient Christian traditions of *theosis* and *theopoiesis*. While this may have been possible without comparative theology, Vedānta's embodied pedagogy uniquely positions us to reconsider *theosis* and *theopoiesis* in light of homiletics. From this new perspective, we can now return to reconsider the two questions raised earlier, prompted by Bultmann's paradox.

Our answer to the first question posed earlier has not changed: *How* is the incarnate Word revealed to the Samaritan woman? She directly and sensually perceives the Word-become-flesh through a personal, highly specific dialogue. Now, however, we can offer a far simpler response to the second question: *How* is the incarnate Word revealed through John's Gospel? It is revealed in nearly the same way: It is sensually perceived through a personal, highly specific sermon by a teacher who embodies the words, wisdom, and pedagogical method (the "how") modeled by the Gospel.

Consistent with John 1:12 and "the ancient formula of theopoiesis,"[96] Cusa becomes a son of God.[97] He becomes a vessel enabling the flow of the Father's living water. By becoming (*theosis*), he begets (*theopoiesis*). By receiving, embodying, and speaking the Word, he mediates revelation, just as a *guru* mediates *śruti*. He (re)incarnates the words of the Word-become-flesh, enabling them to be heard by his Brixen congregation in a manner (*Wie*) that is neither altogether the same as nor altogether different from the way that these eternal words were heard (*śruti*) long ago by an unnamed woman listening beside Jacob's well. Like Śaṅkara's pointing finger, Cusa's pointed speech gestures to the spark of divinity that languishes within his hearers like an untapped well. Intending to stimulate their thirst for justice, Cusa "speak[s] to the rock in their presence."[98]

Comparative Theology as Learning to Hear

As stated in the opening paragraph of this essay, comparative theologians are often driven by an ecology of questions. Formulating and reformulating these questions gives shape to alternative methods of inquiry, different paths for seeking (*quaerens*) understanding(s) of faith. This particular experiment in comparative theology began by reiterating a simple but profound question posed by Rudolf Bultmann: *How* can John's written Gospel reveal the Word-made-flesh? When formulated in this manner, comparative theology would not appear to be a suitable method for approaching this question.

In her critique of Bultmann, however, Gail O'Day reframes the question: *How* might a reader *participate* in John's revelatory dynamic? O'Day shifts our attention to the how (*Wie*) of revelation. That is to say, perhaps John is not simply recounting *that* (*Dass*) the Word-become-flesh was revealed to the Samaritan woman, but is also modeling *how* the Word-become-flesh can be manifestly revealed here and now. The Samaritan woman was not sitting beside Jacob's well, reading scriptures. Rather, she *saw* and *heard* the Word-become-flesh. Because the content (*Was*) of Johannine revelation is the incarnate Word, it cannot be revealed (from Bultmann's perspective, at least) through the written word. Thus, the question was reformulated once more: *How* can scripture reveal its truth beyond the activity of reading?

When posed in this way, comparative theology emerges as a method ideally suited to consider the question for three reasons. First, it invites us to consider how other traditions think about the relationship between scripture and revelation. For Śaṅkara, diligently reading and rereading scripture through the practice of coordination (*upasaṃhāra*) prepares students for the event of revelation because it trains students how to hear *śruti* harmoniously (*samanvaya*). Final realization, however, does not arise through reading, but only in the embodied encounter of teacher and student. The pedagogical dialogues of the Upaniṣads do not simply convey the fact (*das Dass*) of revelation, but also model how (*Wie*) revelation occurs.

Second, delving deeply into another tradition enables the comparative theologian to discover longstanding presumptions latent within our own systematic traditions of thought. In this case, it has enabled us to challenge Bultmann's assumption that John's Gospel is (merely) a text to be read. While John 4 narrates *that* the Word-made-flesh was revealed to the Samaritan woman, it also models *how* the incarnate Word may be seen and heard by Christians today. Like Bultmann, Śaṅkara insists that reading, studying, and interpreting scripture are indispensable activities. Unlike Śaṅkara, however, Bultmann does not seem to regard these as propaedeutic. For Śaṅkara, graceful revelation can occur only in a moment that is devoid of *all* effort and activity, including the act of reading. Revelation arises *after* one has learned to *hear*.

Third, because comparative theology changes how we think, it enables us to rediscover, reclaim, and reconsider elements of our own tradition. In this case, Śaṅkara's embodied pedagogy invites us to reconsider the role of preaching the Gospel. I chose to focus on Cusa's sermon on John 4 primarily because I have studied his writings at length and am most familiar with his thought, but also because his understanding of *theosis* sits comfortably next to Śaṅkara's. Certainly, a different preacher's sermon might have been selected and would likely yield different results. Nevertheless, Śaṅkara's emphasis on the role of a *guru* has made it possible to reconsider the role and responsibility of Christian preachers to mediate scriptural revelation.

Concluding this reflection on *how to do comparative theology*, I emphasize again that comparative theology is an inherently subjective endeavor: a journey of faith seeking understanding.[99] It occurs in what Francis Clooney has described as a "third context." By reading back-and-forth between two contexts, "the engaged reader is 'inscribed' into an ever more complexly composed context, in order to write after and out of it."[100] While always accountable to the particular theologians one studies and writes *about*, the comparative theologian writes *from* a particular theological community and is also distinctively accountable *to* that community.

As a Congregationalist theologian, I am committed to remain in academic dialogue with other Congregationalists on issues that are relevant and timely within our denomination, the United Church of Christ (UCC). For this reason (among others), I have engaged the work of Gail

O'Day, a UCC minister committed to improving UCC homiletics. From pew to pulpit to seminary, Congregationalists are eager for ways to understand the scriptural witness in light of our religiously diverse society. Given the UCC mantra, "God is still speaking," Śaṅkara's theology is particularly insightful insofar as it teaches us new ways to *hear.* This does not necessarily mean that Congregationalists will be compelled to hear *śruti* (though some may be drawn to this). Rather, Śaṅkara's way of thinking about *śruti* compels us to consider that if John's Good News is to be *heard* today, the written Word must be lived, embodied, and (re)incarnated. The preacher's voice is a vessel for this revelation, and is thus imbued with sacred responsibility. Reading Cusa's sermon after Vedānta draws our attention to the flow of teaching from preacher to congregation, and thus to "how" the eternal, living water may gush forth in one who thirsts for justice.

Notes

1. See, for example, Clooney, "Difficult Remainders: Seeking Comparative Theology's Really Difficult Other" in the current volume. Therein, Clooney notes that the method he employs differs from previous work he has done with the same material. Likewise, my method and purpose in this essay differ from my work with this material in my dissertation, Bannon, "Apophatic Measures: Toward a Theology of Irreducible Particularity."
2. John 1:1 and 14, New Revised Standard Version (NRSV).
3. This problem is (arguably) unique to John's Gospel because the synoptic Gospels do not present Christ as a revelation of the incarnate Word.
4. Bultmann, *Theology of the New Testament*, 66.
5. Naturally, Bultmann's position is considerably more nuanced than this. Johannine revelation, according to Bultmann, is also devoid of content because Christ *qua* Son of God reveals nothing about the Father other than the fact (*das Dass*) that Christ is the Son of the Father.
6. Clooney, "Difficult Remainders: Seeking Comparative Theology's Really Difficult Other," current volume. Emphasis added. Likewise, see Clooney, *Thinking Ritually*, and Clooney, "Scholasticisms in Encounter."
7. Clooney, "Difficult Remainders: Seeking Comparative Theology's Really Difficult Other," current volume.
8. Traditionally, there are said to be six orthodox (*āstika*) schools of theology (*darśana*-s): *nyāya*, *vaiśeṣika*, *samkhya*, *yoga*, *mīmāṃsā*, and *vedānta*.
9. This often cited definition of theology derives from St. Anselm's *Proslogion*. The multivalence of the term *quaerens*, connoting "seeking," "questioning," and "questing," and even "striving for" and "desiring," undergirds my method in this essay.
10. Cusa, *Loquimini ad Petram coram Eis* in *Cusanus Texte* I:7; English translation by Jasper Hopkins, *Cusa's Last Sermons 1457–1463*. This sermon was delivered on a Friday

in Brixen to celebrate the feast-day of the Annunciation. The title refers to Numbers 20:8, wherein the Lord instructs Moses to "command the rock before their eyes to yield its water" (NRSV) in order that the physical thirst of the Israelites might be quenched.

11. In contrast to the term "Samarians," referring to "those who live in the region of Samaria," Daniel L. Smith notes that the term "Samaritan" is a religious/sectarian designation signifying "those who believe that God should be worshiped at Gerizim, not Jerusalem." They are divided by regional/tribal differences (not far from modern constructions of "nationality"), ritualistic-doctrinal differences (4:20, not far from modern notions of religious distinctions), and by gender. Smith, *Into the World of the New Testament*, 133.
12. Daube, "Jesus and the Samaritan Woman," 137–47.
13. As Daube notes, it is difficult to imagine what other significance this detail in 4:28 may have. Daube, 138. In contrast, Jesus declines to share the food offered by his disciples (4:31–34).
14. O'Day, "Narrative Mode and Theological Claim," 666, emphasis added.
15. Genesis 32:30.
16. Without intending to imply a canonical reading, my words here paraphrase Paul (Galatians 3:28).
17. O'Day, 667.
18. Bultmann, 72.
19. Lee, "The Gospel of John and the Five Senses," 115–27. Lee demonstrates the significant role played by the five senses throughout John's Gospel.
20. Bultmann, 64.
21. Ibid., 66.
22. Ibid.
23. Ibid., 66 and 72.
24. Ibid., 71–72, referencing John 5:24.
25. O'Day, 666.
26. Genesis 32:30.
27. O'Day, 668.
28. Ibid.
29. Ibid. As discussed earlier, the narrative refers to Jesus's bodily thirst, the water of Jacob's well, and the water-pot as vessel, but simultaneously refers to the woman's spiritual thirst, the Father's living water, and the Word-become-flesh as vessel.
30. See note 94 later in this chapter.
31. O'Day, 666.
32. On the "particularly serious" transgression of purity codes implied by this vessel sharing, see Daube.
33. O'Day, 668.
34. The term "Vedānta" (literally: "end of the Veda") refers to the wisdom revealed by the Upaniṣads, which constitute the fourth and final portion of the Veda. The term "advaita" literally means "not-two," referring to the non-dual relationship of self (*ātmā*) and infinite reality (*brahman*).
35. Rambachan, *A Hindu Theology of Liberation*, 1–2.

36. Ibid., 4. Likewise, see De Smet, "The Theological Method of Sáṃkara"; Clooney, *Theology After Vedānta*; Suthren Hirst, *Śaṃkara's Advaita Vedānta*; Thatamanil, *The Immanent Divine*; and Locklin, *Liturgy of Liberation*. See bibliography for details.
37. For example, Māṇḍūkya Kārika Bhāṣya 4.99. See also Rambachan, *Accomplishing the Accomplished*.
38. See Jaimini's *Pūrvamīmāṃsāsūtra* I.1.5.
39. Likewise, in the introduction to his Bṛhadāraṇyaka Upaniṣad Bhāṣya, Śaṅkara explains that the term *upaniṣad* primarily refers to the libratory truth of the *upaniṣads*, and only secondarily to the books (*grantha*-s) wherein that truth is written down.
40. Clooney, *Theology After Vedānta*, 127.
41. Ibid.
42. The historical veracity of these traditional claims are doubtful and the subject of ample debate. See King, *Early Advaita Vedānta and Buddhism*, and Bannon, "Apophatic Measures," 66ff. Whether historically accurate or not, however, the tradition's emphasis on the flow of teaching (*sampradāya*) is nevertheless pertinent to my thesis.
43. Halbfass, *Studies in Kumārila and Śaṅkara*, 36. For a competing interpretation, see Nakamura, *A History of Early Vedānta Philosophy*. I, 42ff. Nakamura notes that Śaṅkara's student, Sureśvara, offers the oldest extant reference to the MU as *śruti*. For a more extensive discussion of the issue, see Bannon, "Apophatic Measures," 71ff. I have placed *Upaniṣad* in italics because if Halbfass is correct (as I think he is), then *Upaniṣad* is a misnomer when applied to the Māṇḍūkya, from Śaṅkara's perspective. Nevertheless, the Māṇḍūkya is an *upaniṣad* from the perspective of most Hindus today.
44. *Vedāntārthasārasaṅgraha*, Māṇḍūkya Upaniṣad Bhāṣya, Introduction. Śaṅkara describes the Bhagavadgītā in strikingly similar terms.
45. Bādarāyaṇa describes these spiritual exercises in UMS III.3, which P.M. Modi reasonably describes as "the most important portion of the entire Brahmasūtra." Modi, *A Critique of the Brahmasutra (3.2.11–4)*, I, xiii.
46. Here, too, see Clooney, "Difficult Remainders: Seeking Comparative Theology's Really Difficult Other" in the current volume, especially on *Veda-tarka*.
47. For example, MU 5 and MU 7, from Śaṅkara's perspective, coordinate a teaching about salt dissolved in water with a teaching about a man and woman in ecstatic union. *Prima facie*, there is no obvious connection between these teachings. Gradually, however, one understands that when salt is dissolved in water, its salty taste permeates the water, without inside or outside. Similarly, a man and woman know neither inside nor outside when they are united in ecstasy. By coordinating these teachings, one learns to set aside possible misreadings of each and comes to understand that consciousness of the Self does not exist "inside" the body or "outside" the body, but permeates reality (like saltiness) and does not distinguish between inside and outside (like ecstatic union). For our purposes, the point is that coordination is a practice that trains one to make certain decisions by learning to hear diverse teachings in harmony with one another.
48. Clooney, *Theology After Vedānta*, 127.
49. See, for example, UMSBh IV.1.1–2.
50. Bannon, "Thou, That, and An/Other," 53–56.

51. The three movements may be divided as follows: MU 1, MU 2–7, and MU 8–12. For a more detailed analysis, see Bannon, "Apophatic Measures," especially Chapter 1, "Learning to Hear Harmoniously: Method and Structure of the Māṇḍūkya Kārika." MU 6, on *Īśvara* ("the Lord"), is somewhat anomalous, interrupting the otherwise clear parallels between the three movements. While this is a critically important point, it is beyond the scope of this essay. Thomas Wood (see bibliography) offers a very different interpretation of the MU, arguing that MU 6 is the hermeneutic key to unlocking its meaning. Without affirming or denying the merits of Wood's argument, it is clear that his intention is not to expound the *bhāṣyakāra*'s interpretation, whereas this is precisely my goal.
52. Bultmann, 71–72.
53. Rambachan, *A Hindu Theology of Liberation*, 38.
54. Muṇḍaka Upaniṣad I.2.12, Rambachan, *A Hindu Theology of Liberation*, 30.
55. Śaṅkara, *Muṇḍaka Upaniṣad Bhāṣya* I.2.12, Rambachan, *A Hindu Theology of Liberation*, 51.
56. Rambachan, *A Hindu Theology of Liberation*, 47.
57. Ibid., 43, 47.
58. Ibid., 48, my emphasis added.
59. Ibid., 46–48.
60. Bannon, "Thou, That, and An/Other," 54, drawing upon Upad I.18. In that essay, I also argue that the grammatical indexicality of the word "thou" in Vedānta's great sentence, "Thou art that" only performs its meaning when it is uttered by a teacher, directly and particularly, to a student. Only in this intimate, embodied encounter is the student able to grasp that the word "thou" im-mediately signifies him/her.
61. Karl Barth's trifold dictum from *Church Dogmatics* comes to mind: Faith alone. Scripture alone. Grace alone.
62. Again, *śruti* literally means "that which is *heard*." From Śaṅkara's perspective, the Veda is called *śruti* not only (or even primarily) because these eternal, unauthored words were *heard* by sages in some distant past, but because they have been continuously *heard* throughout the ages by those who relinquish all action and agency in order to hear *śruti*'s graceful revelation.
63. Rambachan, *A Hindu Theology of Liberation*, 38.
64. *Śruti* cannot be summarized, distilled, or reduced; its truth cannot be abstracted. Nevertheless, four sentences are regarded as particularly concise expressions of Advaita Vedānta's truth. As Rambachan explains, the tradition understands these "great sayings" (*mahāvākya*-s) as the "unequivocal affirmation of the identity of *ātmā* [Self] and *brahman*, the infinite." Rambachan, *A Hindu Theology of Liberation*, 65. Deriving from each of the four branches of the Veda, they include: "Thou art that" (Chāndogya Upaniṣad 6.8.7), "Awareness is Brahman" (Aitareya Upaniṣad 5.3), "I am Brahman" (Bṛhadāraṇyaka Upaniṣad 1.4.10), and "This Self is Brahman" (Māṇḍūkya Upaniṣad 2).
65. Śaṅkara, MUBh 2, my translation.
66. This is the topic of Śaṅkara's commentary on MU 1. See Bannon, "Apophatic Measures," 94ff.
67. In addition to MUBh (Māṇḍūkya Upaniṣad Bhāṣya) 2; MKBh (Māṇḍūkya Kārika Bhāṣya) 4.99; and MuUBh (Muṇḍaka Upaniṣad Bhāṣya) I.2.12 mentioned earlier, see

also MKBh 2.32, BUBh (Bṛhadāraṇyaka Upaniṣad Bhāṣya) II.1.20; and especially UMSBh (Uttaramīmāṃsāsūtra Bhāṣya) IV.1.2.

68. Śaṅkara, MUBh 2.
69. Ānandagiri, MUBh Ṭīkā 2. Śaṅkara, *Upaniṣadbhāṣyam*, I, 218.
70. This does not contradict my claim that Śaṅkara does not consider the MU to be *śruti*. As I have argued, the MU is paradigmatic of a method propaedeutic for hearing *śruti*. Śaṅkara's commentary, here and throughout the MU, repeatedly points to the *mahāvākya*, "Thou art that," which is, most certainly, *śruti*.
71. Clooney, *Theology After Vedānta*, 7.
72. See note 10, earlier in the chapter.
73. Cusa, Sermon 247, Hopkins trans., 168, paragraph 4.
74. Ibid., 168–69, paragraph 5.
75. "Now, it was about the sixth hour of the day of the world (when the sun reaches its maximum height) with respect to Christ Jesus, who as Sun of Justice, was Fullness of the Spirit of Light, enlightening every [person]." Hopkins 169, paragraph 5. Cf. Malachi 4:1–2: "See, the day is coming, burning like an oven, when all the arrogant and all evildoers will be stubble; the day that comes shall burn them up . . . . But for you who revere my name the Sun of Righteousness shall rise, with healing in its wings."
76. See note 75.
77. Cusa, Sermon 247, paragraph 6.
78. Ibid., paragraph 12 (John 4:11).
79. Ibid., paragraph 12: *Attende quomodo haurire necesse est cum labore et ingenio omnem aquam, quia omni homini "puteus altus est."*
80. O'Day, 668. See note 29 earlier in the chapter.
81. Numbers 20:8. See note 10 earlier in the chapter.
82. Cusa, Sermon 247, paragraph 6.
83. Ibid., Hopkins 172, paragraph 13.
84. Ibid., Hopkins 173, paragraph 14.
85. Clooney, *Theology After Vedānta*, 127.
86. Ibid.
87. Cusa, Sermon 247, paragraph 12.
88. Ibid., Hopkins 169, paragraph 5.
89. Ibid., Hopkins 170, paragraph 7.
90. Credit goes to Elizabeth Bannon for pointing out to me this aspect of Cusa's sermon.
91. On this topic, see Sermon 248, delivered two days later. See note 93.
92. Rambachan, *A Hindu Theology of Liberation*, 43, 47.
93. See especially Cusa's *De filiatione Dei*. On March 27, 1457, Cusa preached a sermon entitled "We Are Not Children of the Bondwoman" (Sermon 248) wherein he coordinates Galatians 4:31, John 1:12, the Theotokos, and the birth of Isaac to Abraham and Sarah.
94. While the gendered nature of this term is lamentable and stands in need, now as always, of unsaying, the ontological relationality should not be occluded. While the term "Parent" succeeds in some ways, it lacks intimacy and strikes me, as a "daddy," as lamentably impersonal.

95. Keller, *Cloud of the Impossible*, 308. As Keller indicates in note 5 (368), Athanasius is paraphrasing Irenaeus. Older still, the statement synoptically interprets John 1:12 and John 1:14, as I discuss shortly.
96. Keller, *Cloud of the Impossible*, 308.
97. A substantial difference must be noted between *theosis* in Vedānta and Cusa. When a student of Vedānta realizes his/her inherent identity with Brahman, the student becomes established in Brahman (*brahmaniṣṭham*) and attains liberation. The *theosis* modeled by Cusa, however, is transient, unlike Christ's incarnation of the Word. As previously discussed, the Father's eternal, living waters are always already "there," ready to gush forth, but only do so in one who thirsts for those waters. The water is eternal, but the thirst is ephemeral.
98. Numbers 20:8. See note 10, earlier in the chapter.
99. Axel Takács, a fellow contributor to this anthology, comments: "The analogy of the musical piece comes in handy here . . . One can play and hear the same musical piece in unique, different ways; how I hear music is different from you, and likewise, how one music conductor and orchestra plays a piece is different from another, despite the fact that the notes on the page are identical."
100. Clooney, *Theology After Vedānta*, 7.

14 Living Interreligiously

ON THE "PASTORAL STYLE" OF COMPARATIVE THEOLOGY

Michael Barnes, S.J.

Comparative Theology commends an imaginative entry into another religious world. In so doing it raises some difficult questions about what it means to live and act "interreligiously." How to recognize continuities, acknowledge discontinuities, build creative analogies, without getting stuck into some sort of self-serving colonizing of the other? How to ensure that the complex business of mediating across religious borders does not ignore the demands of truth—and justice? How to keep alive the discipline of obedience that arises from the hearing of the Word while yet taking seriously the myriad words that are inseparable from life in a thoroughly pluralist world? What, in short, are the parameters in which Comparative Theology as a type of "theological hospitality" can be exercised with integrity?

Interreligious dialogue may be the imperative of our times, but whatever answers there may be to such questions, they come not with some theoretical framework that patronizes the other but through the practical and often unstructured engagement that begins "in the middle of things" and seeks somehow to make sense of what is found in this particular moment and place. For that reason I prefer the term "conversation" to "dialogue," not because it conjures up images of genial informality but because it recognizes that, whether applied in a metaphorical sense to the close reading of texts or in a more literal sense to the everyday encounter between persons, to live interreligiously is to keep open the possibility of further learning. To that extent, I think of Comparative Theology less as a formal "school" with its traditional lineage and method and more a "style" of theology. In this essay, I want to argue that, as a way of bringing tradition into dialogue with the reality of everyday life, it has close affinities with another theological development that also has its roots in the post-conciliar renewal of the Catholic Church, namely Pastoral Theology. I write as a theologian who began as a textual scholar with a specialization in the religions of India and has spent most of the last twenty-five years in close contact with local communities of faith in West London. If I have learned anything from this experience, it is that informal conversation with neighbors as much as serious debate with peers from another religious community requires spiritual and intellectual support. To cross any sort of border, let alone the physical boundary of a place of worship, is to enter a world that is at once familiar yet strange.

There are three major sections in what follows. I begin with Pastoral Theology as an ecclesiocentric practice, and a sketch of its methodology in terms of the correlation of the normative tradition and the everyday experience of a people committed to a particular way of life and mission. I then bring in my Comparative Theology "micro-study"—the description of a particular place of worship and the devotional life of the community it supports. Finally, I turn to a number of brief theological reflections that emerge from the engagement. My argument is that the meditative "style" of Comparative Theology is in many ways similar to the discernment of the typically Christian praxis of Pastoral Theology. Bringing the two disciplines together provides the necessary framework for a prayerful "reading" of another world that can both inspire and communicate faith at whatever level.

The Virtues of Living in an Engaged Church

Pastoral Theology used to be the preserve of the clergy—the intellectually undemanding set of skills that spelled out the practical implications at the end of the more systematic process of clerical formation. That has changed dramatically. No longer does it refer to a handful of peripheral "extras" but is concerned primarily with a holistic theological formation based on the acquisition of deeply theological virtues of self-reflexivity, discernment, and attentiveness that run through and inform all forms and styles of theology—from the reading of scripture to the philosophically nuanced elucidation of a Christian account of truth. More specifically, this is a way of doing theology that is consciously focused on the life of the Church, both its "inner life" in terms of liturgy and prayer, and its "outer life" as evidenced in the various relationships that can be said to define the Church. In this sense, Pastoral Theology attends equally to all manner of human relationships—with fellow Christians seeking to live out their baptismal commitment; with the poor, the marginalized, and the disadvantaged; with those living on the fringes of the Church; with those who profess to be agnostic or atheist; or with those who owe allegiance to another of the great religions.

This is not the place to analyze this shift of Pastoral Theology from the periphery to the center of theological reflection. Sufficient, perhaps, to note the words of Henri-Jerome Gagey reflecting on the renewal of Catholic Pastoral Theology in the wake of Vatican II, that it is "the result of a deep break which made the timeless conception of Christian life . . . unsustainable."[1] The retrieval of a more culturally sensitive historical consciousness has focused attention on *how* the mystery of faith is lived out in the community of believers. In this sense, ecclesial practice must take account of the broader philosophical and cultural influences that shape society as a whole. Thus, running alongside the retrieval of a more biblically centered process of learning about the ways of God with human beings is a more diffuse practical philosophy that seeks to reinstate the role of practical wisdom within the wider concerns of reason and theory. I do not just refer to the retrieval of the ethical relation as intrinsic to the sense of personhood, as in Levinas, or to a greater sensitivity to the way in which language is used, as in Wittgenstein, or to a broadening of the concept of hermeneutics to include all ways of understanding what it means to be human, as in the writings of Paul Ricoeur and Hans-Georg Gadamer. I mean all of this and more: texts and artifacts, places and monuments, ancient traditions and more contemporary cultural icons, act as a *moral witness* that both shapes practical concerns and challenges the limits of purely theoretical or technical reason. It is not that in our postmodern world culture relativizes philosophy (though there is, of course, that danger), but that philosophy is much more responsive to the plurality of cultural forms. Nor is it that understanding leads to or dominates application in any straightforwardly linear sense. Rather, practice itself—the ways in which we interact with each other and our world—is recognized as possessing its own inner logic, a much more complex dialectical movement that seeks to uncover as well as critique the levels of inherited meaning to which human beings are constantly subject.

This does not make Pastoral Theology a new form of fundamental theology, an anchoring of theory in praxis from which everything else flows. In rooting theological reflection in the inner life and outer relations of the Church, Pastoral Theology recognizes a critical dialectic between, on the one hand, the normative revelation of truth given in Jesus Christ and, on the other, the necessarily unending *performance* of that truth by Christians as they seek to engage with the meaning-giving practices that make up the wider world. In setting Comparative Theology within this overall pastoral perspective, my point is that we are dealing with just such a performative practice of faith that seeks to correlate a familiar formulation of Christian truth and an analogous formulation from another religious world. This is to set Comparative Theology within a venerable Catholic tradition of what in the modern jargon is called "inculturation": bringing the Gospel into a creative encounter with local culture and religious custom. If the Word of God is to be heard, then the words of the one called to speak have to be translated. This is no straightforwardly mechanical exercise. In the first place, it demands a perseverance in learning the terms of the culture, and the fortitude and determination to enter deeply into that world. But it also requires other virtues, perhaps most obviously the sort of patience learned ultimately from the Paschal Mystery of the Death and Resurrection, not a passive waiting but a willingness to absorb a certain suffering. Whether we are talking about scholars engaged with the inner meaning of a textual tradition, or pastoral workers attempting to discern how the Spirit of God is at work in all manner of interpersonal encounter, or those who hesitantly aspire to some hybrid of both, pastoral theologians need to seek a personal translation, to acquire the *habitus* of living "in between." The "micro studies" or "thought experiments" that make up the "matter" of Comparative Theology may lead to all sorts of positive insights, but perhaps more important is to learn from the "style" itself, the *manner* of engagement—what "living interreligiously" does to the sense of self.

This is what I myself have learned from my experience of entering the world of Buddhism, both through the practice of Zen and *Vipassana* meditation and in study and teaching. Christianity and Buddhism are manifestly different traditions, yet the fact that there is so much space between them leaves room for the imagination to operate. Both traditions speak a truth for all people—and are prepared to adapt and accommodate; indeed both traditions only become *properly alive* when they seek to communicate with and enter into another religious world. Even if for a Christian the challenge is to remain theological, to acknowledge the continuing significance of God, the paradox set deep in both traditions is that to be faithful is to engage with and risk change. In the "micro-study" that follows, I do not begin with the "big questions," about the nature of God, about human selfhood and salvation, about the very possibility of language about ultimate reality. I come at these questions in a round-about fashion not in order to avoid them but to foreground the profound puzzlement that always precedes any attempt to cross the threshold into another religious world. This particular example of Comparative Theology is not intended to illustrate some implicit "theology of Buddhist-Christian relations." It is a brief meditation that emerges from and seeks to extend the Christian's sense of being inextricably caught up in the Trinitarian *Missio Dei*, the sending by the Father of the Son and the Spirit into the world for the salvation of humankind. That's what the Church is: a community of people who have heard God's invitation—maybe *God's question*—and go on seeking out the mystery of what is properly God's action.

What follows is a description of a place of worship—a snapshot of decorations, artifacts, rituals, devotions, faith *at work*. In an obvious sense, such a place is the context within which a religious practice is situated. To that extent, it is also an extension of a textual tradition. By reading the place as one would read a text, one begins to notice and attend to the disarming edges where the unknown opens up a conversation with what is known. This conversation is necessarily open-ended. It is not that some sort of analogous truth from the Buddhist world is bolted on to a pre-existent Christian edifice, but that the very building of a synthesis is enriched by the act of watching and waiting, a thoughtful attentiveness that is sensitive to the risks of jumping to premature conclusions. This does not ignore the "big questions"; it sets them in the context of an experience of faith that finds itself put in question and then learns to see things differently.

Exploring the Limits of Freedom

The Buddhapadipa Temple, a few minutes' walk from the green expanse of Wimbledon Common in South London, is built in traditional Thai style, its red and white exterior crowned with ornate finials and delicate gilded tracery. Formally opened in 1982 by members of the British and Thai royal families, its community of Theravadin monks welcomes devotees from all over the country and an increasing number of young people who come to practice simple mindfulness exercises surrounded by hundreds, perhaps thousands, of Buddhas and bodhisattvas who

time by that original act of writing or painting, but neither are they indeterminate, dependent on purely contingent factors or the whim of the moment. The imagination works within certain constraints—which is not to say that the task of making connections and reconciling differences is inevitably reductionist. On the contrary, it is to enter into a chaos of imagery, ancient and modern, confident that it is possible to weave further variations out of the strands that are already there. Any given artifact, whether written document or oral narrative or a decorated place like the Buddhapadipa Temple, consists at one and the same time of a certain form that *limits* freedom and what I shall simply call a spirit or energy that presumes to *explore* it.

Bringing Something of the Word to Birth

The most familiar forms of Comparative Theology are those that involve the close reading of texts, a sort of interreligious *lectio divina* in which the familiar dual imperative of any sort of interreligious dialogue—faithfulness to what is known and openness to what is unknown—is given a particular intensity. What I am proposing here is an approach that is more consciously contextual, not because I have any doubt about the value of bringing texts on analogous themes into a correlation, but because the practice of dialogue with which I have become familiar consists of negotiating that ill-defined area "between" one religious world and another, an area populated by persons of faith trying to make sense of all manner of artifacts, from texts and paintings to the architecture that houses them. The particular skill of the comparative theologian is to track a way across a threshold, picking up hints and taking cues from certain words and symbols and concepts in order to build up, if not continuities, then at least positive analogies. At the same time, a hermeneutic of suspicion avoids premature judgments. Whatever is said is prefaced with humility and to be understood as only ever partial and preliminary. As with Pastoral Theology, Comparative Theology demands virtues of patience and fortitude and practical skills of discernment and attentiveness. In this sense, Comparative Theology shares with Pastoral Theology an intensely self-reflexive sensitivity to engagement with the other. What demands attention is not just what is heard and seen and tasted in some way but what goes on *in the mind and heart of the theologian* as he or she seeks to make sense of that religious world and receives something unexpected from its cultural specificity. The question of what catches the imagination is utterly mysterious; more open to scrutiny is the response to what may be given through what the early Fathers of the Church called "seeds of the Word." Something of the Word springs to birth in the heart of the discerning theologian.

That traditional Patristic image can be intensely problematic when Christians enter into a Buddhist religious world. In one particular regard, these two traditions share a common space. Buddhism, as I have noted, addresses the same sort of questions as Christianity about the need for cross-cultural accommodation between consciously universalist traditions. "Inculturation" raises much the same dilemma for Buddhists, the sort of questions with which I began, especially about how one affirms *and* challenges culture. How to negotiate that mysterious overlap that both joins and separates religious worlds?

My argument is that the actual resolution of such dilemmas—should such ever be possible—is secondary to a more profound difference. Where Christians speak of the Word and confidently expect to find "seeds of the Word" scattered across other religious spaces, including Buddhism, the Buddhist tends to keep silence. The Buddha's silence can be interpreted in a number of ways. Sometimes it seems to express agnosticism. Sometimes it amounts to a nihilistic insistence that language is only a source of mystification. More often, we find elements of both. Thus, according to early Buddhist traditions, the Buddha refused to answer certain metaphysical propositions; this was on the pragmatic grounds that speculation about ultimate reality would only distract from the pursuit of liberation. Whatever the explanation, the focus on silence is a major challenge to what the Christian might call the "question of God." In what sense can a dialogue that performs a radical critique of religious language be understood as somehow participating in God's own act of self-revelation? The Christian answer is always deeply Trinitarian. If the reading of texts or their broader aesthetic contexts is indeed set between the acknowledging of form or Logos and the following of the energy or Pneuma it unleashes, then any work of interpretation is theological—at least in the sense that it acts as a provocation to self-transcendence.

This is where Comparative Theology leads us. In moving toward the limits of what can be said and in building an ever greater sensitivity about the words we use to say it, Comparative Theology takes us to the edges of contemplation, where the familiar begins to intersect with what is disarmingly other. Thus, the method I use comes not from Systematic but from Pastoral Theology, what I understand as a hermeneutical exercise that seeks to uncover the traces of God's self-revealing action within the myriad relations that make up the Church. Evangelization, catechesis, works of mercy, the struggle for justice, the fourfold forms of dialogue,[3] all are rooted in liturgy, prayer, and the Church's sacramental inner life. Put like that, Comparative Theology consists of particular examples of "living interreligiously." This is what makes Comparative Theology an intensely pastoral and ecclesial exercise: not a bit of elitist speculation or pious escapism but a generous response to God's call that refuses to recognize any bounds to the extent of God's love, beyond—as Karl Rahner would remind us—the domain of human sin.

So how to be faithful to that Trinitarian vision in the middle of a world which seems at times antagonistic to all that is central to Christianity? And how, on the other hand, to keep open the possibility that even in an unremittingly anthropocentric tradition such as Buddhism traces of transcendence are forever to be perceived? I seem to have spent an inordinate amount of my life puzzling over such questions, very often when reading Buddhist texts, or in company of Buddhist teachers and practitioners, or just sitting in a Buddhist temple and wondering how to make sense of it all. The common stereotype of Buddhism sets belief in a personal God against a vision of the interrelatedness of all things. There is clearly some truth in this, but if the instinct of the comparative theologian is to seek out the widest extent of God's grace, then the drawing of oppositions that risks bringing dialogue to an end needs to be complemented by the search for more satisfactory analogies. Buddhism, with or without its crowds of attendant *deva*-figures, is often spoken of as non-theistic or even atheistic on the grounds that so much of the early teaching is based on a denial of the significance of talk about ultimate reality. Moreover, as Jayatilleke insists, Buddhism is critical of all "pseudo-religions" or false or *unskillful* opinions that inhibit enlightenment, including not just materialism, because its vision of reality is untrue, but theism as well because by projecting hopes and fears onto *Ishvara*, the Lord, or some personalized god-figure, it encourages complacency and takes away any sense of free will or responsibility.[4] Only on pragmatic grounds is belief in a personal God to be encouraged, as a "step in the right direction."[5] There is, of course, a strong apologetic thrust to Jayatilleke's essay; it is nothing if not a robust defense of Theravada Buddhist specificity. And yet, to spend time in the Buddhapadipa Temple is to remember that, however different its core beliefs and guiding ideas, this place is a devotional centre which supports a life of faith just as much as my own Catholic parish church a mile or so away.

Devotion, Imagination, and the Inner Life of a School of Faith

In strictly Buddhist terms, it is correct to say that what is to be "read" in the richness of the paintings and the practices of devotees is no more than an intermediate stage on the path of enlightenment. Yet Buddhism constantly surprises us—and I do not just mean jokey asides about punk rockers and prime ministers being made subject to the great cycle of *samsara*. I am thinking of something more directly subversive of everyday expectations. Is there, I keep asking myself, something more to the practice of Buddhist devotion than mere "popular religion"? Could it be that everyday rituals—invoking the name of the Buddha, the taking of the refuges, chanting the words of Pali hymns—say something to a Christian faith that is itself deeply devotional, touching the senses as well as appealing to the intellect? Aloysius Pieris—who has spent a lifetime engaging with the different dimensions of Theravada Buddhism and Sinhalese culture—is reluctant to make an arbitrary distinction between lay practices and scholastic philosophy. Strictly speaking, the *devas* are "cosmic forces," which are subordinate to the "meta-cosmic" or transcendent goal of Nibbana.[5] They are invoked to help people with their everyday needs, whereas the Buddha remains the exemplar of enlightenment itself. That, however, is very far from relegating such practices to the realm of the religiously unsophisticated; there is—as Richard Gombrich demonstrated in his masterly study of the Theravada in rural Śri Lanka more than forty years ago[6]—a strong continuity between textual tradition and contemporary religious behavior. Imaginative depictions of myths and legends are not secondary accretions intended to accommodate ancient tradition to modern needs; they are a vital part of the tradition itself. Indeed, one of the dominating myths of early Buddhism allows for a positive role for the theistic tradition in the life of the Buddha who only decided to speak about Dharma out of compassion for suffering sentient beings and at the specific request of the god Brahma. If our model of religion is "the system," then the gentle chaos in which concepts and ideas, symbols, and devotional practices are forever mingling and challenging each other raises problems. Shift to the model of the school and it does not.

Buddhist spirituality is not normally thought of in liturgical or devotional terms, but in all traditions it is impossible to ignore many ritual-like elements in the practice of the Noble Eightfold Path, not just the central practice of meditation with its formal structures but the homage to the Buddha and the taking of the refuges and precepts. In the Theravada the salutation to the Buddha sounds like a confession of faith as titles are piled one on another:

> Such is that blessed one, the worthy one, the perfectly and completely awakened one, perfect in his understanding and conduct, happy, one who understands the world, an unsurpassed trainer of unruly persons, the teacher of both gods and human beings, a blessed Buddha.[7]

The chanting of salutations to the Three Jewels, Buddha, Dharma, and Sangha, goes hand in hand with the offering of flowers, the burning of incense and a repeated personal commitment to the principal signs of the Buddha's continuing presence, through relics and representations.

> This mass of flowers, fresh-hued, odorous and choice, I offer at the sacred lotus-like feet of the noble sage. With diverse flowers, the Buddha I adore; through this merit may there be release.
>
> Even as these flowers must fade, so does my body march to a state of destruction.
>
> To the blessed one, the worthy one, the perfectly-awakened one—seated as if arisen from the most supreme ecstasy—with these flowers, reverentially I make offering, reverentially I make offering, reverentially I make offering.
>
> With perfumed incense, compounded from odorous substances, I revere the exalted one, worthy of reverence, a fit receptacle for our offerings.
>
> Take pity on us, master, and accept, most high one, for compassion's sake, the food and drink that we present.
>
> I salute every *cetiya* [burial mound] that may stand in any place, the bodily relics, the great tree of enlightenment, and all images of the Buddha.
>
> I reverence the words of the Teacher, and the last exhortation to earnest pursuit. Every shrine too I salute, my preceptor and teachers. By virtue of this salutation may my mind be freed from all evil!

It is not part of my task to trace links between this *Buddhapuja* and the great movement of *bhakti* religion. With its seminal literary form in the *Bhagavad Gita*—usually dated around fourth century BCE—*bhakti* means "participation" and may be loosely translated as "loyalty;" in the *puranic* tradition, it has connotations of the divine grace poured out on human beings that inspires all forms of heartfelt love. The *Buddhapuja* is quite restrained; the memory of the Buddha is kept by a repetition of words of truth reinforced by vivid imagery which kindles thoughts of enlightenment by appealing to the senses. Let me add just a few verses from the "verses on victory," a sort of benediction on the present moment that channels the earnest desires of the devotee. It begins with reference to some of the myths depicted on the Temple walls:

> Creating thousand hands, with weapons armed, was Mara seated on the trumpeting ferocious elephant, Girimekhala. Him did the lord of sages subdue by means of generosity and other virtues; by its grace may joyous victory be mine.
>
> More violent than Mara was the angry obstinate demon Alavaka, who battled with the Buddha throughout the whole night. Him did the lord of sages subdue by means of his patience and self-control; by its grace may joyous victory be mine.
>
> Nalagiri the might elephant, highly intoxicated, was raging like a forest fire, terrible as a thunderbolt. Sprinkling the waters of loving-kindness this ferocious beast did the lord of sages subdue. By its grace may joyous victory be mine.

The same refrain occurs in each verse. The last verse sums up the good intentions of the devotee:

> The wise one, who daily recites these eight verses of joyous victory of the Buddha, will get rid of diverse misfortunes and gain the bliss of Nibbana.

Another devotional text, the longer "verses of supreme blessings" is more direct, lacking the mythological elements and focusing instead on the central truths of Buddhism—a sort of expansion of the taking of the three refuges.

> The great merciful Lord, for the good of all living beings, practiced all perfections and attained supreme enlightenment. By these true words may joyous victory be mine!

> He who enhanced the happiness of the Sakyas, was victorious at the foot of the *bodhi*-tree. Likewise may there by victory to me, and may I ever be blessed!
>
> I revere the Buddha jewel, highest balm and blest, ever beneficial to gods and men. By the Buddha's glory safely may all obstacles and sufferings cease! . . .
>
> Whatever diverse precious jewels there be in this universe—there is no jewel equal to the Buddha. By this truth let me be prosperous! . . .
>
> There is no other refuge to me. The Buddha is my matchless refuge. By these true words may joyous victory be mine! . . .

This is just a sample of the devotional life of the Theravada, the words reinforcing the message graphically depicted on the wall-paintings. Salutations and ancient *suttas* are recited by the pious laity or chanted by groups of monks on the occasion of a special ceremony: the blessing of a house, initiation services, the great festivals of the year. Underlying them all is the dominating characteristic of Buddhism—the quest for enlightenment, "awakening" to the way things are. This is what the "school" that is Buddhism teaches—and many are the methods it uses to respond to the challenge and promise of the *Buddhadharma*. The Four Noble Truths provide the fundamental structure for all Buddhist practice. The very last words of the Buddha remind his followers that "all compounded things are subject to decay"—from which follows the single imperative: "Work out your own salvation with diligence."[8] Put bluntly like that, it is easy to understand the stereotypical account of the Buddhist as a lonely heroic individualist who ruthlessly brackets out everything that can distract from the single purpose of the Way of Enlightenment.[9]

Reading texts in the context that gives them shape and purpose shifts the perspective from which comparison can be made. As cultural variations within the tradition, artifacts ancient and modern are very often correlated and understood as the teaching devices of the *bodhisattva*'s "skill in means," the ability to adapt the form of the guiding precepts of Buddhist life to the needs and abilities of different people. Something like that is at work in the daily round of devotions in the Buddhapadipa Temple. While Thai iconography is notably different from the more sober decoration to be found in the Sinhalese Temple in West London a few miles away, the purpose is much the same: to provide an ambience which settles the heart as much as it appeals to the head. That, no doubt, is fairly obvious; devotional spiritualities—whether we are talking tensity of Hindu *bhakti* or the love mysticism associated w *devotio moderna*—make a broad appeal to the senses as cata duits of intuitive understanding. There is, however, rather n for the comparative theologian than producing a catalogue phenomena.

No doubt, any serious engagement with the world of "the other" requires a great deal of work in first understanding the phenomena of religious belief and practice. Close examination of what people say and what people do builds a certain sympathetic response—which is not to presume some sort of formula by which the outsider can become an insider. The Christian theologian who seeks to engage with the Buddhist world has to work at a number of different levels, not just because Buddhism makes a radical challenge to any attempt to "be theological," but because there is more to theology than a speculative science that seeks to provide some sort of comprehensive view of things. To return to an earlier point, theology draws out of the Mystery of Christ, which forms all Christian acts of living and loving—not a template that can somehow be adapted to different religious languages but a certain inner capacity *in the theologian* to pick up and reflect upon the traces of what is known in the unknown—or, to put it another way, virtues of patience and wisdom learned through generous practices of discernment. Comparative Theology tends to encourage focused micro-studies that acknowledge the freedom of the Spirit while at the same time driving the faithful thinker deeper into the mystery of divine encounter as it is inscribed in the foundational narratives, texts, and symbols of the "home" tradition. The "fruits of comparison" include a rapidly growing collection of theological studies by Christians of non-Christian texts, technical and scholarly explorations of topics and themes that cross religious frontiers. All of this changes the theological framework within which serious encounter with the other is to be conducted, giving it what I have been describing as a pastoral and contemplative "style." The more familiar that other world becomes, the more easily can human relations be established.

Formal studies are indicative of more ill-defined shifts in the theological culture now being created by interreligious engagements of all kinds, from precise theological critique to the wisdom generated by people of faith as they learn how to live creatively alongside each other. If, some decades back, the prevailing tendency was to seek out continuities, the theologian is now more sensitive to difference, not just to the specificity of tradition but also to neuralgic points which risk real conflict. The experience of "crossing the threshold" demands sustained attention to both.

What "seeds of the Word" are awakened in the theologian by the micro-study I have sketched in this chapter? Before returning to my theme of Comparative Theology and Pastoral Practice, let me briefly make a couple of interrelated points about the experience of the Temple as a school dedicated to educating its pupil-devotees in the way of truth and virtue.

Truth Found in the Present Moment

Each verse of those two Theravadin devotional hymns I have cited ends with a formula that comes under the general category of *patthana*, meaning an earnest wish or desire. Sometimes misleadingly translated as prayer, it can cover a number of aspirations that through faithfulness and integrity something desired may come to pass. Such a statement is often called the "act of truth" and is somewhat equivalent to Christians saying Amen at the end of formal prayer. The most famous example in the canonical literature is the *Angulimala Sutta*. Here we are introduced to a monk called Angulimala who had once been a robber; his name means "garland of fingers" and refers to one of the more unpleasant practices of his earlier life. Now he has been admitted to the *Buddhasangha* and is making progress on the way. One day, he sees a woman in labor. She is suffering greatly and, moved with great compassion, Angulimala asks the Buddha what can be done. The Buddha tells him to go back and say to the woman, "Since being born into the noble life, sister, I have never knowingly taken the life of any living thing. May this my act of truth bring welfare to you and your child."[10] The mother gives birth to her child safely and all goes well with the two of them.

Variations on the "act of truth" are to be found in classical commentaries. Buddhaghosa, for instance, writing in the fifth century CE, ends his great compendium on the religious life, the *Visuddhimagga*—the "Path of Purification"—with the wish that by the merit which has accrued through this book he may gain the reward he desires.[11] This is a popular practice, used as a charm to ward off dangers and evils of all kinds, yet it springs immediately from the point noted above, that Buddhism bases itself on a wisdom and clarity of vision that brings enlightenment not just to the individual but for the welfare of all suffering sentient beings. In that sense, it is not inappropriate to speak of the life and action of the compassionate *bodhisattva* as a gift that in its infinity overflows into the world. On that principle are based forms of theistic Buddhism, such as the Pure Land traditions.

Note that in my two Theravada sets of verses, the longer uses the language of truth: "By these true words may joyous victory be mine!" The shorter uses the language of grace: "By its grace may joyous victory be mine!" The latter seems much closer to Christian theism. The former seems more strictly Buddhist—and with its title of "supreme blessings" appears to trump the "lesser" set. Such distinctions need to be treated with care; discerning the basis of difference is rarely that straightforward. The word translated earlier as grace—in Pali *tejas*—means something like splendor, brilliance, or glory, with connotations of what shines forth, like the brightness of the sun's rays. Set alongside each other in my little book of Pali devotions it might seem words like "truth" and "grace" are equivalents, variations on a theme suitable for different occasions. And no doubt there is something in this; Buddhism tends to take a pragmatic approach to people's needs. But set in the context of the Temple, where the senses are being stimulated, not just by the words of the chant but by the vivid paintings on the walls, not to mention the aroma of incense and the perfume of flowers, a different interpretation of the words becomes possible.

The *Buddhavacanam*, the word of the Buddha, makes itself known in different modes through the different senses. There is, however, no dichotomy between Truth and Grace. What shines forth for those devotees prepared to follow the person of the Buddha or to listen to the chants or to sit in silence surrounded by the imagery that makes up the Buddhist universe, are the "horizons of contemplation" within which all words and formulae of faith have to be set. That splendor can be rendered "grace" in the English translation. It could be interpreted as an involuntary nod in the direction of a different cultural and religious context, namely Theravada Buddhism as it exists in the UK. If so, it opens up an important point of contact: Truth is revealed not just in the spoken word but in all manner of human experience, and sometimes in unexpected and surprising ways. The experience of grace generates a response of gratitude, an idea that is not foreign to the Theravada, a point to which I will return shortly. Meanwhile, to repeat my earlier point, freedom is always limited by the particularity of time and space, but that does not suppress the energy that makes a generous exploration of truth possible.

Bringing together the language of truth and that of grace leads to my second thought—about the figures that stand at the centre of Buddhist and Christian devotional life and give it shape and color. At least in their general outline, the stories of Gotama the Buddha and Jesus the Christ are strikingly similar: birth surrounded by heavenly portents, the experience of harassment by a devil-figure, the gathering of disciples and the peripatetic preaching of a message of salvation, death attended by earthquakes and triumphant visions. There are a number of intriguing parallels—most obviously, the visit of Asita the ascetic who seems to mirror the prophetic role played by Simeon in the Temple. And with the adaptation of tradition to present needs, we find plenty of examples of how the iconography is constantly being "inculturated" to give the different stories a more universal reference. Of course, putative parallels should not be emphasized at the expense of manifest difference. Gotama is at times highly critical of the Brahmin "establishment" but he is not betrayed and killed. Jesus is depicted as in prayer to the Father, but he does not seek personal enlightenment. The Resurrection narratives are quite unlike the descriptions of the apotheosis of the Buddha in the Mahayana. In Buddhism, the human condition is subjected to a complex diagnosis in which various causes are minutely analyzed; for Jesus, on the other hand, sin is the breakdown of a personal relationship with a loving God. And behind the "wise sayings" in the Gospel and such Buddhist scriptures as the *Dhammapada* are very different visions of what human beings are saved *to*, the *summum bonum*.

It would be surprising if the founding narratives, the stories and teachings of Jesus and Buddha, did not manifest certain lines of similarity. But this—perhaps paradoxically—is precisely because the texts are more than biographies. What holds them together is less the content of the teaching, or the structure of the story, than the purpose for which they are written: to draw devotees into a way of life. The ways differ in important respects, but the underlying dynamic of devotional practices, the manner in which they draw people into a more intensely felt devotion, may not. However desirable it may be, a dialogue between Christology and Buddhology would take us far away from the limited focus of this little experiment in Comparative Theology; my purpose here has been to note that the process of bringing the Word to birth in the soul has to begin somewhere—in a school of faith, a community of learning and teaching. What is taught in any school is specific to that school; the *way* in which it is taught, raising questions, stimulating the imagination, moving the heart, often crosses boundaries. The "conversion" and "enlightenment" narratives that typify Christianity and Buddhism respectively draw people not into some other-worldly intuition but into the realm of the everyday where they are most deeply human. Jesus preaches a breaking in of the Kingdom, the truth that "God reigns." For the Buddha, enlightenment is only achieved through constant attention to the present, by being "mindful" of what is here and now, what is "given" in the present moment. Once that point has been attained, and only then, can the Christology-Buddhology debate move to a different level, beyond the lining up of points of similarity and difference, to an engagement set within the life-giving practices of "schools of faith" where alone these respective narratives make sense.

Such a focus on the everyday may allow us a glimpse of a way beyond that troublesome distinction between Christianity as theistic and Buddhism as irredeemably non-theistic. There is no doubt that Christianity is doxological. God's Word is encountered by an act of self-attestation—the confession of the prophet: "Here I am"; the experience of being called into life leads to prayers of praise and thanksgiving. It seems as if there is nothing like that in Buddhism. But close attention to text *and practice* indicates otherwise. In the early texts a relationship is built up between enlightened teacher and the searching pupil. The pupil puts his faith, it is said, in the teacher.[12] Of course, the end of the path is to cultivate a *personal* realization of truth, not something that *depends* on the other. But that is very far from a sort of splendid isolation. For the Buddhist, a potential solipsism is overcome by a variety of strategies, all of which have as their purpose the configuring of Wisdom and Compassion: *Prajña* and *Karuna*. It is too easy to get fixated on the "end of the way," as if the *summum bonum* of Buddhism is *Nirvana*, when it is more exactly about the building of those virtues of right living and acting that make *Nirvana* possible: a wise-compassion or a compassionate-wisdom.

Such an ethical composite is more typical of the Mahayana than the Theravada. Yet the same interaction between the cognitive and affective dimensions of enlightenment is there in both traditions. There is a Pali word that appears in various Theravada texts, and also in another of those devotional hymns. I like to think that it is reflected in some of those intrigued and horrified faces looking at that graphic depiction of the first Noble Truth. The word is *katañňuta*—literally "knowing or recognizing what has been done"—and it often goes along with the term *katavedi*, which can be translated as "making what has been done known." It is difficult not to translate it as "gratitude," a rejoicing in what has been given. One of the many signs of progress on the way is a gratitude that both rejoices in truth and finds ways of sharing that truth with other suffering sentient beings. Acts of praise and thanks are not that distant from a supposedly "non-theistic" tradition.

The Pastoral "Style" of Comparative Theology

Lest these all too tentative remarks, culled from a "micro study" that focuses on the diffuse practices of devotional spirituality, be dismissed as little more than a temporary distraction from the "big questions" which dominate dialogue between Buddhists and Christians, let me now return to my earlier point about the "matter" and "style" of Comparative Theology. I have argued that Comparative Theology has many of the characteristics of Pastoral Theology in its attentiveness to the God-revealing potential of a theological reflection that begins "in the middle of things." To quote Gagey again:

> The truth claimed by the [Christian] message is not the object of some kind of informative knowledge. It is not to be completed by more information. It is to be fulfilled (performed, realized, accomplished) in the life of the one who welcomes it. Consequently, this truth is not only announced in words claiming intellectual assent. It communicates itself through all the mediations (narrative, symbolic systems, ritual, social, etc.) that give shape to the existence of those who believe in the Gospel.[13]

If Gagey is correct, the positive insights that aid interreligious understanding arise not just directly from study and observation, but indirectly from the manner of "living interreligiously" that changes the way in which the world is perceived. It is the latter that requires analysis.

Pastoral or Practical Theology attends to the terms in which the practice of a community of faith is seen to correlate with the norms inscribed in tradition. A continuous cycle of practice, reflection, and focused action builds up a sensitivity to the various "voices" with which the Word of God is spoken in the world and apprehended in the life of the community. These include, but are not exhausted by, the normative or formal authority found in scripture and creeds, the systematic reflections of academic theology, and the faithful practice of people seeking to live out their sense of mission. The last practice I have referred to as "living interreligiously"—and it involves a responsibility not just to face the "home" tradition with integrity but to touch another world of faith that has its own norms and traditions with respect and delicacy. If there are answers to the "big questions," they often turn out to be no more than tentative glimpses of a bigger picture made possible by a persistent attention to what is learned in "the middle of things." While any philosophically coherent work of comparison aspires to extract itself from the contingencies of the moment, there is never any magisterial "view from nowhere." To return to my second reflection in the preceding text, attention to the aesthetic and devotional context of *Buddhapuja* acts as a corrective to those accounts of Nirvana that emphasize the cognitive at the expense of the affective. To say that Buddhist enlightenment is about awakening to the truth of things is not to privilege the sense of sight at the expense of hearing, tasting, touching, and so on.

The principle is clear enough. Just as for the insider all the senses are to be stimulated in order that the whole person comes to terms with the transformative truth about things, so only the broadest and most generous interpretation of Buddhist practice and belief will make it possible for the outsider to enter into and understand this particular religious world. Plausible constructs such as the theism/non-theism distinction may be true at a certain level of generality; they may perform a valuable pedagogical function in mapping out the territory within which interreligious comparison can take place. But care needs to be taken not to turn a useful heuristic tool into a rigid template that stops forming thought and subtly *de*forms it. Distinctions are not oppositions. In any work of comparison one needs to recognize a certain tension between the virtues of faith and hope, between an obedient exploration of memory and tradition and a generous openness to what always remains mystery and beyond comprehension. The tension becomes palpable in any religious artifact once it is understood not as "mere" decoration and aesthetic enhancement but as a continuation of a narrative of truth that engages heart as much as head. That is not to meld the theistic into the non-theistic, as if the distinction is no longer significant. But it does argue for a context of practice—the inner life of a community—where alone such constructions begin to make sense.

The artists responsible for the paintings in the Buddhapadipa Temple were engaged in a practice of faith akin to the "pastoral cycle" sketched earlier. The normative authority of the great *Buddhadharma* is not exercised in any "top-down" fashion, but exists in constant dialogue with the practical demands of the moment. I have argued that what motivated them was the need to communicate Buddhist truth in a contemporary mode—a bit of Buddhist "inculturation." How is the energy inherent in tradition to be translated into a form that touches the devotee, the visitor, and even the comparative theologian seeking out the traces of transcendent truth in a strange world? There are little corners and rather grander sweeps where the artists have felt free to insinuate something new and provocative. It is, of course, arguable that all we have in these friezes is a Buddhist nod in the direction of the post-modern, a sort of eclectic "hommage" to other cultures and styles with their own ways of representing the human desire to communicate deeply felt convictions about the meaning of human living. The concept of intertextuality is now a commonplace; texts repeat other texts, and every textual reading has to be related to the cultural context from which both author and reader draw the codes that direct the work of interpretation. The same is true of plays and films, paintings and sculpture, and all manner of artistic creation—even of Buddhist illustration with its impish delight in contemporary glimpses of the Four Noble Truths. Nevertheless, the sensitive comparativist will always discern something more going on.

Let me close by repeating the point that Comparative Theology as a form of Pastoral Theology is itself a performative act. For the Christian, Comparative Theology is a practice of faith, appropriate for religious living in a pluralist world, which seeks to understand and communicate the Truth manifested in the revealed Word of God. In focusing on practice as an activity of the Church that begins in liturgy and the life of the sacraments and continues in acts of prayer, study, and social relations in the broadest sense, I have used the act of reading as a metaphor for a religious life conducted "in the middle of things." Any artifact or cultural construct, as much as a text or written record, can be "read." I have not attempted more than the most rudimentary analysis of the stages of a pastoral cycle, which seeks to be true to both the normative and personal or practical dimensions of any encounter with the Word made Flesh. Nor have I touched on the tricky issue of artistic inspiration, that mysterious originating "spark" that gives a shape or direction to a tradition of thought. Here, I have been more interested in the equally mysterious process of close reading that Comparative Theology as a practice of faith seeks to promote. What a text or place or artifact does is give us a fixed point around which a school of faith orientates itself, what Ricoeur memorably speaks of as the symbol that gives rise to thought. "Fixed" does not imply static; rather, what is given is not to be explained away and substituted by something else. Human beings cannot manage without the form or structure that classic texts and imaginative artifacts provide for their thinking. But neither can they avoid the invitation to explore the connections and resonances they open up. Whatever is meant by "inculturation," it depends not on applying some prescribed pattern to the flux of human interaction but more simply, on a responsible and generous commitment to "living interreligiously." Before culture is a noun, an object, it is a verb, an action; it is what the writer or artist—or indeed theologian—does.

Notes

1. Gagey, "Pastoral Theology as a Theological Project," 80–98.
2. The idea is taken from the thought of Nicholas Lash, especially *The Beginning and the End of "Religion"* (Cambridge: Cambridge University Press, 1996). See Barnes, *Interreligious Learning*, 32.
3. The now familiar fourfold dialogue—common life, common action, religious experience, and theological exchange—is first noted in the 1984 document from the Secretariat for non-Christian Religions: "The attitude of the Church towards the followers of other religions," *Bulletin* 1/2 (1984), 126–41. It is repeated in John Paul II's encyclical, *Redemptoris Missio*, para 57 (1990), and in the 1991 joint document from the Pontifical Council for Inter-religious Dialogue and the Congregation for Evangelisation, "Dialogue and Proclamation: reflections and orientations on inter-religious dialogue and the proclamation of the Gospel of Jesus Christ," *Bulletin* 26/2 (1991), 210–50.
4. See Jayatilleke, "The Buddhist attitude to other religions."
5. See E. G. Pieris, 128–29.
6. Gombrich, *Precept and Practice.*
7. Pali text taken from *A Buddhist's Manual.*
8. *Mahaparinibbana Sutta, Digha Nikaya* ii 156.
9. For an exercise in Comparative Theology on this theme see Barnes, "Way and Wilderness."
10. *Majjhima Nikaya* ii 98–105.
11. *Visuddhimagga*, translated by Bhikkhu Ñanamoli, 4th edition; Kandy: Buddhist Publication Society (1976), 837.
12. See Barnes, "Way and Wilderness" and discussion of the various texts that take their rise from the *Samaññaphala Sutta, Digha Nikaya* i.47ff.
13. "Pastoral Theology as a Theological Project," 92.

15 Theologizing for the Yoga Community?

COMMITMENT AND HYBRIDITY IN COMPARATIVE THEOLOGY

Stephanie Corigliano

Comparative theology is a transformative academic pursuit. To name but a few examples, James Fredericks, Paul Knitter, Catherine Cornille, and Francis X. Clooney all argue in different ways that comparative theology is a study that begins with a theologian who is rooted in a particular faith tradition. In this way, the learning about and from another tradition, as Knitter describes, is an act of passing over, which necessarily entails a passing back, or return to one's home tradition.[1]

This essay questions the idea that an explicit faith commitment is a necessary criterion for comparative theology. Conversely, I propose that for some, comparative theology is a way of exploring and even forming faith identity, thus faith commitments may be unclear or not "rooted" in a particular tradition at the beginning of a comparative exercise. As such, the comparative discussion might be navigated between three points, the two historical traditions (and associated texts) being compared and that of a modern community (religious, spiritual, or otherwise) or a particular question that arises from the contemporary context.[2]

This methodological approach may further the scope and impact of comparative theology by expanding the possibilities for who can do comparative theology. It also has implications for how it might be used in settings such as the classroom, where faith-identity is not a prerequisite for enrollment. Comparative theology can be a means for thoughtfully engaging more than one religious tradition in a way that relates to philosophical questions and the personal search for meaning and life-understanding. Further, comparative theology is an effective method for studying New Religious Movements or New Spiritual Practices and contemporary expressions of religious faith.[3] Thus, the criteria of commitment or the "rooted" position of faith may need to be re-examined in light of communities and faith-positions that are ill-defined, in process, or newly forming.

To explore the importance of having an explicit faith commitment as a criterion for doing comparative theology, I will look at select works of leading theologians in the field and why or how this criterion is presented.[4] I will then discuss my 2015 dissertation research on detachment in Hinduism, Christianity, and Yoga in modern times as an example of my thesis that, for some, comparative theology can be a way of examining and forming faith identity.

"Rooted" Perspectives in Comparative Theology

JAMES L. FREDERICKS

James L. Fredericks is an early proponent of comparative theology. In his 1999 book *Faith Among Faiths: Christian Theology and Non-Christian Religions*, he proposes two fundamental goals for comparative theology. It is, first of all, a way for Christians to develop creative and practical skills for living responsibly with non-Christians. Second, according to Fredericks, it is a way for Christians to explore and deepen their own faith in dialogue with non-Christians. Since the writing of Fredericks's book, an increasing number of scholars from traditions outside of Christianity have begun to take interest in the potential of comparative theology for increasing peace and dialogue between traditions.[5] Thus, it might similarly be suggested, comparative theology is a way for Muslims to explore and deepen their Islamic faith and so forth.

Fredericks highlights a creative tension that is necessary within comparative theology.[6] He states, "In doing theology comparatively, there will always be a tension between our commitments to the Christian tradition, on the one hand, and, on the other, to the allure of other religious traditions."[7] Curiosity or sense of anticipation that something new might be learned is crucial to inter-religious scholarship. Subsequently, according to Fredericks, without a lasting commitment to a particular religious tradition, we run the risk of relativism. He explains,

> By "remaining rooted" I do not mean closing ourselves off from the demanding and transforming truths of other religious traditions. This is the unhelpful legacy of exclusivist theologies. I am cautioning against adopting some meta-religious position that no actual religion holds.[8]

According to Fredericks, the "meta-religious position" is the problematic legacy of pluralism, a late development in the theology of religions that attempts to find a common ground between diverse religions by suggesting that all religions worship the same transcendent reality. This perspective is echoed in the common refrain that "all religions are more or less saying the same thing."[9] Any devout religious individual is likely to disagree with this kind of analysis, and so the pluralist perspective and associated "meta-religious positions" are not successful models for actually engaging people from different religions. As Fredericks concisely states: "Failing to take the teaching of other religious traditions seriously is intolerance, although certainly a subtle form of intolerance."[10] From this perspective, relativism whitewashes religious diversity and ignores the aspects of religious life that are most important to religious individuals and communities.

However, when relativism or fear of dogmatic religious tradition is the starting point (as is the case for many students at the undergraduate level), comparative theology also has the potential for demonstrating the value of religious praxis, belief, and even doctrine. I will discuss this point in more detail with examples from my own work in the sections on relativism and hybridity that follow. It is also the case that proponents of the various forms of new or secular spiritual practice (such as Yoga, contemporary meditation, or even tradition-free pluralists) have valuable and challenging perspectives to offer. Thus, expanding the notion of who can do comparative theology by rethinking the criterion of "rootedness" in comparative theology can actually contribute to Fredericks' first goal for comparative theology: for Christians to develop creative and practical skills for living responsibly with non-Christians.

PAUL F. KNITTER

Paul F. Knitter is a specialist in the field of theology of religions[11] and though he may not identify as a comparative theologian, his contribution to the discussion of methods and comparative theology is important. Like Fredericks, he similarly discusses the tension between vulnerability and loyalty in his 2002 book *Introducing Theologies of Religions*, yet he frames the goal of the comparative project somewhat differently:

> What the comparative theologian learns about another religion will be something not only that s/he can write books about; it may also be some-

> thing that the theologian has to live and integrate into his/her own life. This means that what is true of all theology (and what makes the difference between theology and religious studies) is also true of comparative theology: faith is at stake—one's own and that of one's community.[12]

For Knitter, the identity of the theologian is tied to vocation and the fundamental purpose of theology. Like Fredericks, Knitter is ultimately also concerned with dialogue and peacemaking through interreligious engagement and study. To do theology is to seek truth and to enrich faith. It cannot be limited to the objective study of texts and history; it must bear upon a personal and communal quest for understanding.

In the 2009 text *Without Buddha I Could Not Be a Christian*, Knitter details a method for "passing over" to a different religious tradition and then "passing back" to one's own tradition. In this, he exemplifies the value and method of beginning from a position of faith, addressing questions and concerns that arise from that perspective, then turning to another tradition to see how similar questions or concerns are explained or addressed. This is clearly a quest for understanding. Yet Knitter's own process also demonstrates the risk and complexity involved in deep encounters with the religious other. To learn deeply from and about another tradition can change how one views the world and how one relates to his/her own religious tradition. In the final chapter of this later work, he discusses the issue of hybridity and his own experience of double religious belonging. Drawing upon the work of Jeannine Hill Fletcher, Knitter explains that identity, including religious identity, is always in process:

> [Religious identity] takes shape through an ongoing process of standing in one place and stepping into other places, of forming a sense of self and then expanding or correcting that sense as we meet other selves. There is no such thing as a neatly defined, once-and-for-all identity.[13]

In this way, Knitter suggests that double religious belonging is, in a sense, an explicit expression of a more common attribute of identity formation. Identity and the significance or the conceptualization of the various aspects of identity change over time. More importantly, Knitter argues that his own engagement with Buddhism (and his official pronouncement of Buddhist vows) actually strengthens his belief in Christ and his ability to be Christian. Knitter acknowledges the importance of commitment to a religious tradition. As stated, the notion of the "rooted" theologian, for Knitter (and Fredericks), relates to the vocation of the theologian at large. Yet, as evidenced in Knitter's work, "rootedness" and commitment are not necessarily in opposition to religious hybridity and the concept of fluid identity formation.

CATHERINE CORNILLE

Catherine Cornille, too, is a specialist in the field of theology of religions, interreligious dialogue, and comparative theology with a primary focus on questions of theory and methods. Like Knitter, the value of "hybrid positions" is recognized in her work where she acknowledges the profound insight, humility, and struggle of monks such as Bede Griffiths (1906–93) and Henri Le Saux (1910–73) who sought to engage and learn from Hindu monks.[14] However, for monks such as Le Saux and his companion, Jules Monchanin (1895–1957), the unfolding of a Hindu-Christian belonging was a slow and often painful process. Both Le Saux and Monchanin were deeply committed to their Christian faith and only through a prolonged immersion and dialogue with Hindu texts and monks did they come to accept shared truths between both traditions.[15] This process was marked by a difficult struggle to be both open to the truth of the other and also faithful to the Christian Gospel.[16] Cornille recognizes the inter-monastic dialogue as "one of the most enduring and fruitful forms of interreligious dialogue."[17] She goes on to state,

> It might be above all a life of immersion in the cultivation of humility that generates a greater attention and receptivity to the truth of other religions. Conversely, the monastic experience of dialogue with other religions also seems to reinforce the attitude of humility about one's own tradition.[18]

Thus, Cornille recognizes that a possible (even common) outcome of inter-monastic dialogue is epistemic and doctrinal humility, an increased humility with regard to ultimate truth and the truth of one's own tradition. In addition, it may often be the case (although not necessarily for Le Saux or Monchanin) that individuals drawn to dialogue often already stand at the margins of a particular tradition or may view the very concept of tradition as a hindrance to genuine openness in dialogue. Cornille's 2008 work, *The Im-Possibility of Interreligious Dialogue*, discusses dialogue without commitment and finally argues that commitment is an important criterion for interreligious dialogue and comparative theology.[19]

Like Fredericks, Cornille points to the problem of relativism. Citing the late nineteenth century Theosophical Society as a predecessor to the New Age movement, Cornille suggests that both are distinguished by a belief in the unity of all religions, a rejection of institutional authority, and the practice of "integrating the best of all religious traditions in the course of one's own religious or spiritual quest."[20] This position contrasts with the more general methodological considerations of John Hick (discussed in Frederick's work above) because the Theosophical Society formed a distinct community and propounded a kind of mystical philosophy that supported their particular community through written works, group lectures, and meditation practice.

In addition, Cornille points to post-modern philosophy and the shift from an external sense of authority to a sense of internal authority where "the individual self becomes the final norm."[21] Consistently, Cornille acknowledges the positive side of this approach, pointing to the work of figures like Mohandas Gandhi, who freely explored a personal sense of truth across religious boundaries and rose to become a great spiritual and political leader.

Nonetheless, with regard to interreligious dialogue, Cornille lists several problems that may arise from the early expression of New Age philosophy. Namely, the potentially arbitrary selection of particular ideas and practices from diverse traditions tends towards individualistic forms of spiritual practice that risk being self-serving and indulgent. Next, the urge to learn from new traditions can also become a means for "endless wandering," leading to (often) shallow encounters that lack the aspects of challenge and depth that a deeper commitment would allow for.[22] Last, according to Cornille, the lack of singular commitment can also lead to a lack of coherence, such that the individualized spiritual experience cannot be communicated or shared with a larger community.[23]

By contrast, Cornille defines religious commitment as a "deliberate identification with the teachings and practices of a particular tradition."[24] She further argues that this is a vital component for interreligious dialogue:

> For one's interlocutor, it offers the basis for confidence that one is effectively engaged in a dialogue with a genuine religious tradition, rather than with an arbitrary individual. And for the individual, it provides the

> strength and security that comes by appeal to the authoritative voice of the tradition, as opposed to speaking solely in one's own name.[25]

Thus, religious commitment in dialogue bridges communities, rather than isolated individuals. Of course, this also entails a level of informed religious commitment and willingness for critical reflection on the teachings and practices of a particular religious community. For Cornille, one of the most important reasons to emphasize commitment in dialogue is the question of audience:

> Return to the tradition entails, among other things, exposure of one's own insights to the collective authority of the tradition . . . the ultimate goal of dialogue is growth in the truth, not only for disparate individuals who have the capacity and the luxury to engage in such dialogue, but for the tradition itself.[26]

Dialogue and comparative study will be most fruitful if it can be shared with a larger community. This relates to the concerns expressed in the work of Fredericks and Knitter: that comparative theology is a means for developing creative ways for Christians to live with and learn from other traditions. Working from and maintaining a faith commitment to a particular community may be one of the more effective ways to do this. However, like Knitter, Cornille also acknowledges the risks involved in deeply engaging with another tradition. Commitment to a faith tradition and to learning from and with another tradition can profoundly transform the individual in ways that will not always be appreciated by the larger faith community.[27]

Cornille returns to the issue of double religious belonging and intermonastic dialogue to discuss several prominent figures who, while controversial in their approach to doctrine and commitment, have nonetheless contributed positively to interreligious understanding. She argues that the step of returning to one's initial faith community despite personal transformation and a potentially (new) complex sense of identity is essential for interreligious dialogue to have any impact beyond individual experience. This again requires humility and a sense of openness to learn from one's home community. For Cornille, interreligious dialogue in its fullest sense requires an initial commitment to a particular faith community, followed by a willing effort to engage and learn from the other, and a subsequent return to the initial faith community. Return to one's home tradition may be difficult, but it is also an important step.

However, we may be at a juncture in the history of religions where it is increasingly necessary to consider (and include in dialogue) persons of ill-defined and complex religious identities. Such complex religious identities are found among the pioneers of inter-monastic dialogue discussed in Cornille's work, like Henri Le Saux, Bede Griffiths, and Raimon Panikkar (to name only a few). These individuals were also prolific authors and leaders who have contributed to more pluralistic and, yes, relativist ways of imagining faith. Thus, we now have a generation who may need to pick up where these brave thinkers left off.

FRANCIS X. CLOONEY

The issue of commitment as a primary criterion for comparative theology is also considered in the work of Francis X. Clooney. As a founder and one of the most prolific authors in the field, Clooney offers the following definition for comparative theology:

> *Comparative theology—comparative* and *theological* beginning to end—marks acts of faith seeking understanding which are rooted in a particular faith tradition but which, from that foundation, venture into learning from one or more other faith traditions. This learning is sought for the sake of fresh theological insights that are indebted to the newly encountered tradition/s as well as the home tradition.[28]

The term "comparative theology," coined by Clooney in the 1980s, set apart a new academic venture of combining traditional, faith-based, theological inquiry with the careful study of another tradition.[29] This is distinct from the field of comparative religions, in which the scholarly ideal is the objective study of two or more traditions and the intended audience is primarily fellow scholars or a more general public. Comparative theology is also academically rigorous and needs to be accountable to a scholarly community, yet it operates from an acknowledged faith perspective and with a broader faith community in mind.

Like the previous authors, the criterion of the "rooted" position of faith in Clooney's work is primarily related to the vocation of the theologian. Yet Clooney goes on to recognize the limits of this position:

> My strong emphasis on faith and tradition may seem to marginalize readers who do not identify with any particular religious tradition . . . it is true that I do not wish to move to a tradition neutral stance, as if to

> suggest that traditional foundations do not really matter. Nor do I wish to define "tradition" so loosely that it turns out that everyone has a tradition, like it or not.[30]

It is important to retain an understanding of the commitment to a religious tradition as distinct from New Age curiosity and casual religious learning. Yet, Clooney does later recognize that some individuals may have thoughtful faith commitments and community networks despite their lack of affiliation with an established tradition. He suggests that these individuals may be able to contribute to comparative theology by reflecting on their own particular questions in dialogue with established religious traditions. Interestingly, while readers who do not identify with any particular religious tradition are acknowledged as potentially marginalized here, later in the text (like Knitter and Cornille) Clooney goes on to discuss the inherent and potentially inevitable marginalization of comparativists in relation to their home traditions:

> Comparative study leaves her, if she is successful, at the border between two worlds, in a space distinguished by a seeming multiplication of loyalties. She exists in between, no longer a sure fit in a theological world defined within one community. While she may not abandon her home tradition, she is likely then to remain a marginal figure, though of a kind valuable to that community and also to the wider religiously diverse society.[31]

Similarly, Clooney suggests, the comparative theologian may also be located on the margins of the academic community because she treads between the disciplines of comparative religion and traditional theology. Nonetheless, the discomfort of this margin may also be crucial to the important, creative work of addressing diversity with academic integrity, heartfelt questions, and a deep awareness of the complexity of our present moment.[32]

It is here that a contradiction surfaces in Clooney's work, one that he may readily acknowledge because above all else in the discussion of methods, Clooney emphasizes the need to postpone grand judgments and hasty conclusions. On the one hand, he suggests the need for the comparativist to have an established foundation in one tradition. Yet he also boldly states:

> But I also expect important contributions to comparative theology from readers who are not committed to any formal religious tradition at the present moment and from those who never had such commitments.

> While I do insist that comparative theology will for the most part be rooted in familiar religious traditions, there is no reason not to welcome other voices arising in less familiar contexts. The challenge facing such readers, of course, is to practice faith seeking understanding, in their own ways.[33]

This is a fresh turn in the discussion of methods, one that even in Clooney's work seems to hide between pages, toward the back of his text instead of being set forth in the opening chapters. Yet leading theologians do recognize the reality of complex religious identities that result from the prolonged and careful study of a second religious tradition. This being the case, it makes sense to understand that as faith communities coexist in increasingly close proximity to one another, the next generation is already faced with a world where clear-cut choices for exclusive faith commitments may not come naturally. This reality requires new and creative ways for engaging with the "spiritual but not religious." Our understanding of this phenomenon cannot be limited to a reproach of the superficial, relativistic, or New Age movement.

The quest to understand faith within and outside of established religious traditions is a powerful and important pursuit. In fact, the value of commitment to a particular religious faith and practice may increasingly need to emerge out of a deep encounter with diversity. As stated in my introduction, comparative theology may be a way of forming and cultivating faith identity or at least a way to cultivate a deeper understanding of those who elect for strong faith commitments.

"Aerial" Perspectives in Comparative Theology

The banyan tree has aerial roots, ones that grow above ground either sprouting up from roots below or reaching down from existing branches. Because the banyan initially grows from a seed planted on a host tree, over time the actual trunk of the host tree can be difficult to decipher from the many roots that stand around it in clusters. In this next section, I propose that for a new generation, the criterion of the "rooted" identity of the theologian must be revised to accommodate the idea of aerial roots.[34] That is, roots that sprout from unusual places but may, nonetheless, take shape into large and interesting trees. Thus, I argue that an important function of comparative theology may be the ability to better understand and explore faith identity. Rather than understanding comparative theology as arising out of already-in-place commitments, it can be formative of commitment.

The authors discussed earlier in this essay engaged in interreligious dialogue and cross-cultural studies, and began comparing texts and practices across religious traditions at a time when the Christian-Catholic perspective toward other traditions was largely marked by a history of suspicion. Past efforts toward interreligious dialogue were commonly directed toward evangelization and the frontier of theology of religions was the "inclusivist" theory propounded by Karl Rahner and supported in the document of Vatican II, *Nostra Aetate*.[35] Since this period, Fredericks, Knitter, Cornille, and Clooney each independently pieced together their interreligious education and began exploring across religious traditions as an addition to their foundations in Christian theology.

Owing much to the contributions and efforts of the four discussed here, I am now part of a newer generation of scholars who are able to specialize in comparative theology as a sub-field within theology. My training is focused in depth on both theory and methods of theology and religious studies and in comparative study. From the outset of my graduate work, I was able to focus on learning about and from two religious traditions (Christianity and Hinduism) and to think theologically about what this learning means for my own faith formation and for the question of religious belonging in general.

The opportunity to enter graduate work with a comparative focus opens up the field for more sustained and in-depth comparative work at an early point in an individual's career. It also affects the basic parameters for comparative study because the individual may be less steeped in the academic study of a "home" tradition and instead will engage in learning from and about two traditions simultaneously. The issue of religious belonging and rootedness in a particular tradition as a basic criterion for the comparative theologian was likely an assumed characteristic of early comparative work because the turn to comparative work usually came at a later point in the individual's career. As the field expands, this criterion will need to be reconsidered. The following section of this essay will look at my 2015 dissertation and how my particular approach and perspective impacts five methodological points: theological orientation, textual choices, relativism, hybridity, and audience. The first two criteria relate to beginning the comparative study. The final three are points for consideration related to the criterion of rootedness that have evolved from my comparative project.

My 2015 dissertation, "Towards a Hermeneutic of Yoga in Modern Times: Practice and Detachment in Hinduism and Christianity," offers a constructive analysis of Yoga in modern times and the practice of detachment through a comparative study of both Hindu and Christian texts. In this, I seek to further a scholarly understanding of contemporary Yoga practice by considering the dialectical tension between life-affirming goals in Yoga (health, balance, well-being) and the world-renouncing asceticism of traditional texts such as Patañjali's *Yogasūtras*. As such, I take seriously the self-understanding of particular modern gurus (namely, within the teaching tradition of T. Krishnamacharya[36]) and construct an analysis of practice and authoritative texts that bridge insider perspectives with contemporary scholarly debates.

The practice of comparative theology is perhaps most effective at creating a new light with which the individual can freshly examine another tradition. In particular, when the study is centered on a common concept, the differences between the two traditions can help to bring out new perspectives that might otherwise have gone unnoticed. For example, the core concept of detachment, while prominent throughout the *Yogasūtras*, appears to be at odds with the modern tradition, which emphasizes attachment-oriented goals like health and well-being. Thus, in the dissertation, I introduce a comparative study of detachment in the work of the eighteenth-century Jesuit, Jean Pierre de Caussade, in order to further consider the dialectic between detachment, action, and love. In this way, my own work is an example of my initial thesis: that the comparative discussion might be navigated between three points, the two historical traditions (and associated texts) being compared and that of a modern community (religious, spiritual, or otherwise—in my study this "modern community" is Yoga practitioners in the tradition of T. Krishnamacharya). In this model, the comparative study between the two historical traditions works to highlight distinctive characteristics of the contemporary question or community. For a new generation often marked by ambiguous and complex faith identities (aerial roots!), comparative theology can be a means of understanding and forging identity.

THEOLOGICAL ORIENTATION

My project is fundamentally a work of constructive, comparative theology. Yet I stand in the liminal space between the worlds of academic, theological study and a more popular Yoga culture. As a theologian, I start from a position of faith and commitment to practice and it is from this position that I formed the questions that drove the dissertation. It is as a practitioner of Yoga that the concept of detachment is especially important, challenging, and interesting to me. The experience of Yoga as a practice that engenders health and strength (attachment!) is difficult to reconcile with the claims made within various Yogic texts (here, specifically the *Yogasūtras*), which suggest that detachment is necessary.[37] Thus my study focuses on why detachment is important. How is it actually practiced? What might be gained or changed within the modern practice of Yoga if the challenge of detachment were taken more seriously?

Theology is usually a term reserved for the study of Christianity (by Christians). While my theological perspective is undeniably influenced by my own rootedness in Catholicism, the faith and practice that I primarily recognize in this work is a concrete, daily practice of physical Yoga *āsana* (posture).[38] The assertion of Yoga practice as a formal position of faith and spiritual commitment may be somewhat incredulous to many scholars, both in the fields of Theology and in South Asian studies. Indeed, when I began my Master's studies in Catholic Theology in 2007, I lacked both the courage and conviction to make this statement. For some, particularly scholars of religion, Yoga is not really thought of as a living "faith" tradition. The study of contemporary Yoga in theology seemed like a side project, too trendy to be taken seriously.

I am grateful to the groundbreaking works in the study of Yoga (Edwin Bryant, Christopher Key Chapple, Gerald James Larson, Elizabeth De Michelis, Stuart Ray Sarbacker, Mark Singleton, Ian Whicher, David Gordon White, and others) that have emerged in the past two decades. These works have provided a language, community, and validity to all future academic studies of Yoga. Yet, by and large, they have been written from the field of South Asian studies, by individuals who sometimes admit to practicing Yoga in passing (or else make a point to declare that they do not), but who have, until recently, avoided explicit constructivist claims. The linchpin of theology, the question of how faith or commitment can be advanced through the effort to link the historical studies to particular modern communities has been implied, yet largely undervalued. In fact, this possibility of exploring theological questions has often been understood as a threat to the overall integrity of the objective field of religious studies and South Asian studies.

Yet in the past several years, the community I am a part of, an international and interreligious group, many of whom have maintained a daily practice of physical Yoga for 10–30+years, has continued to grow and mature.[39] This community is increasingly seeking ways to communicate the depth and value of the practice of Yoga to outside communities in the forms of social outreach, work in schools, prisons, hospitals, and addiction recovery centers. This community has also been affected by recent scholarship, which at times appears to diminish the value of core precepts of the community and to question the historical authenticity of the practice.[40] These challenges are immensely important and valuable because they force constructive responses.

Thus, in this dissertation, I do have a "rooted" position, although it is not a conventional position of faith. Further, I have found that it is through my study of multiple traditions that I have come to understand this liminal "rooted" position and have begun to consider the ways in which it can be studied, challenged, and further developed in intentional ways. Throughout this essay, I argue for the possibility and value of doing comparative theology from a less "rooted" faith perspective, like that of many contemporary Yoga practitioners. Yet I also contend that Yoga, both in individual and community contexts, would greatly benefit from concerted efforts of theological study.

TEXTUAL CHOICES

Doing comparative theology between three points of comparison (two historical traditions and a contemporary community/question) requires three stages of comparison. This may begin with a question or topic that arises from the contemporary community. My own study focuses on detachment in contemporary Yoga practice. The first comparative stage is then between the contemporary community and a historical text. In my work, I compared the practice of detachment (or lack of detachment) in contemporary Yoga with the understanding of detachment in the *Yogasūtras*. The second comparative stage takes up the issue (for example, detachment) in, a study of an outside tradition. Here I turned to study the practice of detachment in the work of the Catholic, Jean Pierre de Caussade. Finally, the third comparative stage is a comparison between the first two parts and how this overall study informs the contemporary community or initial question. Textual choices arise from the context of particular communities and from the questions raised in the first comparative part.

Yoga today is a transnational phenomenon. As a physical discipline, individuals from around the world take up Yoga to improve flexibility, health, and concentration. In the theory component of many contemporary teacher trainings, one of the primary texts presented is Patañjali's *Yogasūtras*. This can be partially attributed to the legacy of T. Krishnamacharya (1888–1989), who is often referred to as the founder of many of the forms of Yoga that are popular today and who used the *Yogasūtras* to contextualize his innovative teachings.

As such, the first comparative aspect of my study engages the historical [Hindu] text, *Yogasūtras*, with a study of Yoga in modern times. I look closely at the written works of Krishnamacharya to gain a better understanding of his philosophical approach to Yoga and precisely why and how he employed the *Yogasūtras*. I also examine the written works and the use of the *Yogasūtras* by three of the students who learned from Krishnamacharya and who later became international Yoga gurus: K. Pattabhi Jois, BKS Iyengar, and TKV Desikachar. This broad study of Yoga in the tradition of Krishnamacharya and its relationship to the classic text articulates a theoretical understanding of Yoga in modern times that accounts for insider perspectives (Yoga gurus and practitioners) as well as outsider critiques (scholars and journalists).[41] It also raises certain questions regarding the practice of Yoga and detachment (or lack thereof).

The choice to focus on the Hindu text *Yogasūtras* was a starting point for my analysis because it is already a prominent text within modern Yoga. The association of the *Yogasūtras* with Yoga today has also been a source of debate and critical scholarship because there is little obvious connection between the physical forms of Yoga and Patañjali's text. The *Yogasūtras* define Yoga as absorbed concentration, or the cessation of mental fluctuation.[42] Early in the text it states that this absorbed concentration is attained through practice and detachment.[43] The text lists various forms of practice, including ethical precepts and physical observances, but the primary focus is the withdrawal from ordinary consciousness toward *samādhi* (absorption) or *kaivalya* (liberation). As noted, an important aspect of my study is the inclusion of the commentaries and texts from the modern gurus, which grounds the practice of *āsana* (physical posture) within the purview of the historical text yet I also take into consideration critiques of these modern gurus (and their use of the *Yogasūtras*) from relevant scholars.[44]

The second comparative aspect of my study turns to an outside tradition. Here I look at the practice of detachment in the work of the Catholic, Jesuit Jean-Pierre de Caussade (1675–1751) as a devotional practice of eighteenth-century Christianity. I turn to Caussade in order to give a fresh perspective on the contrasting dynamics of attachment (love), practice, and detachment. He lived in the wake of one of the last great persecutions of heresy by the Catholic Church, Quietism. The great threat of Quietism was its practice of absolute passivity, a non-engagement with the world and Church. For the Catholic Church, this took the practice of detachment too far; it neglected the commandment to love and the commitment to receive the sacraments. In light of this controversy, Caussade carefully balances love, duty, and surrender.

Of course, this is not to suggest that Yoga practitioners today make a habit of reading Caussade![45] As noted, the purpose of the comparative study in comparative theology is to shed new light on an existing issue or subject within another (usually the "home") tradition. I chose to focus on the Christian author Caussade because he is a great exemplar of active detachment. He valued a complete surrender to God through an active engagement with the world and an appreciation for everyday life and mundane tasks. The prose attributed to Caussade directly addresses the difficultly of balancing achievement and love with the practice of detachment.[46] Thus, his work nicely corresponds to the core questions raised in my comparative study between the *Yogasūtras* and contemporary Yoga.

The comparison between detachment in the *Yogasūtras*, modern Yoga, and in the Christian texts broadens the conceptual analysis of detachment, in practice and theory. Both the modern gurus and the Christian author Caussade discuss detachment in terms of devotion and focus, yet the goals of the *Yogasūtras* remain distinct from those of Christianity. The following three sections will consider outcomes of the comparative study and how they relate to the question of methods and criteria.

LEARNING THROUGH COMPARISON—AGAINST RELATIVISM

Relativism is one of the primary reasons that the theologians discussed in the first part of the essay suggest that commitment to a single religious tradition is important for comparative theology. However, in the work of my dissertation I have found that the comparative study of a particular concept or idea in two or more traditions highlights the distinctive goals of those traditions, such as liberation or salvation. It also draws attention to how key concepts are interpreted differently within different traditions. In this way, comparative theology works against relativism regardless of the author's religious commitments (or lack thereof).

For example, Christian detachment is distinct from Patañjali's *vairāgya* (detachment) in ways that help to clarify both the purpose and the limits of the *Yogasūtras* text. The *Yogasūtras* is a nonsectarian text that emphasizes the efficacy of devotion to God as a way to focus the mind. Devotion is primarily functional because it is a practice that focuses the mind. The term used for God throughout the *Yogasūtras* is *īśvara*, a generic name for God. The use of *īśvara* (as opposed to a specific name for God like Sīva, Krishna, or Jesus) allows for different groups to read and interpret the *Yogasūtras* according to their own specific understanding of God. Indeed, devotion appears to be one option for practice among several.

Practice in the *Yogasūtras* is directed toward the complete stilling of the mind and the attempt to withdraw (or detach) from the influences of attraction, aversion, and daily activity. As the mind becomes focused or absorbed, the practitioner is strengthened and can experience a certain level of understanding, proficiency and some associated benefits.[47] For Yoga, the ability to discern the eternal (*puruṣa*) from the temporary (*prakṛti*) is the key to *kaivalya* (liberation). This is learned through practice and detachment.[48]

By contrast, for Caussade, devotion is the goal of daily practice with salvation as the ultimate goal. Sacraments, duty, and prayer are all directed toward the veneration of God and the perfection of devotion. Caussade discusses detachment as an abandonment of self or complete surrender. This form of detachment is based on the Jesuit practice of ordering desire, the first exercise in Ignatius of Loyola's *Spiritual Exercises*. Everything the individual does and desires is in relation to her primary desire to love God. This perspective makes the practice of detachment concrete. It also allows for detachment to be understood as compassionate and kind. The intuitive urge to care for children, creatures, the earth, etc., is not denied, but rather understood as an extension of God's love. Loving God above all else is an attempt to purify one's love and subtract (or detach) selfish desires from the act.

For Caussade, devotion is the means to cultivate detachment from destructive impulses. Time and again throughout his writing, Caussade emphasizes a process of abandonment of the self to the will of God, accepting the present moment, and responding (acting) according to one's duty.[49] As noted, the *Yogasūtras* also recognize the efficacy of devotion.

Yet, within Yoga philosophy, the eternal self (*puruṣa*) has no will of its own. In *Yogasūtra* 2.5 the soul (*ātman*) is described as "joyful, pure, and eternal"; it is the seer (*draṣṭṛ*), never the cause of action.[50] This points to a fundamental difference between Christian theology and Yoga philosophy. For Christians, God wills creation into being, yet he allows it free will. Caussade suggests that his ultimate freedom is in the alignment of his personal will with the will of the creator. For Yoga philosophy according to the *Yogasūtras*, devotion is functional and a theological understanding of God is not defined within the text. Ultimate freedom in the *Yogasūtras* is the complete stilling of the mind and the discernment between *puruṣa* and *prakṛti*.

Thus, Yoga philosophy and Christian theology are radically different. The worldview assumed by each shapes the purpose and meaning of practice. Looking at a particular concept in each tradition demonstrates this in a concrete way. It pushes the reader to go beyond the obvious similarities and consider how the full meaning and goals of the tradition comes to affect its basic sense of practice and prose.

Comparative theology can shed light on particular aspects of practice and how they are interpreted differently in various traditions. This contextual understanding of tradition and practice works against relativistic theories, which might, for example, assume that detachment or devotion are the same in Christianity and Hinduism. The urge to simply co-opt aspects of a tradition stands out when both traditions are studied in the particular. Thus, the comparative study shows details of particular traditions and gives depth to how texts are read. This might be especially important for newer religious communities that tend toward a less careful appropriation of texts. Thus, looking closely at specific examples in comparison with another tradition can be a remedy for relativism because it brings out data that undercuts an "all is the same" theory.

CONSIDERING HYBRIDITY AND CULTURAL BORROWING

While the Yoga community at large is composed of individuals from a variety of religious and non-religious backgrounds, the close comparative study of the historic texts demonstrates the value of commitment to a particular practice and understanding of God. This is not to say that Yoga, properly understood, aligns with one religious identity. Rather, from both the Hindu-Yogic perspective and from the Christian perspective, religious identity and commitment shape the nature of practice. While many individuals who practice Yoga will remain in a kind of "liminal" position with regard to religious identity, understanding the value of tradition and commitment can contribute to a more intentional approach to Yoga practice—that is, an approach to Yoga texts and practice that is grounded in an awareness of history and contexts. Cultural borrowing and appropriation are most problematic when they are done with little to no regard for the borrowee. Yet, hybridity remains a fact of our time. I propose that comparative study has the potential to avoid some of the pitfalls of cultural appropriation such that learning (and borrowing) from other cultural and religious traditions is done respectfully and in a way that ultimately contributes to the more peaceful coexistence of religious and non-religious persons.

For example, in the comparative study of Caussade's work, it is clear that a particular understanding of Christ shapes Caussade's understanding of holiness. Thus, even in the momentary appreciation of daily practice and mundane tasks, a definite Christ-centered standard is raised by which these efforts are evaluated. Ideals and standards impact our self-understanding and the basic ways that we evaluate the world we live in. Getting clear about the subject of devotion (for Caussade, that is Christ) directly impacts practice. Reading Caussade on devotion highlights this aspect of Krishnamacharya's work. In particular, it is interesting that Krishnamacharya states that the practice of devotion must be more than a desire.[51] Remembering God in a particular form, with words, images, or particular rituals contributes to the moral and social implications of practice.

As a nineteenth-century proponent of Yoga and a devout South Indian Vaiṣṇava, Krishnamacharya taught the *Yogasūtras* as the authoritative text on Yoga. He was also deeply committed to his family and to the ritual practices and duties of his Vaiṣṇava heritage. He emphasized the importance of devotion to God as a component of Yoga practice, although he was careful to note that anyone could do Yoga and that devotion to God could be expressed through different religious traditions. Thus, for contemporary Yoga practitioners (in the tradition of Krishnamacharya), the comparative study between the work of Krishnamacharya and Jean Pierre de Caussade raises the questions: How is God imagined? What commitments are necessary to live a life of faith?

Comparative theology can demonstrate the value of particular faith commitments. Even in the context of a non-sectarian practice, setting a clear intention and considering the specificity of certain aspects of practice through a comparative study with different religious traditions can challenge practitioners to approach texts, practices, and specific teachings with greater care and attention. Comparative study also involves acute curiosity and patience to learn from and about the historical contexts of modern practice, such that religious hybridity and cultural borrowing can become acts of genuine appreciation and respect.

AUDIENCE

Comparative study of a specific concept or practice in two or more traditions is an excellent way to demonstrate both similarity and distinction between the traditions. In the classroom, this is an effective way to learn about and from the two traditions while respecting the unique integrity of each. This demonstrates for students that all religions are, in fact, not saying the same thing. As an exercise in theology, the comparative study also invites the student to consider questions of truth and faith in relation to the material studied. Thus, in the classroom, comparative theology can work for students regardless of their explicit religious commitment. If successful, it helps to move students beyond tolerance toward dialogue and the possibility of enriching their own perspective in the world through and with the radical differences they find in others.

Outside the classroom, a major consideration for how to do comparative theology relates to who its intended audience is. The term theology indicates that research should not be exclusively directed to an academic community, but must also take into account and attempt to address a larger community of faith. For some, the effort to affect or address a community of faith is where religious studies, strictly speaking, becomes theology. For individuals who are not writing from a traditional religious community, this takes some additional consideration.

Most specifically, in my work, my community is the people with whom I learned to practice Yoga with in Mysore, India and with whom I continue to share and learn in various locations and shalas around the world. These individuals are familiar with the same daily routines and practices that I follow. More broadly, my community might be all individuals who are committed to a consistent practice of Yoga (in a variety of forms) and who share a common knowledge of particular terms, habits, and texts.[52] It is this broad sense of community that I speak of throughout the first chapter of my dissertation in my analysis of *Yogasūtras* and Yoga today.[53] I contend that the discussion of ethics, goals, and key terms, such as detachment, will be enriched and improved through this expanded sense of community.

The question of audience is important. Scholarship is of little use if the author has no audience in mind. My point in this section is that the lack of a conventional "rooted" position does not necessarily limit or eliminate the possibility of audience. It does, however, take some additional consideration. A Catholic writing for a community of scholars and for other Catholics in general can have in mind the idea of advancing the tradition through their scholarly work. A person without a traditional religious commitment will need to consider the goals and implications of their work more explicitly by defining how they understand their particular community and explaining what they hope to accomplish with their work.

Concluding Comments: From the "Rooted" to the "Aerial"

My work, therefore, contributes to three distinct conversations. The first would be the emerging academic field of Yoga studies that seeks to articulate the modern phenomenon of Yoga and its relation (or lack thereof) to traditional schools of Hindu philosophy. Second, as noted previously, I am concerned with addressing practitioners of Yoga in modern times. The third conversation involves comparative theology, the methodology of interreligious study and the multi-vocal discourse of Hindu-Christian dialogue. Throughout this essay, I highlight this third aspect and argue that the phenomena of contemporary Yoga and Yoga studies offer a perspective that is missing in some of the more "rooted" examples discussed in the first half of the article. Newer communities of practice can benefit from comparative study for a number of reasons outlined already (such as avoiding relativism and becoming aware of cultural appropriation). They can also contribute to the wider discussion of comparative theology (and theology in general) by demonstrating the value of particular practices (such as embodied or meditative practices) and the particular shape of new spiritual communities.

The first part of this essay looked at four prominent scholars in the field of comparative theology and the theology of religions to consider the importance of commitment and the "rooted" identity as a basic criterion for comparative theology. Each of the four emphasized various goals for comparative theology and reasons why commitment to a single tradition is a valued criterion. In turn, I have argued that with the expansion of the field of comparative theology, this criterion needs to be re-evaluated. James L. Fredericks proposed two goals for comparative theology, which are generally supported in the work of all four scholars discussed. In short, comparative theology in the broadest sense is aimed at promoting peace and at deepening faith (or an understanding of one's own faith commitments).

Following from this, both Frederick's study of pluralism and Catherine Cornille's study of the New Age argue that relativism is problematic for dialogue and therefore not helpful for promoting peace. In response, I point out that the relativistic view of religions is a starting point for many, although it may indeed be problematic. Acknowledging this relativistic perspective as a starting point opens the door for comparative theology to affect how individuals approach interreligious learning by introducing methods for historical, contextual study. Further, I have suggested that the careful approach set forth in comparative theology for learning from and about multiple traditions may actually be a means for some individuals to come to a better understanding of their own faith perspective(s).

Religious hybridity or multiple religious belonging is also a common result of prolonged study and engagement with another tradition. This is evidenced in the examples of inter-monastic dialogue raised in the work of Cornille and in the work of Knitter, who though Catholic, after many years of study and practice has now also taken Buddhist vows. Here, hybridity is much more intentional and careful than relativism, but it nonetheless combines religious traditions such that the individual's "rooted" identity may come into question. Paul F. Knitter's discussion of hybridity and the acknowledgment of identity formation as an on-going process of experimentation and learning also supports my suggestion that comparative theology can be done from a less "rooted" perspective.

Theological learning is personal. The vocation of the theologian relates academic learning to a personal and communal understanding of faith and practice. Without an explicit faith commitment at the outset of a comparative project, it becomes more difficult to ground new learning in a context of faith and community. One might wonder what it means to pursue "faith seeking understanding" if the individual lacks an explicit faith commitment. In the analysis of my own work, I have demonstrated how individuals who identify with a new, liminal, or interreligious community can still account for their particular faith commitments and community involvement. This also relates to the question of audience (addressed in Cornille's critique of individualistic learning), which, I argue, takes some additional consideration for those who write from a less "rooted" position. However, as demonstrated in my own example, in today's eclectic religious milieu, communities of faith do exist that cross traditional religious boundaries and yet connect individuals in important and meaningful ways.

Francis X. Clooney acknowledges the possibility of learning from individuals associated with new forms of spiritual practice and those who lack explicit faith communities. However, Clooney resists bending the notion of tradition too far; it is still important to recognize the particularity and value of explicit faith commitments even as the field of comparative theology expands. In the second part of the essay I suggest that the method of learning from and about two traditions can actively work against relativism and some of the more problematic expressions of cultural appropriation. By turning the lens back onto one's own faith position, however ill-defined it may be, comparative theology raises important questions for those who seek greater depth in the religious and spiritual practices that they practice.

The "spiritual, but not religious" has long been associated with New Age thought and the lackadaisical attitude of spiritual consumerism. To object that the New Age category does not measure up to the scope and historicity of the traditional categories of religion is to ignore one of the most widespread and challenging voices within the study of contemporary spirituality. Those who participate in new, liminal, or interreligious communities are, in a sense, "rooted" in a tradition, even if that tradition remains ill-defined. The issues that emerge from these diverse communities can be examined in the particular and in dialogue. Like the tenuous aerial roots of the banyan tree, it may begin with a shallow hold that grows and develops unexpectedly. For a new generation, the practice of comparative theology is a way of challenging and cultivating a better understanding of religious belonging and identity. As such, an important aspect of theology, especially comparative theology, may be to maintain a dialogical awareness of shifting cultures and new traditions. Ultimately, this approach can help develop creative, practical, and meaningful skills for living responsibly with religious and non-religious neighbors.

Notes

1. Of course, for Knitter, this passing back to one's home tradition can be difficult and the theologian can be radically changed through the encounter with the different tra-

dition. Given the relative newness of the field, it is also important to note that both Knitter and Catherine Cornille (discussed later) may not explicitly identify their work as comparative theology. Yet they both study more than one tradition and have made significant contributions to the discussion of methods and criteria of the theology of religions and comparative theology.

2. Similarly, in general, good theology that is non-comparative navigates between a tradition and a contemporary question(s). However, here I suggest that a contemporary community or phenomenon (such as Yoga today) can be studied through a comparative analysis of two traditions and select corresponding texts.
3. This might be done by comparing an aspect of a New Religious Movement/Contemporary Spiritual Practice to a similar aspect of an existing tradition or, as in my dissertation (discussed later) with aspects from two established traditions.
4. In this section, I focus on four scholars who explicitly discuss the importance of commitment as a starting point in comparative theology. It should be noted that Keith Ward, Robert C. Neville, Mark Heim, Michael Barnes, S.J., and several others have also made significant contributions to the field and all approach the role of commitment in somewhat different ways.
5. See, for example, the work of John Makransky as well as Shoshana Razel Gordon Guedalia and Muna Tatari (both featured in this book).
6. Francis X. Clooney also addresses the need for a creative tension between faith commitment and openness to the other in *Theology After Vedanta*, 5.
7. James L. Fredericks, *Faith Among Faiths*, 170.
8. Ibid.
9. Fredericks devotes several chapters to the discussion of *Pluralism* and its more sophisticated proponents. John Hick, Huston Smith, Paul Knitter, Wilfred Cantwell Smith, and Stanley Samartha are among those discussed, none of whom would be so careless to say that "all religions are saying the same thing." This refrain echoes a more casual approach to religious diversity that, in the attempt to be ultimately tolerant, actually exhibits intolerance for the concerns and particularity of religious communities.
10. James L. Fredericks, *Faith Among Faiths*, 164. Yet, to be fair, Hick and others argue that taking the other seriously involves moving to a meta-position. Hick explains this meta-position as a *hypothesis* that suggests that the major religions of the world each contain a partial understanding of the whole. Thus, dialogue is necessary in order to gain a fuller understanding of ultimate religious truth, (Ibid., 105). The main point against this perspective, according to Fredericks, is that it does not represent or account for how believers understand their own faith commitments.
11. Theology of religions is an academic discipline that examines how (primarily Christian) people from a particular religious faith relate to and understand other religions.
12. Paul Knitter, *Introducing Theologies of Religions*, 208.
13. Paul Knitter, *Without Buddha I Could Not Be a Christian*, 214.
14. Catherine Cornille, *The Im-Possibility of Interreligious Dialogue*, 27; 73–78. See also: Cornille, *The Guru in Indian Catholicism*.
15. Henri Le Saux eventually accepted a double religious belonging, along with a Hindu name, Swami Abhishiktananda. The development of his thought can be found in the collected works: Abhishiktānanda, *Swami Abhishiktananda*. Jules Monchanin, who

became ill and passed away quite early in his career, was more determined to maintain his Catholic identity and to learn from Hindus in order to strengthen his ability to teach them about Christianity. However, it is also clear from his work that he came to deeply appreciate and incorporate aspects of Hindu spirituality into his own Christian practice. See, for example, Jules Monchanin, *In Quest of the Absolute*.

16. Le Saux, Monchanin, and Griffiths all lived and wrote prior to the formation of contemporary comparative theology. However, I would argue that any serious engagement across religious traditions is, in a sense, comparative theology.
17. Cornille, *Im-Possibility*, 27. The inter-monastic dialogue involved textual, historical, and contextual learning as much as it did inter-personal dialogue. In this way, inter-monastic dialogue is as much an act of comparative theology as it is of interreligious dialogue.
18. Ibid.
19. It should be noted that Cornille identifies her focus as interreligious dialogue and not as comparative theology. While the distinction between these two categories is certainly not fixed, the former is normally associated with actual dialogue between individuals or groups and the latter can be primarily based on the (textual) study of two or more traditions. Nonetheless, Cornille is active in the discussion of methods for comparative theology and her insight applies to both means for interreligious learning.
20. Cornille, *Im-Possibility*, 63.
21. Ibid. She adds, "Accordingly, religious truth is measured only by the degree to which a particular teaching or practice comes to enhance one's personal sense of well-being or wholeness."
22. Ibid., 64.
23. Ibid. Cornille explains, "While such personal syncretism of ideas coming from different religious traditions may possess a certain relevance and coherence for the individual, there is on the whole little to no concern with the larger, that is to say shared, intelligibility of one's religious insights."
24. Ibid., 66.
25. Ibid., 67.
26. Ibid., 73.
27. Noted previously, Cornille discusses several examples of "liminality," as used in the work of Michael Amaldoss for individuals who "exist on the border between two communities and their symbolic universes, feeling at ease within both, and who experience religious solidarity with each of the two communities." In Cornille, *Im-Possibility*, 74–78 and in Michael Amaladoss, "Le double appartenance religieuse," 52.
28. Francis X. Clooney, S.J., *Comparative Theology*, 10.
29. A kind of "comparative theology" was also practiced by Jesuit missionaries in India beginning in the sixteenth century. In this early discipline, the goal of the comparative study was to enhance missionary efforts through the careful study of the religions and culture of India. Clooney devotes a chapter to this history and the differences between this early comparative work and the contemporary discipline in his text *Comparative Theology*, 24–40. The early comparative theology is also discussed in detail in Tomoko Masuzawa's *The Invention of World Religions*.
30. Clooney, *Comparative Theology*, 21.

31. Ibid., 158.
32. One might distinguish between comparativists who were at one time rooted in a particular tradition and, by way of study and/or dialogue, moved to the margin and those whose initial starting point is fluid because they never had a firm grounding in a tradition. While these two positions are very different, both point to the need to reconsider the criterion of "rootedness" in comparative theology.
33. Clooney, *Comparative Theology*, 165.
34. Aerial roots function in a variety of ways: for propagation, to provide support to existing branches, to help a vine attach and grow, to absorb nutrients, and in some cases like the banyan tree, the aerial roots can "strangle" the host tree. Though lacking the space in this essay, the analogy could be taken further to discuss benefits and problems of aerial roots.
35. *Inclusivism*, which argues that individuals faithful to traditions other than Christianity could be saved through the truth and light present in those traditions, was a step forward from Karl Barth's *exclusivist* theology of religions, which firmly maintained that the only way to salvation was through the Christian Church. See Karl Rahner, "Christianity and the Non-Christian Religions," 115–34. On Karl Barth, see *Church Dogmatics*, 297–325.
36. Krishnamacharya (1888–1989) was the primary teacher/spiritual master, or Guru, for B. K. S. Iyengar, K. Pattabhi Jois, T. K. V. Desikachar, Indra Devi, and a number of other significant contemporary teachers of Yoga. Collectively, these teachers are directly responsible for the forms of physical Yoga that are currently most prevalent outside of India. For example, American "Power Yoga" and all types of "Vinyasa/Flow Yoga" are derived from the methods originally taught by Krishnamacharya.
37. It should be noted that detachment in the *Yogasūtras* involves learning to control one's consciousness such that the individual is without craving of any kind. Both attachment and aversion are presented as problematic because they cause turbulence in the mind. See *sūtras* 1.15 and II.2–11.8.
38. I understand Catholicism and Yoga as two distinct ideologies. Thus, my own rootedness in both is a kind of double belonging. In the work of this dissertation, I emphasize questions that arise from the Yoga community and from my own practice of Yoga.
39. I practice Ashtanga Yoga in the tradition of Pattabhi Jois. This is part of the broader tradition of Yoga practice descended from the teaching tradition of T. Krishnamacharya (1888–1989).
40. The various schools of Yoga that have descended from the teaching tradition of T. Krishnamacharya commonly uphold the *Yogasūtras* as a core text for Yoga practitioners. Recent scholarship (discussed at length in the dissertation) question the connection between this esoteric text and modern practice, suggesting that the *Yogasūtras* may have been arbitrarily linked to modern Yoga practice (for the purpose of popular validation and authority) yet do not have a coherent connection.
41. In particular, I look at the work of Gudrun Bühnemann (2007), Mark Singleton (2008, 2010), and David Gordon White (2014).
42. *Yogasūtra* 1.2 states, *yogaś citta-vṛtti-nirodhaḥ*, "Yoga is the stilling of the changing states of the mind." Throughout this essay, translation of the *Yogasūtras* is from Edwin F. Bryant, *The Yoga Sūtras of Patañjali*.

43. *Sūtra* 1.12 states, *abhyāsa-vairāgyabhyāṁ tan-nirodhaḥ*, "[The *vṛitti* states of mind] are stilled by practice and dispassion." Ibid.
44. Often, the criticism of linking contemporary Yoga practice to historical texts is presented as a minor comment in a larger work. I address this broader trend in the dissertation and then look specifically at the work of Mark Singleton and David Gordon White.
45. My own study focuses on understanding the concept of detachment in Yoga. Caussade's work helps to bring out certain aspects of this concept that might otherwise be overlooked. Additional studies of other historical figures and/or texts, possibly from entirely different religious backgrounds, would add still new perspectives and new layers of understanding to this concept and practice.
46. In a recent study of the original materials of Caussade's compilation and treatise, Dominique Salin, S.J. notes inconsistencies both in style and content of the various letters and writing. Salin suggests that the collections attributed to Caussade may represent more than one author. See Dominique Salin, S.J., 24–27. However, in my dissertation, I refer to Caussade as an author much in the same way that I refer to Patañjali as an author, both names representing a body of work more than particular, historical individuals.
47. This is generally categorized as *siddhi* (Yogic power) in the *Yogasūtras*. It is the topic of Chapter 3 in the *Yogasūtras* and discussed at length in my dissertation, Chapter 4.
48. *Yogasūtra* 1.12, quoted previously.
49. As a Jesuit, Caussade believes that God has a will and plan for creation, and can communicate this to us through the Church, through reason, and through discernment.
50. *Yogasūtra* 2.5: *anityāśuci-duḥkhānātmasu nitya-śuci-sukhātma-khyātir avidyā*, "Ignorance is the notion that takes the self, which is joyful, pure, and eternal, to be the nonself, which is painful, unclean and temporary."
51. In reference to Krishnamacharya's work, his son, T. K. V Desikachar explains, "But this devotion to God must not remain just a desire. It must become a regular practice, as this alone, when regularly done, can prevail upon the past tendencies of the mind. The practice involves remembering God in some form, in words, images, rituals, offering flowers or visiting temples, taking great care that it does not become mechanical . . ." See T. K. V Desikachar, *The Yoga of T. Krishnamacharya*, 46–47.
52. Admittedly, this "expanded sense of community" will include forms and approaches to Yoga that I may personally find distasteful. It is likely that this is equally true for Christian (etc.) scholars who write for a broader audience of Christians.
53. In this way, the shared effort to read and understand a text like the *Yogasūtras* works to form a broad sense of community. When a community holds a text in high regard, that text has the potential to inform, develop, and challenge the community. Thus, my claim (echoing the gurus in the tradition of Krishnamacharya), that physical *āsana* practice is Patañjali Yoga, has obvious benefits for the ongoing formation and self-understanding of Yoga in modern times.

BIBLIOGRAPHY

Abhinavagupta. *Paratrisika-Vivarana: The Secret of Tantric Mysticism*. Translated by Jaideva Singh. Edited by Bettina Baumer. Delhi: Motilal Banarsidass, 1988.

———. "The Short Gloss on the Supreme, The Queen of the Three, *Paratrisikalaghuvrttih*." In *The Triadic Heart of Siva: Kaula Tantricism of Abhinavagupta in the Non-dual Shaivism of Kashmir*, translated by Paul Eduardo Muller-Ortega, 202–32. Albany: SUNY Press, 1989.

Abhishiktānanda. *Swami Abhishiktananda: Essential Writings*. Edited by Shirley Du Doulay. New York: Orbis Books, 2007.

Abou el-Fadl, Khaled. "Islam and the Challenge of Democracy. Can Individual Rights and Popular Sovereignty Take Root in Faith?" *Boston Review* (April/May 2003).

Abu Zaid, Nasr Hamid. "Was bedeutet der Begriff Gewissheit?" In *Verwundete Gewissheit. Strategien zum Umgang mit Verunsicherungen in Islam und Christentum*, edited by Jürgen Werbick, Muhammad Kalisch, and Klaus von Stosch, volume 3 of *Beiträge zur Komparative Theologie*. Paderborn: Ferdinand Schoenigh, 2010.

Ahmed, Shahab. *What Is Islam?: The Importance of Being Islamic*. Princeton: Princeton University Press, 2016.

Aklé, Yvette et alia. *Der Schwarze Christus. Wege afrikanischer Christologie*. Volume 12 of *Theologie in der Dritten Welt*. Freiburg-Basel-Wien: Herder, 1989.

Alpyagil, Recep. "Trying to Understand Whitehead in the Context of Ibn ʿArabi." *Islamic Philosophy* Yearbook 3 (2012), edited by Yanis Eshots. Lativa: University of Lativa, 220–29. Moskow: Moskow Literatura Publishers, 2012.

Amaldoss, Michael. "Le double appartenance religieuse." In *Vivre de Plusieurs Religions: Promesse ou Illusion?* Edited by D. Gira and J. Scheuer. Paris: Les Editions de l'Atelier, 2000.

Andrae, Tor. *Der Ursprung des Islam und das Christentum*. Uppsala: Almquist and Wiksell, 1926.

Antepli, Abdullah T. "Muslim Mary and Jesus." *American Baptist Quarterly* 26 (2007): 298–312.

Aquinas, Thomas. *Summa Theologica*. Volume I. Translated by the Fathers of the English Dominican Province. New York: Benzinger Brothers, 1948.

Aš-Šāṭibī Abū Isḥāq, *al-Muwāfaqāt fī uṣūl aš-ṣarīʿa*. Neu herausgegeben von Ibrāhīm Ramaḍan, 4 Vol, Bairūt 1994.

Asscher, Maarten. *Apples and Oranges: In Praise of Comparisons*. Translated by Brian Doyle Du-Breuil. San Francisco: Four Winds Press, 2015.

Aviner, Shlomo, Tzvi Fishman, and David Samson, trans. and comp. *Torat Eretz Yisrael of HaRav Tzvi Yehuda HaCohen Kook*. Jerusalem: Ateret Kohanim, 1991.

Ayoub, Mahmoud. *A Muslim View of Christianity: Essays on Dialogue by Mahmoud Ayoub*. Edited by by Irfan A. Omar. Maryknoll, N.Y.: Orbis Books, 2007.

Ayres, Lewis. *Nicaea and Its Legacy*. New York: Oxford University Press, 2004.

Balthasar, Hans Urs von. *Explorations in Theology*. Volume I. Translated by A. V. Littledale with Alexander Dru. San Francisco: Ignatius Press, 1989.

Bannon, R. Brad. "Apophatic Measures: Toward a Theology of Irreducible Particularity." Doctoral dissertation, Harvard Divinity School, 2015.

———. "Thou, That, and An/Other: Hearing Śaṅkara's Indexicals and Finding Cusa's Seeking God." *Journal of Hindu-Christian Studies* 27 (November 2014): 48–61.

Bareau, André. *Les Sectes Bouddhiques du Petit Véhicule*. Saïgon: École Française d'Extrême-Orient, 1955.

Barnes, Michael. *Interreligious Learning: Dialogue, Spirituality and the Christian Imagination*. Cambridge: Cambridge University Press, 2012.

———. *Theology and the Dialogue of Religions*. Cambridge: Cambridge University Press, 2002.

———. "Way and Wilderness, an Augustinian Dialogue with Buddhism." in *Augustine and the World Religions*, edited by Brian Brown, John Doody, and Kim Paffenroth, 115–40. Lanham: Lexington Books, 2008.

Barnes, Michel René. "The Fourth Century as Trinitarian Canon." In *Christian Origins: Theology, Rhetoric, and Community*, edited by Lewis Ayers and Gareth Jones. New York: Routledge, 1998.

Barnes, Timothy D. *Athanasius and Constantius*. Cambridge: Harvard University Press, 1993.

Barth, Karl. *Church Dogmatics*, vol. 1. Edited by G. W. Bromiley and T. F. Torrance. Edinburgh: T. & T. Clark, 1956.

Bauer, Walter. *Orthodoxy and Heresy in Earliest Christianity*. Edited by Robert A. Kraft and Gerhard Krodel. Philadelphia: Fortress, 1971.

Bäumer, Bettina. *Abhinavagupta's Hermeneutics of the Absolute: Anuttaraprakriya, An Interpretation of His Paratrisika Vivarana*. Shimla: Indian Institute of Advanced Study, 2011.

Bauschke, Martin. *Jesus—Stein des Anstoßes: Die Christologie des Korans und die deutschsprachige Theologie*. Vol. 29 of *Kölner Veröffentlichungen zur Religionsgeschichte*. Köln: Böhlau Verlag, 2000.

Bazargan, Mehdi. *Und Jesus ist sein Prophet: Der Koran und die Christen*. With an introduction by Navid Kermani and translated from Persian by Markus Gerold. München: Beck, 2006.

Beattie, Tina. *Theology After Postmodernity: Divining the Void—A Lacanian Reading of Thomas Aquinas*. Oxford: Oxford University Press, 2013.

Bell, Catherine. "Ritual Tensions: Tribal and Catholic." *Studia Liturgica* 32 (2002): 27.

Berger, Alan and David Patterson. *Jewish-Christian Dialogue: Drawing Honey From the Rock*. Minnesota: Paragon House, 2008.

Berman, Harold J. *Law and Revolution: The Formation of the Western Legal Tradition*. Cambridge: Harvard University Press, 1983.

Bloor, David. "Two Paradigms for Scientific Knowledge?" *Science Studies* 1 (1971): 101–15.

Boys, Mary. *Has God Only One Blessing? Judaism as a Source of Christian Self-Understanding?* New York: Paulist Press, 2000.

Brick, David. "Transforming Tradition into Texts: The Early Development of '*Smṛti*.'" *Journal of Indian Philosophy* 34:3 (June 1, 2006): 287–302.

Brinkmann, Martien E. "Christian-Muslim dialogue: The relationship between Jesus and God." *Reformed World* 59 (2009): 103–10.

Bronkhorst, Johannes. *Buddhism in the Shadow of Brahmanism*. Leiden: Brill, 2011.

———. *Greater Magadha*. Leiden: Brill, 2007.

Brueggemann, Walter. "A Fissure Always Uncontained." In *Strange Fire: Reading the Bible after the Holocaust*, edited by Tod Linafelt, 62–75. Sheffield: Sheffield Academic Press, 2000.

Bryant, Edwin F. *The Yoga Sūtras of Patañjali: A New Edition, Translation, and Commentary with Insights from the Traditional Commentators*. New York: North Point Press, 2009.

Buddhaghosa, Bhadantacariya, *The Path of Purification: Visuddhimagga*, translated by Bhikkhu Ñanamoli; 4th ed. Kandy: Buddhist Publication Society, 1976.

Bühnemann, Gudrun. *Eighty-four Āsanas in Yoga: A Survey of Traditions*. New Delhi: D.K. Printworld, 2007; 2011.

Bultmann, Rudolf. *Theology of the New Testament*, Vol. 2. Translated by Kend Grobel. Waco: Baylor University Press, 2007.

Bürkle, Horst. "Jesus und Maria im Koran." In *Wege der Theologie: An der Schwelle zum dritten Jahrtausend*, edited by Günter Risse, Heino Sonnemans, Burkhard Thess, 575–86. Paderborn: Bonifatius GmbH, 1996.

Campbell, Charles L. *Preaching Jesus: New Directions for Homiletics in Hans Frei's Postliberal Theology*. Grand Rapids, Mich.: Eerdmans, 1997.

Châu, Thich Thiên. "Les Réponses des Pudgalavādin aux Critiques des Écoles Bouddhiques." *Journal of the International Society for Buddhist Studies* 10, no. 1 (1987): 33–53.

Chenchiah, Pandipeddi. *Ashrams Past and Present*. Indian Christian Book Club, 1941.

Chittick, William C. *The Self-Disclosure of God. Principles of Ibn al-ʿArabī's Cosmology*. Albany: SUNY Press, 1998.

———. *The Sufi Path of Knowledge: Ibn Al-ʿArabi's Metaphysics of Imagination*. Albany: SUNY Press, 1989.

Clooney, Francis X. *Beyond Compare: St. Francis de Sales and Śrī Vedānta Deśika on Loving Surrender to God*. Washington: Georgetown University Press, 2008.

———. *Comparative Theology: Deep Learning Across Religious Borders*. Oxford: Wiley-Blackwell, 2010.

———. "Contribution and Challenge of Mimamsa to the Dream of a Global Hermeneutics." In *Musings and Meanings: Hermeneutical Ripples . . .*, edited by Nishant Alphonse Iruyadason. Christian World Imprints and Jnana-Deepa Vidyapeeth, 135–51.

———. "Discerning Comparison: Between the *Garland of Jaimini's Reasons* and Catholic Theology." In *The Past, Present, and Future of Theology of Interreligious Dialogue*, edited by Terrence Merrigan and John Friday. New York: Oxford University Press, 2017.

———. *Hindu God, Christian God: How Reason Helps Break Down the Boundaries Between Religions*. Oxford: Oxford University Press, 2001.

———. *His Hiding Place Is Darkness: A Hindu-Christian Theopoetics of Divine Absence.* Stanford: Stanford University Press, 2014.

———. "Introduction to the Role of *Śruti* in Hindu Theology." *The Journal of Hindu Studies* 7 (2014): 1–5.

———. "Mādhava's *Garland of Jaimini's Reasons* and His Elaboration VI.1: On Conditions Governing Eligibility to Perform Sacrifices." Presentation handout at the Comparative Studies Colloquium, Harvard University, April 2015.

———. "Mādhava's *Garland of Jaimini's Reasons* as Exemplary Mīmāṃsā Philosophy." In *Oxford Handbook of Indian Philosophy*, edited by Jonardon Ganeri. New York: Oxford University Press. Currently online at Oxford Handbooks Online, and to appear in book form in 2017.

———. "Mīmāṃsā as Introspective Literature and as Philosophy." In *The Encyclopedia of Indian Religions*, edited by Arvind Sharma. Dordrecht: Springer Publishing, 2017.

———. "Mīmāṃsā for the Mīmāṃsaka-s: Distinctiveness of Style in Mādhavācārya's Jaiminīyanyāyamālā, *Brahmavidya: Adyar Library Bulletin* 17 (2014–15): 487–518.

———. "On the Scholar's Contribution to the Contemplative Work of Hindu-Christian Studies." *Journal of Hindu-Christian Studies* 27 (2014): 3–10.

———. "Passionate Comparison: The Intensification of Affect in Interreligious Reading of Hindu and Christian Texts." *Harvard Theological Review* 98 (2005): 367–90.

———. "Reading as a Way of Disclosing the Truth in a Religiously Diverse World." In *The Wiley Blackwell Companion to Religious Diversity*, edited by Kevin Schilbrack. Oxford: Wiley-Blackwell, 2015.

———. "Reading Interreligiously as Theological Comparison." For a thematic issue of *Religion*, edited by Oliver Freiberger. Forthcoming in 2018.

———. "Scholasticisms in Encounter: Working through a Hindu Example." In *Scholasticism: Cross-Cultural and Comparative Perspectives*, edited by José Ignacio Cabezón, 177–200. Albany: SUNY Press, 1998.

———. *Seeing Through Texts: Doing Theology Among the Śrīvaiṣṇavas of South India.* Albany: SUNY Press, 1996.

———. *Theology after Vedānta: An Experiment in Comparative Theology.* Albany: SUNY Press, 1993.

———. *Thinking Ritually: Rediscovering the Pūrva Mīmāṃsā of Jaimini.* Vienna: Sammlung De Nobili Institut für Indologie der Universität Wien, 1990.

———. "Toward a Complete and Integral Mīmāṃsā Ethics: Learning with Mādhava's *Garland of Jaimini's Reasons.*" In *The Bloomsbury Research Handbook of Indian Ethics*, edited by Shyam Ranganathan. New York: Bloomsbury Publishing, 2016, 299–318.

———. *The Truth, the Way, the Life: Christian Commentary on the Three Holy Mantras of the Srivaisnava Hindus*. Leuven: Peeters, 2008.

Cohen, Gerson. "Esau as a Symbol in Early Medieval Thought." In *Jewish Medieval and Renaissance Studies*, edited by Alexander Altmann, repr. *Studies in the Variety of Rabbinic Cultures*, 243–69. Philadelphia: Jewish Publication Society, 1991.

Collins, Steven. *A Pali Grammar for Students.* Chiang Mai: Silkworm Books, 2005.

———. *Selfless Persons.* Cambridge: Cambridge University Press, 1982.

Coriden, James. *An Introduction to Canon Law.* Mahwah, N.J.: Paulist Press, 2004.

Cornille, Catherine, ed. *Christian Commentary on Non-Christian Sacred Texts.* Six unnumbered volumes. Leuven: Peeters Publishing, 2006.

———. "Conditions for Interreligious Dialogue." In *The Wiley-Blackwell Companion to Interreligious Dialogue*, edited by Catherine Cornille, 20–32. Chichester: Wiley-Blackwell, 2013.

———. "The Confessional Nature of Comparative Theology." *Studies in Interreligious Dialogue* 24, no. 1 (2014): 9–17.

———. *The Guru in Indian Catholicism: Ambiguity or Opportunity of Inculturation?* Louvain: Peeters Press, 1991.

———. *The Im-possibility of Interreligious Dialogue.* New York: Crossroads, 2008.

———. "Multiple Religious Belonging." In *Understanding Religious Relations*, edited by David Cheetham, Douglas Pratt, and David Thomas. Oxford: Oxford University Press, 2013.

Cragg, Kenneth. *Jesus and the Muslim: An Exploration.* London: Oneworld Publications, 1985.

Cusa, Nicholas of. *Cusa's Last Sermons 1457–1463.* Translated by Jasper Hopkins. Minneapolis: Jasper Hopkins, 2011.

———. Sermon 274, "Loquimini ad Petram coram Eis." In *Cusanus Texte* I:7, edited by Josef Koch. Heidelberg: Carl Winter's Universitätsbuchhandlung, 1942.

Daube, David. "Jesus and the Samaritan Woman: The Meaning of συγχράομαι." *Journal of Biblical Literature* 69, no. 2 (June 1, 1950): 137–47.

Davis, Donald, Jr. *The Spirit of Hindu Law.* Cambridge: Cambridge University Press, 2010.

De Lubac, Henri. *Amida: Aspects du Bouddhisme.* Paris: Editions du Cerf, 1955.

Desikachar, T. K. V. *The Yoga of T. Krishnamacharya.* Madras, India: Krishnamacharya Yoga Mandiram, 1982.

De Smet, Richard. *La Quête de l'Éternel, Approches Chrétiens de l'Hinduisme.* Paris: Desclée de Brouwer, 1967.

———. "The Theological Method of Sáṃkara." Pontificia Universitas Gregoriana, 1953.

Dobie, Robert J. *Logos & Revelation: Ibn 'Arabi, Meister Eckhart, and Mystical Hermeneutics.* Washington, D.C.: Catholic University of America Press, 2010.

Duerlinger, James. *Indian Buddhist Theories of Persons: Vasubandhu's "Refutation of the Theory of a Self."* New York: Routledge, 2003.

Ehrlich, Uri. *The Nonverbal Language of Prayer*, translated by Dena Ordan. Tubingen, Germany: Mohr Siebeck, 2004.

Eißler, Friedmann. "Jesus und Maria im Islam." In *Jesus und Maria im Judentum, Christentum und Islam*, edited by Cristfried Böttrich, Beate Ego, Friedmann Eißler, 120–205. Göttingen: Vandenhoeck and Ruprecht, 2009.

Elon, Menachem. "Interpretation." In *Encyclopaedia Judaica*, edited by Michael Berenbaum and Fred Skolnik, 2nd edition, vol. 9. Detroit: Macmillan Reference USA, 2007.

Eltschinger, Vincent. "Dharmakīrti." *Revue Internationale de Philosophie* 64 (2010): 397–440.

Eltschinger, Vincent and Isabelle Ratié. *Self, No-Self, and Salvation.* Wien: Österreichische Akademie der Wissenschaften, 2012.

Emerson, Ralph Waldo. "Self-Reliance." In *The Selected Writings of Ralph Waldo Emerson*, 132–53. New York: Random House, 1992.

Emet, Dabru. "Jewish Statement on Christians and Christianity." In *The Jewish People and Their Sacred Scriptures in the Christian Bible*. Pontifical Biblical Commission (2001). http://www.jcrelations.net/Dabru_Emet_-_A_Jewish_Statement_on_Christians_and_Christianity.2395.0.html.

Emon, Anver M. "Ḥuqūq Allāh and Ḥuqūq al-ʿIbād: A Legal Heuristic for a Natural Rights Regime." *Islamic Law and Society* 13 (2006): 325–91.

———. *Religious Pluralism and Islamic Law. Dhimmīs and Others in the Empire of Law.* Oxford: Oxford University Press, 2012.

Ensminger, Sven. *Karl Barth's Theology as a Resource for a Christian Theology of Religions.* London: Bloomsbury, 2014.

Faber, Roland. *Gott als Poet der Welt. Anliegen und Perspektiven der Prozesstheologie.* Darmstadt: WBG, 2003.

Flannery, John. "Christ in Islam." *One in Christ* 41 (2006): 27–36.

Flood, Gavin. *The Ascetic Self: Subjectivity, Memory, and Tradition.* Cambridge: Cambridge University Press, 2004.

———. *Body and Cosmology in Kashmir Saivism.* San Francisco: Mellen, 1993.

Fredericks, James L. *Buddhist and Christians: Through Comparative Theology to Solidarity.* Maryknoll, N.Y.: Orbis Books, 2004.

———. *Faith among Faiths: Christian Theology and Non-Christian Religions.* Mahwah, N.J.: Paulist Press, 1999.

Frei, Hans. *Types of Christian Theology.* Edited by George Hunsinger and William C. Placher. New Haven: Yale University Press, 1992.

Gadamer, Hans-Georg. *Wahrheit und Methode. Grundzüge einer philosophischen Hermeneutik* [*Truth and Method*]. (Gesammelte Werke, Band I). Tübingen: Mohr Siebeck, 1990.

Gagey, Henri-Jerome, "Pastoral Theology as a Theological Project." In *Keeping Faith in Practice: Aspects of Catholic Pastoral Theology*, edited by James Sweeney, Gemma Simmonds and David Lonsdale, 80–98. London: SCM Press, 2010.

Geertz, Clifford. *The Interpretation of Cultures: Selected Essays.* New York: Basic Books, 1973.

———. "Making Experience, Authoring Selves." In *The Anthropology of Experience*, edited by Victor Turner and Edward Bruner. Urbana: University of Illinois Press, 1986.

———. "Person, Time, and Conduct in Bali." In *The Interpretation of Cultures: Selected Essays.* New York: Basic Books, 1973.

Gellman, Yehuda. "The Akedah and Covenant Today." In *Two Faiths, One Covenant? Jewish and Christian Identity in the Presence of the Other*, ed. Eugene Korn and John Pawlikowksi, 35–44. Oxford: Rowman and Littlefield Publishers, 2005.

Gnilka, Joachim. *Die Nazarener und der Koran. Eine Spurensuche.* Freiburg-Basel-Wien: Herder, 2007.

Gombrich, Richard. *How Buddhism Began.* Atlantic Highlands: Athlone, 1996.

———. *Precept and Practice: Traditional Buddhism in the Rural Highlands of Ceylon.* Oxford: Oxford University Press, 1971.

Gómez, Luis O. "Proto-Mādhyamaka in the Pali Canon." *Philosophy East and West* 26, no. 2 (1976): 137–65.

Gordon, Rabbi Dr. Menachem-Martin Gordon. *Studies in Modern Orthodoxy.* Jerusalem: Urim Publications, 2011.

Gordon Guedalia, Shoshana Razel. "Jerusalem Is Burning." Cambridge: *The Wick*, 2013.

———. "Lethal Wives and Impure Widows." In *Hindu and Jewish Philosophy and Religion: Comparative Perspectives*, edited by Yehudit Greenberg and Ithamar Theodor. Lanham, Md: Lexington Books, 2017.

———. "The 'Pesaqratic Oath': Good Faith Presumption in the Spirit of Religio-Legal Rulings." *Keren Journal* (July 2013).

Gort, Jerald D., et al., eds. *On Sharing Religious Experience: Possibilities of Interfaith Mutuality.* Grand Rapids, Mich.: Eerdmans, 1992.

Grant, Sara. *Toward an Alternative Theology: Confessions of a Non-Dualist Christian.* Bangalore: Asian Trading Company, 1991.

Griffiths, Bede. *Marriage of East and West.* Springfield, Ill.: Templegate, 1982.

Griffiths, Paul. "On the Future of the Study of Religion in the Academy." *Journal of the American Academy of Religion* 74, no. 1 (2006): 66–74.

Grillmeier, Alois. *Jesus der Christus im Glauben der Kirche. Bd. 2/4: Die Kirche von Alexandrien mit Nubien und Äthiopien nach 451.* Unter Mitarbeit von Theresia Hainthaler. Freiburg-Basel-Wien: Herder, 1990.

———. *Jesus der Christus im Glauben der Kirche. Bd. 2/3: Die Kirchen von Jerusalem und Antiochien nach 451 bis 600.* Edited by Theresia Hainthaler. Freiburg-Basel-Wien: Herder, 2002.

Grossman, David. Presentation at Harvard Science Center, 2013.

Hacker, Paul. "Ānvīkṣikī." *Wiener Zeitschrift für die Kunde Süd- und Ostasien* 2 (1958): 54–83.

Hainthaler, Theresia. *Christliche Araber vor dem Islam. Verbreitung und konfessionelle Zugehörigkeit. Eine Hinführung.* Vol. 7 of *Eastern Christian Studies.* Leuven–Dudley, Mass.: Peeters, 2007.

Halbfass, Wilhelm. *India and Europe: An Essay in Understanding.* Albany: SUNY Press, 1988.

———. *Studies in Kumārila and Śaṅkara.* Reinbek: Verlag für Orientalistische Fachpublikationen, 1983.

Halbwachs, Maurice. *The Collective Memory*, translated by Francis J. Ditter and Vida Yazdi Ditter. New York: Harper and Row, 1980.

Hallaq, Wael. "Was the Gate of *Ijtihad* Closed?" *International Journal of Middle East Studies* 16, no. 1 (March, 1984): 3–41.

Handelman, Susan. *The Slavers of Moses: The Emergence f Rabbinic Interpretation in Modern Literary Theory.* Albany: SUNY Press, 1982.

Hanson, R. P. C. *The Search for the Christian Doctrine of God.* Grand Rapids, Mich.: Baker Academic, 1988.

Harvey, Van A. "Hermeneutics (1987 and 2005)." In *Encyclopedia of Religion*, edited by Lindsay Jones, 3930–36. Detroit: Macmillan Reference USA, 2005.

Haslam, Molly C. *A Constructive Theology of Intellectual Disability: Human Being as Mutuality and Response.* New York: Fordham University Press, 2012.

Hedges, Paul. "The Old and New Comparative Theologies: Discourses on Religion, the Theology of Religions, Orientalism and the Boundaries of Tradition." *Religions* 3/4 (2012): 1120–37.

Helmholz, R. H. *The Spirit of Classical Canon Law*. Athens: University of Georgia Press, 2010.

Hengel, Martin. *The Cross of the Son of God*. Translated by John Bowden. London: SCM Press, 1977.

Hill Fletcher, Jeannine. "As Long as We Wonder: Possibilities in the Impossibility of Interreligious Dialogue." *Theological Studies* 68, no. 3 (2007): 531–54.

———. *Motherhood as Metaphor: Engendering Interreligious Dialogue*. New York: Fordham University Press, 2013.

———. "Shifting Identity: The Contribution of Feminist Thought to Theologies of Religious Pluralism." *Journal of Feminist Studies in Religion* (2003): 5–24.

Hillgardner, Holly. *Longing and Letting Go: Hindu and Christian Practices of Passionate Non-attachment*. New York: Oxford University Press, 2016.

Hoffman, Lawrence A. *Beyond the Text: A Holistic Approach to Liturgy*. Bloomington: Indiana University Press, 1989.

Höhn, Hans-Joachim. *Gott-Offenbarung-Heilswege* [*God-Revelation-Ways of Salvation*]. *Eine Fundamentaltheologie*. Würzburg: Echter, 2011.

Holdrege, Barbara A. *Veda and Torah: Transcending the Textuality of Scripture*. Albany: SUNY Press, 1996.

———. "What's Beyond the Post? Comparative Analysis as Critical Method." In *A Magic Still Dwells*, edited by Kimberly Patton and Benjamin Ray, 77–91. Berkeley: University of California Press, 2000.

Hurtado, Larry W. "Christ Devotion in the First Two Centuries: Reflections and a Proposal." *Toronto Journal of Theology* 12:1 (1996): 17–33.

———. *Lord Jesus Christ*. Grand Rapids, Mich.: Eerdmans, 2003.

Ibn al-ʿArabī. *Al-Futūḥāt Al-Makkīyah*. Edited by ʿUthmān Yaḥyá and Ibrāhīm Madkūral. Qāhirah: al-Hay'ah al-Miṣrīyah al-ʿĀmmah lil-Kitāb, 1972.

———. *The Bezels of Wisdom* [=*Fuṣūṣ Al-Ḥikām*]. Translated by R. W. J. Austin. New York: Paulist Press, 1980.

———. *Fuṣūṣ Al-Ḥikām*. Edited by Abū al-ʿIlā Afīfī. Cairo: Isā al-Bābī al-Ḥalabī, 1946.

Imbach, Josef. *Wem gehört Jesus? Seine Bedeutung für Juden, Christen und Moslems*. München: Kösel, 1989.

Irenaeus (Lugdunensis). Against the Heresies. Edited by Dominic J. Unger. New York: Paulist, 2012.

Isaac, Jules. *The Teaching of Contempt: Christian Roots of Anti-Semitism*. New York: Holt, 1964.

Izutsu, Toshihiko. *Sufism and Taoism. A Comparative Study of Key Philosophical Concepts*. Berkeley: California University Press, 1984.

Jāmī. *Naqd al-Nuṣūṣ fī sharḥ Naqsh al-Fuṣūṣ*. Edited by William Chittick and Jalāl al-Dīn Āshtiyānī. Tehran: Anjuman-i Shāhanshāhī-i Falsafah-'i Īrān, 1977.

Jayatilleke, K. N. "The Buddhist Attitude to Other Religions." In *Christianity Through Non-Christian Eyes*, edited by Paul Griffiths, 141–52. Maryknoll, N.Y.: Orbis, 1990.

Johanns, Pierre. *To Christ Through the Vedanta*. Bangalore: United Theological College, 1930, 1996.

Jordan, Henry Louis. *Comparative Religion: Its Genesis and Growth*. New York: Charles Scribner's Sons, 1905.

Joselyn-Semiatkoski, Daniel. "Comparative Theology and the Status of Judaism: Hegemony and Reversals." In *The New Comparative Theology*, edited by Francis Clooney, 89–108. New York: Continuum, 2010.

Kant, Immanuel. *Die Religion innerhalb der Grenzen der bloßen Vernunft*, edited by Bettina Stangneth. Hamburg: Meiner, 2003.

———. *Kritik der reinen Vernunft*. In *Werkausgabe III*, edited by Wilhelm Weischedel. Frankfurt a.M.: Suhrkamp 1974.

Kapstein, Matthew T. *Reason's Traces*. Boston: Wisdom Publications, 2001.

———. "Śāntarakṣita's Tattvasaṃgraha: A Buddhist Critique of the Nyāya View of the Self." In *Buddhist Philosophy: Essential Readings*, edited by William Edelglass and Jay L. Garfield, 320–33. New York: Oxford University Press, 2009.

Karimi, Milad. *Die Beziehung von Mensch und Gott aus islamischer Perspektive*. In *"Der stets größere Gott." Gottesvorstellungen in Christentum und Islam*, edited by Andreas Renz a.o., 231–40. Regensburg: Pustet 2012.

———. *Hingabe. Grundfragen der systematisch-islamischen Theologie*. Freiburg, 2015.

———. *Identität–Differenz–Widerspruch. Hegel und Heidegger*. Berlin a.o.: Rombach, 2012.

———. *Versuch einer ästhetischen Hermeneutik des Qur'ān*. In *Herausforderungen an die Islamische Theologie in Europa—Challenges for Islamic Theology in Europe*, edited by Mouhanad Khorchide, Klaus von Stosch, 14–30. Freiburg a.o.: Herder, 2012.

———. *Zur Frage der Erlösung im religiösen Denken des Islam*. In *Streitfall Erlösung*, edited by Klaus von Stosch, Aaron Langenfeld, 17–37. Paderborn a.o.: Schöningh, 2015.

Kasper, Cardinal Walter. Foreword to *Christ Jesus and the Jewish People Today: New Explorations of Theological Interrelationships*. Edited by Philip Cunningham and Joseph Sievers. Grand Rapids, Mich.: Eerdmans, 2011.

Katz, Steven T. "The 'Conservative' Character of Mystical Experience." In *Mysticism and Religious Traditions*, edited by Steven T. Katz, 3–60. Oxford: Oxford University Press, 1983.

Keenan, John. *The Meaning of Christ: A Mahayana Theology*. Maryknoll, N.Y.: Orbis Books, 1989.

———. "The Promise and Peril of Interfaith Hermeneutics." In *Interreligious Hermeneutics*, edited by Catherine Cornille and Chris Conway, 184–202. Eugene: Cascade Books, 2010.

Keith, A. B. "Pre-Canonical Buddhism." *The Indian Historical Quarterly* 12 (1936): 3–20.

Keller, Catherine. *Cloud of the Impossible: Negative Theology and Planetary Entanglement*. Insurrections: Critical Studies in Religion, Politics, and Culture. New York: Columbia University Press, 2014.

Kelly, J. N. D. *Early Christian Creeds*. London: Longman, 1972.

———. *Early Christian Doctrines*. San Francisco: Harper and Row, 1978.

Kermani, Navid. *Gott ist schön. Das ästhetische Erleben des Koran*. München: Beck, 2007.

Kessler, Edward. "Jacob." In *Dictionary of Jewish-Christian Relations*, edited by Edward Kessler and Nell Wenborn. Cambridge: Cambridge University Press, 2005.

Khorchide, Mouhanad. *Das Jenseits als Ort der Transformation statt des Gerichts—Eine andere Lesart der islamischen Eschatologie*. In *Glaubensgewissheit und Gewalt. Eschatologische Erkundungen in Islam und Christentum*, edited by Jürgen Werbick, Sven Kalisch, Klaus von Stosch, 37–48. Paderborn a.o.: Schöningh, 2011.

Khoury, Adel Theodor. "Jesus Christus im Koran." *Communio* 40 (2011): 466–73.

King, Richard. *Early Advaita Vedānta and Buddhism: The Mahāyāna Context of the Gauḍapādīya-Kārikā.* SUNY Series in Religious Studies. Albany: SUNY Press, 1995.

Klein, Ralph. "Promise and Fulfillment." In *Contesting Texts: Jews and Christians in Conversation about the Bible*, edited by Meredith Knowles et. al., 47–63. Minneapolis: Fortress, 2007.

Klostermaier, Klaus. *Hindu and Christian in Vrindaban.* London: SCM Press, 1971.

Knitter, Paul F. *Introducing Theologies of Religions.* Maryknoll, N.Y.: Orbis Books, 2002; 2008.

———. *Without Buddha I Could Not be a Christian.* Oxford: Oneworld, 2009.

Krishna, Daya. "The Mīmāṁsaka vs. the Yājñika," in *Contrary Thinking: Selected Essays of Daya Krishna*, edited by Nalini Bhushan, Jay L. Garfield, and Daniel Raveh, 228–44. New York: Oxford University Press, 2011.

Krokus, Christian. *The Theology of Louis Massignon: Islam, Christ, and the Church.* Washington, D.C.: Catholic University of America Press, 2017.

Kuhn, Thomas S. "The Function of Dogma in Scientific Research." In *Scientific Change*, edited by A. C. Crombie, 347–69. London: Heinemann, 1963.

Lakatos, Imre. "Falsification and the Methodology of Scientific Research Programmes." In *The Methodology of Scientific Research Programs*, edited by John Worrall and Gregory Currie, 8–101. New York: Cambridge University Press, 1978.

———. "History of Science and Its Rationalist Reconstructions." In *The Methodology of Scientific Research Programs*, 102–38.

Lammens, Henri. "Les chrétiens à la Mecque à la veille de l'hégire." In *L'Arabie occidentale avant l'hégire*, 1–49. Beyrouth: Impr. Catholique, 1928.

Lander, Shira and Daniel Lehmann. "New Wine for New Wineskins." *Religious Education* 91 (1996): 519–28.

Lane, Edward William. *Arabic-English Lexicon.* Beirut: Librairie du Liban, 1968.

Langenfeld, Aaron. *Das Schweigen brechen. Christliche Soteriologie im Kontext islamischer Theologie.* Paderborn a.o.: Schöningh, 2016.

Largen, Kristen. *Baby Krishna, Infant Christ.* New York: Orbis Books, 2011.

Lash, Nicolas. *The Beginning and the End of "Religion."* Cambridge: Cambridge University Press, 1996.

Lawrence, David Peter. *Rediscovering God with Transcendental Argument: A Contemporary Interpretation of Monistic Kashmiri Saiva Philosophy.* Albany: SUNY Press, 1999.

Lee, Dorothy. "The Gospel of John and the Five Senses." *Journal of Biblical Literature* 129, no. 1 (April 1, 2010): 115–27.

Legenhausen, Muhammad. Preface to *Jesus through the Qur'an and Shi'ite narrations*, selected by Mahdi Muntazir Qa'im, translated by Al-Hajj Muhammad Legenhausen. Qom: Tahrike Tarsile Qur'an, 2009.

Le Saux, Henri. *Saccidananda: A Christian Approach to the Advaitic Experience.* London: ISPCK, 1970.

Levinas, Emmanuel. *Difficult Freedom: Essays on Judaism.* Translated by Sean Hand, London: Athlone Press, 1990.

———. *Ethics and Infinity*, Pittsburgh: Duquesne University Press, 1985.

Lienhardt, Joseph T. "Did Athanasius Reject Marcellus?" In *Arius after Arius*, edited by Michel R. Barnes and Daniel H. Williams, 65–80. Edinburgh: T and T Clark, 1993.

Linafelt, Tod, ed. *Strange Fire: Reading the Bible after the Holocaust.* Sheffield: Sheffield Academic Press, 2000.

Lincoln, Bruce. *Gods and Demons, Priests and Scholars.* Chicago: University of Chicago Press, 2012.

Lindbeck, George. *The Nature of Doctrine: Religion and Theology in a Postliberal Age.* Philadelphia: Westminster, 1984.

Lindtner, Christian. "The Problem of Precanonical Buddhism." *Buddhist Studies Review* 14, no. 2 (1997): 109–39.

Locklin, Reid B. *Liturgy of Liberation: A Christian Commentary on Shankara's* Upadesasahasri. Leuven: Peeters and Grand Rapids, Mich.: Eerdmans, 2011.

Lonergan, Bernard J. F. *Method in Theology.* Toronto: University of Toronto Press, 1990.

Lopez, Donald S. "Do Śrāvakas Understand Emptiness?" *Journal of Indian Philosophy* 16 (1988): 65–105.

Maclean, Derryl N. *Religion and Society in Arab Sind.* New York: Brill, 1989.

Madigan, Daniel A. "Revelation and Inspiration." In *Encyclopedia of the Qur'ān*, edited by Jane McDammen Auliffe, Vol. 4, 431–47. Leiden et.al.: Brill, 2004.

Maimonides, Moses. "Book of Mada, Laws of Torah Study." In *Mishneh Torah*, translated by Shoshana Razel Gordon Guedalia.

———. "Laws of Tzitzit," in *Sefer HaMitzvot*, translated by Shoshana Razel Gordon Guedalia.

———. "Sefer Hamitzvot." In *A Maimonides Reader*, translated by Isadore Twersky. New Jersey: Behrman House, 1972.

Makransky, John. "A Buddhist Critique of, and Learning from, Christian Liberation Theology." *Theological Studies* 75, no. 3 (September 2014): 635–57.

Maraldo, John C. "A Call for an Alternative Notion of Understanding in Interreligious Hermeneutics." In *Interreligious Hermeneutics*, edited by Catherine Cornille and Christopher Conway, 89–115. Eugene, Ore.: Cascade Books, 2010.

Martin, Richard and Mark P. Woodward, with Dwi S. Atmaja. *Defenders of Reason in Islam: Mu'tazilism from Medieval School to Modern Symbol.* Oxford: Oneworld, 1997.

Masuzawa, Tomoko. *The Invention of World Religions: Or, How European Universalism Was Preserved in the Language of Pluralism.* Chicago: University of Chicago Press, 2005.

McCauley, Robert N. *Why Religion Is Natural and Science Is Not.* New York: Oxford, 2011.

McCrea, Lawrence. "Hindu jurisprudence and scriptural hermeneutics." In *Hinduism and Law: An Introduction*, edited by Donald R. Davis, Jr., Jayanth K. Krishnan, and Timothy Lubin. Cambridge: Cambridge University Press, 2010.

McGovern, Nathan Michael. "Buddhists, Brahmans, and Buddhist Brahmans: Negotiating Identities in Indian Antiquity." PhD. diss., University of California Santa Barbara, 2013.

McIntosh, Mark Allen. *Christology from Within: Spirituality and the Incarnation in Hans Urs von Balthasar.* Notre Dame: University of Notre Dame Press, 1996.

———. *Mystical Theology: The Integrity of Spirituality and Theology.* Malden, Mass.: Blackwell, 1998.

Meier, John P. "On the veiling of hermeneutics." *Catholic Biblical Quarterly* 40, no. 2 (1978): 212–26.

Menke, Karl-Heinz, *Das unterscheidend Christliche: Beiträge zur Bestimmung seiner Einzigkeit*. Regensburg: Pustet, 2015.

Modi, P. M. *A Critique of the Brahmasutra (3.2.11–4)*. Bhavnagar: Modi, 1943–56.

Monchanin, Jules. *In Quest of the Absolute: The Life and Work of Jules Monchanin*, edited and translated by J. G. Webe. Kalamazoo: Cistercian Publications, 1977.

Moosa, Ebrahim. *Ghazālī and the Poetics of Imagination*. Chapel Hill: University of North Carolina Press, 2005.

———. "Transitions in the 'Progress' of Civilization: Theorizing History, Practice, and Tradition." In *Voices of Change*, edited by Omid Safi, volume 5 of *Voices of Islam*, general editor Vincent J. Cornell, 115–30. Westport and London: Praeger, 2007.

Morris, James W. "How to Study the Futûhât: Ibn 'Arabī's Own Advice." *Muhyiddin Ibn 'Arabi: A Commemorative Volume*. Edited by S. Hirtenstein & M. Tiernan, 73–89. Rockport, Mass.: Element, 1993.

———. "Ibn 'Arabi's Rhetoric of Realisation: Keys to Reading and 'Translating' the *Meccan Illuminations*. Part I: Ibn 'Arabi's Audiences and Intentions." *Journal of the Muhyiddin Ibn 'Arabi Society* 33 (2003): 54–98.

———. "Ibn 'Arabi's Rhetoric of Realisation: Keys to Reading and 'Translating' the *Meccan Illuminations*. Part II." *Journal of the Muhyiddin Ibn 'Arabi Society* 34 (2003): 103–44.

Moyaert, Marianne and Joris Geldhof, eds. *Ritual Participation and Interreligious Dialogue*. London: Bloomsbury Academic, 2015.

Moyaert, Marianne. "Abraham's Strangers: A Hermeneutic Wager." In *Hosting the Stranger between Religions*, ed. R. Kearney and J. Taylor, 95–108. Continuum: London, 2011b.

———. "Christianity as the Measure of Religion? Materializing the Theology of Religions." In *Twenty-First Century Theologies of Religions*, edited by P. Hedges, E. Harris, and S. Hettiarachchi, 239–61. Amsterdam/New York: Brill, 2016a.

———. *Fragile Identities: Towards a Theology of Interreligious Hospitality*. Amsterdam/New York: Brill/Rodopi, 2011a.

———. "From Soteriological Openness to Hermeneutical Openness: Recent Developments in the Theology of Religions." *Modern Theology* 28 (2012a): 35–52.

———. "Inappropriate Behavior? On the Ritual Core of Religion and Its Challenges to Interreligious Hospitality." *Journal for the Academic Study of Religion* 7 (2014): 1–21.

———. *In Response to the Religious Other: Ricoeur and the Fragility of Interreligious Encounters*. Lanham, Md.: Lexington Books, 2014.

———. "On Vulnerability: Probing after the Ethical Dimensions of Comparative Theology." *Religions* 3 (2012b), special issue on European Perspectives on Comparative Theology: 1144–61.

———. "Who Is the Suffering Servant? A Comparative Theological Reading of Isaiah 53 after the Shoah." In *Comparative Theology: Insights for Systematic Theological Reflection*, edited by Michelle Voss Roberts, 216–38. New York: Fordham, 2016b.

Muller-Ortega, Paul Eduardo. *The Triadic Heart of Siva: Kaula Tantricism of Abhinavagupta in the Non-Dual Shaivism of Kashmir*. Albany: SUNY Press, 1989.

Nakamura, Hajime and Trevor Leggett. *A History of Early Vedānta Philosophy*. Vol. 1. Delhi: Motilal Banarsidass, 1983.
Nasr, Seyyed Hossein et al. *The Study Quran: A New Translation and Commentary*. New York: HarperOne, 2015.
Neusner, Jacob. *Genesis Rabbah. The Judaic Commentary to the Book of Genesis. A New American Translation. Parashiyyot Sixty-Eight through One Hundred on Genesis 28:10–50:26*. Brown Judaic Studies 106. Atlanta: Scholars Press, 1985a.
———. *The Talmud of the Land of Israel: A Preliminary Translation and Explanation*, Vol. 23. Chicago: University of Chicago Press, 1985b.
———. *Transformations in Ancient Judaism: Textual Evidence for Creative Response to Crisis*. Peabody: Hendrickson, 2004.
Neuwirth, Angelika. *Der Koran als Text der Spätantike: Ein europäischer Zugang*. Frankfurt a.M.: Verlag der Weltreligionen, 2010.
Neville, Robert and Wesley Wildman. "On Comparing Religious Ideas." In *The Human Condition*, edited by Robert C. Neville, 9–20. Albany: SUNY Press, 2001.
Nicholson, Hugh. *Comparative Theology and the Problem of Religious Rivalry*. Oxford: Oxford University Press, 2011.
———. "The New Comparative Theology and the Problem of Theological Hegemonism." In *The New Comparative Theology: Interreligious Insights from the Next Generation*, ed. Francis Clooney, 43–62. London: T and T Clark, 2010.
———. "The Reunification of Theology and Comparison in the New Comparative Theology." *Journal of the American Academy of Religion* 77, no. 3 (2009): 609–45.
Nyanatiloka. *Buddhist Dictionary*. Kandy: Buddhist Publication Society, 2004.
Oberhammer, Gerhard. "Der frühe Nyāya: Bemerkungen zur inneren Gestalt seines Denkens." In *Gerhard Oberhammer: Ausgewählte kleine Schriften*, edited by Utz Podzeit, 337–52. Vienna, Austria, 2007.
———. "Pakṣilasvāmin's Introduction to his Nyāyabhāṣyam." *Asian Studies* 2, no. 3 (1964): 302–22.
O'Day, Gail R. "Narrative Mode and Theological Claim: A Study in the Fourth Gospel." *Journal of Biblical Literature* 105, no. 4 (December 1, 1986): 657–68.
O'Donnell, Emma. *Remembering the Future: The Experience of Time in Jewish and Christian Liturgy*. Collegeville, Minn.: Liturgical Press, 2015.
Oeldemann, Johannes. *Die Kirchen des christlichen Ostens. Orthodoxe, orientalische und mit Rom unierte Ostkirchen*. Kevelaer: Topos, 2008.
O'Leary, Joseph S. *Questioning Back: the overcoming of metaphysics in Christian tradition*. Minneapolis: Winston, 1985.
Otto, Rudolph. *The Idea of the Holy*. Translated by John W. Harvey. London and New York: Oxford University Press, 1973.
———. *Mysticism East and West. A Comparative Analysis of the Nature of Mysticism*. Wheaton: Quest Books, 1987 (original German version in 1936).
Padilla, Elaine. *Divine Enjoyment: A Theology of Passion and Exuberance*. New York: Fordham University Press, 2015.
Panikkar, Raimundo. "The Dialogical Dialogue." In *The World's Religious Traditions*, edited by Frank Whaling, 201–21. Edinburgh: T and T Clark, 1984.
———. *The Rhythm of Being*. Maryknoll, N.Y.: Orbis Books, 2013.

———. "What Is Comparative Philosophy Comparing?" In *Interpreting across Boundaries*, edited by Gerald Larson and Elliot Deutsch, 116–36. Princeton: Princeton University Press, 1988.

Pasnau, Robert. *Thomas Aquinas on Human Nature: A Philosophical Study of* Summa Theologiae *Ia 75–89*. Cambridge: Cambridge University Press, 2002.

Patton, Kimberly and Benjamin Ray, eds. *A Magic Still Dwells*. Berkeley: University of California Press, 2000.

Pieris, Aloysius. *Love Meets Wisdom: A Christian Experience of Buddhism*. Maryknoll, N.Y.: Orbis Books, 1989.

———. *Prophetic Humour in Buddhism and Christianity*. Colombo: Ecumenical Institute for Study and Dialogue, 2005.

Pöhlmann, Horst Georg. "Jesus im Islam und Christentum." In *Verantwortete Exegese. Hermeneutische Zugänge—exegetische Studien—systematische Reflexionen—praktische Konkretionen, FS F.G.* Untergaßmair, edited by H.G. Pöhlmann. Berlin: LIT Verlag, 2006.

Pollefeyt, Didier. "Christology after Auschwitz: A Catholic Perspective." In *Jesus Then and Now: Images of Jesus in History and Christology*, ed. Marvin. Meyer, 229–45. Harrisburg: Trinity Press International, 2001.

Poya, Abbas. "'*Iǧtihtād*' und Glaubensfreiheit. Darstellung einer islamisch-glaubensfreiheitlichen Idee anhand sunnitisch-rechtsmethodologischer Diskussionen." *Der Islam* 75 (1998): 226–58.

Priestley, Leonard. *Pudgalavāda Buddhism*. Toronto: University of Toronto, 1999.

Pröpper, Thomas. *Erlösungsglaube und Freiheitsgeschichte. Eine Skizze zur Soteriologie*. München: Kösel, 1991.

———. *Theologische Anthropologie*. Freiburg: Herder,. 2012.

Prothero, Stephen. *God Is Not One*. New York: Harper Collins, 2010.

Rahman, Fazlur. *Islam and Modernity: Transformation of an Intellectual Tradition*. Chicago: University of Chicago Press, 1982.

Rahner, Karl. *Grundkurs des Glaubens. Einführung in den Begriff des Christentums*. Freiburg a.o.: Herder, 1976.

———. *Theological Investigations V*. Translated by Karl H. Kruger. Baltimore, Md.: Helicon Press, 1966.

Rambachan, Anantanand. *Accomplishing the Accomplished: The Vedas as a Source of Valid Knowledge in Śaṅkara*. Honolulu: University of Hawaii Press, 1991.

———. *A Hindu Theology of Liberation: Not-Two Is Not One*. Albany: SUNY Press, 2015.

Regamey, Constantin. "Le problème du bouddhisme primitif et les derniers travaux de Stanislaw Schayer," *Rocznik Orientalisticzny* 21 (1957): 37–58.

Reinhart, A. Kevin. *Before Revelation: The Boundaries of Muslim Moral Thought*. New York: SUNY Press, 1995.

Ricœur, Paul. *Interpretation Theory*. Fort Worth: Texas Christian University Press, 1976.

———. "The Metaphorical Process." *Semeia* 4 (1975): 75–106.

Roberts, Tyler. "Exposure and Explanation: On the New Protectionism in the Study of Religion." *Journal of the American Academy of Religion* 72:1 (2004): 143–72.

Ruben, Walter. "Zur Frühgeschichte der indischen Philosophie." In *Beiträge zur Literaturwissenschaft und Geistesgeschichte Indiens (Festgabe H. Jacobi)*, 346–57. Bonn: Kommissionsverlag F. Klopp, 1926.

Ruparell, Tinu. "Inter-Religious Dialogue and Interstitial Theology." In *The Wiley-Blackwell Companion to Inter-Religious Dialogue*, edited by Catherine Cornille, 117–32. Oxford: Wiley-Blackwell, 2013.

Rusch, William G., trans. *The Trinitarian Controversy*. Philadelphia: Fortress Press, 1980.

Saddhatissa, H. and Russell Webb. *A Buddhist's Manual*. London: British Mahabodhi Society, 1976.

Salin, S.J. Dominique, ed. and introduction. *L'Abandon á la Providence Divine-Autrefois attribué á Jean-Piere de Caussade*. France: Desclee de Brouwer, 2006.

Sanderson, Alexis. "Saivism and the Tantric Traditions." In *The World's Religions: The Religions of Asia*, ed. Friedhelm Hardy, 128–72. London: Routledge, 1988.

Sandmel, David. "Philosemitism and Judaizing' in the Contemporary Church." In *Transforming Relations: Essays on Jews and Christians Throughout History in honor of Michael A. Singer*, edited by F. Harkins, 405–20. Notre Dame: University of Notre Dame Press, 2010.

Śaṅkara, *Upaniṣadbhāṣyam: Samagrabhāṣyasya Śrīmadānandagiryācāryakṛtaṭīkayā*. Edited by Subrahmanya Shastri. Māuṇṭa Ābū: Maheśa-Anusandhāna-Saṃsthānam, 1979.

Schayer, Stanislaw. *Ausgewählte Kapitel aus der Prasannapadā*. Krakow: Polska Akademja Umiejetności, Prace Komisji Orjentalistycznej, 1931.

———. "New Contributions to the Problem of the Pre-Hīnayistic Buddhism." In *On Philosophizing of the Hindus*, 169–78.

———. "Precanonical Buddhism." In *On Philosophizing of the Hindus*, edited by Marek Mejor, 121–32. Warsaw: Polish Scientific Publishers, 1988.

Schedl, Claus. *Muhammad und Jesus: Die christologisch relevanten Texte des Koran*. Freiburg-Basel-Wien: Herder, 1978.

Schmucker, Werner. *Die christliche Minderheit von Nağran und die Problematik ihrer Beziehungen zum frühen Islam*. Vol. 27/1 of *Bonner Orientalische Studien*. Bonn: Universität Selbstverlag des Orientalischen Seminars, 1973.

Sells, Michael. *Approaching the Qur'ān: The Early Revelations*. Ashland: White Cloud Press, 1999.

Shomali, Mohammad Ali. "Mary, Jesus, and Christianity: An Islamic Perspective." In *Catholics and Shi'a in dialogue: Studies in Theology and Spirituality*, edited by Anthony O'Mahony and Wulstan Peterburs, 71–86. London: Melisende, 2011.

Simonetti, Manlio. *La Crisi Ariana nel IV Secolo*. Rome: Augustinianum, 1975.

Singh, Jaideva. *Pratyabhijnahrdayam: The Secret of Self-Recognition*. Delhi: Motilal Banarsidass, 1982.

———, trans. *Vijnanabhairava or Divine Consciousness: A Treasury of 112 Types of Yoga*. Delhi: Motilal Banarsidass, 1979.

Singleton, Mark. "The Classical Reveries of Modern Yoga." In *Yoga in the Modern World: Contemporary Perspectives*, edited by Mark Singleton and Jean Byrne. New York: Routledge Hindu Studies Series, 2008.

———, *Yoga Body: The Origins of Modern Posture Practice*. Oxford: Oxford University Press, 2010.

Skilling, Peter. "A Note on King Milinda in the *Abhidharmakośabhāṣya*." *Journal of the Pali Text Society* 24 (1998): 81–101.

Slage, Walter. "Niśreyesam im alten Nyāya." *Wiener Zeitschrift für die Kunde Südasiens* 30 (1986): 163–77.

Smith, Daniel Lynwood. *Into the World of the New Testament: Greco-Roman and Jewish Texts and Contexts*. New York: Bloomsbury Publishing, 2015.

Smith, Jonathan Z. *Imagining Religion: From Babylon to Jonestown*. Chicago: University of Chicago Press, 1982.

Soloveitchik, Rabbi Joseph B. *The Seder Night: An Exalted Evening: The Passover Haggadah*, edited by Rabbi Menachem Genak. New York: Orthodox Union Press, 2009.

Stang, Charles M. "Being Neither Oneself Nor Someone Else: The Apophatic Anthropology of Dionysius the Areopagite." In *Apophatic Bodies: Negative Theology, Incarnation, and Relationality*, 59–78. Transdisciplinary Theological Colloquia. New York: Fordham University Press, 2010.

Stosch, Klaus von and Aaron Langenfeld, eds. *Streitfall Erlösung*. Volume 14 of *Beiträge zur Komparativen Theologie*. Paderborn: Ferdinand Schöningh, 2015.

Stosch, Klaus von and Hamideh Mohagheghi, eds. *Moderne Zugänge zum Islam. Plädoyer für eine Dialogische Theologie*. Volume 2 of *Beiträge zur Komparativen Theologie*. Paderborn: Ferdinand Schöningh, 2010.

Stosch, Klaus von and Muna Tatari, editors. *Gott und Befreiung. Befreiungstheologische Konzepte in Islam und Christentum*. Volume 5 of *Beiträge zur Komparativen Theologie*. Paderborn: Ferdinand Schöningh, 2012.

———. *Trinität—Anstoß für das islamisch-christliche Gespräch*. Volume 7 of *Beiträge zur Komparativen Theologie*. Paderborn: Ferdinand Schöningh, 2013.

Stosch, Klaus von. "Das besondere Verhältnis von Judentum und Christentum als Lernort Komparativer Theologie." In *Das Heil der Anderen. Problemfeld "Judenmission*," edited by Hubert Franemölle and Josef Wohlmuth, 113–36. Freiburg-Basel-Wien: Herder, 2010.

———. *Glaubensverantwortung in doppelter Kontingenz. Untersuchungen zur Verortung fundamentaler Theologie nach Wittgenstein*. Regensburg: Pustet, 2001.

———. "Jesus im Qur'ān. Ansatzpunkte und Stolpersteine einer qur'ānischen Christologie." In *Handeln Gottes—Antwort des Menschen*, ed. Klaus von Stosch and Muna Tatari, 109–33. Volume 11 of *Beiträge zur Komparativen Theologie*. Paderborn: Ferdinand Schöningh, 2014.

———. *Komparative Theologie als Wegweiser in der Welt der Religionen*. Volume 6 of *Beiträge zur Komparativen Theologie*. Paderborn: Ferdinand Schöningh, 2012.

———. "Philosophisch verantwortete Christologie als Komplizin des Antijudaismus?" *Zeitschrift für Katholische Theologie* 125 (2003): 370–86.

———. "Versuch einer ersten diachronen Lektüre der Jesusverse des Qur'ān." In *Streit um Jesus. Muslimische und christliche Annäherungen*, edited by Mouhanad Khorchide and Klaus von Stosch. Paderborn: Ferdinand Schöningh, 2016.

———. ed., *Wirtschaftsethik interreligiös*. Volume 12 of *Beiträge zur Komparativen Theologie*. Paderborn: Ferdinand Schöningh, 2014.

Suthren Hirst, Jacqueline. *Śaṃkara's Advaita Vedānta: A Way of Teaching*. New York: RoutledgeCurzon, 2005.

Sydnor, Jon Paul. *Ramanuja and Schleiermacher: Toward a Constructive Comparative Theology.* Eugene: Wipf and Stock, 2011.

———. "Shaivism's *Nataraja* and Picasso's *Crucifixion*: An Essay in Comparative Visual Theology." *Studies in Interreligious Dialogue* 15, no. 1 (2005): 86–100.

Tamari, Meir. *Truths Desired by God: An Excursion into the Weekly Haftara.* Jerusalem: Gefen Publishing House, 2011.

Tardy, René. *Najrân. Chrétiens d'Arabie avant l'Islam.* Beirut: Dar el-Machreq, 1999.

Tatari, Muna. *Gott und Mensch im Spannungsverhältnis von Gerechtigkeit und Barmherzigkeit. Versuch einer islamisch bergründeten Verhältnisbestimmung [God and Human in Relation to Justice and Mercy: Attempt of an Islamic Positioning.].* PhD diss., Münster: Waxmann, 2016.

———. "Plädoyer für die Klage vor Gott [Plea for a complaint against God]." In *Islam in der deutschen und türkischen Literatur*, edited by Michael Hofmann and Klaus von Stosch, 279–85. Paderborn: Ferdinand Schönigh, 2012.

te Velde, Rudi A. *Participation and Substantiality in Thomas Aquinas.* Leiden: Brill, 1995.

Teitelbaum, Rabbi Yoel. *Vayoel Moshe.* N.Y.: Beit Mischar Seforim Jerusalem, 1961.

Thatamanil, John J. "Binocular Wisdom: The Benefits of Participating in Multiple Religious Traditions." *The Huffington Post.* http://www.huffingtonpost.com/john-thatamanil/binocular-religious-wisdo_b_827793.html.

———. *The Immanent Divine: God, Creation, and the Human Predicament.* Minneapolis: Fortress Press, 2006.

Thomas, M. M. *The Acknowledged Christ of the Hindu Renaissance.* London: SCM Press, 1969.

Tiele, C. P. "On the Study of Comparative Theology." In *A Museum of Faiths*, edited by Eric J. Ziolkowski, 75–84. Atlanta: Scholars Press, 1993.

Tiemeier, Tracy Sayuki. "Engendering the 'Mysticism' of the Alvars." *Journal of Hindu Studies* 3.3 (2010): 337–53.

Tracy, David. "Comparative Theology." In *Encyclopedia of Religion*, edited by Lindsay Jones, vol. 13, 9125–34. Detroit: Macmillan, 1986, 2005.

———. "Kenosis, Sunyata, and Trinity: A Dialogue with Masao Abe." In *The Emptying God*, edited by John B. Cobb and Christopher Ives, 135–54. Maryknoll, N.Y.: Orbis Books, 1990.

Triebel, Johannes. "Das koranische Evangelium. Kritische Anmerkungen zur koranischen Darstellung der Person und Botschaft Jesu." *Theologische Beiträge* 38, no. 4/5 (2007): 269–82.

Trimingham, Spencer. *Christianity Among the Arabs in Pre-Islamic Times.* London, New York: Longman, 1979.

Twersky, Isadore. *Introduction to the Code of Maimonides: (Mishneh Torah).* New Haven: Yale University Press, 1980.

Upadhyaya, Brahmabandhab. *The Writings of Brahmabandhab Upadhyaya.* Bangalore: United Theological College, 1991.

Vaggione, Richard Paul. *Eunomius of Cyzicus and the Nicene Revolution.* Oxford: Oxford University Press, 2000.

Venkataramanan, K. "Sāmmitīyanikāya Śāstra." *Visva-Bharati Annals*, Vol. V, edited by P. C. Bagchi, 155–243. Santiniketan: Visvabharati, 1953.

Voss Roberts, Michelle. "Beyond Beauty: Aesthetics and Emotion in Interreligious Dialogue." In *Women in Interreligious Dialogue*, edited by Catherine Cornille and Jillian Maxey, 188–208. Eugene, Ore.: Cascade Books, 2013.

———. *Body Parts: A Theological Anthropology*. Minneapolis: Fortress, 2017.

———. *Dualities: A Theology of Difference*. Louisville: Westminster John Knox Press, 2010.

———. *Tastes of the Divine: Hindu and Christian Theologies of Emotion*. New York: Fordham University Press, 2014.

Walleser, Max. *Die Sekten des alten Buddhismus*. Heidelberg: Carl Winter's Universitätsbuchhandlung, 1927.

Ward, Keith. *Religion and Revelation*. Oxford: Oxford University Press, 1994.

Werbick, Jürgen, *Gebetsglaube und Gotteszweifel*, Münster: Lit, 2001.

———. *Theologische Methodenlehre*. Freiburg im Breisgau: Herder, 2015.

———. "'Zur Freiheit hat uns Christus befreit' (Gal 5,1). Was Luthers Wiederspruch gegen Erasmus einer theologischen Theorie der Freiheit heute zu denken gibt." In *Freiheit Gottes und der Menschen. FS Thomas Pröpper*, edited by Michael Böhnke, Michael Bongardt, Georg Essen, and Jürgen Werbick. Regensburg: Pustet, 2006.

White, David Gordon. *The Yoga Sūtra of Patañjali: A Biography*. Princeton: Princeton University Press, 2014.

Whitney, William Dwight. *The Roots, Verb-Forms and Primary Derivatives of the Sanskrit Language*. Delhi: Motilal Banarsidass Publishers Private Limited, 2003.

Whittemore, Robert C. "The Process Philosophy of Sir Muhammad Iqbal." *Toulane Studies in Philosophy* 2, no. 24 (1975): 113–30.

Wildman, Wesley and Robert Neville. "How Our Approach to Comparison Relates to Others." In *Ultimate Realities*, edited by Robert C. Neville, 211–36. Albany: SUNY Press, 2001.

Wiles, Maurice. *Archetypal Heresy*. New York: Oxford University Press, 1996.

Williams, Paul. *Mahāyāna Buddhism: The Doctrinal Foundations* (2nd Edition). New York: Routledge, 2009.

Williams, Rowan. *Arius: Heresy and Tradition*. Grand Rapids, Mich.: Eerdmanns, 2002.

Williamson, Clark. "Doing Christian Theology with Jews: The Other, Boundaries and Questions." In *Introduction to Christian Theology. Contemporary North American Perspectives*, ed. Roger Badham, 37–52. Louisville: Westminster John Knox Press, 1998.

Winkler, Ulrich. *Zum Projekt einer Komparativen Theologie*. In *"Mit euch bin ich Mensch . . ." FS Friedrich Schleinzer*, edited by Georg Ritzer, 115–47. Innsbruck-Wien: Tyrolia, 2008.

Wittgenstein, Ludwig. *Philosophische Untersuchungen*. In *Werkausgabe I*, 225–580. Frankfurt a.M.: Suhrkamp, 2006.

Wood, Thomas E. *The Māṇḍūkya Upaniṣad and the Āgama Śāstra: An Investigation into the Meaning of the Vedānta*. Honolulu: University of Hawaii Press, 1990.

Wright IV, William M. "The Literal Sense of Scripture According to Henri De Lubac: Insights from Patristic Exegesis of the Transfiguration." *Modern Theology* 28, no. 2 (April 2012): 252–77.

Wynn, Mark. "Religion and the Revelation of Value: The Emotions as Sources for Religious Understanding." In *Comparative Theology: Essays for Keith Ward*, edited by T. W. Bartel, 44–54. London: SPCK, 2003.

Yuval, Israel. *Two Nations in Your Womb: Perceptions of the Jews and Christians in Late Antiquity and the Middle Ages*. Berkley: University of California Press, 2006.

CONTRIBUTORS

BRAD BANNON received his ThD from Harvard University. He is an adjunct faculty member at Boston College and Fitchburg State University.

MICHAEL BARNES is Professor of Interreligious Relations at Heythrop College, University of London.

FRANCIS X. CLOONEY, S.J., is the Parkman Professor of Divinity and the Director of the Center for the Study of World Religions at Harvard University.

STEPHANIE CORIGLIANO is a Lecturer at Humboldt State University.

CATHERINE CORNILLE is Professor of Comparative Theology and Newton College Alumnae Chair at Boston College.

SHOSHANA RAZEL GORDON-GUEDALIA is a doctoral candidate in Comparative Theology and Law at Harvard University.

AARON LANGENFELD is a research associate at the Center for Comparative Theology and Cultural Studies at the University of Paderborn.

MARIANNE MOYAERT is a professor on the Faculty of Theology, Vrije Universiteit Amsterdam.

HUGH NICHOLSON is Associate Professor of Theology at Loyola University, Chicago.

EMMA O'DONNELL is a postdoctoral research fellow at the Center for Theology and Religious Studies at Lund University.

KLAUS VON STOSCH is Professor for Systematic Theology and Chairman for the Center for Comparative Theology and Cultural Studies at the Institute for Catholic Theology, University of Paderborn.

AXEL MARC OAKS TAKÁCS is a ThD candidate at the Harvard Divinity School.

MUNA TATARI is a Junior Professor at the Institute for Islamic Theology, University of Paderborn.

MICHELLE VOSS ROBERTS is Associate Professor of Theology and Associate Dean of Academic Affairs at Wake Forest University School of Divinity.

GLENN R. WILLIS is Assistant Professor of Religious Studies at Misericordia University.

Comparative Theology / *Thinking Across Traditions*

Loye Ashton and John Thatamanil, series editors

Hyo-Dong Lee, *Spirit, Qi, and the Multitude: A Comparative Theology for the Democracy of Creation*

Michelle Voss Roberts, *Tastes of the Divine: Hindu and Christian Theologies of Emotion*

Michelle Voss Roberts (ed.), *Comparing Faithfully: Insights for Systematic Theological Reflection*

F. Dominic Longo, *Spiritual Grammar: Genre and the Saintly Subject in Islam and Christianity*

Francis X. Clooney, S.J., and Klaus von Stosch (eds.), *How to Do Comparative Theology*